Shojo Beat

Yona of the Dawn

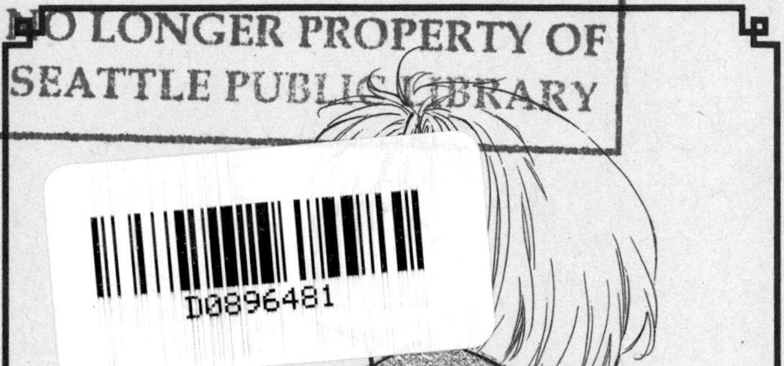

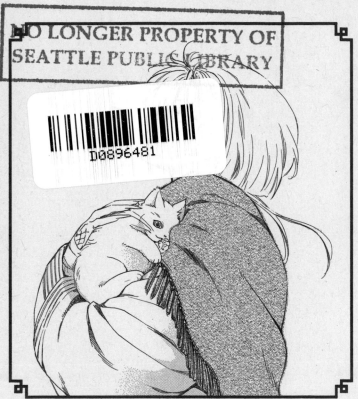

26

Story & Art by
Mizuho Kusanagi

yona of the Dawn
Volume 26

CONTENTS

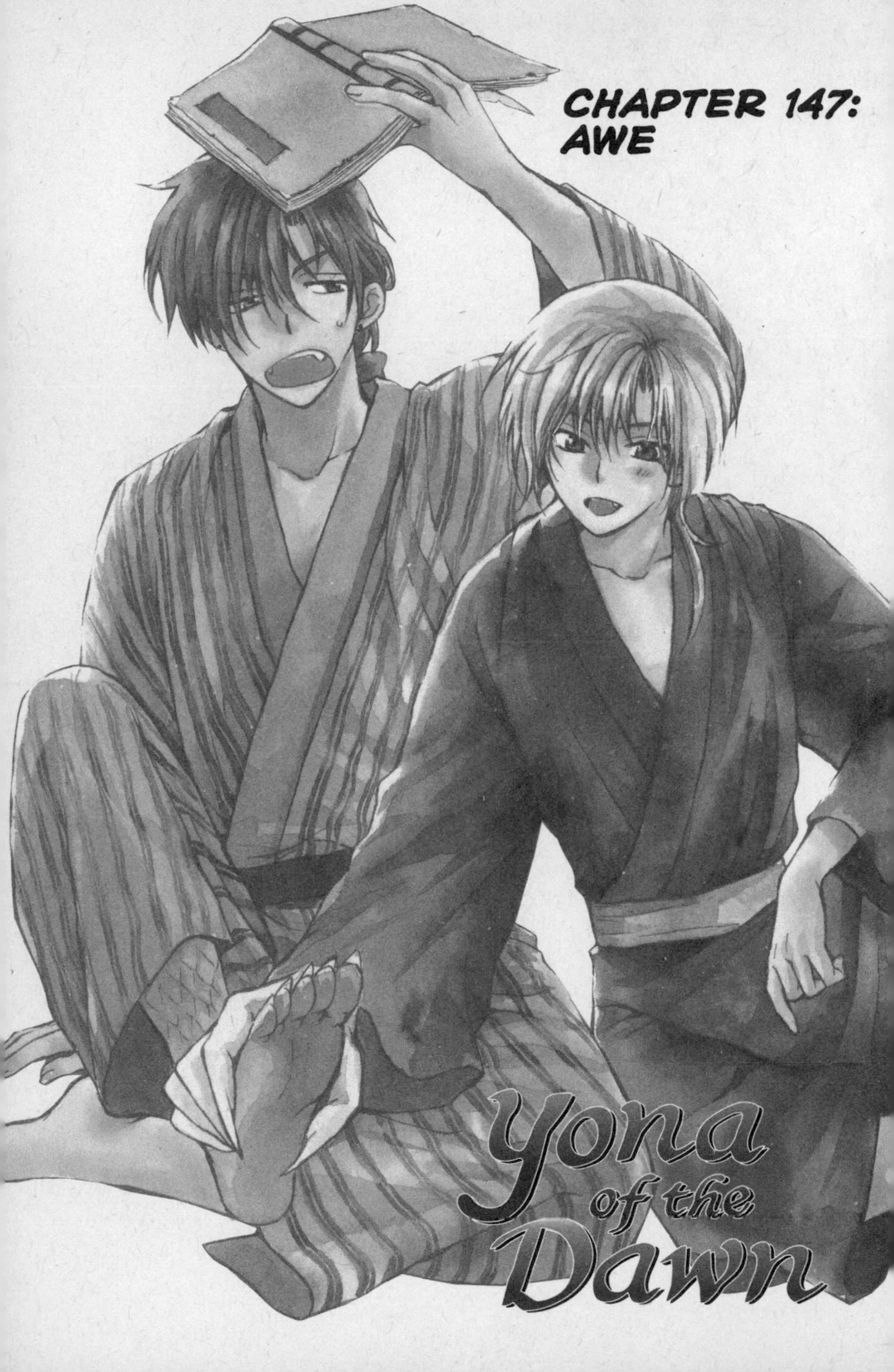
CHAPTER 147:
AWE
Yona of the Dawn

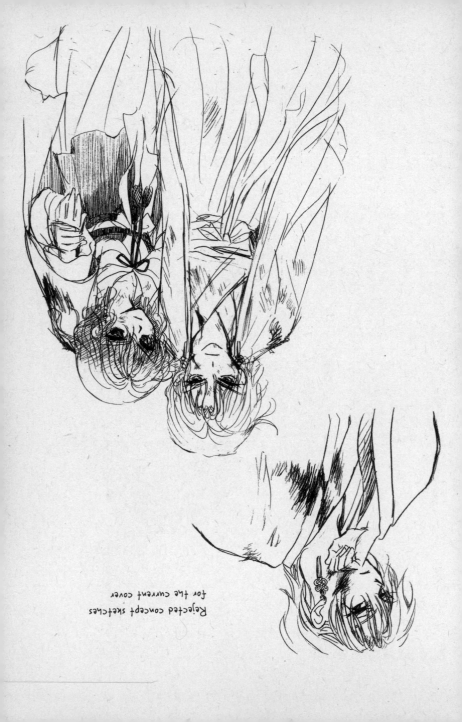

Rejected concept sketches
for the current cover

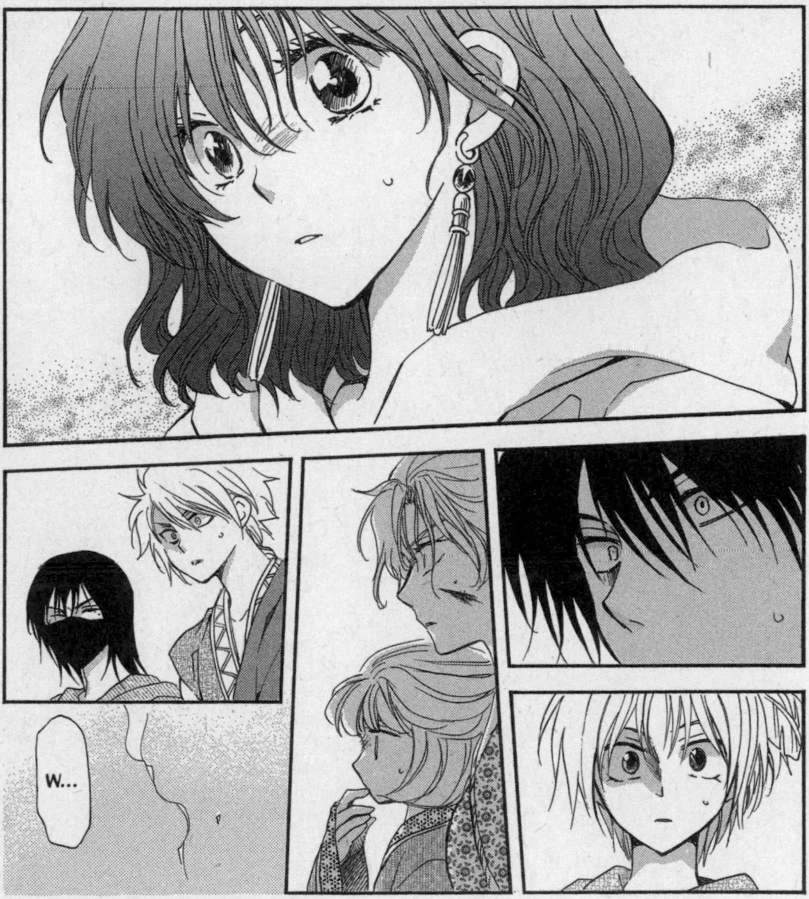
W...

Yona of the Dawn

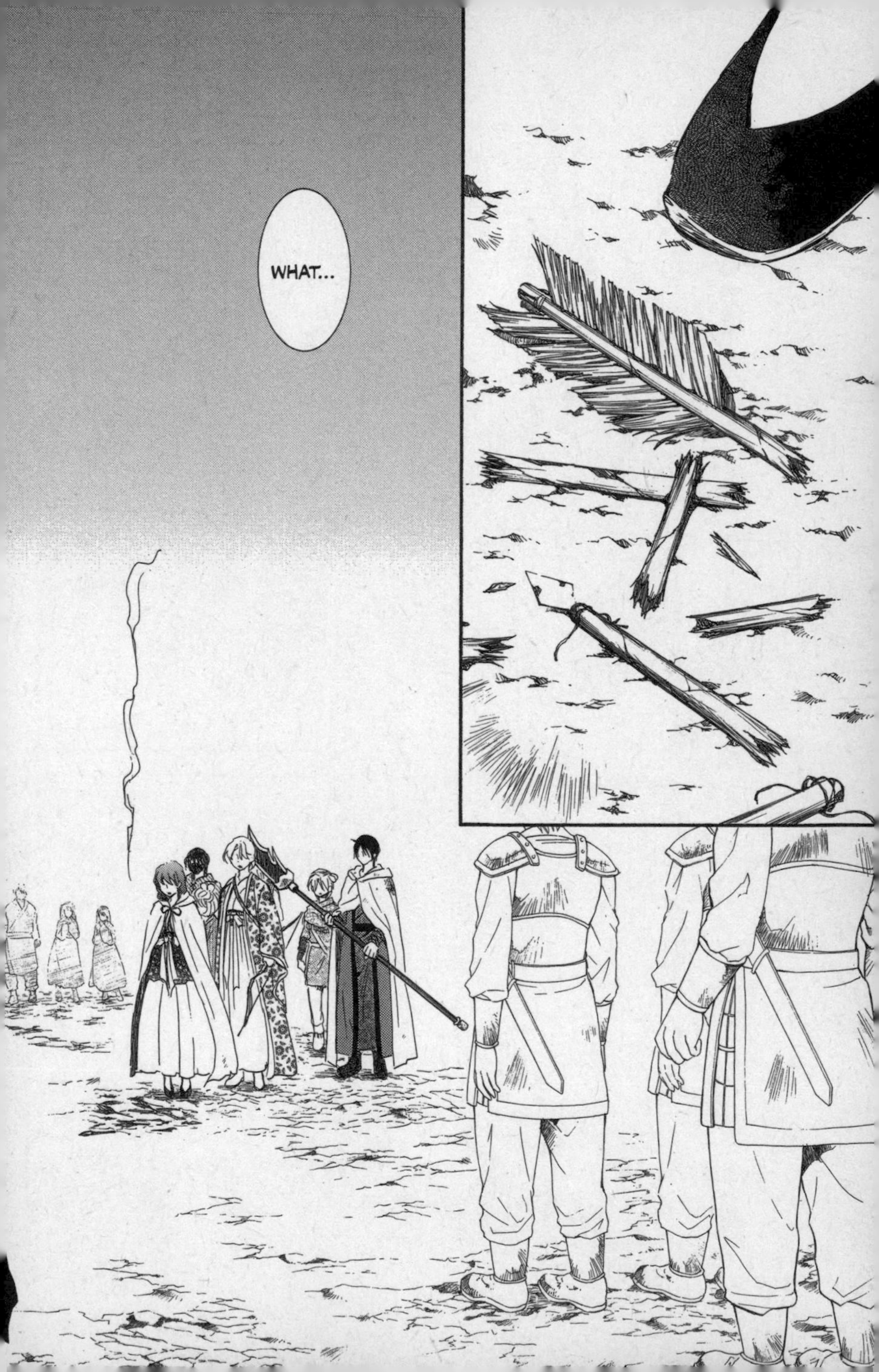
WHAT...

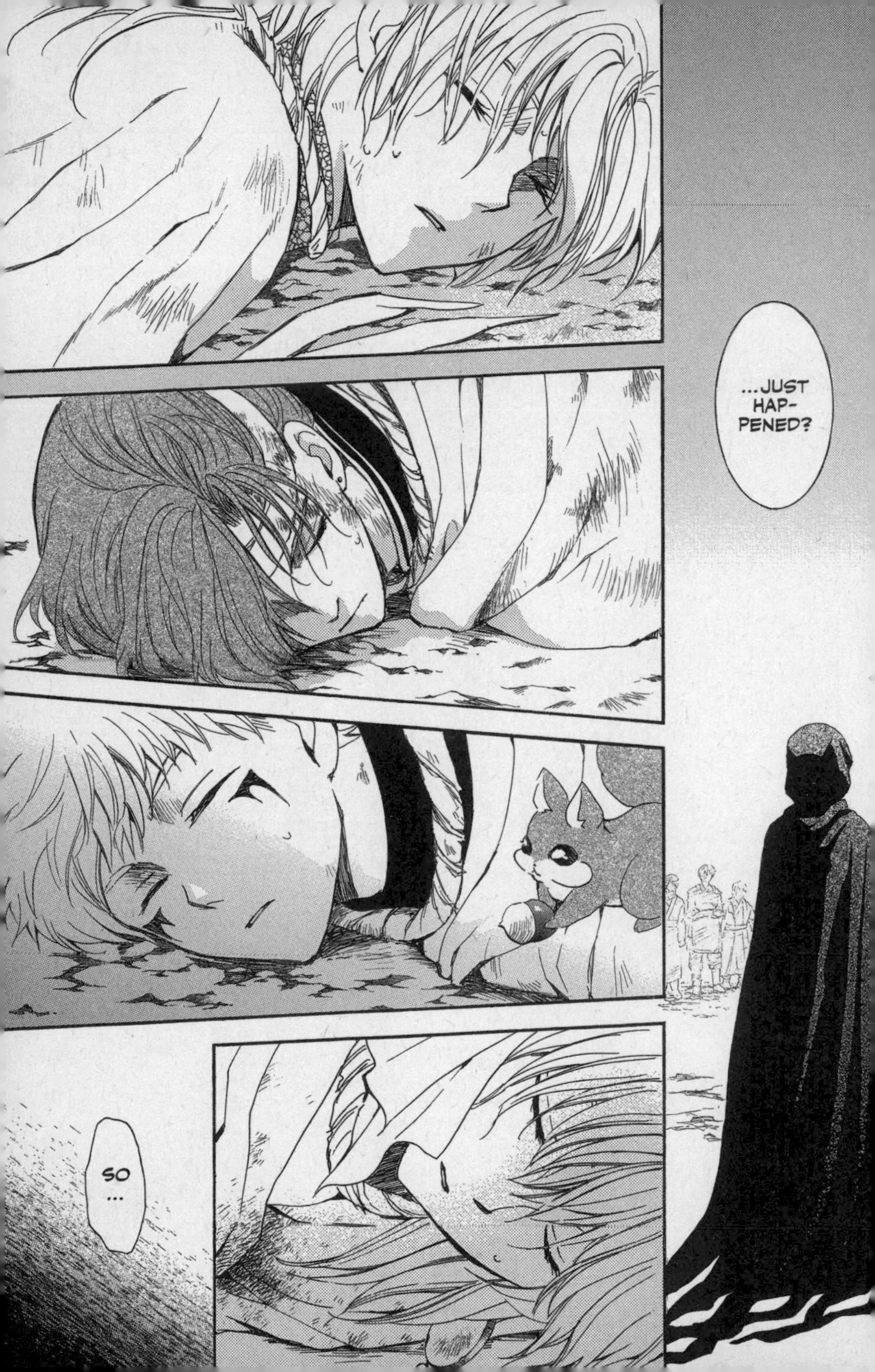
...JUST HAP-PENED?
SO ...

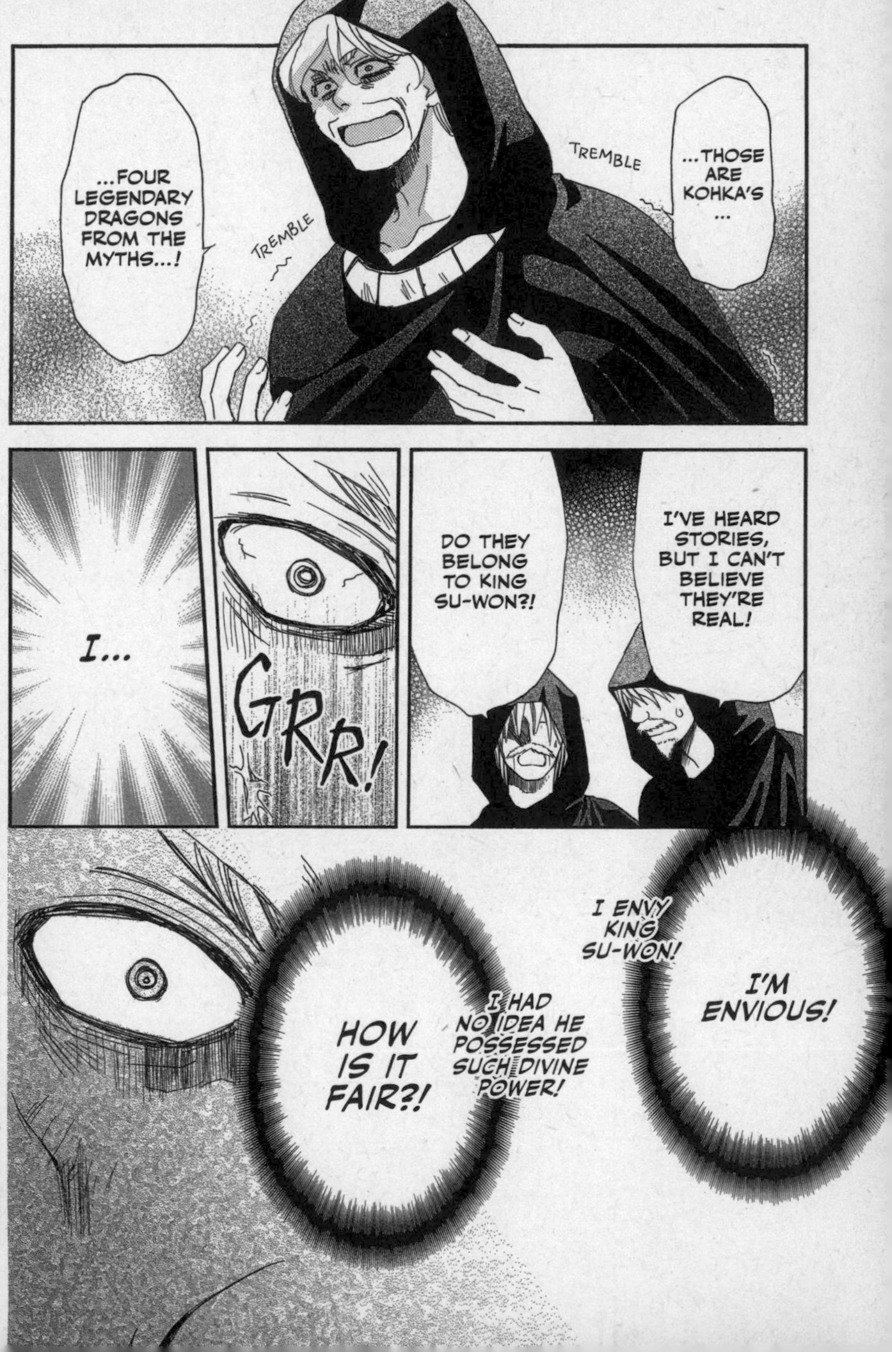
...THOSE ARE KOHKA'S ...
TREMBLE
TREMBLE
...FOUR LEGENDARY DRAGONS FROM THE MYTHS...!
I'VE HEARD STORIES, BUT I CAN'T BELIEVE THEY'RE REAL!
DO THEY BELONG TO KING SU-WON?!
GRR!
I...
I'M ENVIOUS!
I ENVY KING SU-WON!
I HAD NO IDEA HE POSSESSED SUCH DIVINE POWER!
HOW IS IT FAIR?!

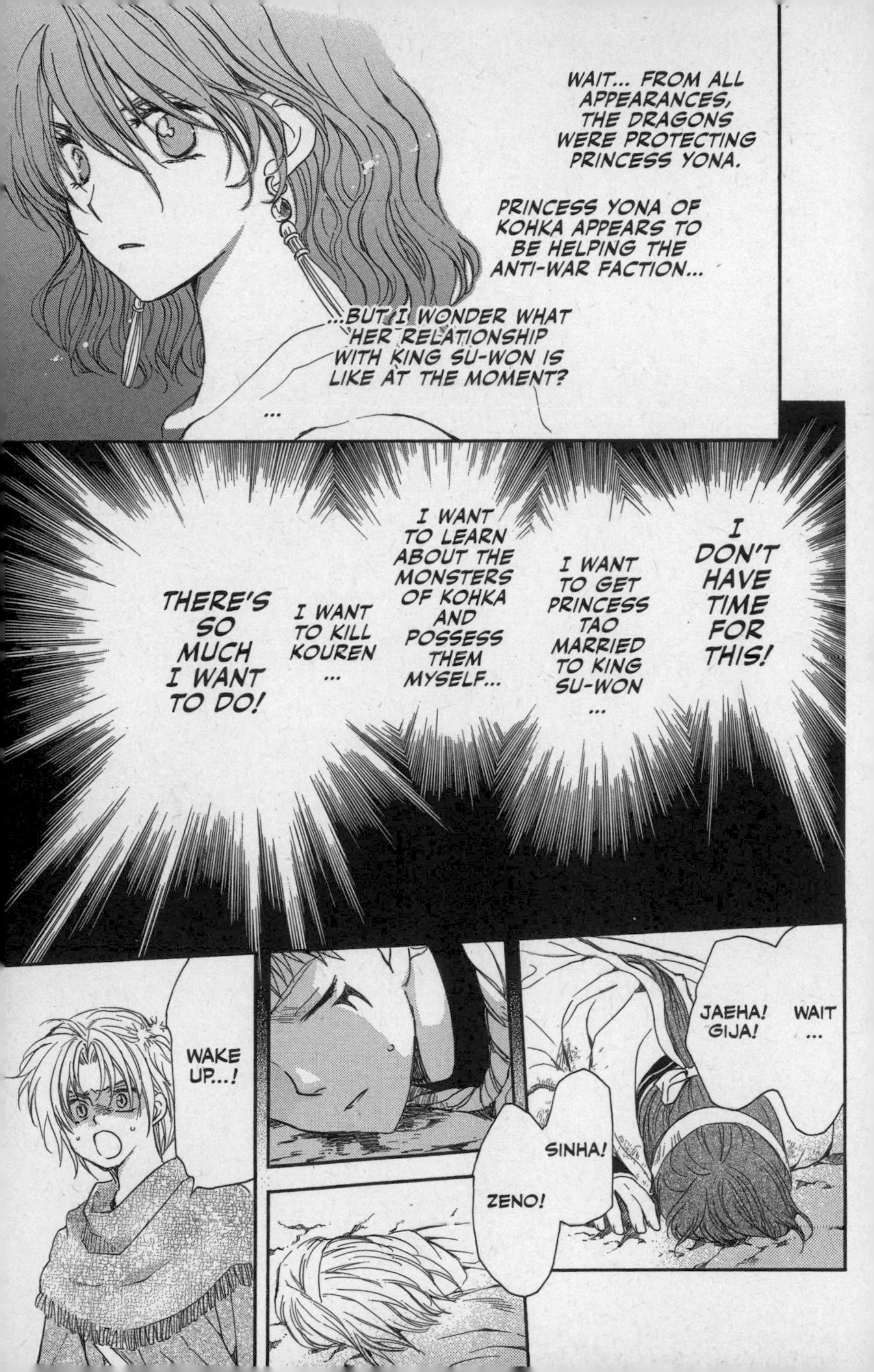
WAIT... FROM ALL APPEARANCES, THE DRAGONS WERE PROTECTING PRINCESS YONA.
PRINCESS YONA OF KOHKA APPEARS TO BE HELPING THE ANTI-WAR FACTION...
...BUT I WONDER WHAT HER RELATIONSHIP WITH KING SU-WON IS LIKE AT THE MOMENT?
...
I DON'T HAVE TIME FOR THIS!
I WANT TO GET PRINCESS TAO MARRIED TO KING SU-WON...
I WANT TO LEARN ABOUT THE MONSTERS OF KOHKA AND POSSESS THEM MYSELF...
I WANT TO KILL KOUREN...
THERE'S SO MUCH I WANT TO DO!
WAIT...
JAEHA! GIJA!
SINHA!
ZENO!
WAKE UP...!

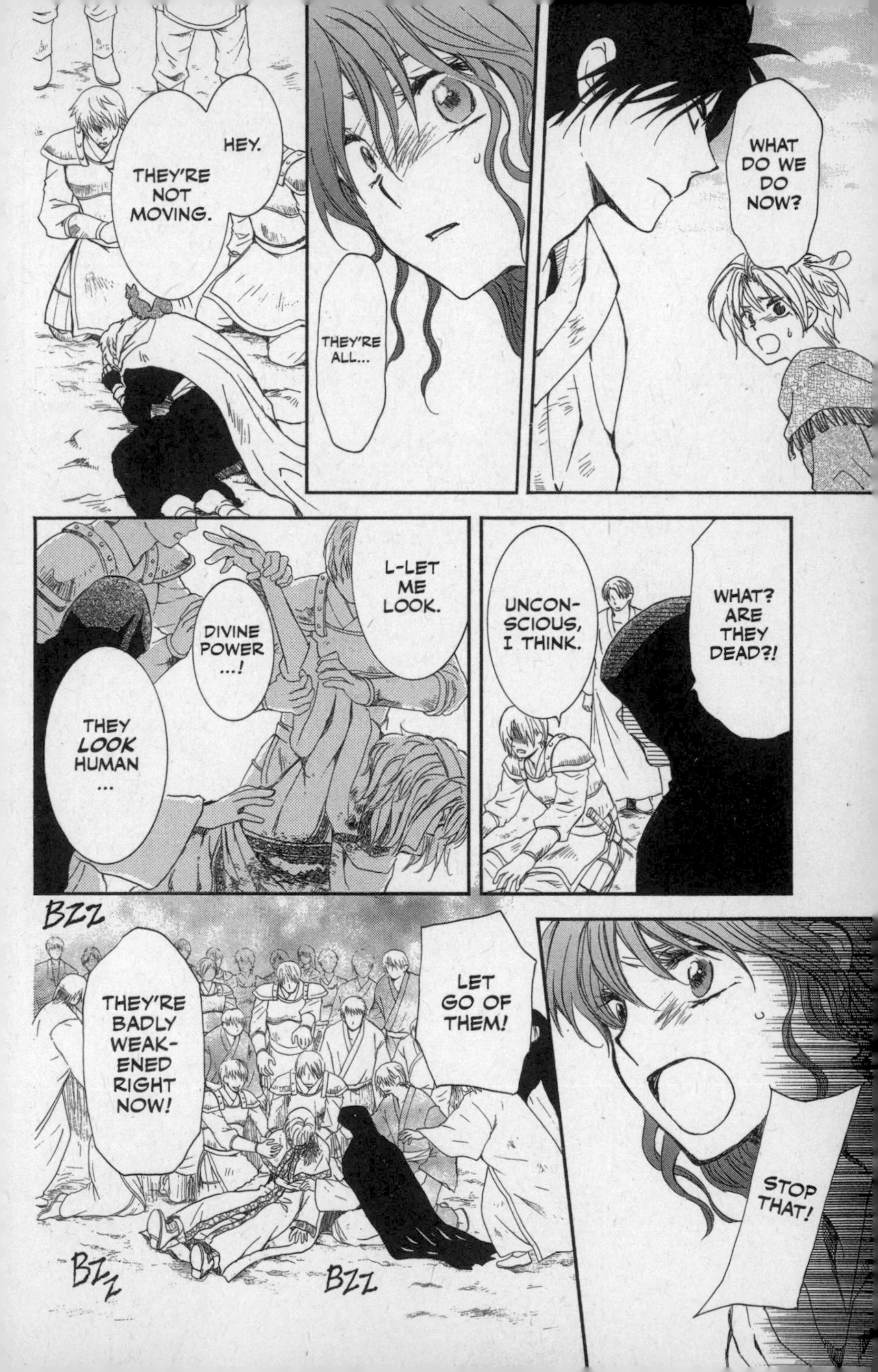
WHAT DO WE DO NOW?
THEY'RE ALL...
HEY.
THEY'RE NOT MOVING.
WHAT? ARE THEY DEAD?!
UNCONSCIOUS, I THINK.
L-LET ME LOOK.
DIVINE POWER ...!
THEY *LOOK* HUMAN ...
STOP THAT!
LET GO OF THEM!
BZZ
THEY'RE BADLY WEAKENED RIGHT NOW!
BZZ
BZZ

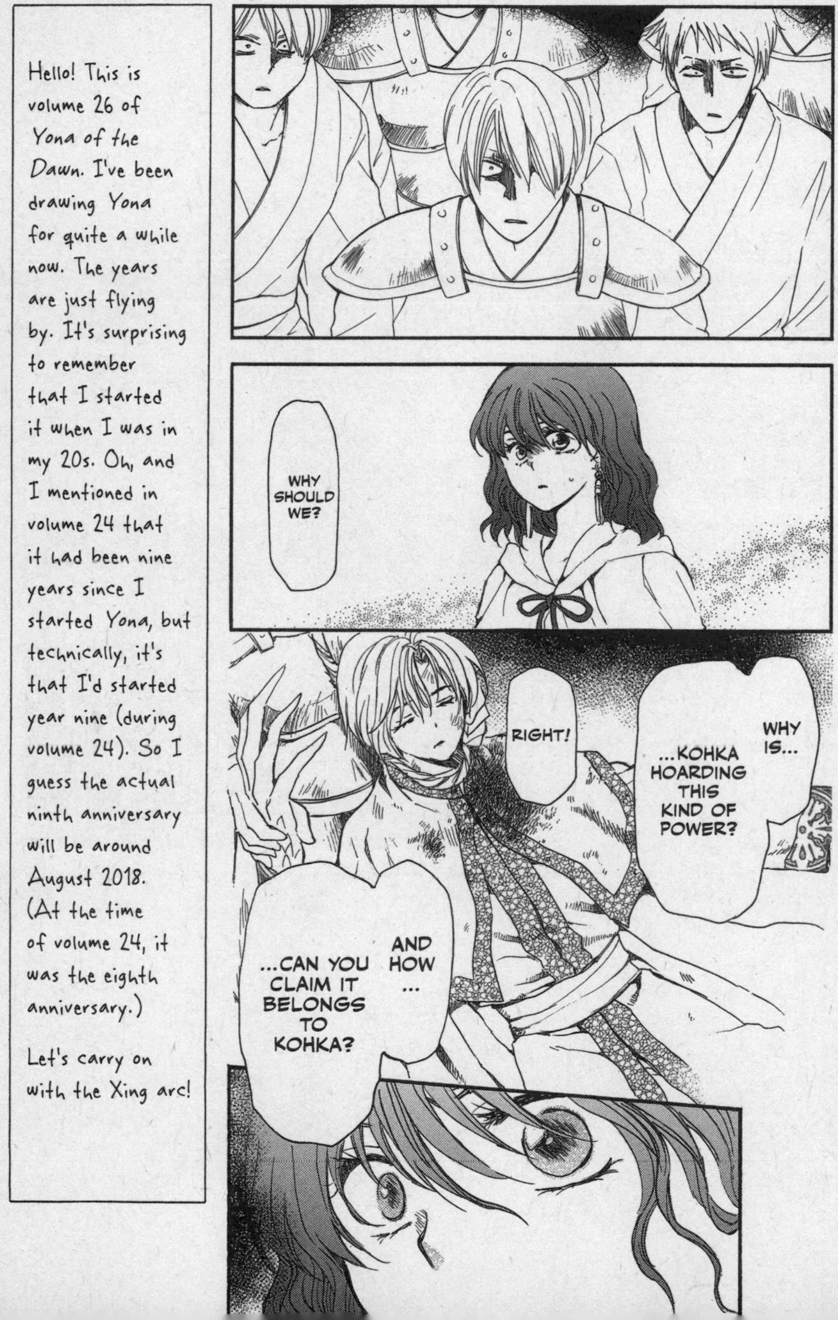
WHY SHOULD WE?
WHY IS...
...KOHKA HOARDING THIS KIND OF POWER?
RIGHT!
AND HOW ...
...CAN YOU CLAIM IT BELONGS TO KOHKA?

Hello! This is volume 26 of Yona of the Dawn. I've been drawing Yona for quite a while now. The years are just flying by. It's surprising to remember that I started it when I was in my 20s. Oh, and I mentioned in volume 24 that it had been nine years since I started Yona, but technically, it's that I'd started year nine (during volume 24). So I guess the actual ninth anniversary will be around August 2018. (At the time of volume 24, it was the eighth anniversary.)

Let's carry on with the Xing arc!

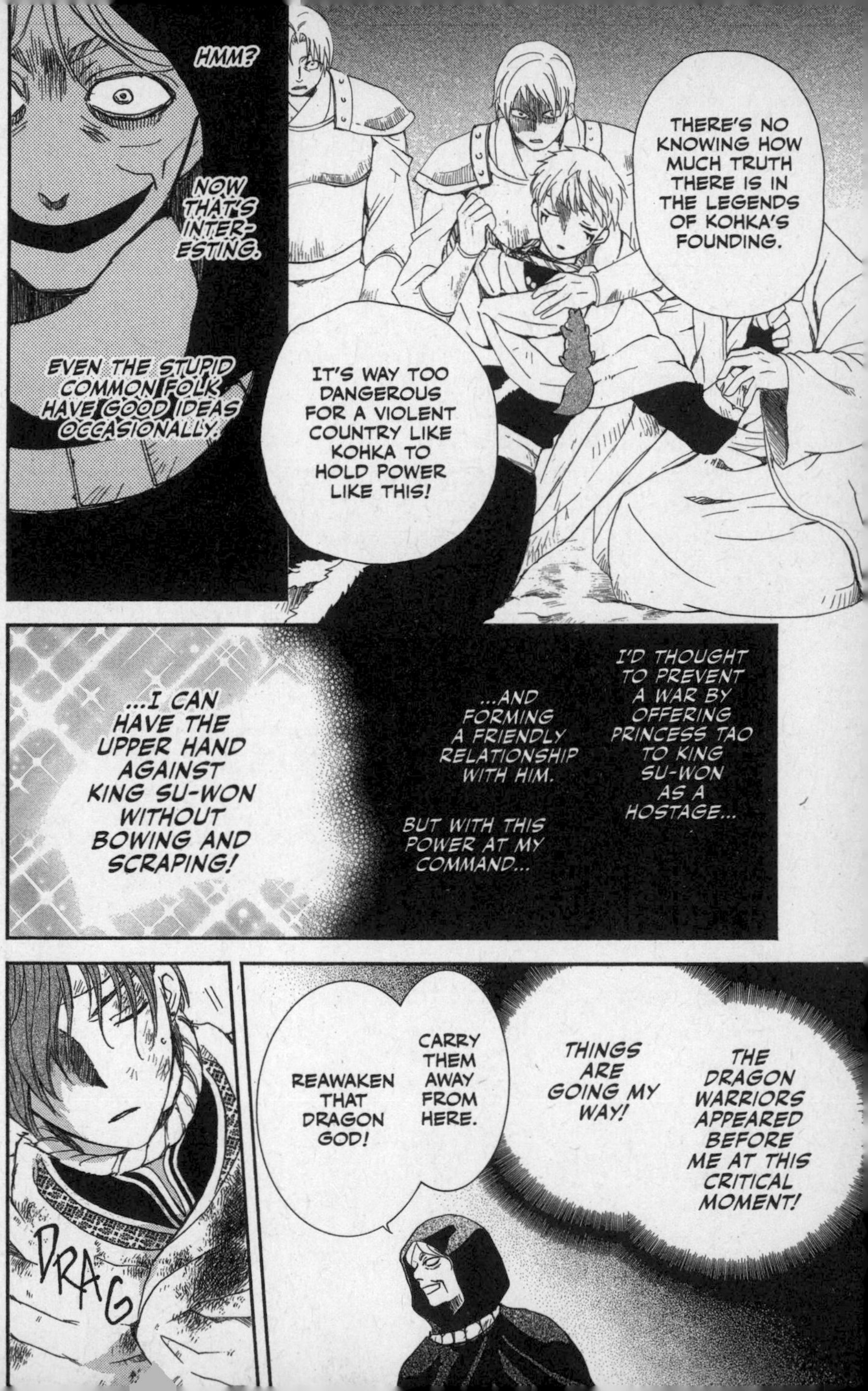
THERE'S NO KNOWING HOW MUCH TRUTH THERE IS IN THE LEGENDS OF KOHKA'S FOUNDING.
IT'S WAY TOO DANGEROUS FOR A VIOLENT COUNTRY LIKE KOHKA TO HOLD POWER LIKE THIS!
HMM?
NOW THAT'S INTER-ESTING.
EVEN THE STUPID COMMON FOLK HAVE GOOD IDEAS OCCASIONALLY.
I'D THOUGHT TO PREVENT A WAR BY OFFERING PRINCESS TAO TO KING SU-WON AS A HOSTAGE...
...AND FORMING A FRIENDLY RELATIONSHIP WITH HIM.
BUT WITH THIS POWER AT MY COMMAND...
...I CAN HAVE THE UPPER HAND AGAINST KING SU-WON WITHOUT BOWING AND SCRAPING!
THE DRAGON WARRIORS APPEARED BEFORE ME AT THIS CRITICAL MOMENT!
THINGS ARE GOING MY WAY!
CARRY THEM AWAY FROM HERE.
REAWAKEN THAT DRAGON GOD!
DRAG

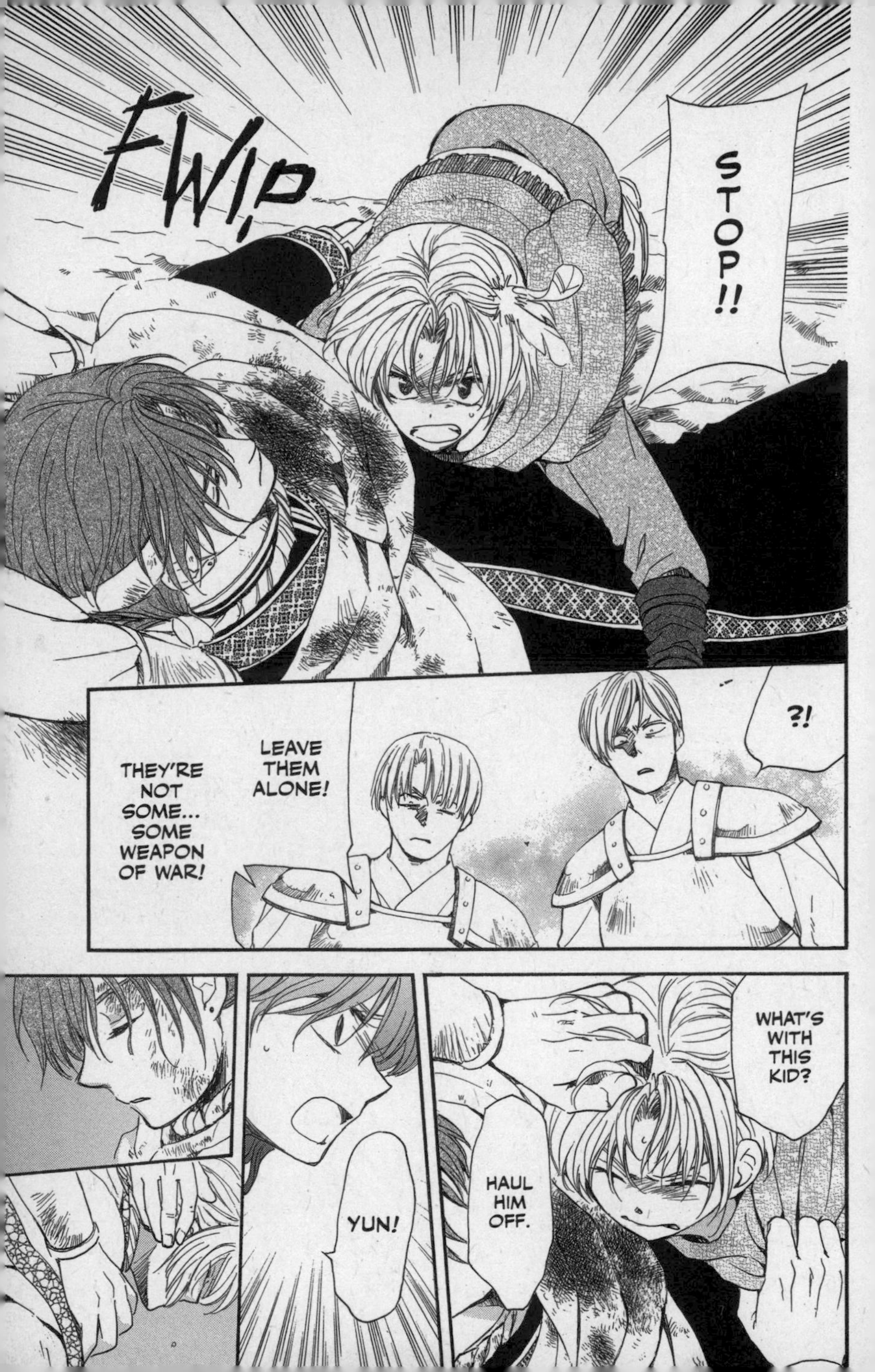
STOP!!
FWIP
?!
LEAVE THEM ALONE!
THEY'RE NOT SOME... SOME WEAPON OF WAR!
WHAT'S WITH THIS KID?
HAUL HIM OFF.
YUN!

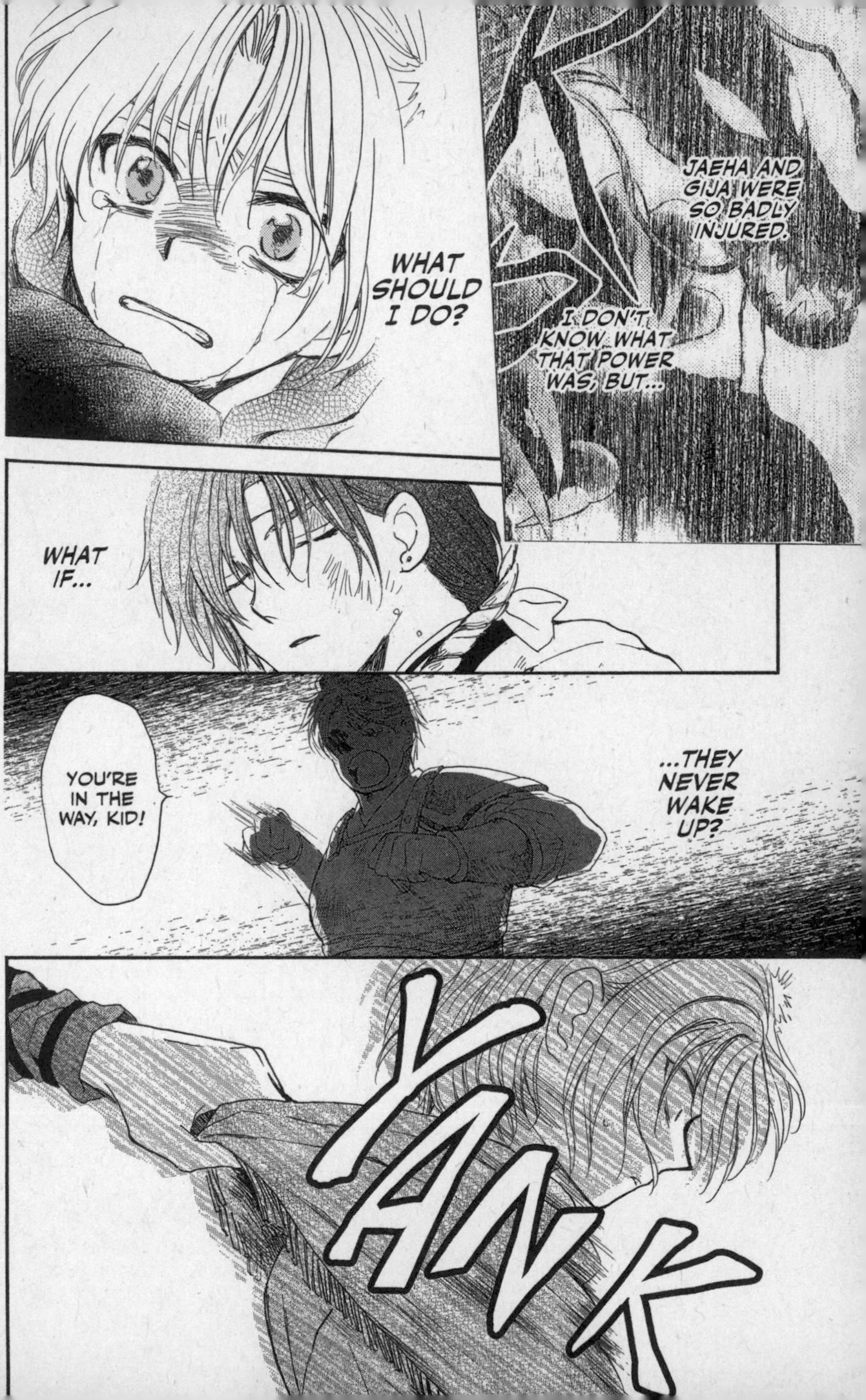
JAEHA AND GIJA WERE SO BADLY INJURED.
I DON'T KNOW WHAT THAT POWER WAS, BUT...
WHAT SHOULD I DO?
WHAT IF...
...THEY NEVER WAKE UP?
YOU'RE IN THE WAY, KID!
YANK

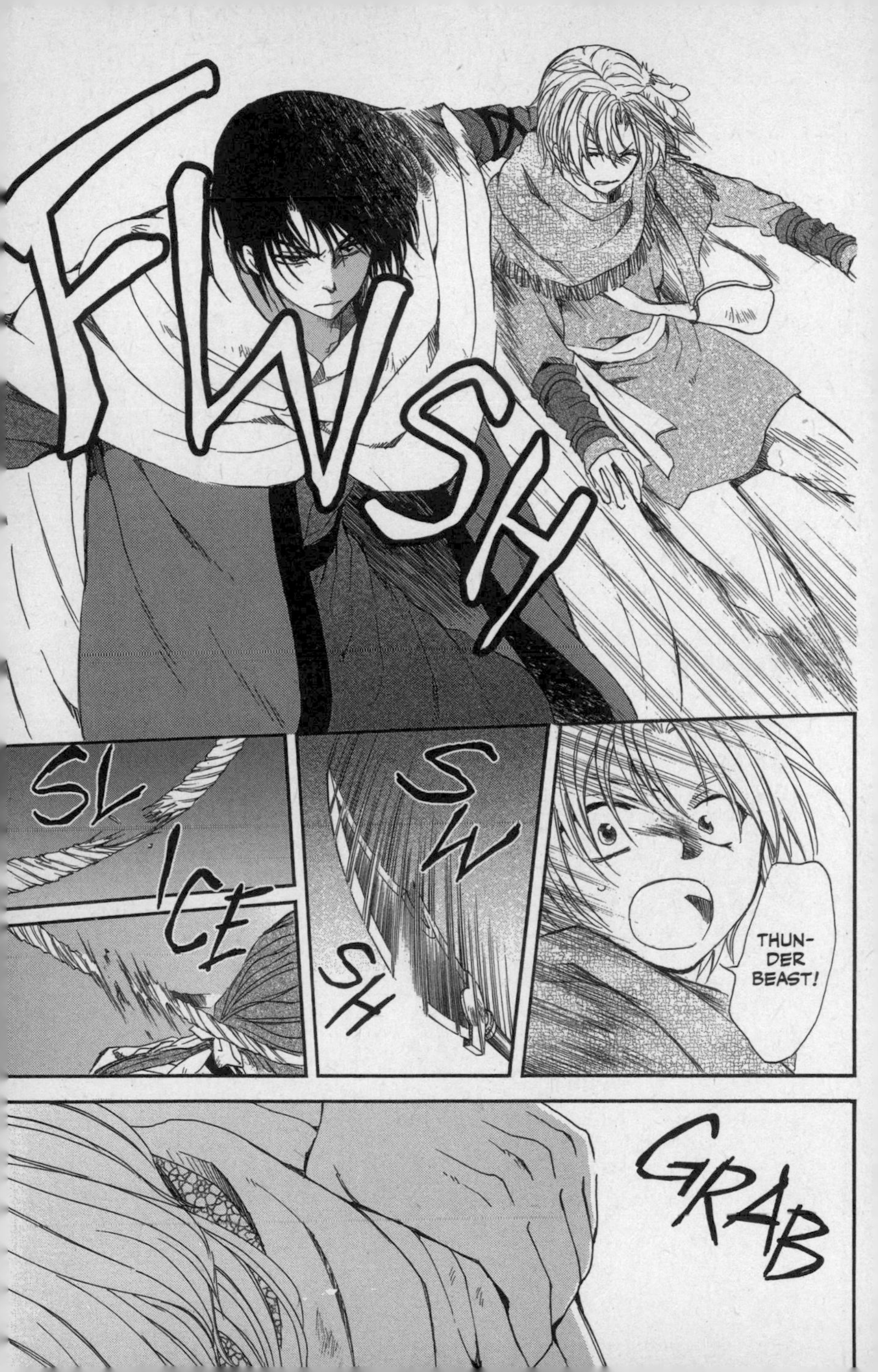
FWISH
THUN-DER BEAST!
SWISH
SLICE
GRAB

...STEAL-
ING THE
DRAGONS!

...
HE'S

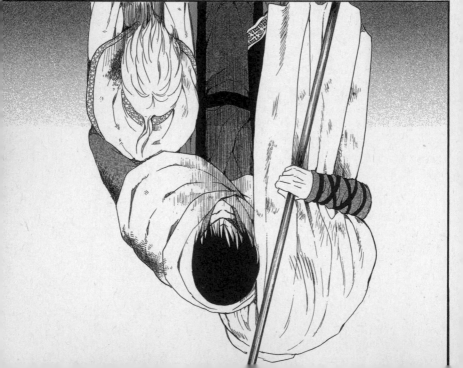

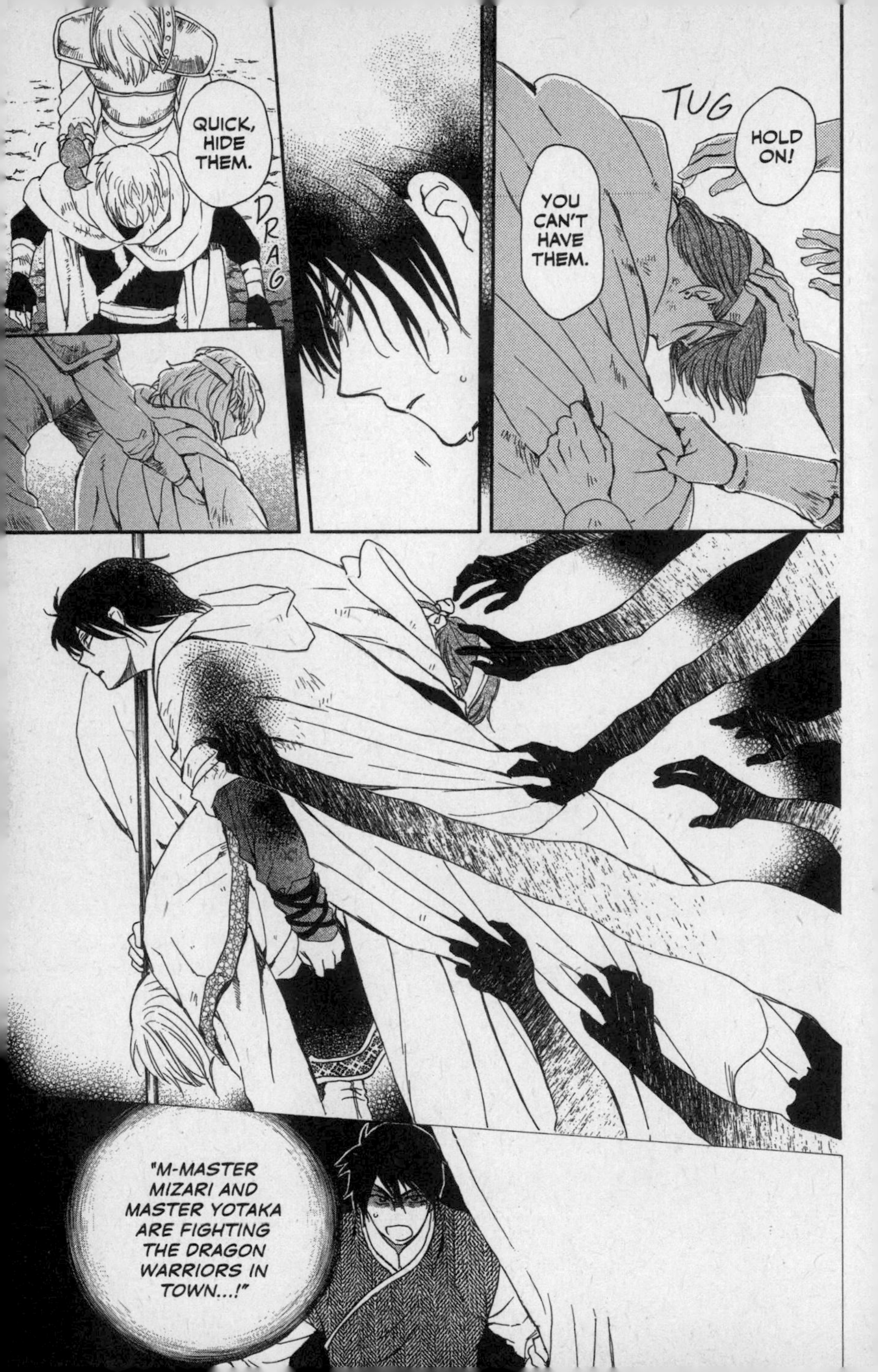
TUG
HOLD ON!
YOU CAN'T HAVE THEM.
QUICK, HIDE THEM.
DRAG
"M-MASTER MIZARI AND MASTER YOTAKA ARE FIGHTING THE DRAGON WARRIORS IN TOWN...!"

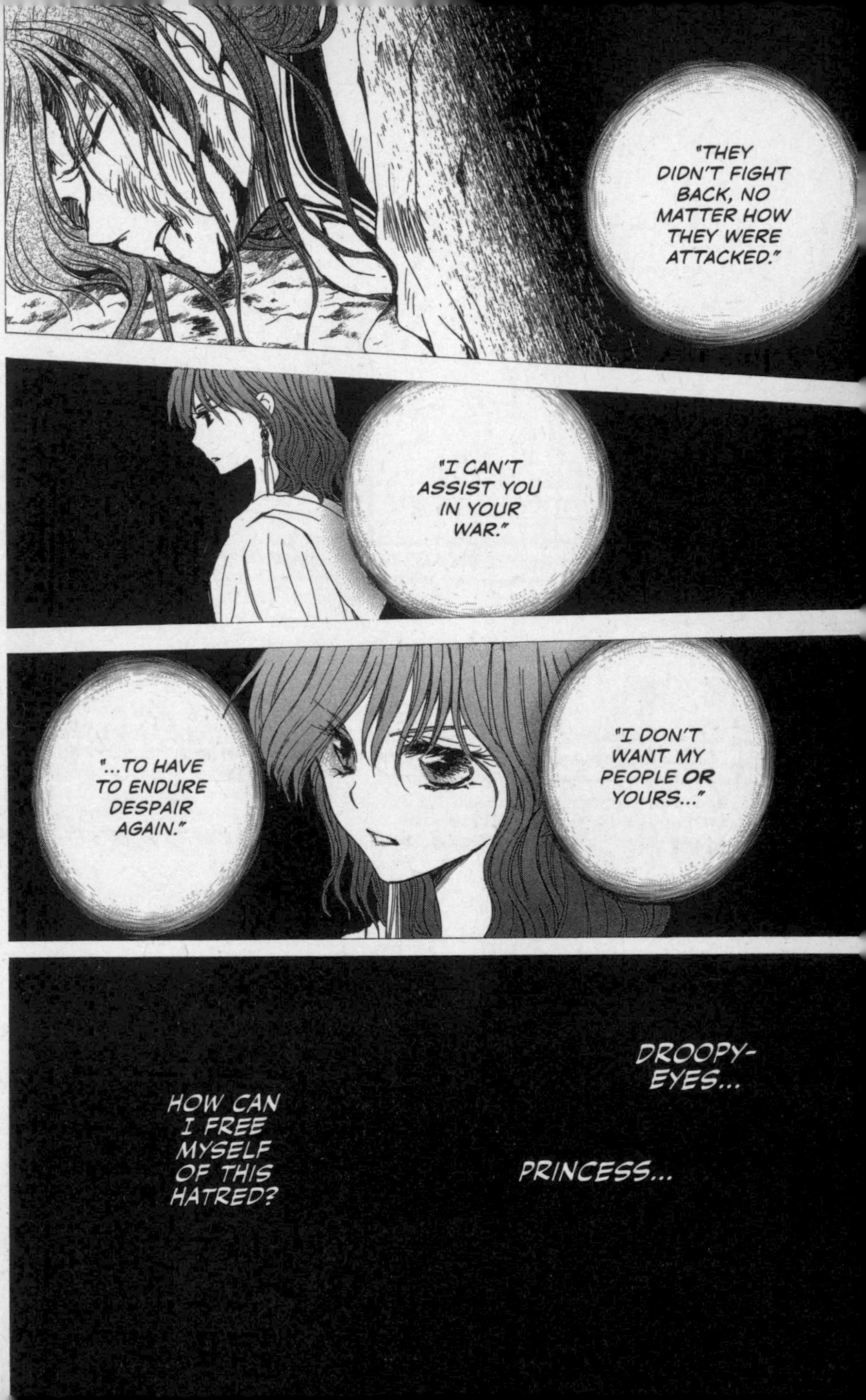
"THEY DIDN'T FIGHT BACK, NO MATTER HOW THEY WERE ATTACKED."
"I CAN'T ASSIST YOU IN YOUR WAR."
"I DON'T WANT MY PEOPLE OR YOURS..."
"...TO HAVE TO ENDURE DESPAIR AGAIN."
DROOPY-EYES...
PRINCESS...
HOW CAN I FREE MYSELF OF THIS HATRED?

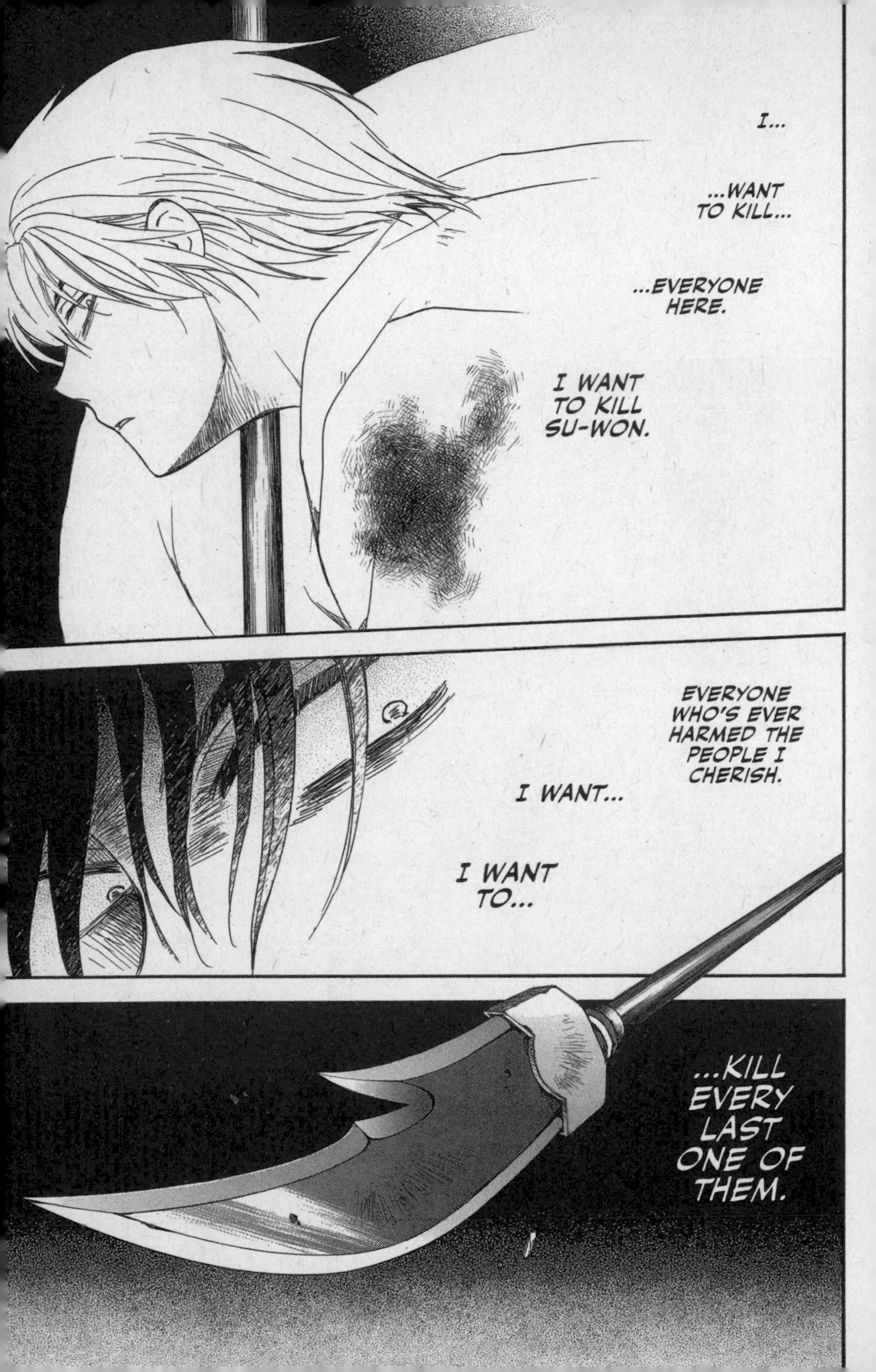
I...
...WANT TO KILL...
...EVERYONE HERE.
I WANT TO KILL SU-WON.
EVERYONE WHO'S EVER HARMED THE PEOPLE I CHERISH.
I WANT...
I WANT TO...
...KILL EVERY LAST ONE OF THEM.

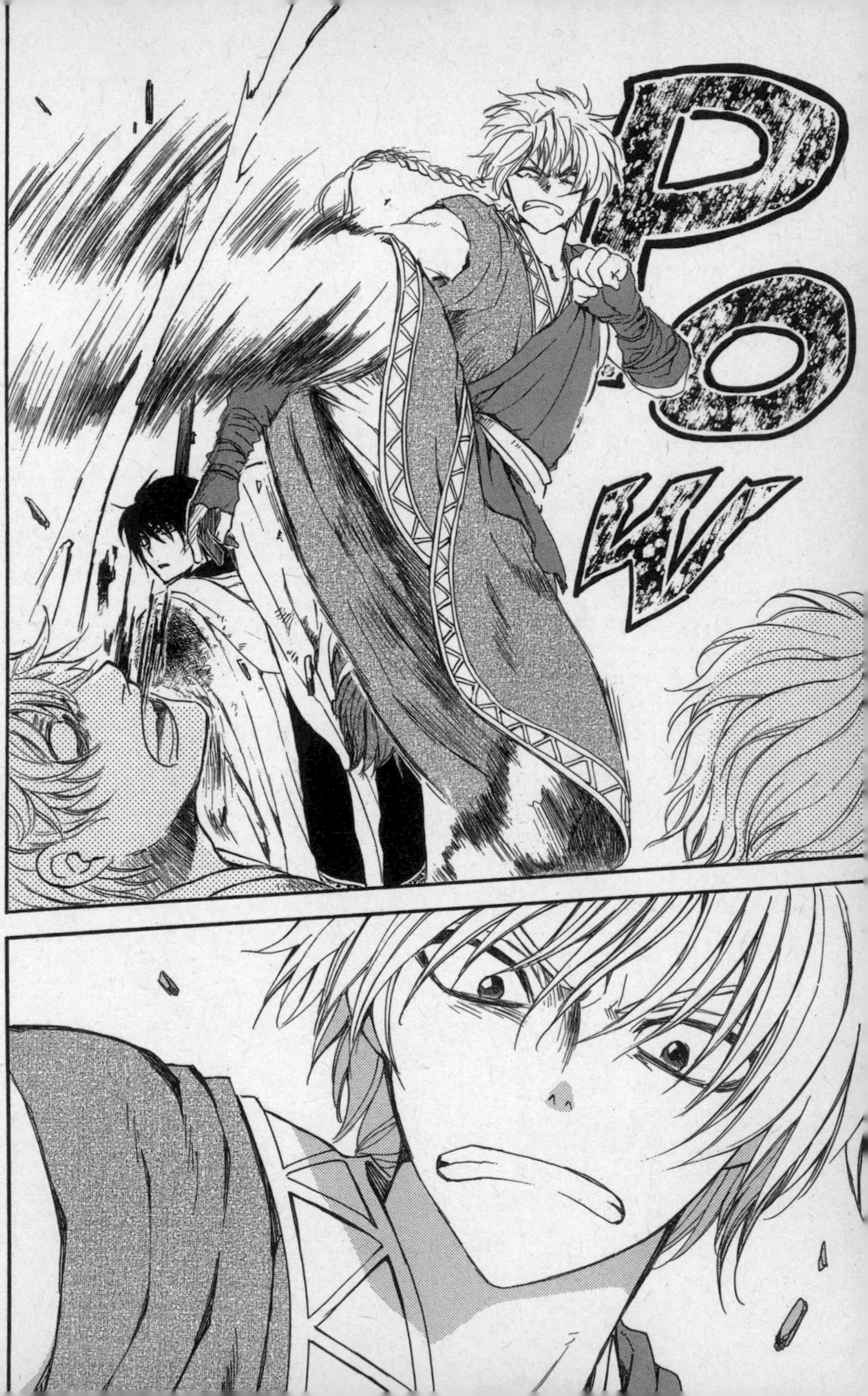
POW

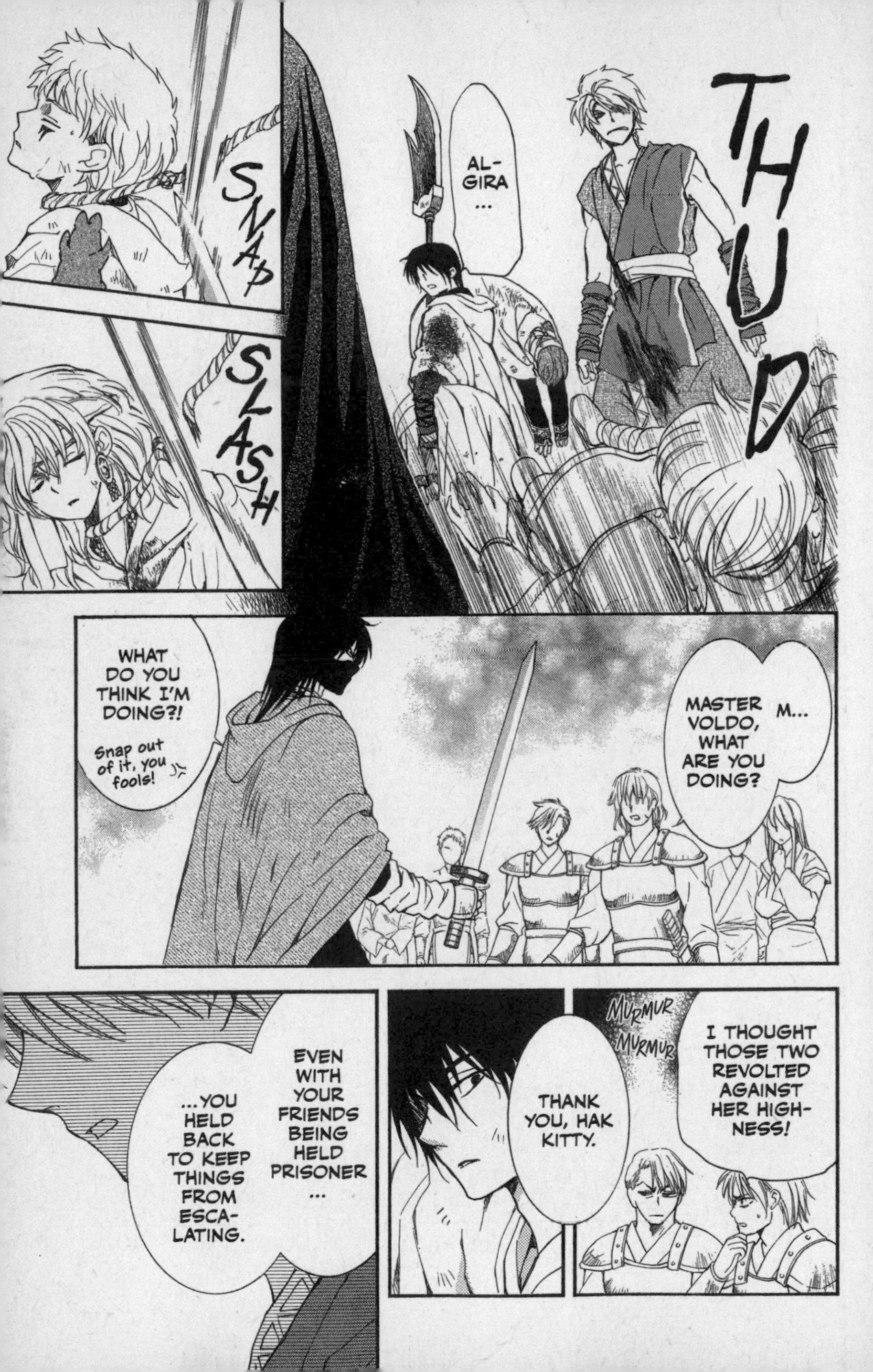
THUD
AL-GIRA...
SNAP
SLASH
MASTER VOLDO, WHAT ARE YOU DOING?
M...
WHAT DO YOU THINK I'M DOING?!
Snap out of it, you fools!
I THOUGHT THOSE TWO REVOLTED AGAINST HER HIGH-NESS!
MURMUR MURMUR
THANK YOU, HAK KITTY.
EVEN WITH YOUR FRIENDS BEING HELD PRISONER...
...YOU HELD BACK TO KEEP THINGS FROM ESCA-LATING.

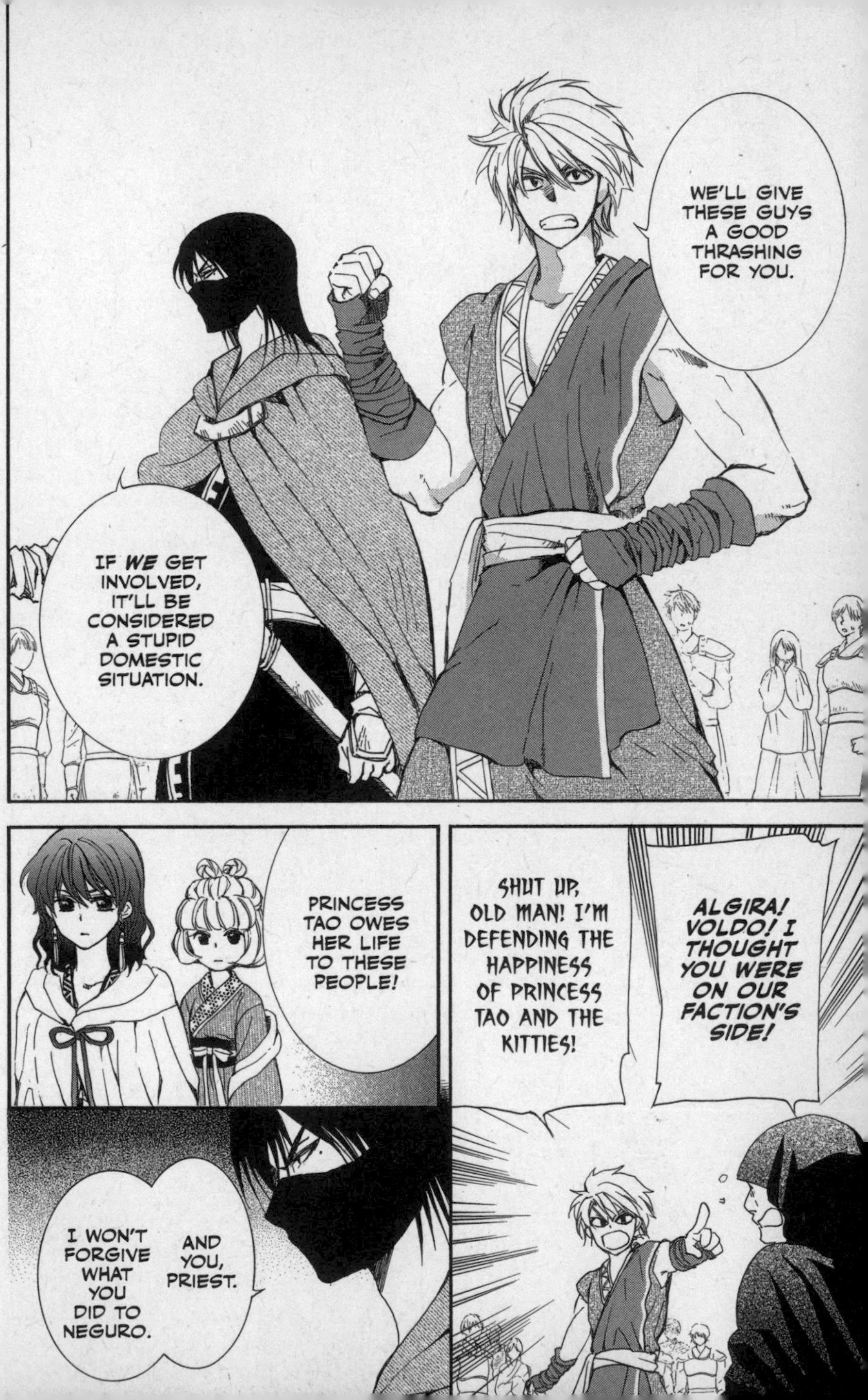
WE'LL GIVE THESE GUYS A GOOD THRASHING FOR YOU.
IF *WE* GET INVOLVED, IT'LL BE CONSIDERED A STUPID DOMESTIC SITUATION.
ALGIRA! VOLDO! I THOUGHT YOU WERE ON OUR FACTION'S SIDE!
SHUT UP, OLD MAN! I'M DEFENDING THE HAPPINESS OF PRINCESS TAO AND THE KITTIES!
PRINCESS TAO OWES HER LIFE TO THESE PEOPLE!
AND YOU, PRIEST.
I WON'T FORGIVE WHAT YOU DID TO NEGURO.

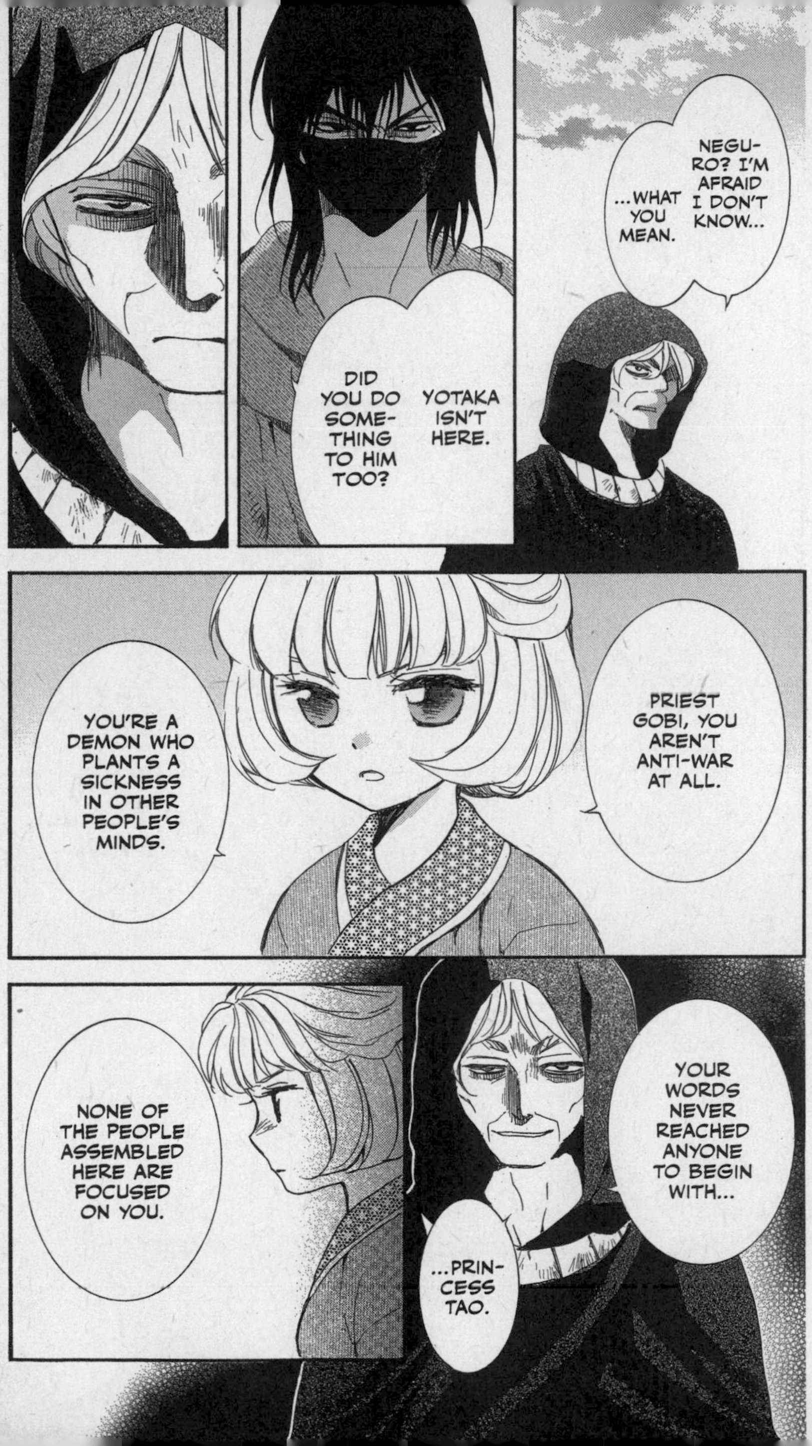
NEGU-RO? I'M AFRAID I DON'T KNOW... ...WHAT YOU MEAN.
YOTAKA ISN'T HERE. DID YOU DO SOME-THING TO HIM TOO?
PRIEST GOBI, YOU AREN'T ANTI-WAR AT ALL.
YOU'RE A DEMON WHO PLANTS A SICKNESS IN OTHER PEOPLE'S MINDS.
YOUR WORDS NEVER REACHED ANYONE TO BEGIN WITH...
...PRIN-CESS TAO.
NONE OF THE PEOPLE ASSEMBLED HERE ARE FOCUSED ON YOU.

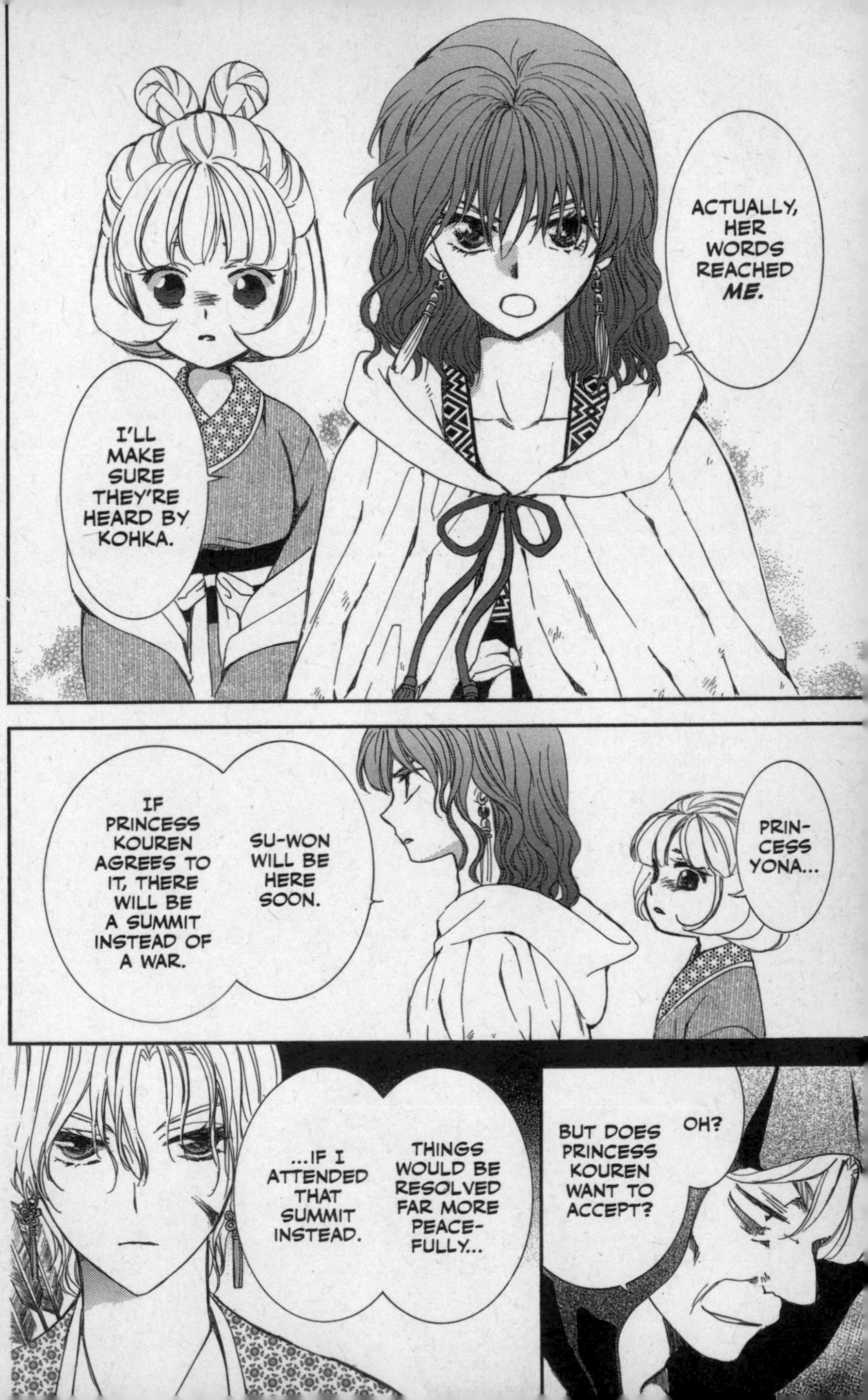
ACTUALLY, HER WORDS REACHED ME.
I'LL MAKE SURE THEY'RE HEARD BY KOHKA.
PRIN-CESS YONA...
SU-WON WILL BE HERE SOON.
IF PRINCESS KOUREN AGREES TO IT, THERE WILL BE A SUMMIT INSTEAD OF A WAR.
OH?
BUT DOES PRINCESS KOUREN WANT TO ACCEPT?
THINGS WOULD BE RESOLVED FAR MORE PEACE-FULLY...
...IF I ATTENDED THAT SUMMIT INSTEAD.

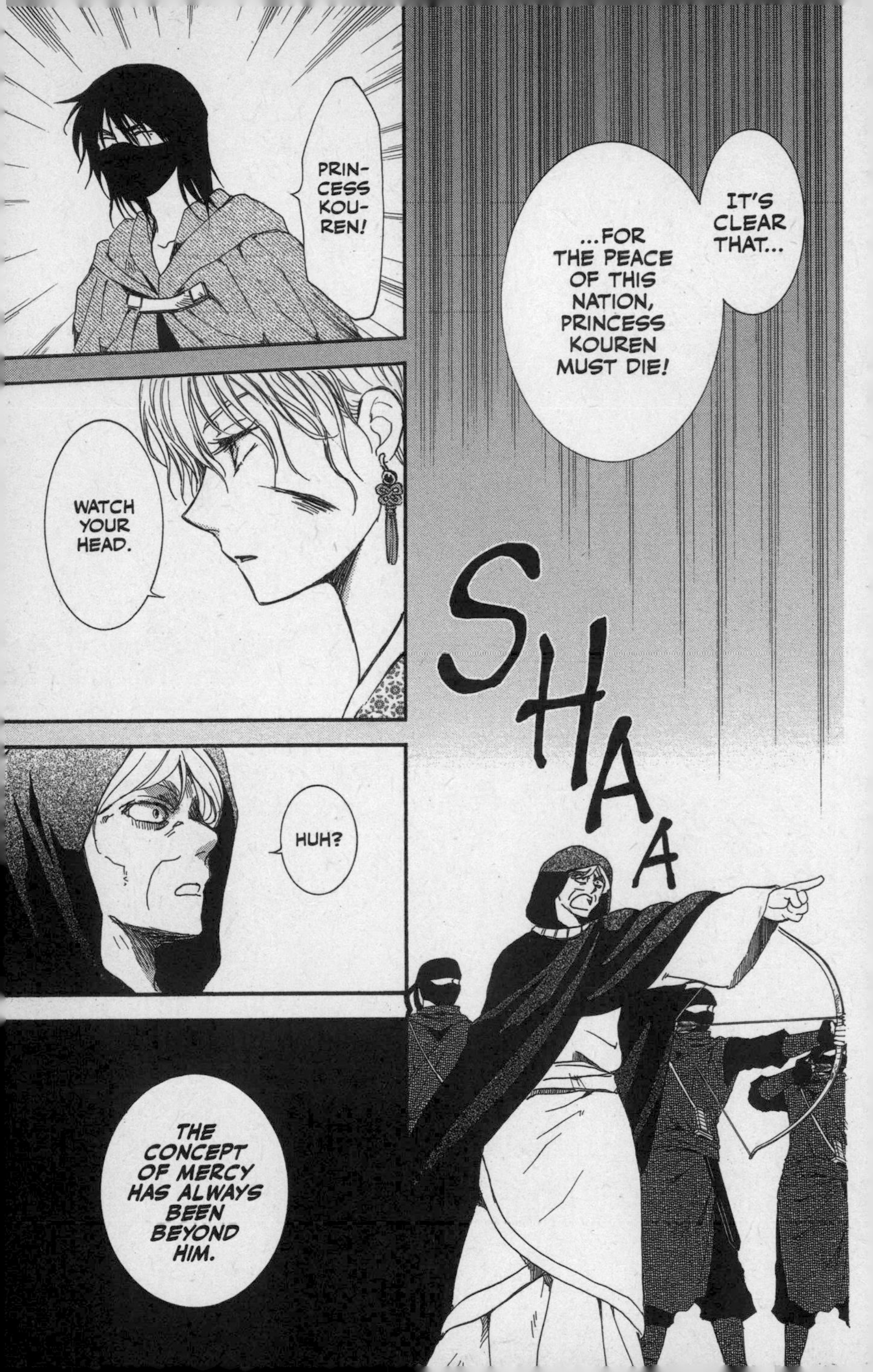
IT'S CLEAR THAT...
...FOR THE PEACE OF THIS NATION, PRINCESS KOUREN MUST DIE!
SHAA
PRIN-CESS KOU-REN!
WATCH YOUR HEAD.
HUH?
THE CONCEPT OF MERCY HAS ALWAYS BEEN BEYOND HIM.

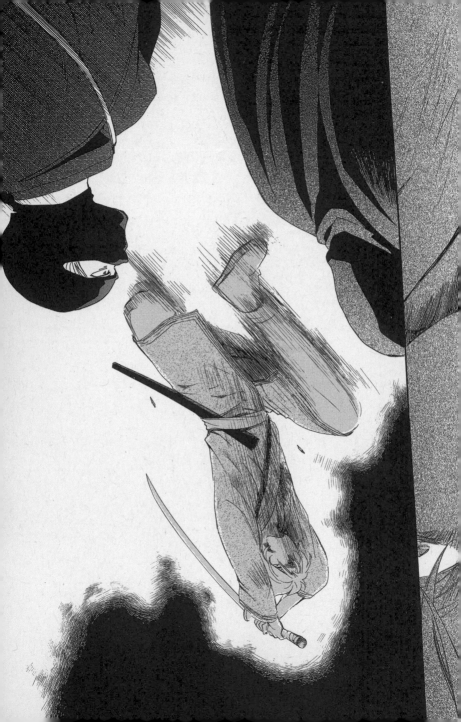

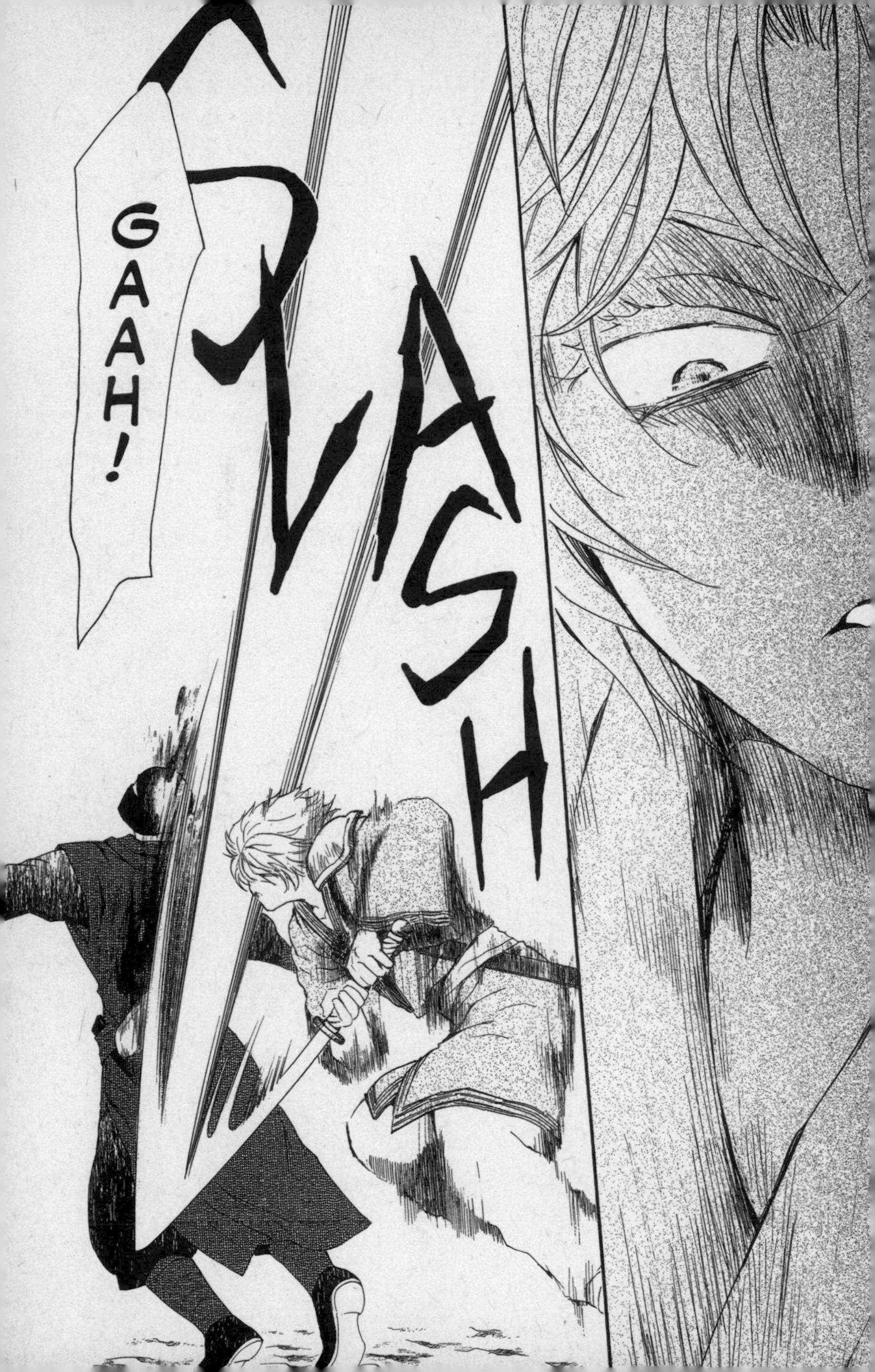
SLASH
GAAH!

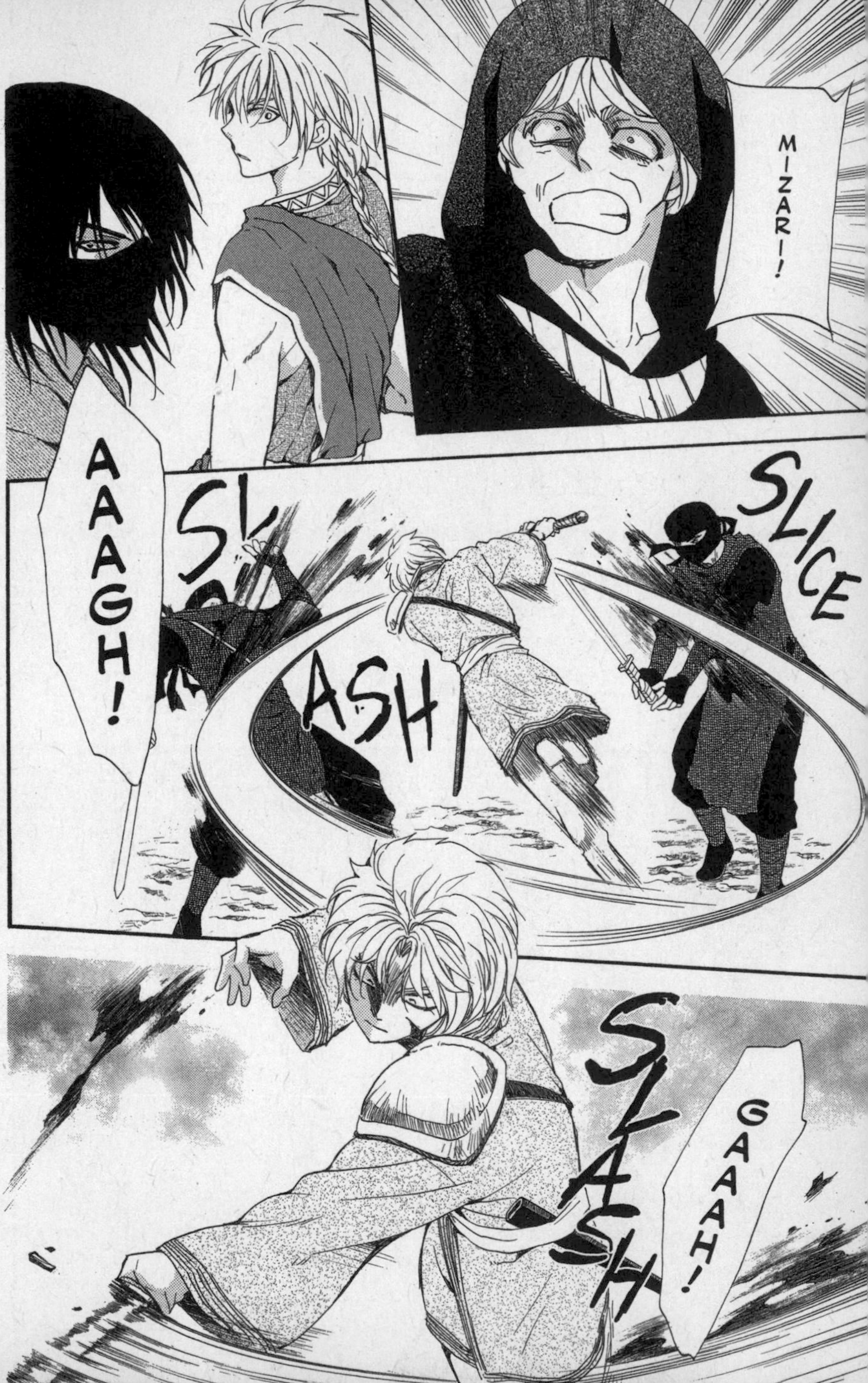
MIZARI!
SLICE
SL
ASH
AAAGH!
GAAAH!
SLASH

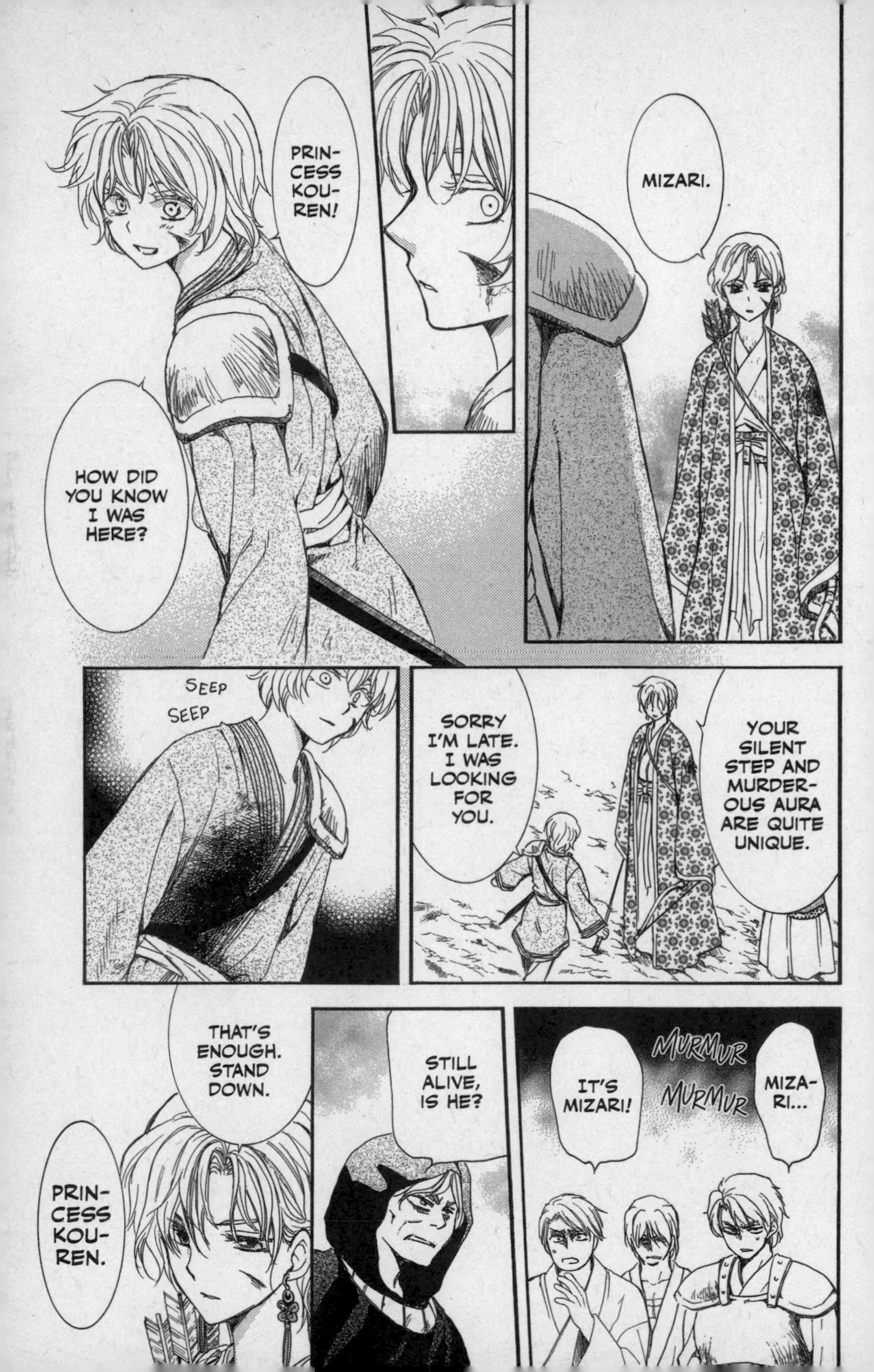
MIZARI.
PRINCESS KOUREN!
HOW DID YOU KNOW I WAS HERE?
YOUR SILENT STEP AND MURDEROUS AURA ARE QUITE UNIQUE.
SORRY I'M LATE. I WAS LOOKING FOR YOU.
SEEP SEEP
MIZARI...
MURMUR MURMUR
IT'S MIZARI!
STILL ALIVE, IS HE?
THAT'S ENOUGH. STAND DOWN.
PRINCESS KOUREN.

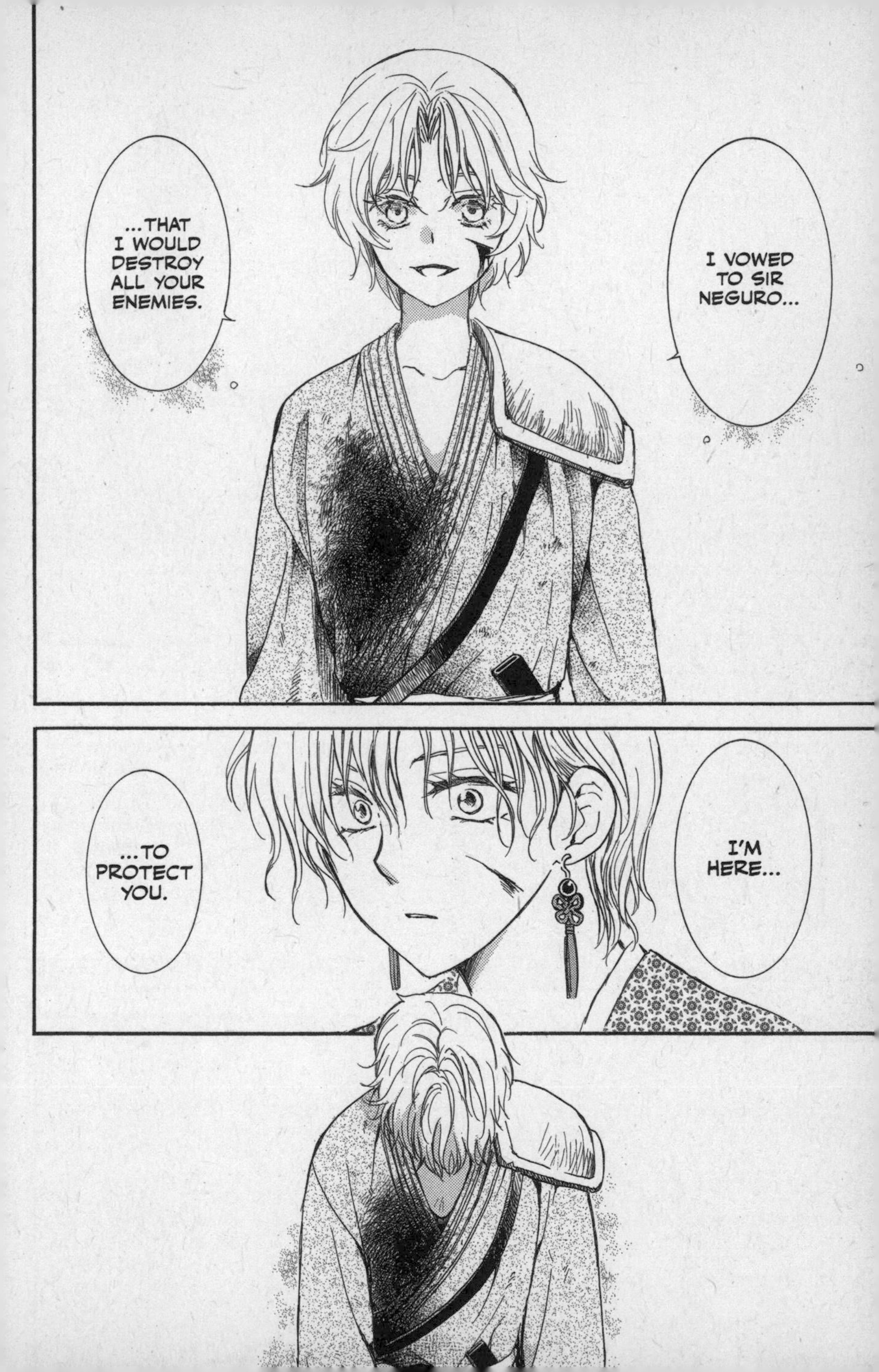
I VOWED TO SIR NEGURO...
...THAT I WOULD DESTROY ALL YOUR ENEMIES.
I'M HERE...
...TO PROTECT YOU.

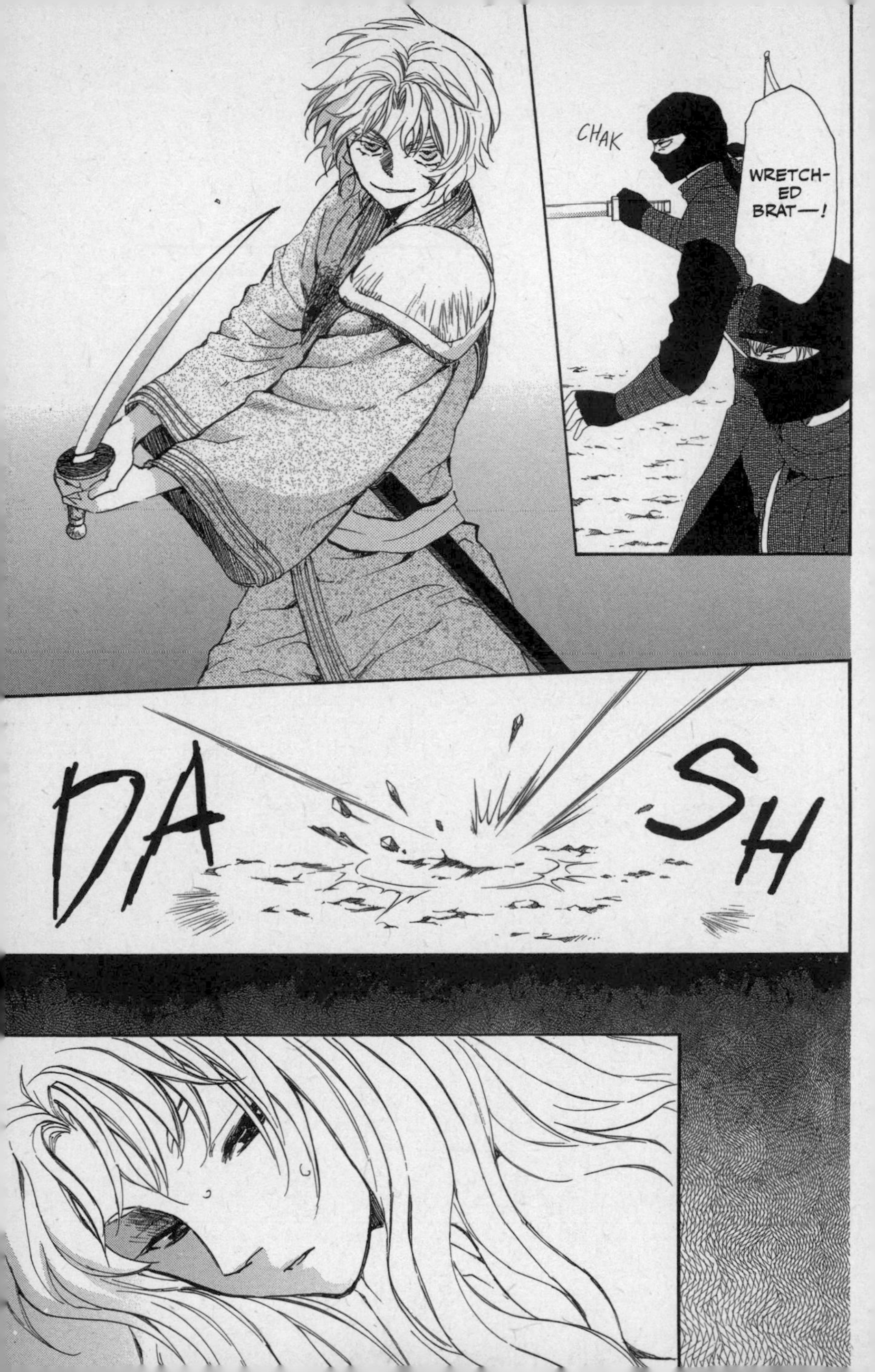
WRETCH-
ED
BRAT—!
CHAK
DASH

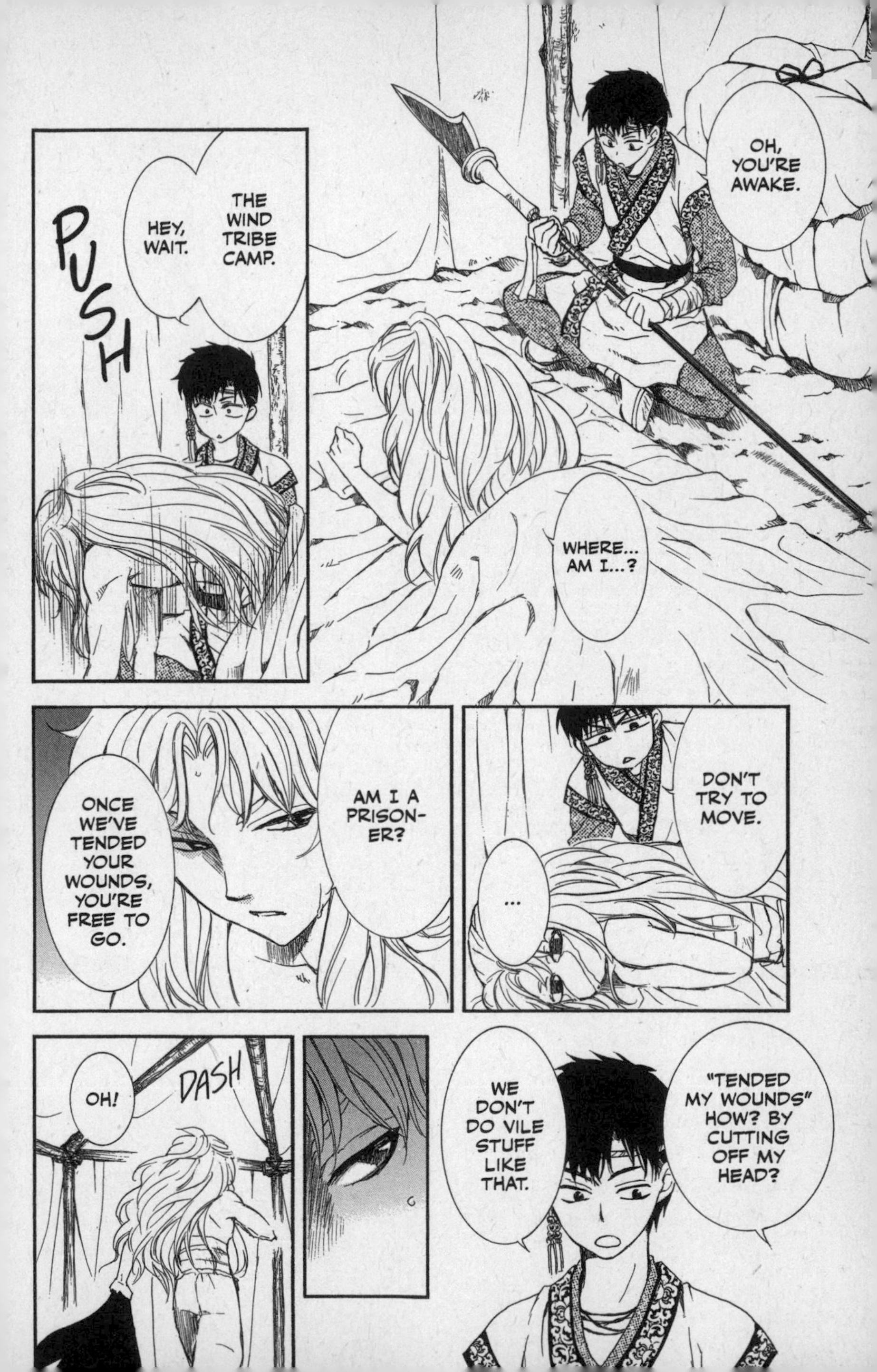
OH, YOU'RE AWAKE.
WHERE... AM I...?
THE WIND TRIBE CAMP.
HEY, WAIT.
PUSH
DON'T TRY TO MOVE.
...
AM I A PRISONER?
ONCE WE'VE TENDED YOUR WOUNDS, YOU'RE FREE TO GO.
"TENDED MY WOUNDS" HOW? BY CUTTING OFF MY HEAD?
WE DON'T DO VILE STUFF LIKE THAT.
DASH
OH!

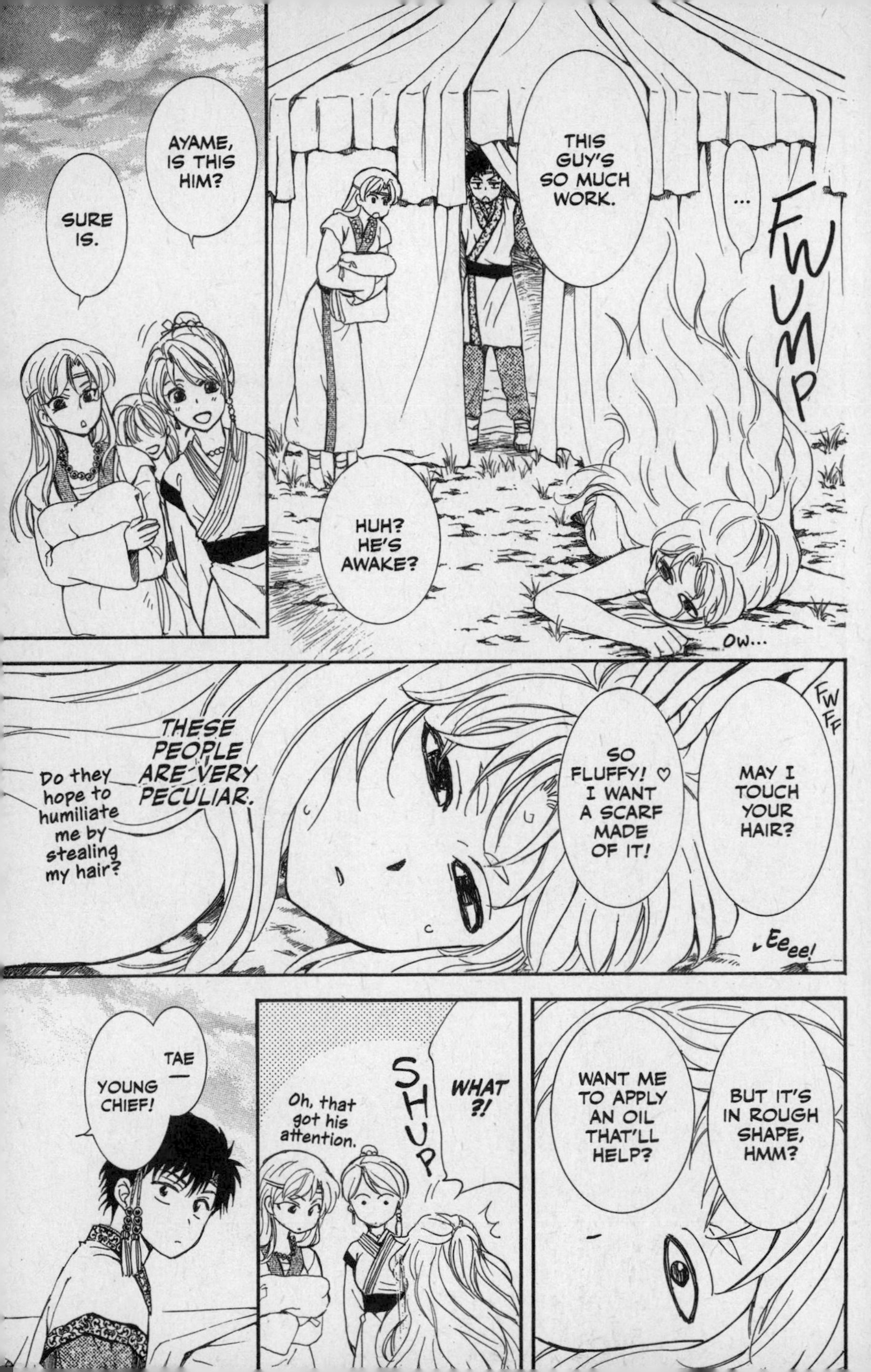
FWUMP
...
THIS GUY'S SO MUCH WORK.
HUH? HE'S AWAKE?
OW...
AYAME, IS THIS HIM?
SURE IS.
FWFF
MAY I TOUCH YOUR HAIR?
SO FLUFFY! ♡ I WANT A SCARF MADE OF IT!
Eeee!
THESE PEOPLE ARE VERY PECULIAR.
Do they hope to humiliate me by stealing my hair?
BUT IT'S IN ROUGH SHAPE, HMM?
WANT ME TO APPLY AN OIL THAT'LL HELP?
WHAT?!
SHUP
Oh, that got his attention.
TAE—
YOUNG CHIEF!

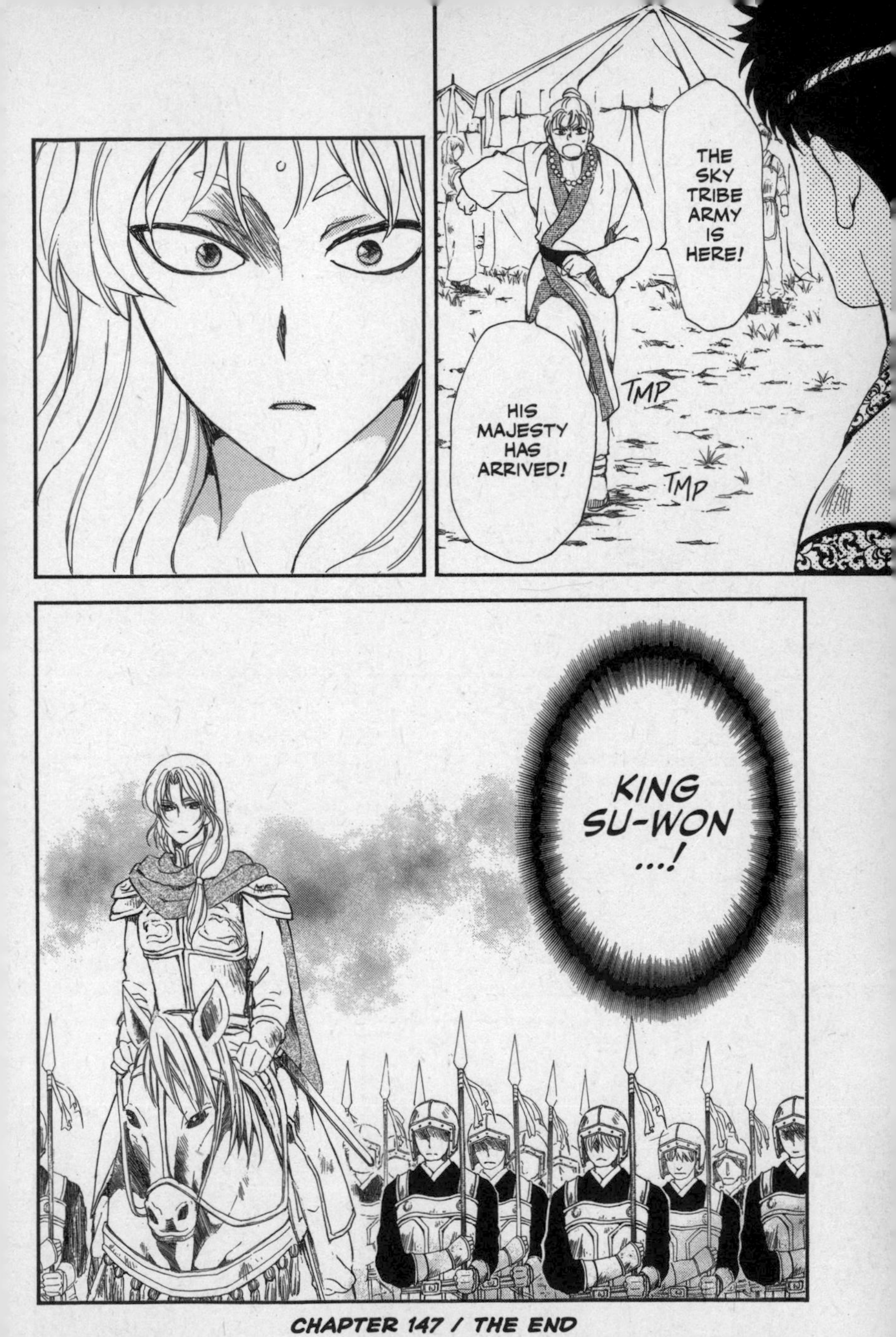
THE SKY TRIBE ARMY IS HERE!
HIS MAJESTY HAS ARRIVED!
TMP
TMP
KING SU-WON ...!

CHAPTER 147 / THE END

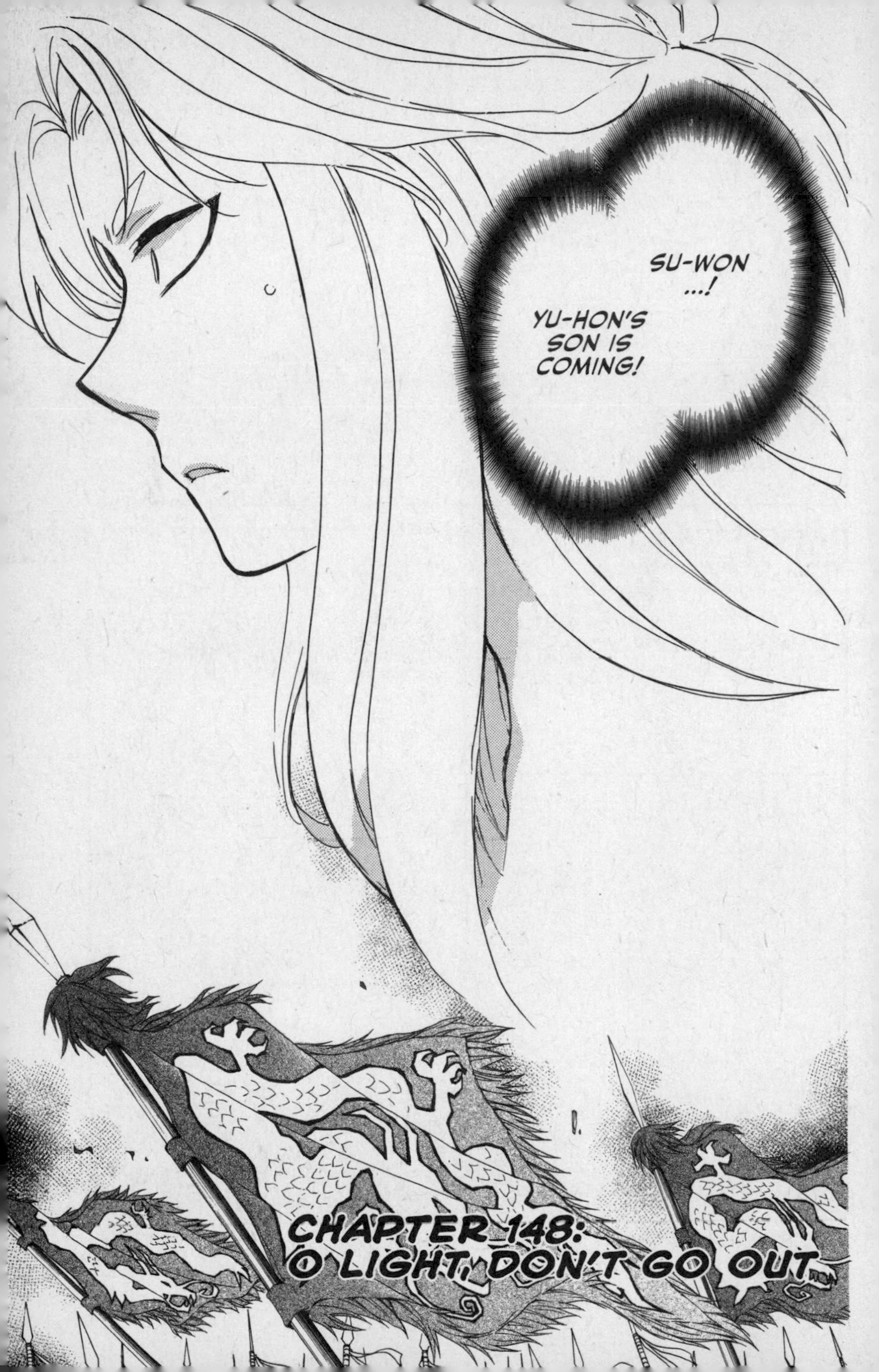
SU-WON ...!
YU-HON'S SON IS COMING!
CHAPTER 148: O LIGHT, DON'T GO OUT

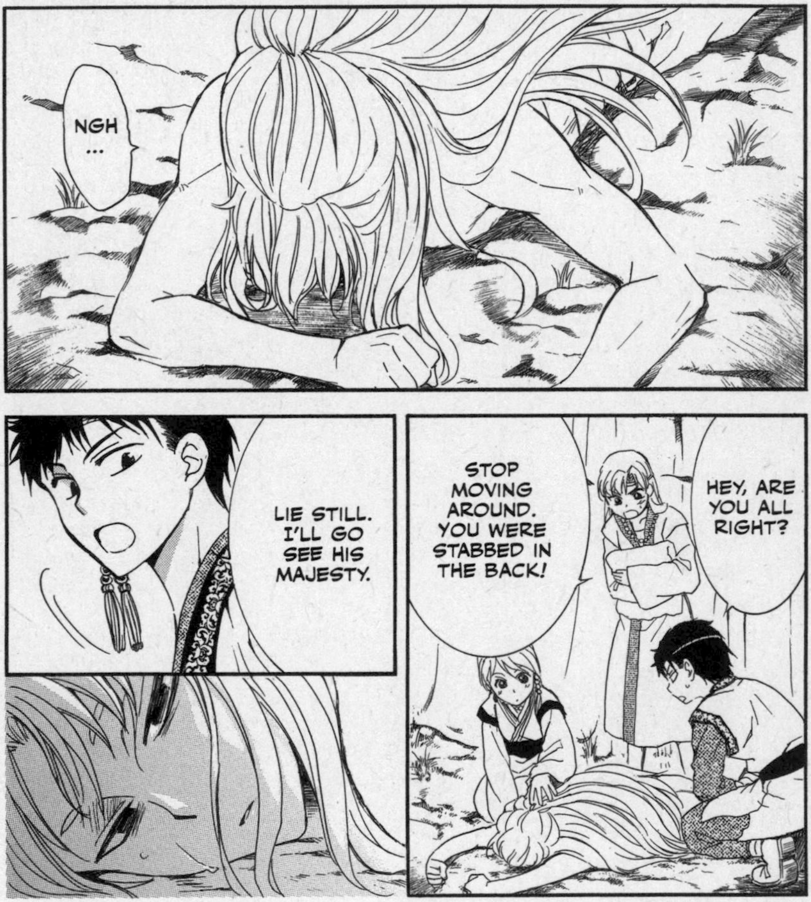
NGH ...
HEY, ARE YOU ALL RIGHT?
STOP MOVING AROUND. YOU WERE STABBED IN THE BACK!
LIE STILL. I'LL GO SEE HIS MAJESTY.

Yona of the Dawn

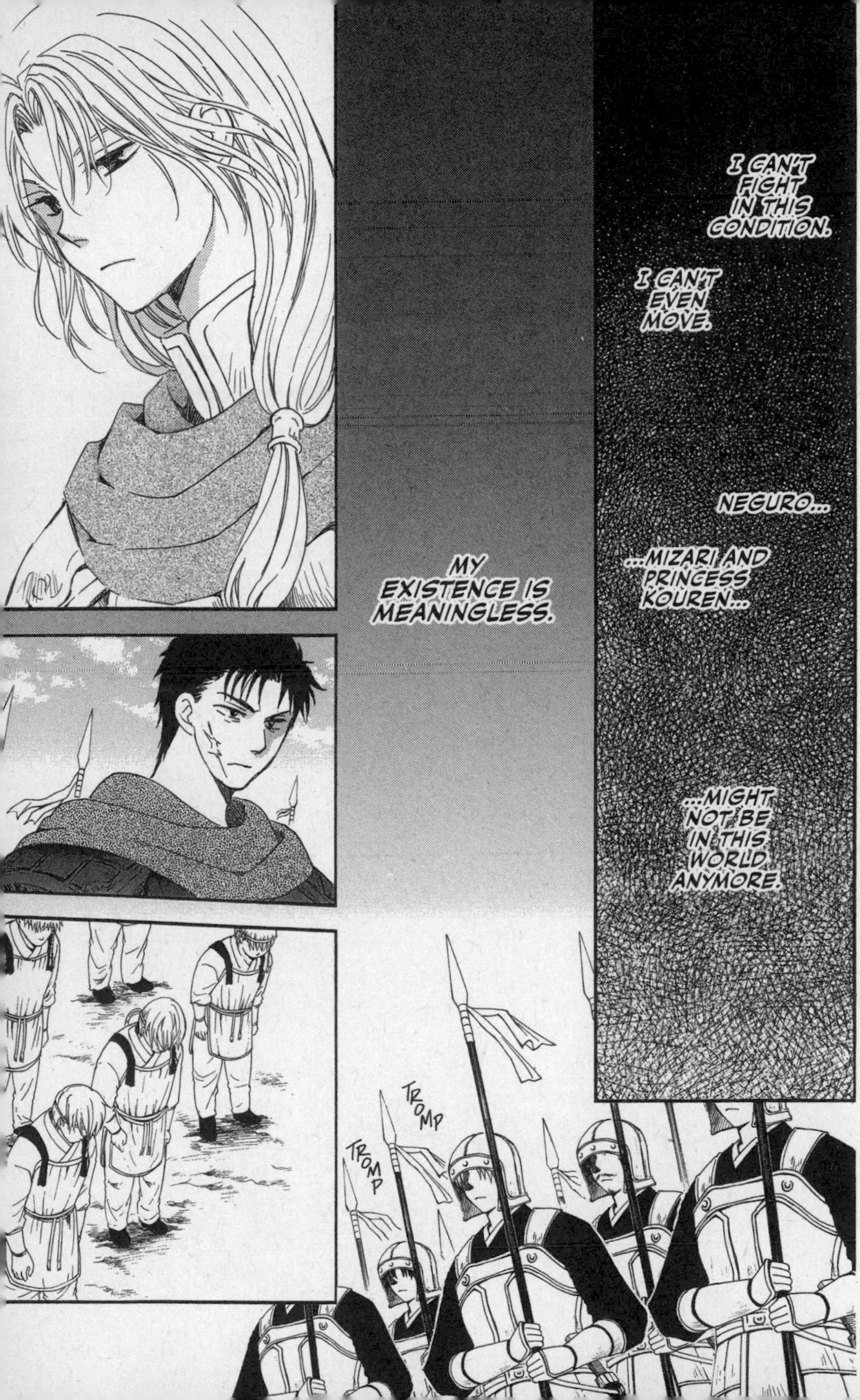
I CAN'T FIGHT IN THIS CONDITION.
I CAN'T EVEN MOVE.
NEGURO...
...MIZARI AND PRINCESS KOUREN...
...MIGHT NOT BE IN THIS WORLD ANYMORE.
MY EXISTENCE IS MEANINGLESS.
TROMP
TROMP

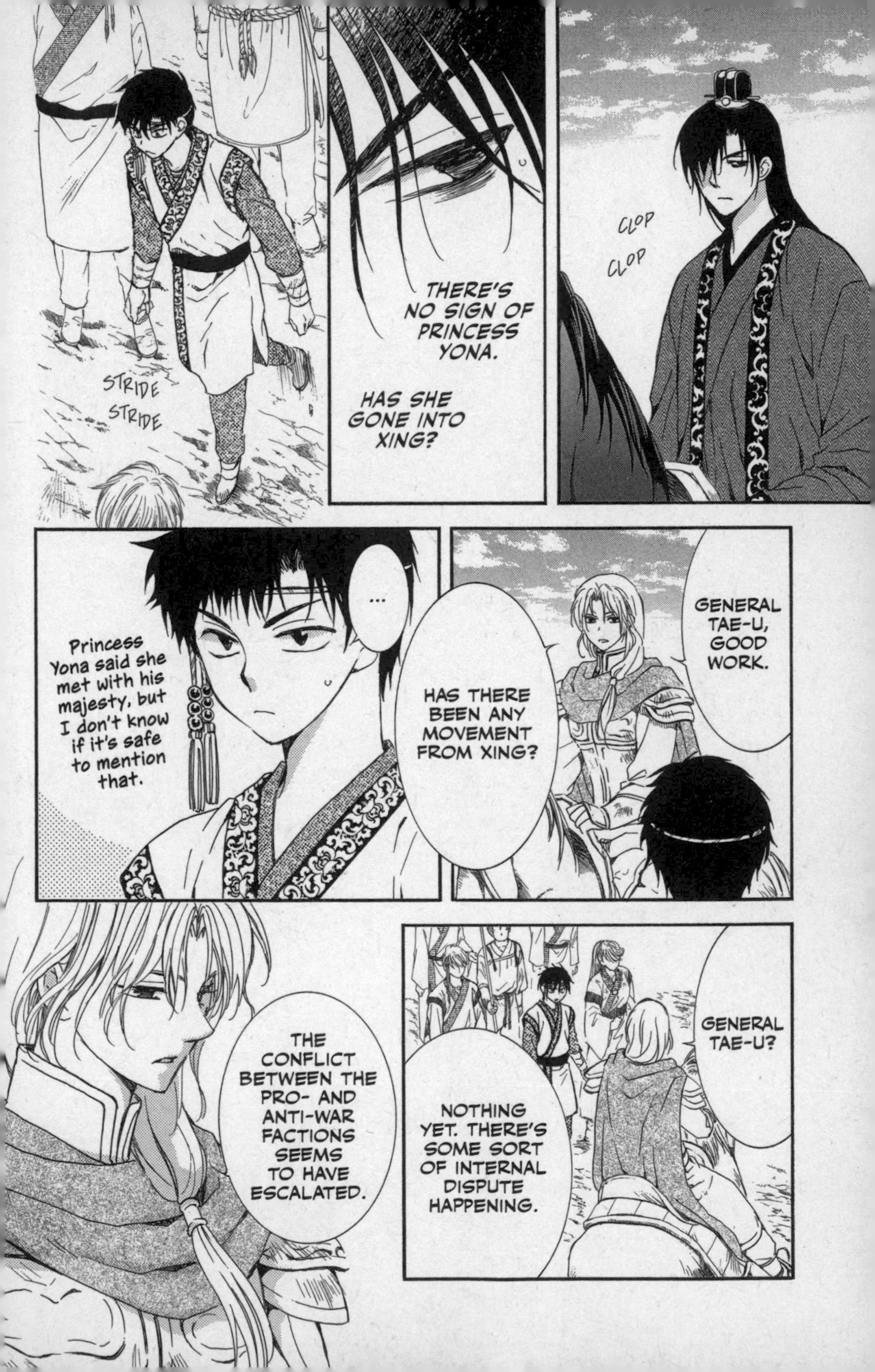
CLOP
CLOP
THERE'S NO SIGN OF PRINCESS YONA.
HAS SHE GONE INTO XING?
STRIDE
STRIDE
GENERAL TAE-U, GOOD WORK.
HAS THERE BEEN ANY MOVEMENT FROM XING?
...
Princess Yona said she met with his majesty, but I don't know if it's safe to mention that.
GENERAL TAE-U?
NOTHING YET. THERE'S SOME SORT OF INTERNAL DISPUTE HAPPENING.
THE CONFLICT BETWEEN THE PRO- AND ANTI-WAR FACTIONS SEEMS TO HAVE ESCALATED.

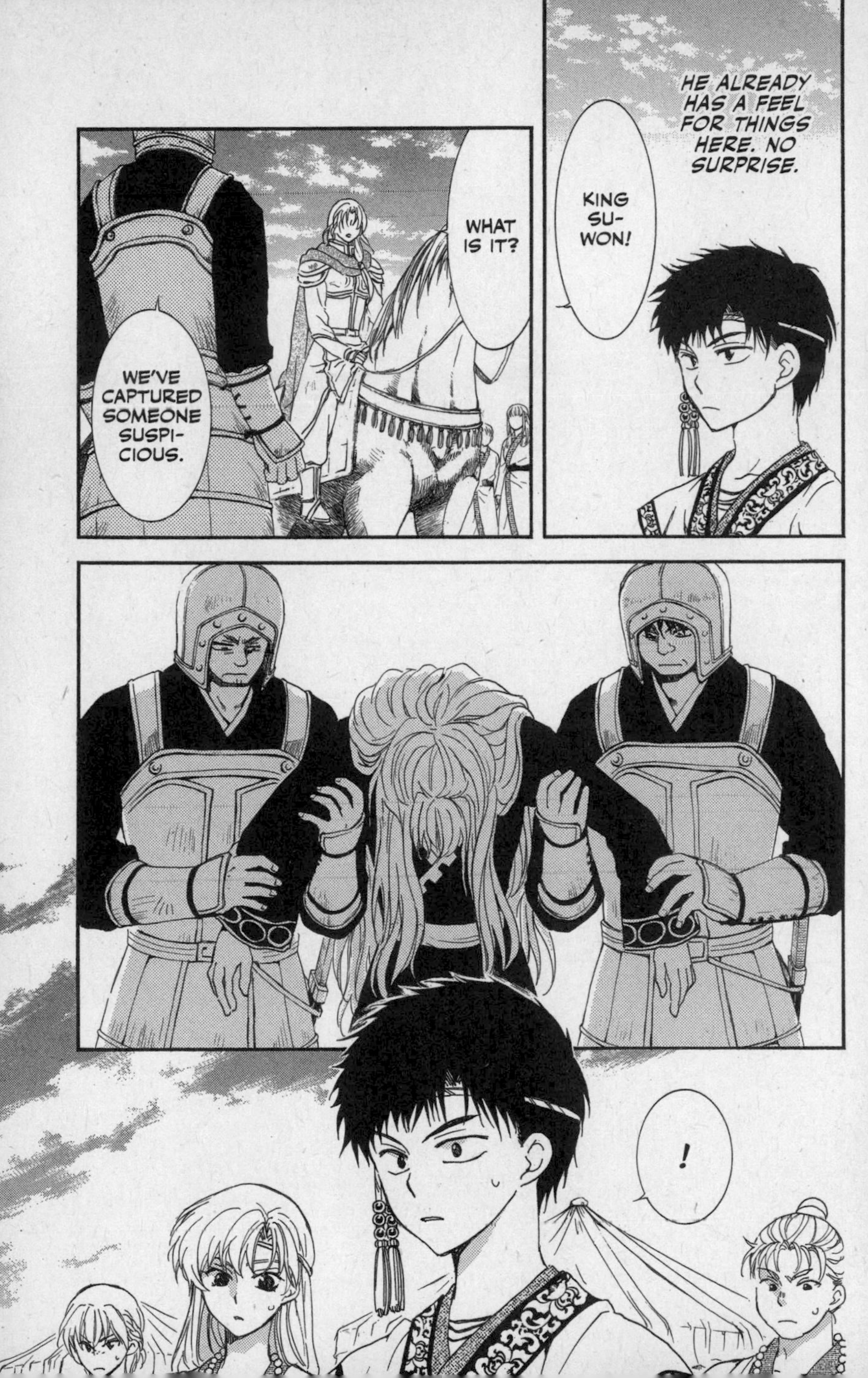
HE ALREADY HAS A FEEL FOR THINGS HERE. NO SURPRISE.
KING SU-WON!
WHAT IS IT?
WE'VE CAPTURED SOMEONE SUSPI-CIOUS.
!

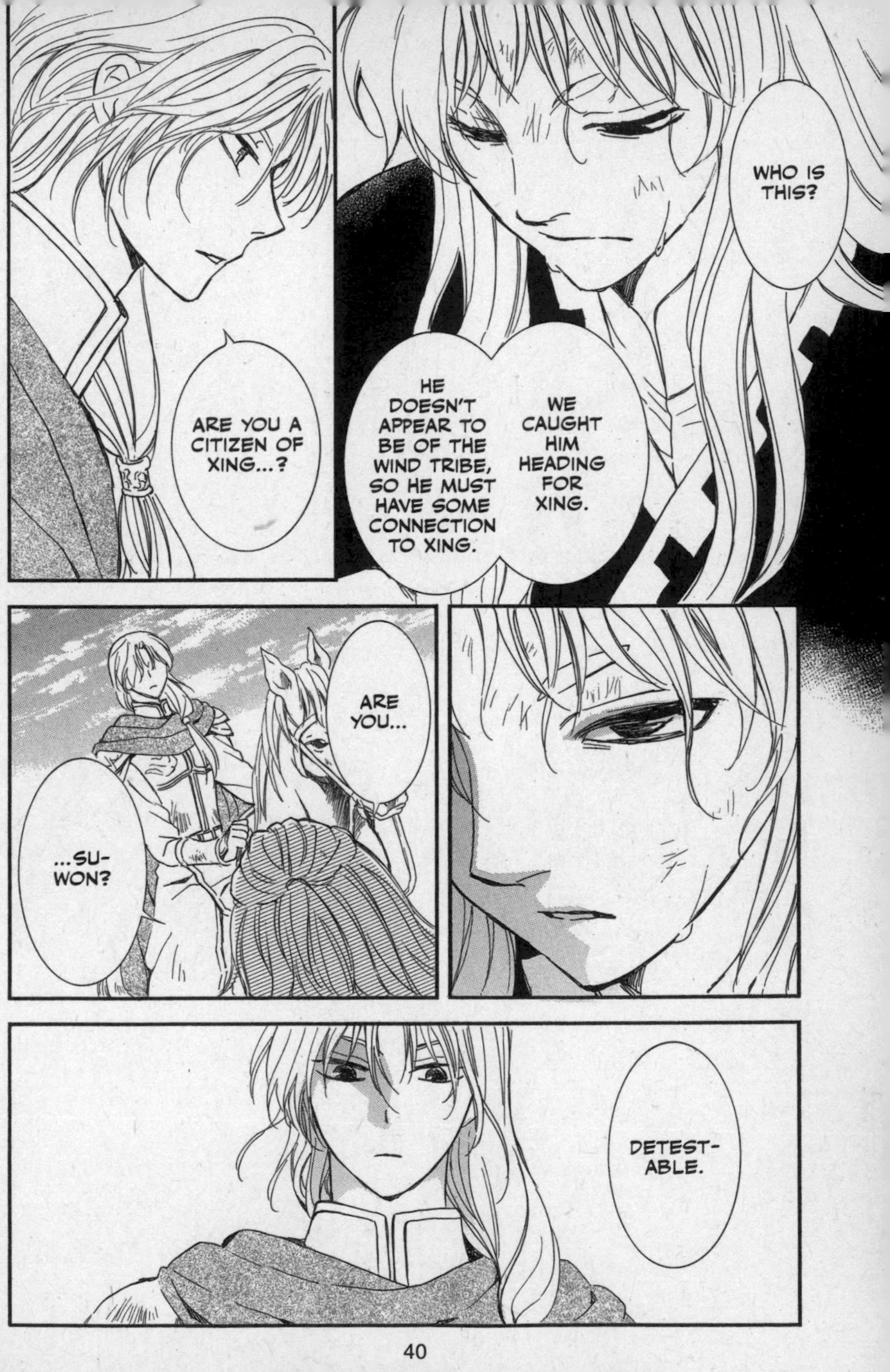
WHO IS THIS?
WE CAUGHT HIM HEADING FOR XING.
HE DOESN'T APPEAR TO BE OF THE WIND TRIBE, SO HE MUST HAVE SOME CONNECTION TO XING.
ARE YOU A CITIZEN OF XING...?
ARE YOU...
...SU-WON?
DETEST-ABLE.

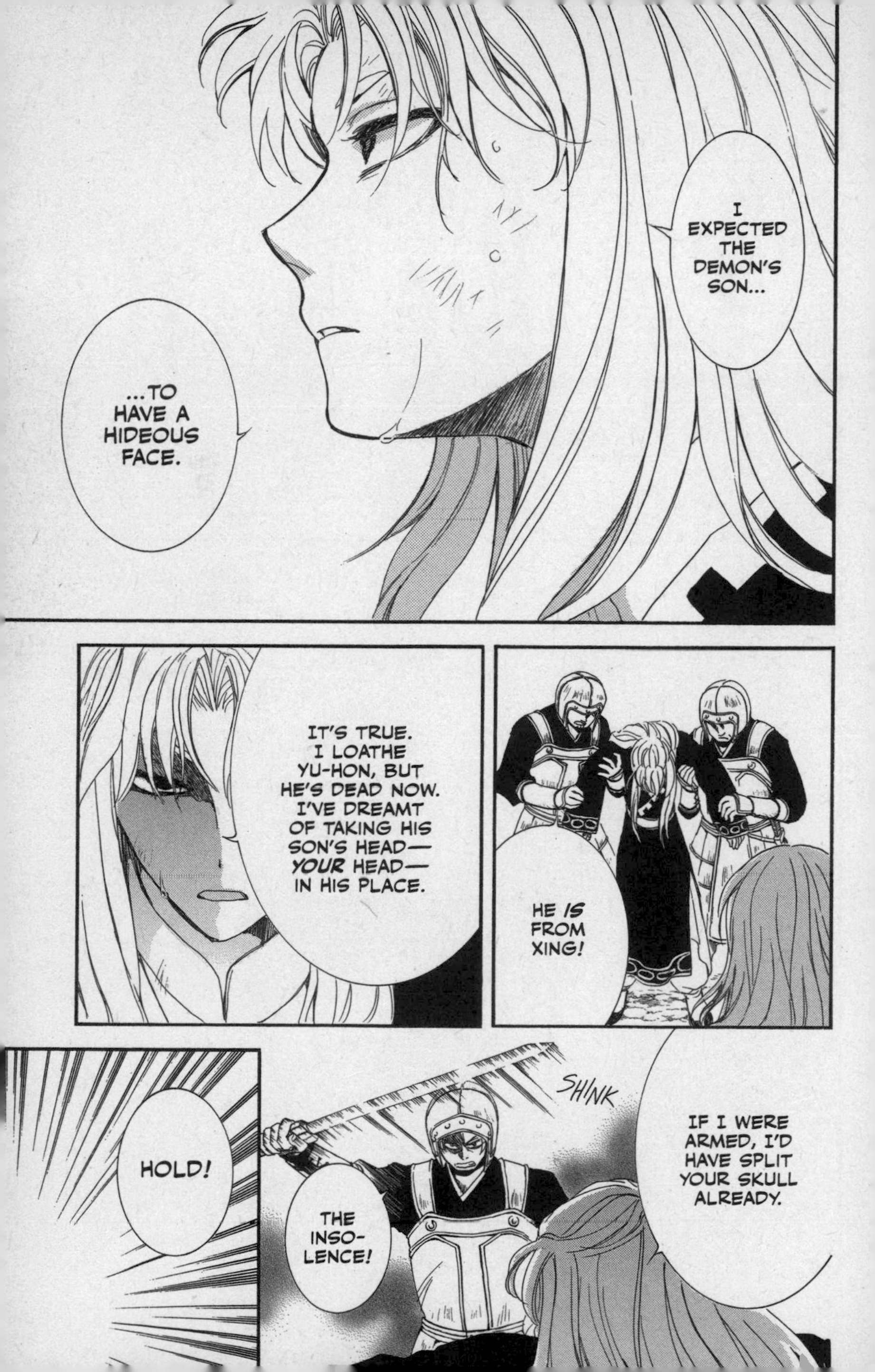
I EXPECTED THE DEMON'S SON...
...TO HAVE A HIDEOUS FACE.
HE *IS* FROM XING!
IT'S TRUE. I LOATHE YU-HON, BUT HE'S DEAD NOW. I'VE DREAMT OF TAKING HIS SON'S HEAD—*YOUR* HEAD—IN HIS PLACE.
IF I WERE ARMED, I'D HAVE SPLIT YOUR SKULL ALREADY.
SHINK
THE INSO-LENCE!
HOLD!

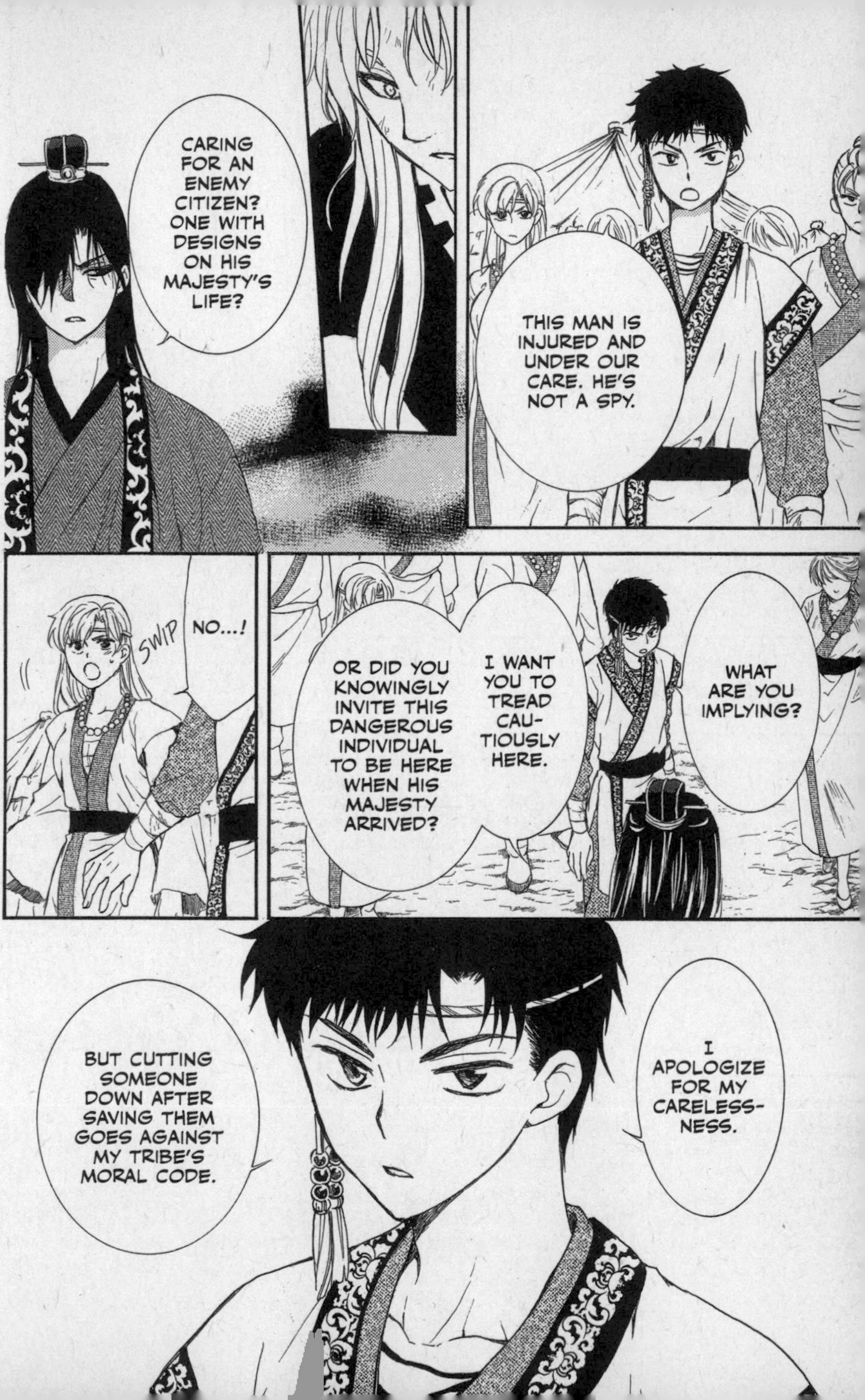
THIS MAN IS INJURED AND UNDER OUR CARE. HE'S NOT A SPY.
CARING FOR AN ENEMY CITIZEN? ONE WITH DESIGNS ON HIS MAJESTY'S LIFE?
WHAT ARE YOU IMPLYING?
I WANT YOU TO TREAD CAU-TIOUSLY HERE.
OR DID YOU KNOWINGLY INVITE THIS DANGEROUS INDIVIDUAL TO BE HERE WHEN HIS MAJESTY ARRIVED?
NO...!
SWIP
I APOLOGIZE FOR MY CARELESS-NESS.
BUT CUTTING SOMEONE DOWN AFTER SAVING THEM GOES AGAINST MY TRIBE'S MORAL CODE.

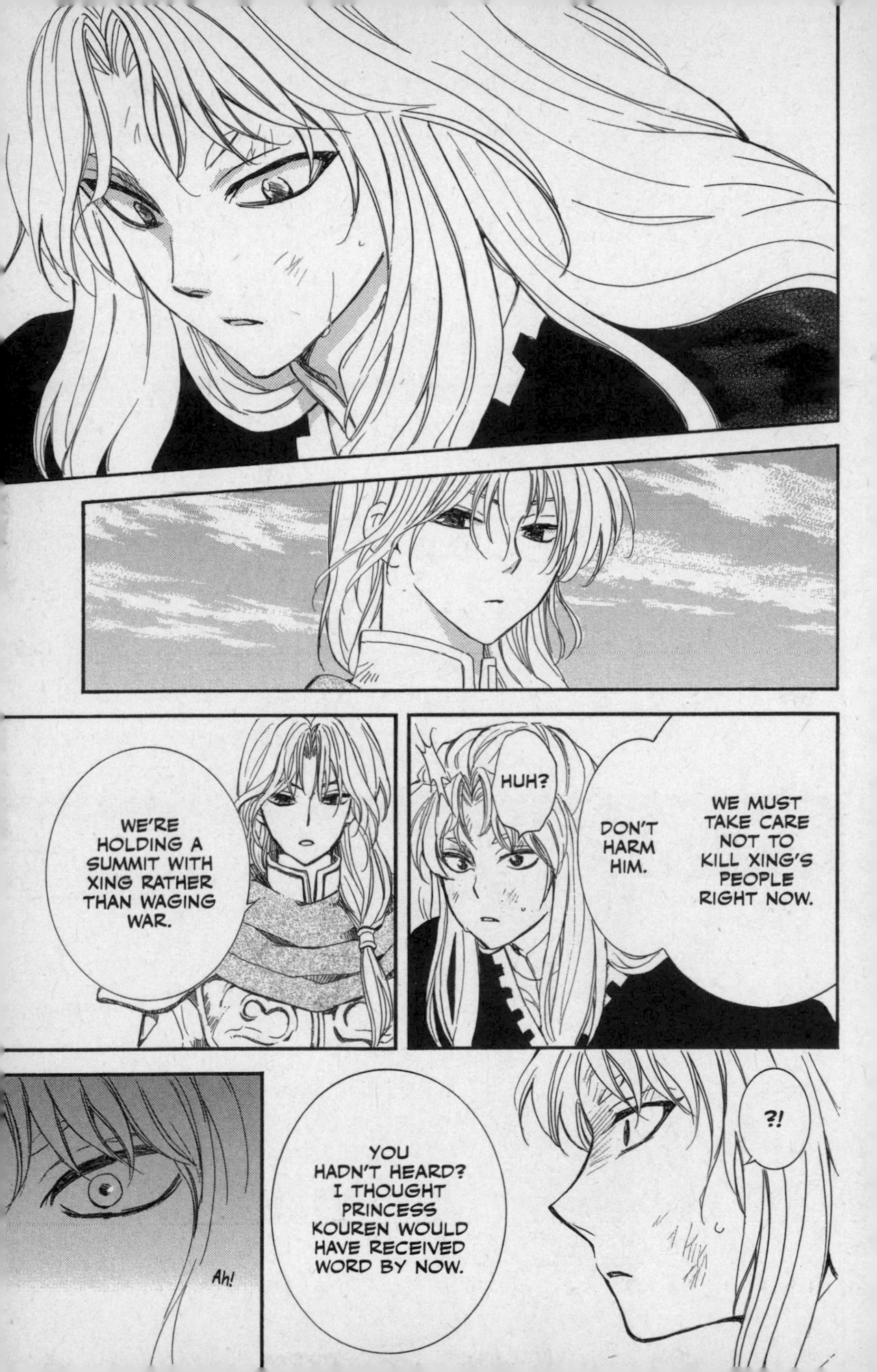
WE MUST TAKE CARE NOT TO KILL XING'S PEOPLE RIGHT NOW.
DON'T HARM HIM.
HUH?
WE'RE HOLDING A SUMMIT WITH XING RATHER THAN WAGING WAR.
?!
YOU HADN'T HEARD? I THOUGHT PRINCESS KOUREN WOULD HAVE RECEIVED WORD BY NOW.
Ah!

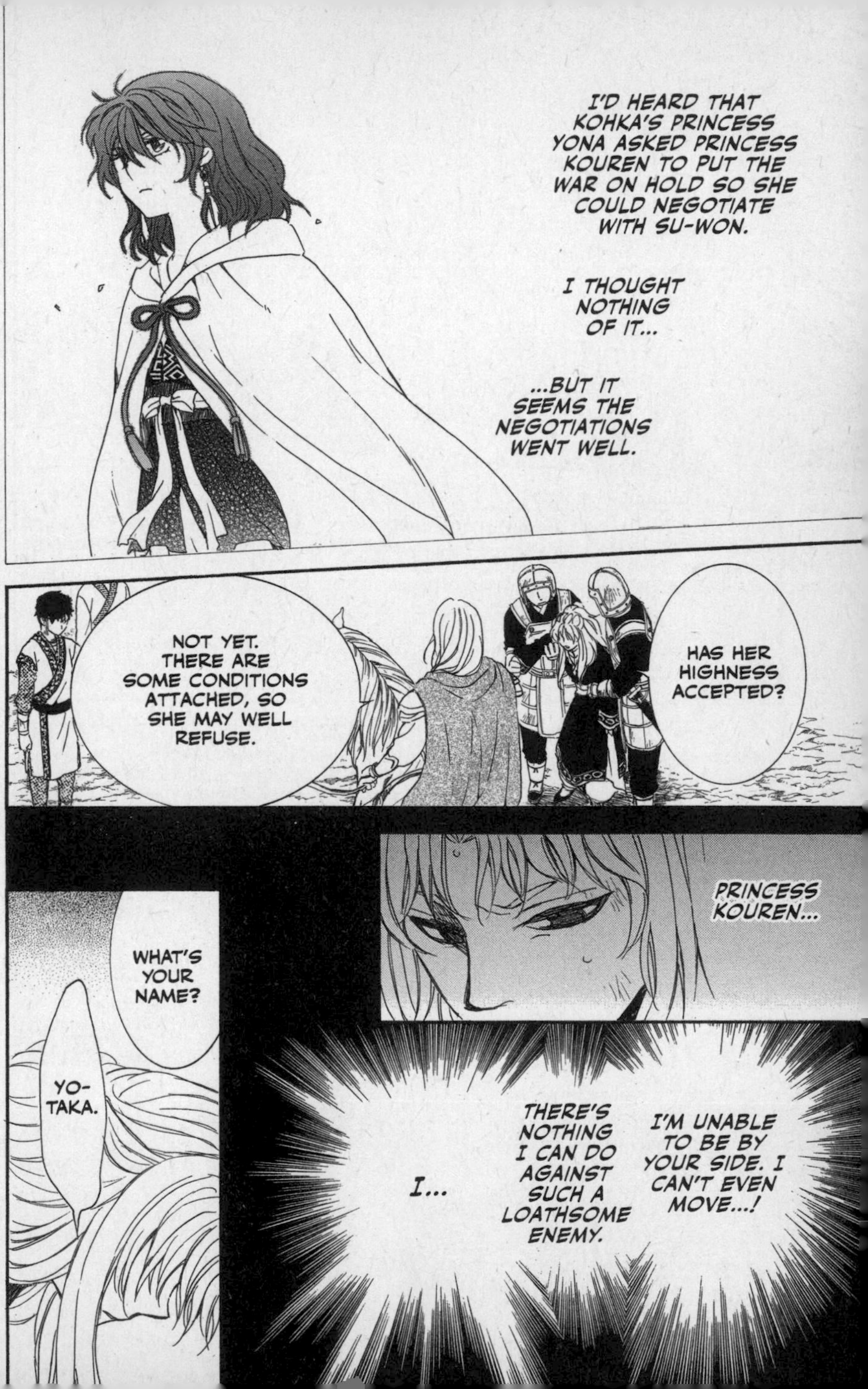
I'D HEARD THAT KOHKA'S PRINCESS YONA ASKED PRINCESS KOUREN TO PUT THE WAR ON HOLD SO SHE COULD NEGOTIATE WITH SU-WON.
I THOUGHT NOTHING OF IT...
...BUT IT SEEMS THE NEGOTIATIONS WENT WELL.
HAS HER HIGHNESS ACCEPTED?
NOT YET. THERE ARE SOME CONDITIONS ATTACHED, SO SHE MAY WELL REFUSE.
PRINCESS KOUREN...
I'M UNABLE TO BE BY YOUR SIDE. I CAN'T EVEN MOVE...!
THERE'S NOTHING I CAN DO AGAINST SUCH A LOATHSOME ENEMY.
I...
WHAT'S YOUR NAME?
YO-TAKA.

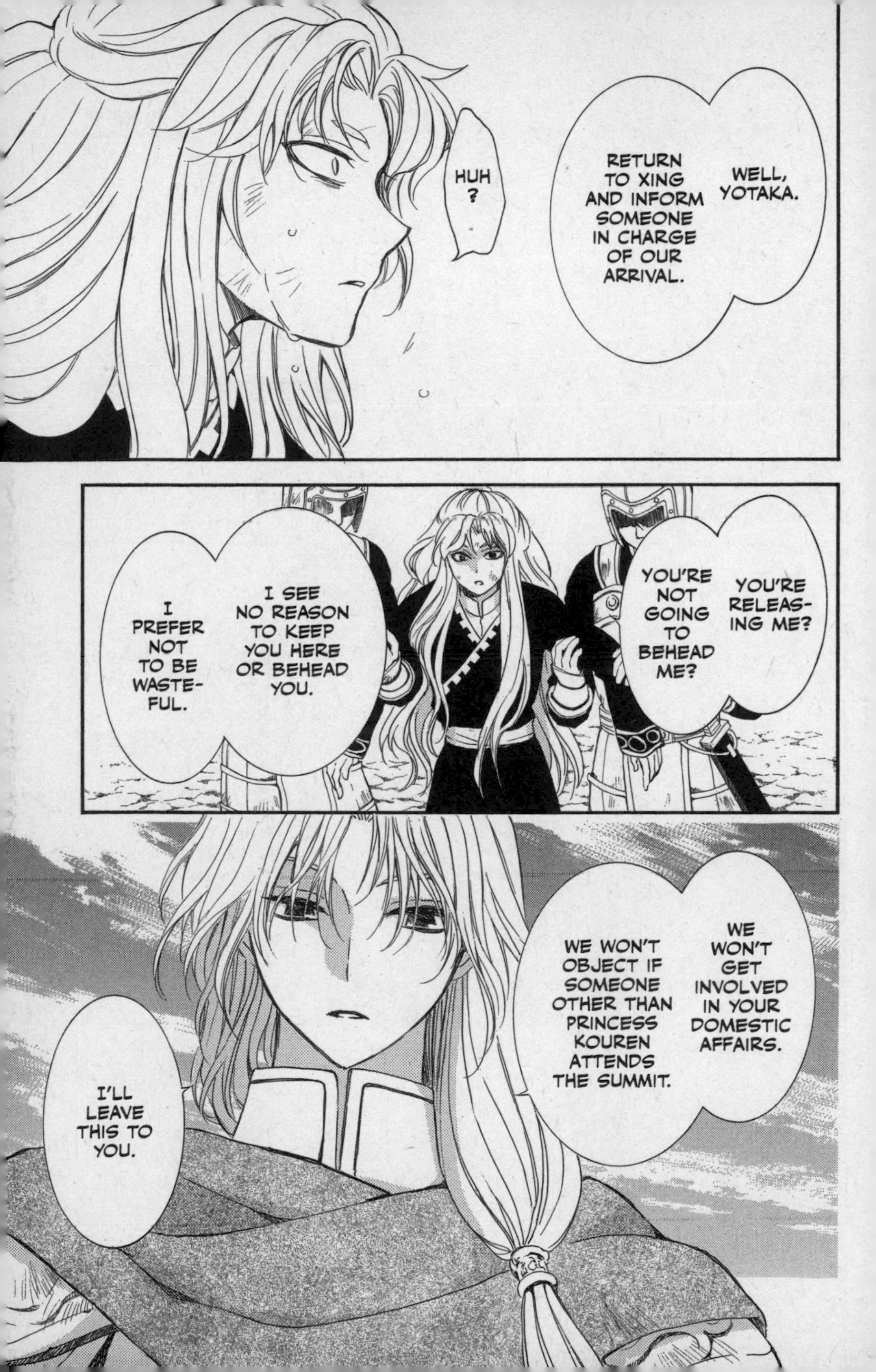
WELL, YOTAKA.
RETURN TO XING AND INFORM SOMEONE IN CHARGE OF OUR ARRIVAL.
HUH?
YOU'RE RELEASING ME?
YOU'RE NOT GOING TO BEHEAD ME?
I SEE NO REASON TO KEEP YOU HERE OR BEHEAD YOU.
I PREFER NOT TO BE WASTEFUL.
WE WON'T GET INVOLVED IN YOUR DOMESTIC AFFAIRS.
WE WON'T OBJECT IF SOMEONE OTHER THAN PRINCESS KOUREN ATTENDS THE SUMMIT.
I'LL LEAVE THIS TO YOU.

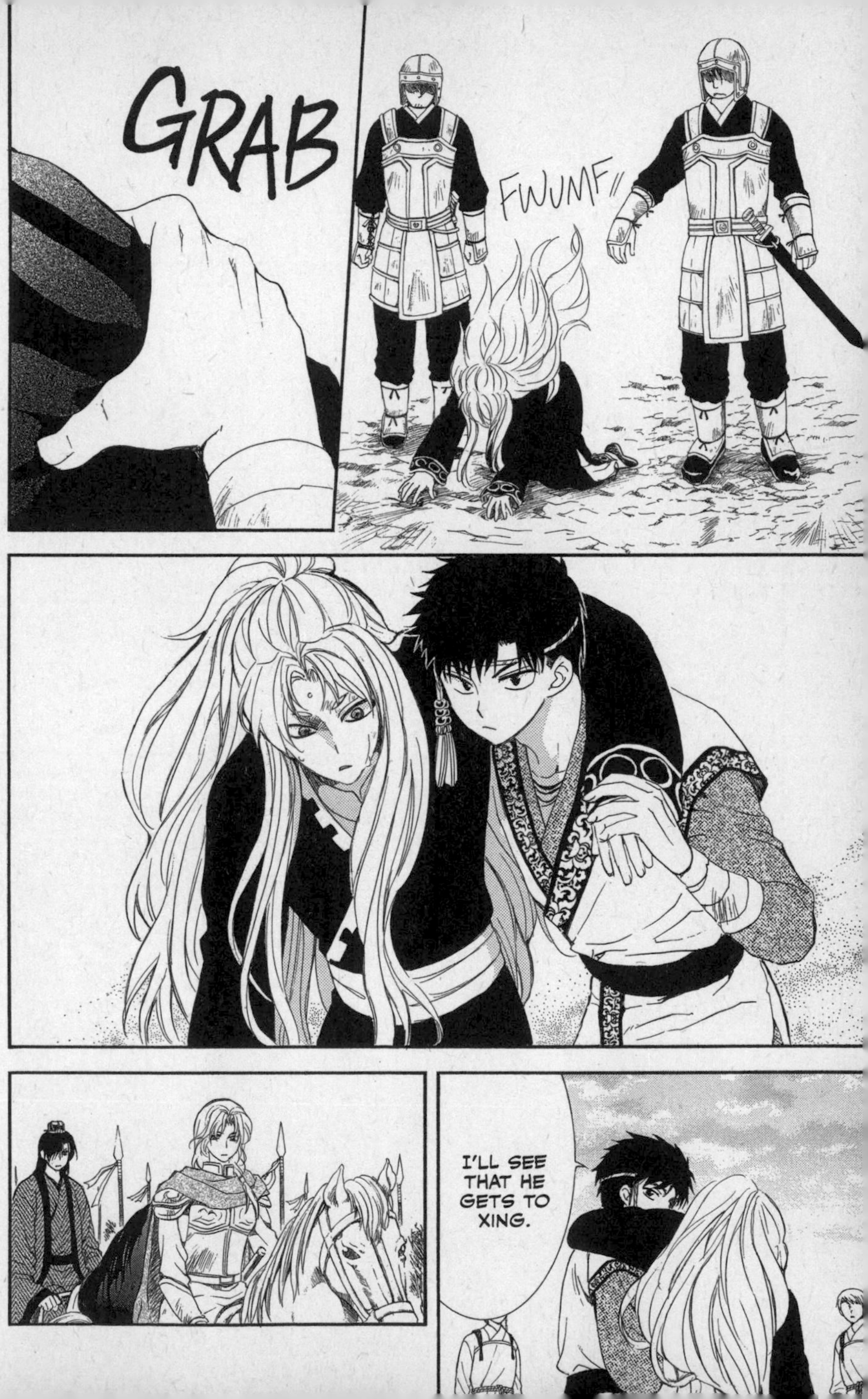
FWUMF
GRAB
I'LL SEE THAT HE GETS TO XING.

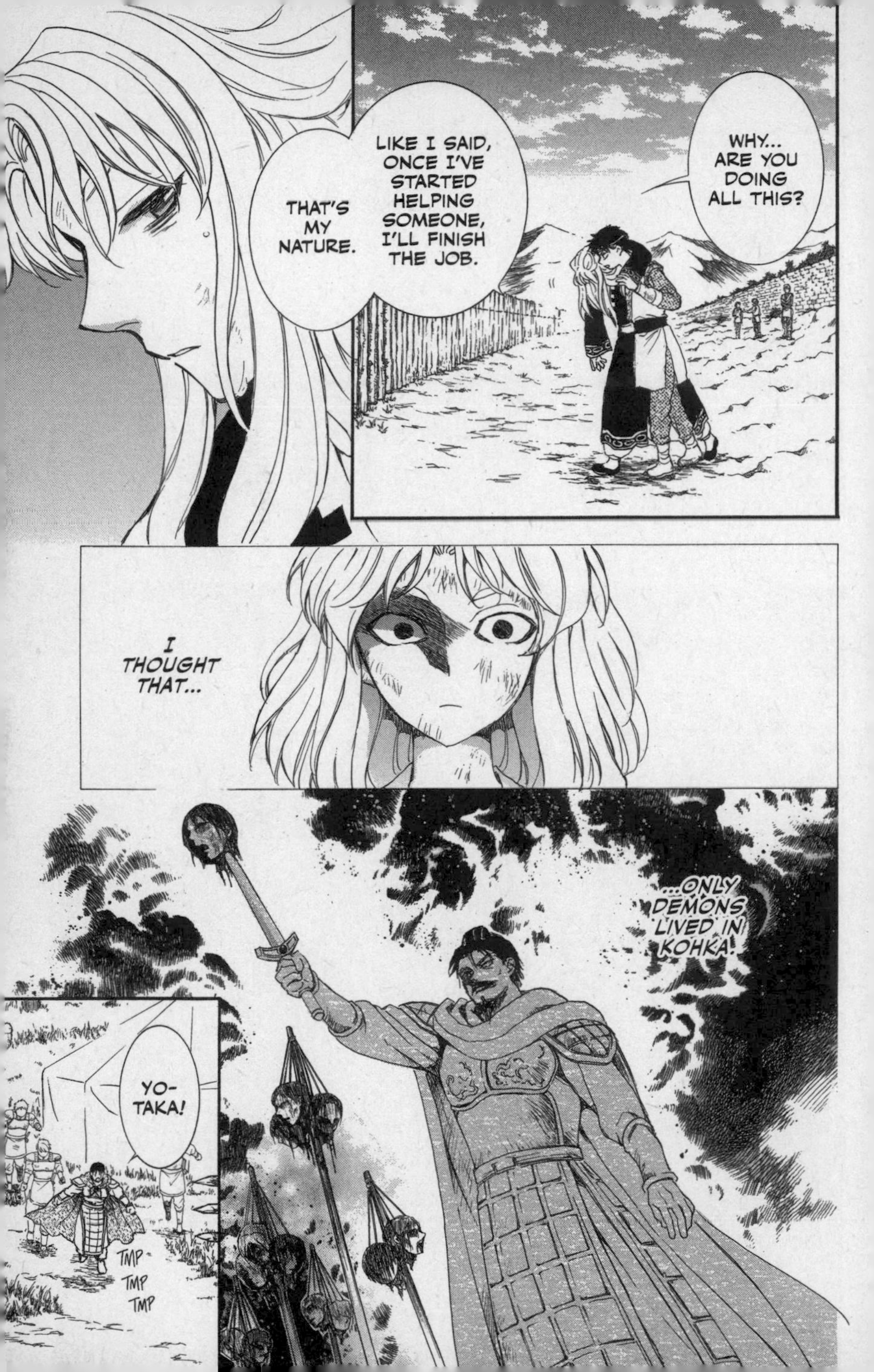
WHY... ARE YOU DOING ALL THIS?
LIKE I SAID, ONCE I'VE STARTED HELPING SOMEONE, I'LL FINISH THE JOB.
THAT'S MY NATURE.
I THOUGHT THAT...
...ONLY DEMONS LIVED IN KOHKA!
YO-TAKA!
TMP TMP TMP

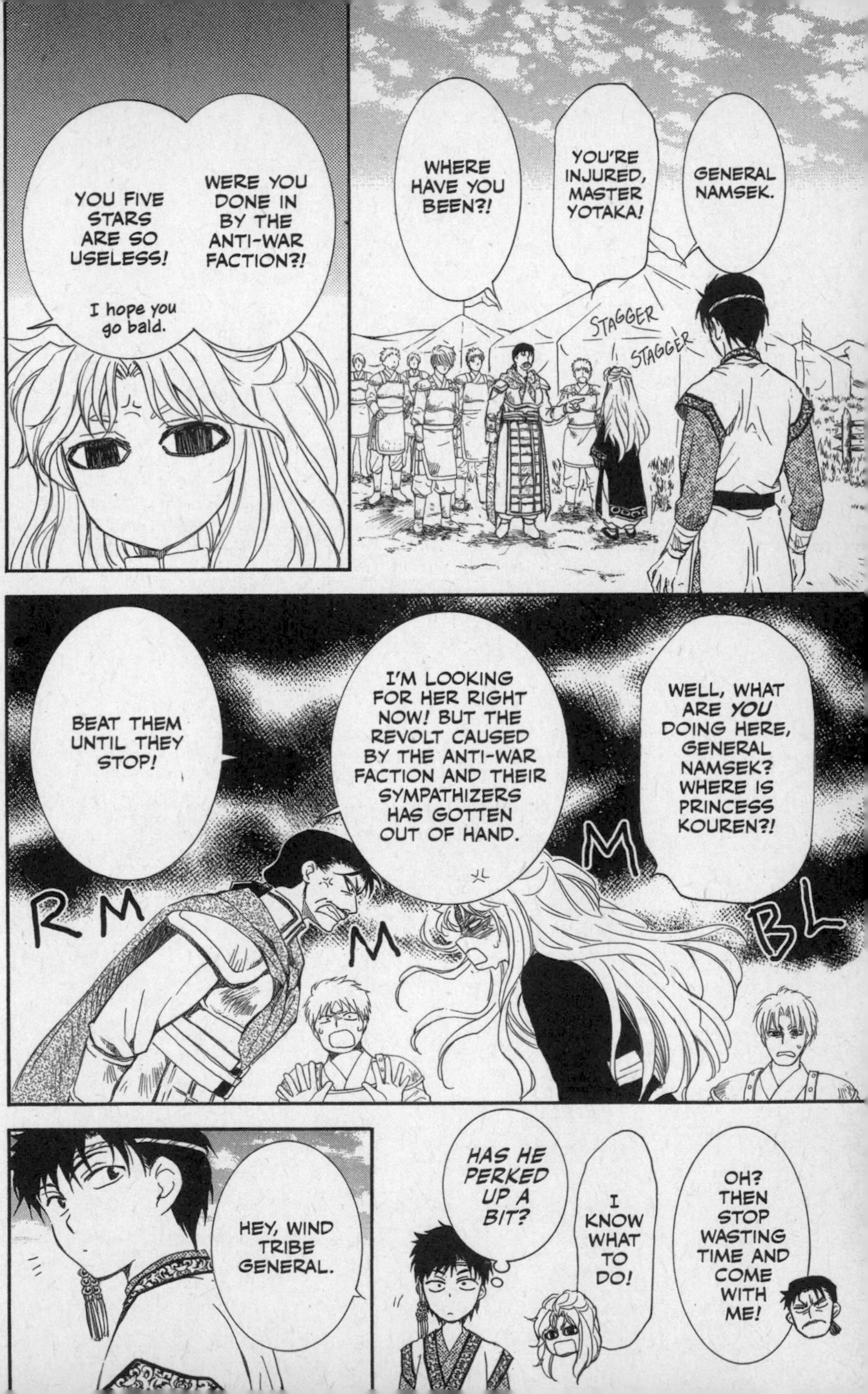
GENERAL NAMSEK.
YOU'RE INJURED, MASTER YOTAKA!
WHERE HAVE YOU BEEN?!
STAGGER
STAGGER
WERE YOU DONE IN BY THE ANTI-WAR FACTION?!
YOU FIVE STARS ARE SO USELESS!
I hope you go bald.
WELL, WHAT ARE *YOU* DOING HERE, GENERAL NAMSEK? WHERE IS PRINCESS KOUREN?!
I'M LOOKING FOR HER RIGHT NOW! BUT THE REVOLT CAUSED BY THE ANTI-WAR FACTION AND THEIR SYMPATHIZERS HAS GOTTEN OUT OF HAND.
BEAT THEM UNTIL THEY STOP!
BL
M
M
RM
OH? THEN STOP WASTING TIME AND COME WITH ME!
I KNOW WHAT TO DO!
HAS HE PERKED UP A BIT?
HEY, WIND TRIBE GENERAL.

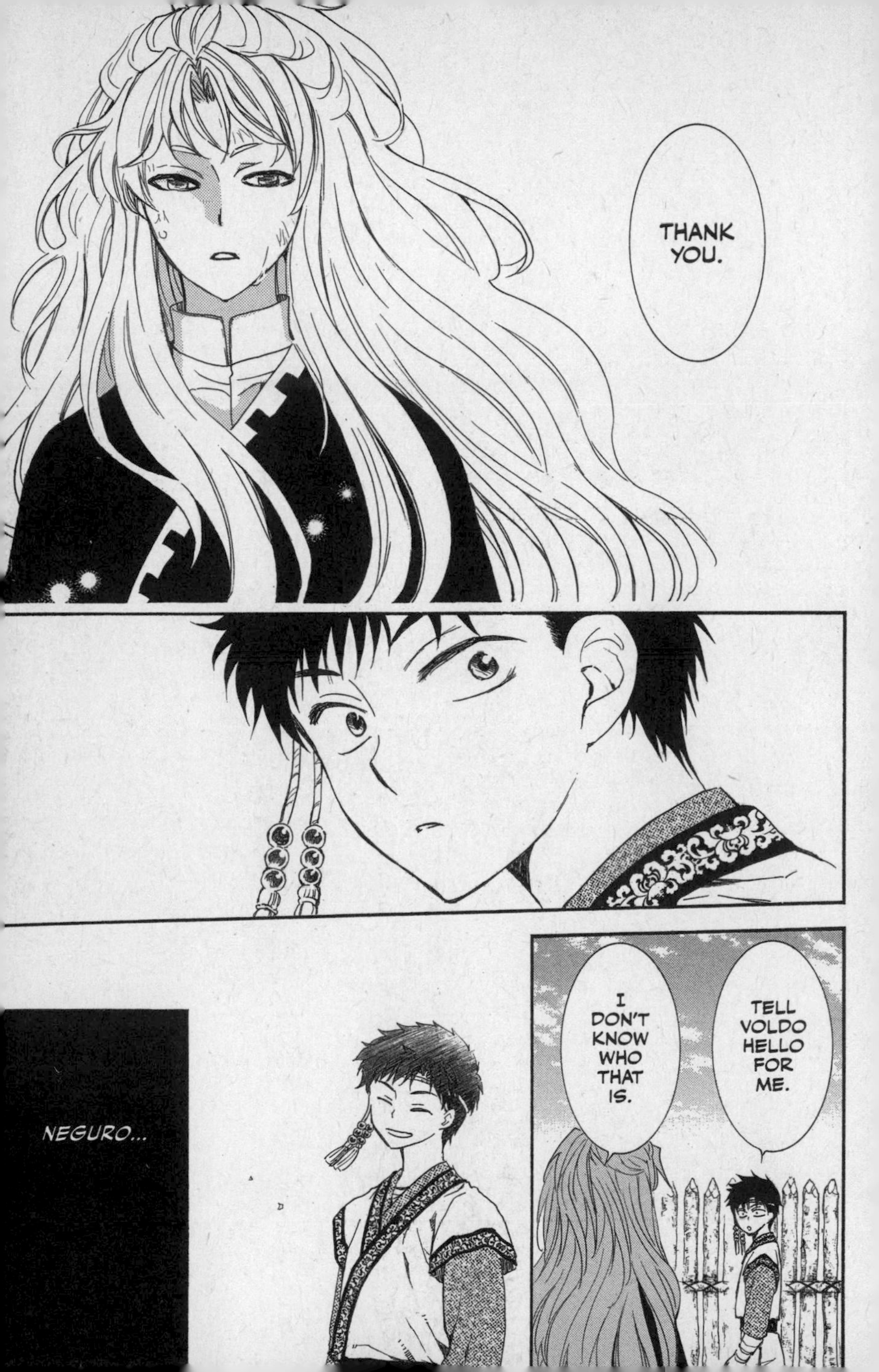
THANK YOU.
TELL VOLDO HELLO FOR ME.
I DON'T KNOW WHO THAT IS.
NEGURO...

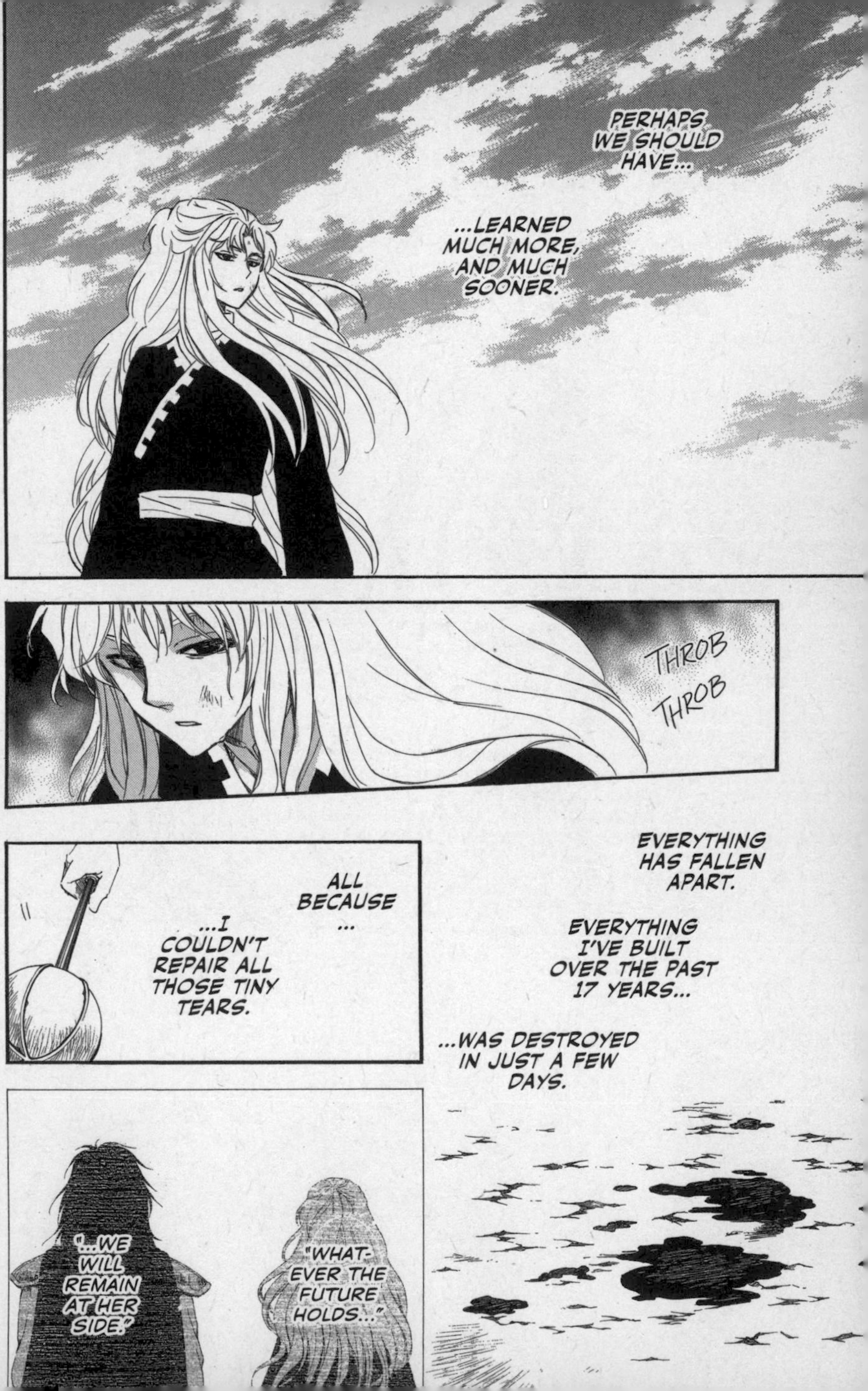
PERHAPS WE SHOULD HAVE...
...LEARNED MUCH MORE, AND MUCH SOONER.
THROB THROB
EVERYTHING HAS FALLEN APART.
EVERYTHING I'VE BUILT OVER THE PAST 17 YEARS...
...WAS DESTROYED IN JUST A FEW DAYS.
ALL BECAUSE...
...I COULDN'T REPAIR ALL THOSE TINY TEARS.
"WHAT-EVER THE FUTURE HOLDS..."
"...WE WILL REMAIN AT HER SIDE."

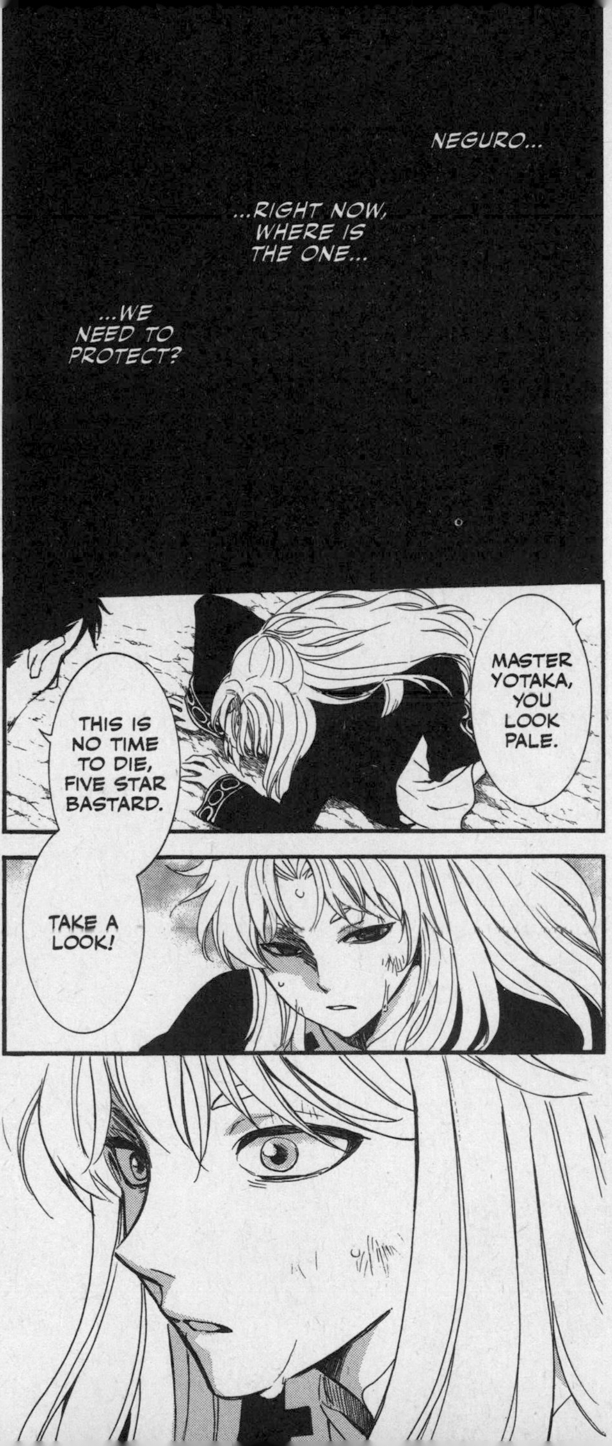
NEGURO...
...RIGHT NOW, WHERE IS THE ONE...
...WE NEED TO PROTECT?
MASTER YOTAKA, YOU LOOK PALE.
THIS IS NO TIME TO DIE, FIVE STAR BASTARD.
TAKE A LOOK!

At signings and in letters, readers have been telling me their ages and professions. It's so interesting to see the wide spectrum of people who are reading this! There are students, of course, but many people around my age too. Sometimes parents come to signings with their children. Occasionally there are men too, all from different fields.

From time to time someone will say that they're embarrassed to be buying *Hana to Yume* at their age, but there are plenty of *Hana to Yume* readers over 30! It's not an issue! (*Ha ha.*)

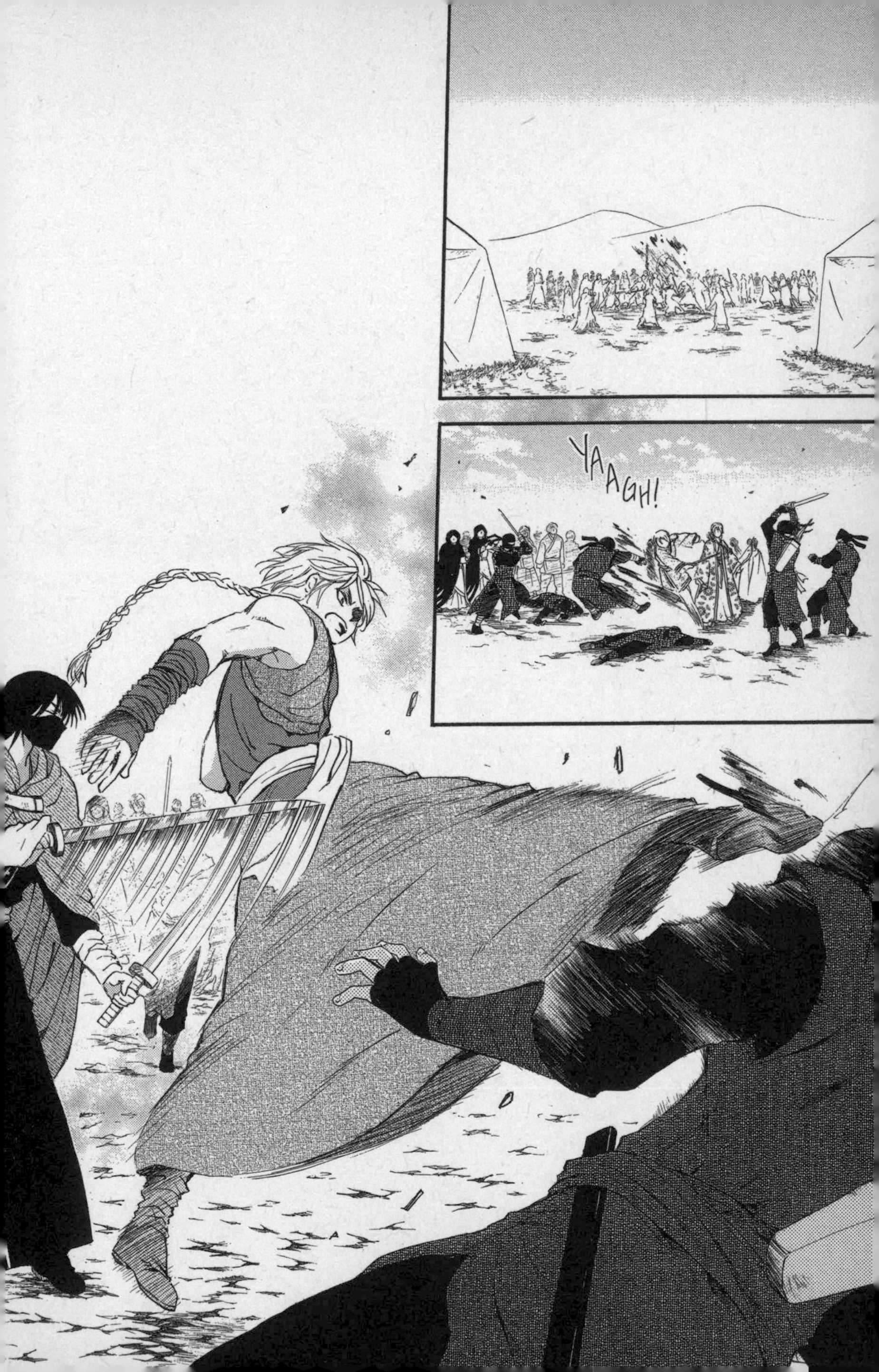
YAAAGH!

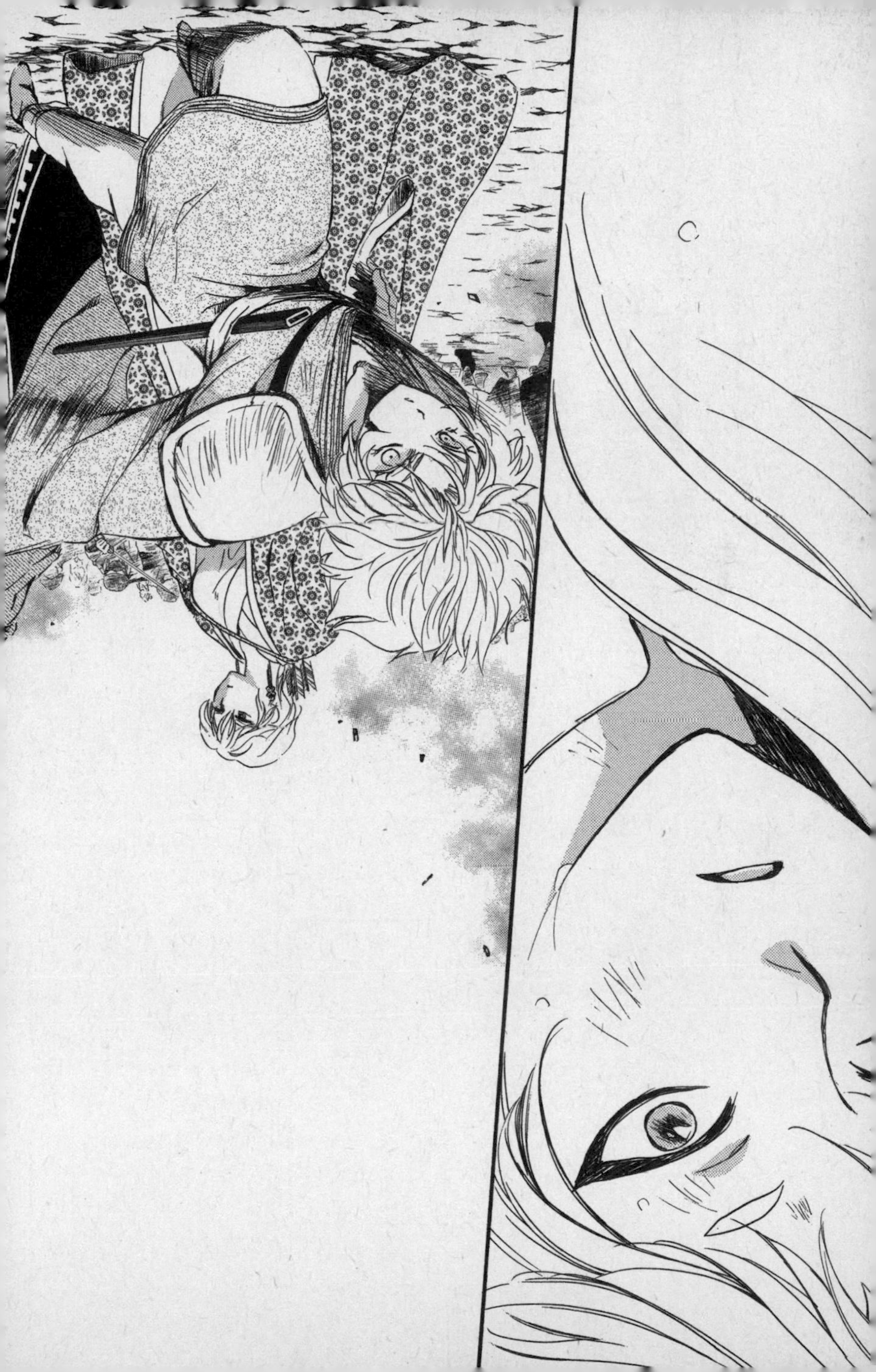

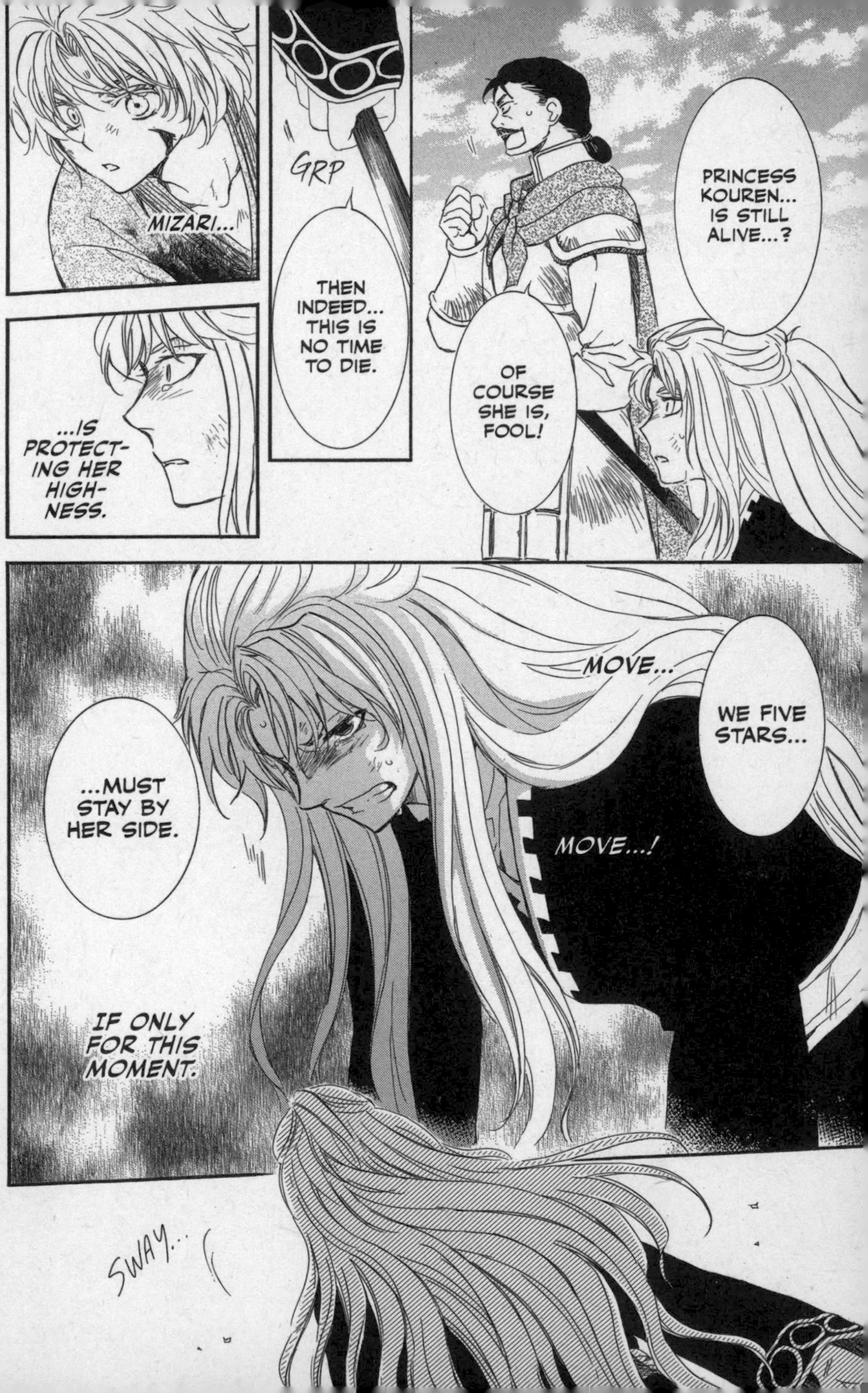
PRINCESS KOUREN... IS STILL ALIVE...?
OF COURSE SHE IS, FOOL!
GRP
THEN INDEED... THIS IS NO TIME TO DIE.
MIZARI...
...IS PROTECTING HER HIGHNESS.
WE FIVE STARS...
MOVE...
MOVE...!
...MUST STAY BY HER SIDE.
IF ONLY FOR THIS MOMENT.
SWAY...

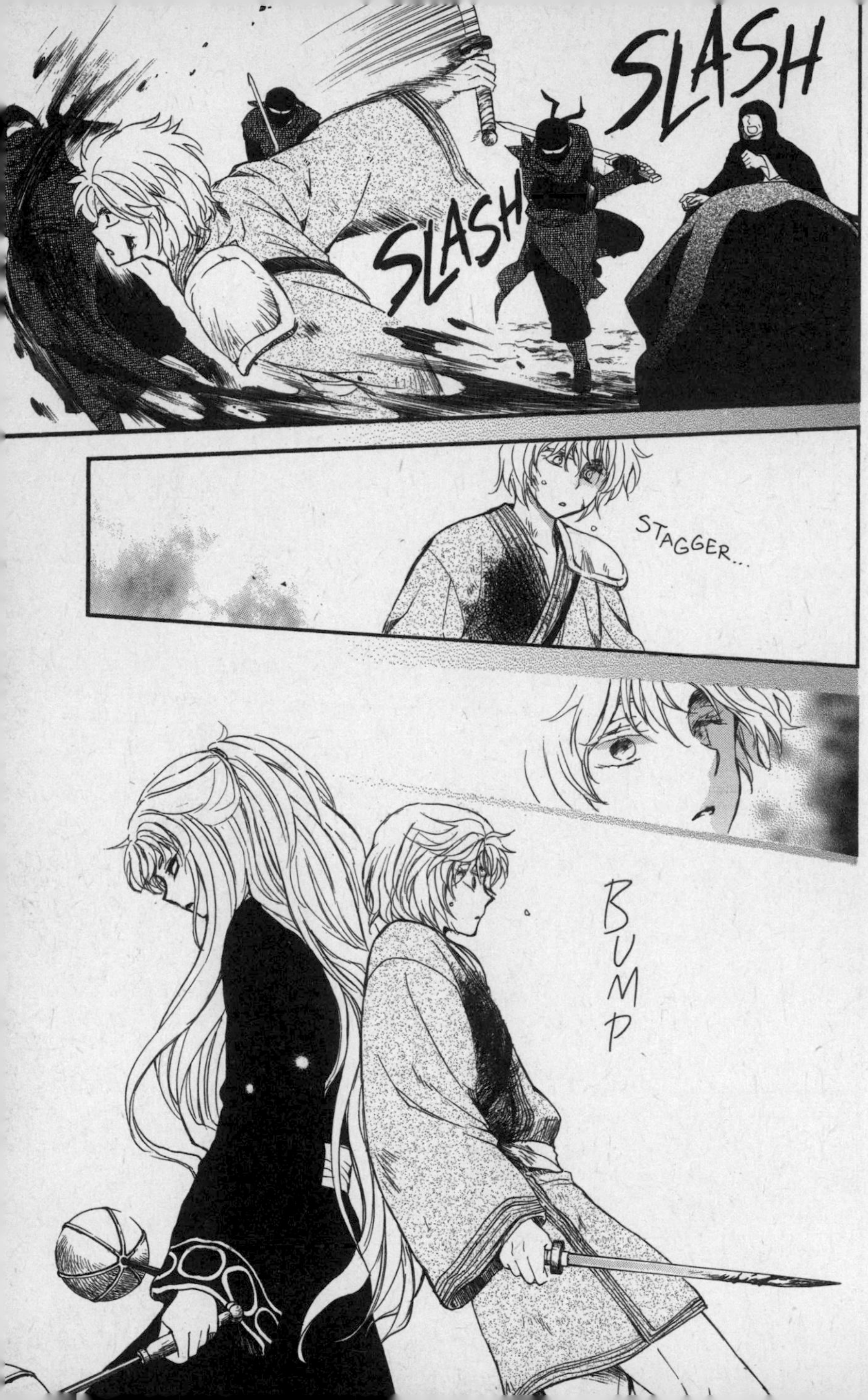
SLASH
SLASH
STAGGER...
BUMP

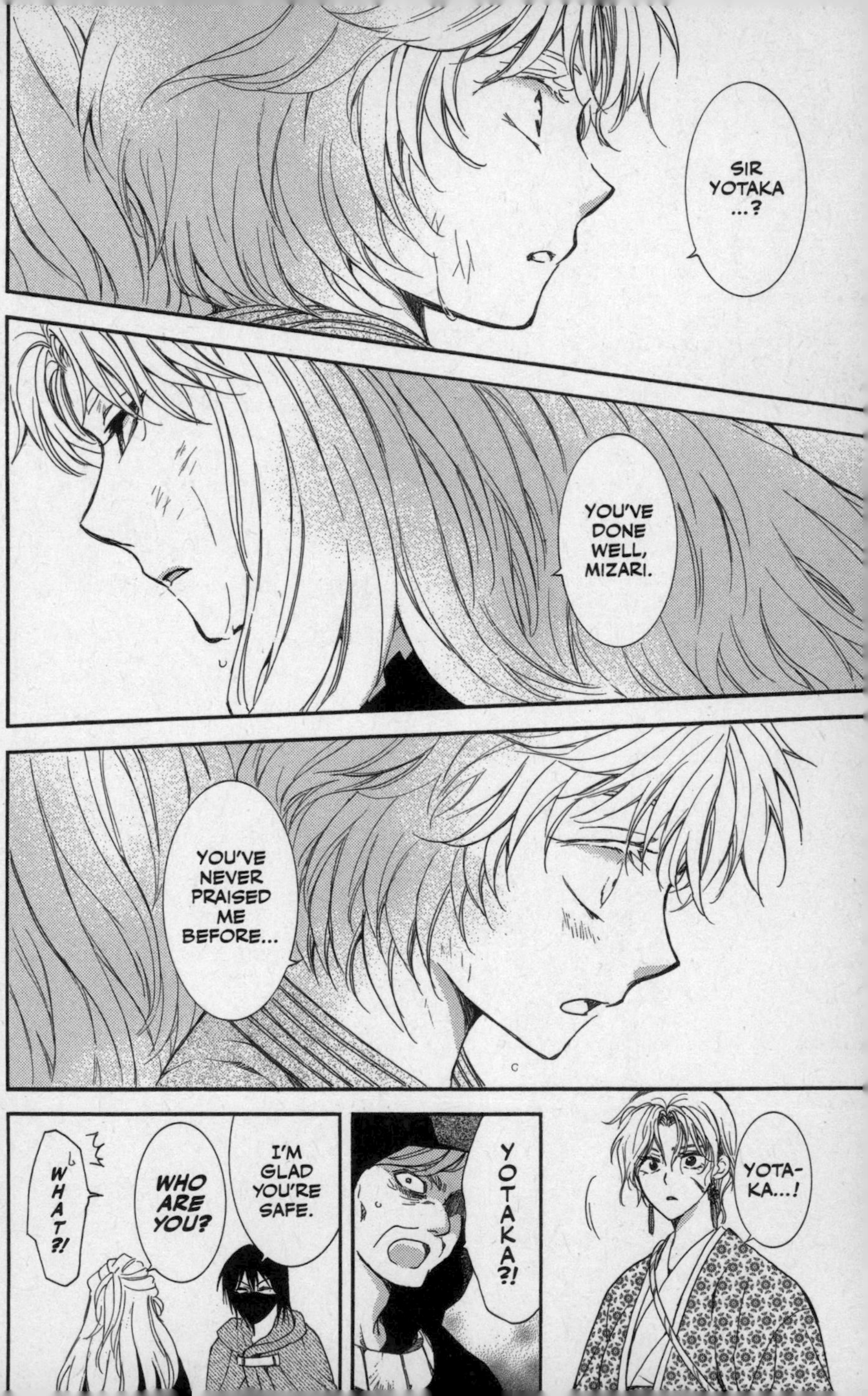
SIR YOTAKA ...?
YOU'VE DONE WELL, MIZARI.
YOU'VE NEVER PRAISED ME BEFORE...
YOTA-KA...!
YOTAKA?!
I'M GLAD YOU'RE SAFE.
WHO ARE YOU?
WHAT?!

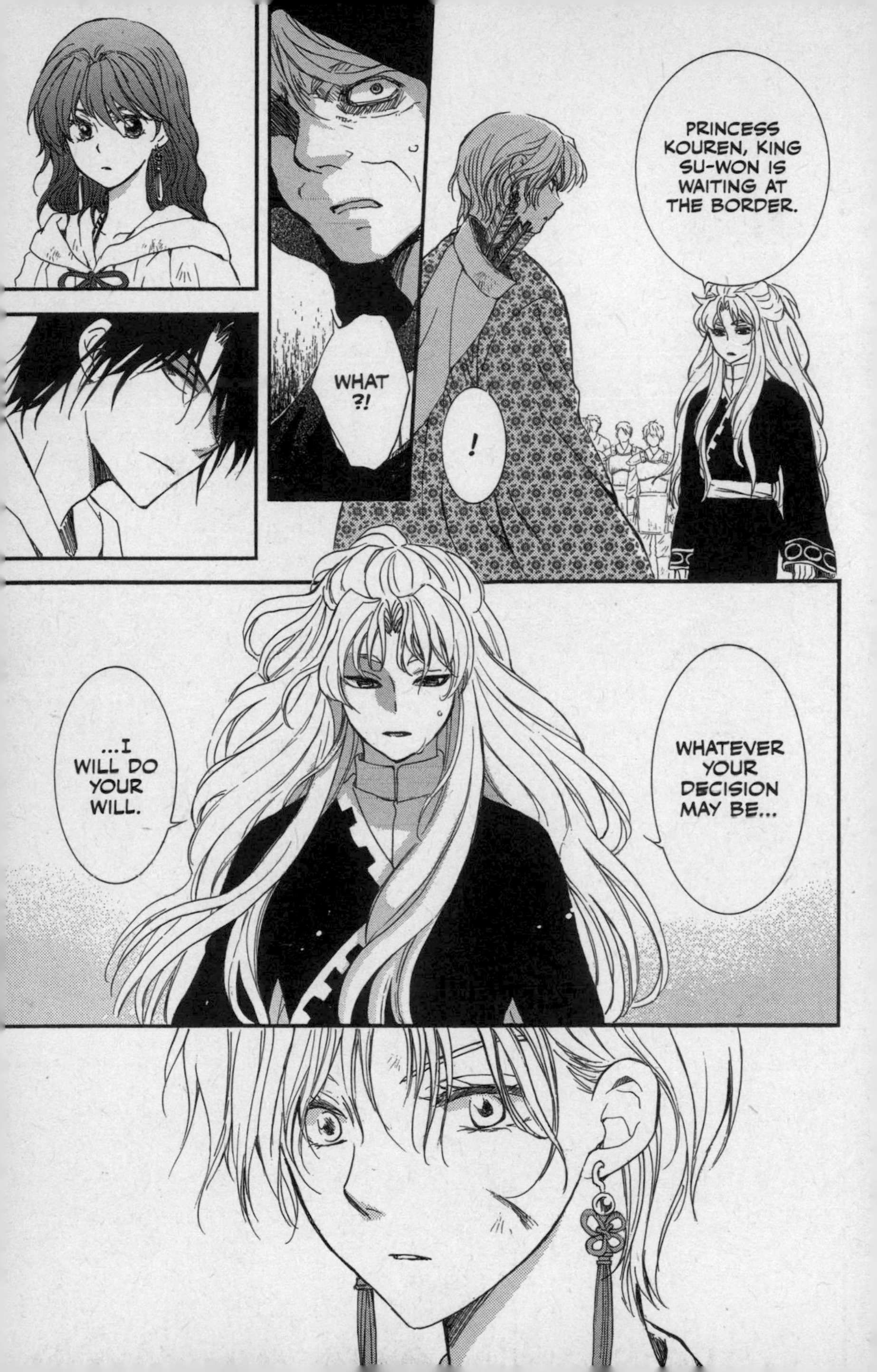
PRINCESS KOUREN, KING SU-WON IS WAITING AT THE BORDER.
!
WHAT ?!
WHATEVER YOUR DECISION MAY BE...
...I WILL DO YOUR WILL.

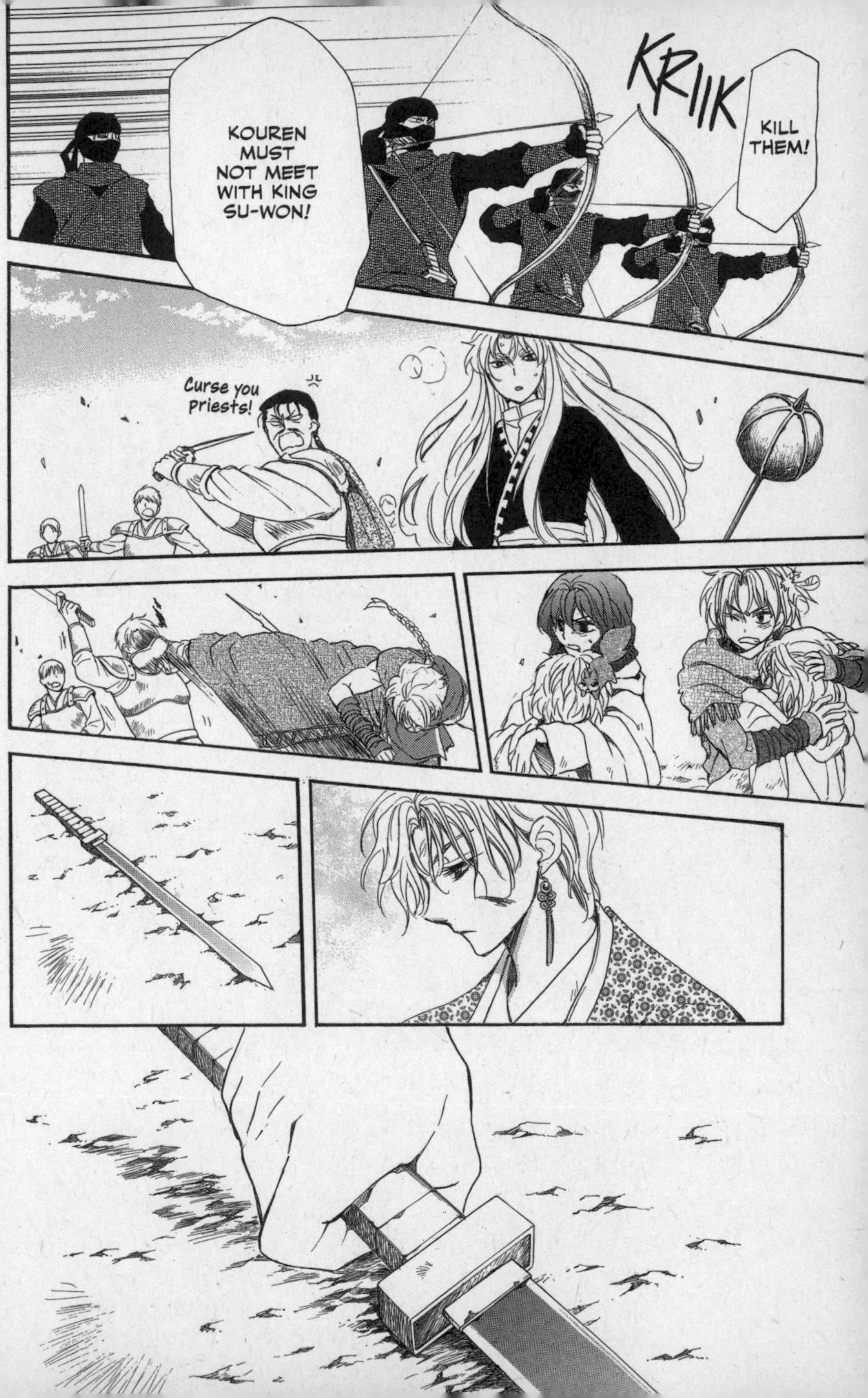
KILL THEM!
KRIIK
KOUREN MUST NOT MEET WITH KING SU-WON!
Curse you priests!

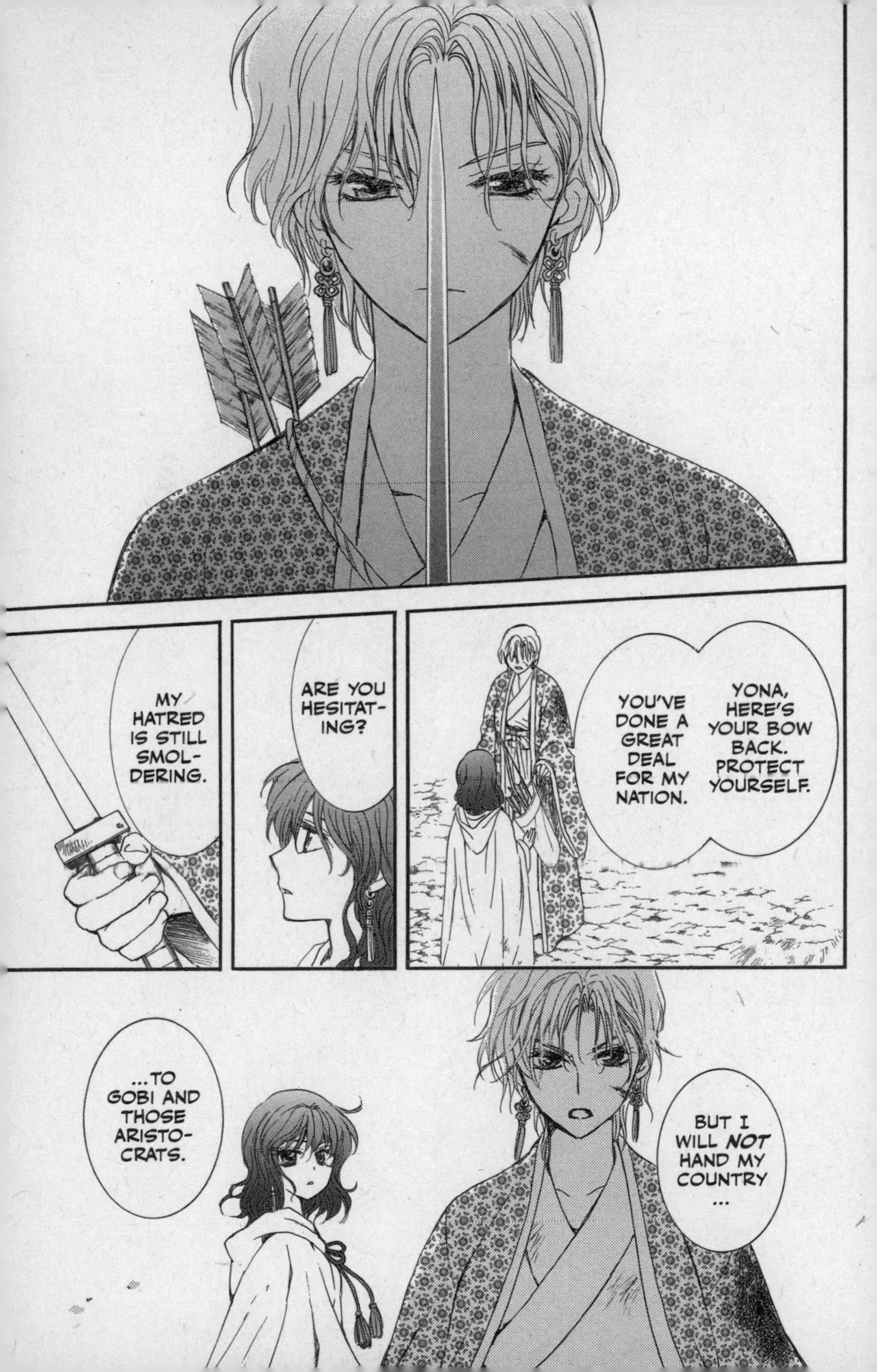
YONA, HERE'S YOUR BOW BACK. PROTECT YOURSELF.
YOU'VE DONE A GREAT DEAL FOR MY NATION.
ARE YOU HESITAT-ING?
MY HATRED IS STILL SMOL-DERING.
BUT I WILL ***NOT*** HAND MY COUNTRY ...
...TO GOBI AND THOSE ARISTO-CRATS.

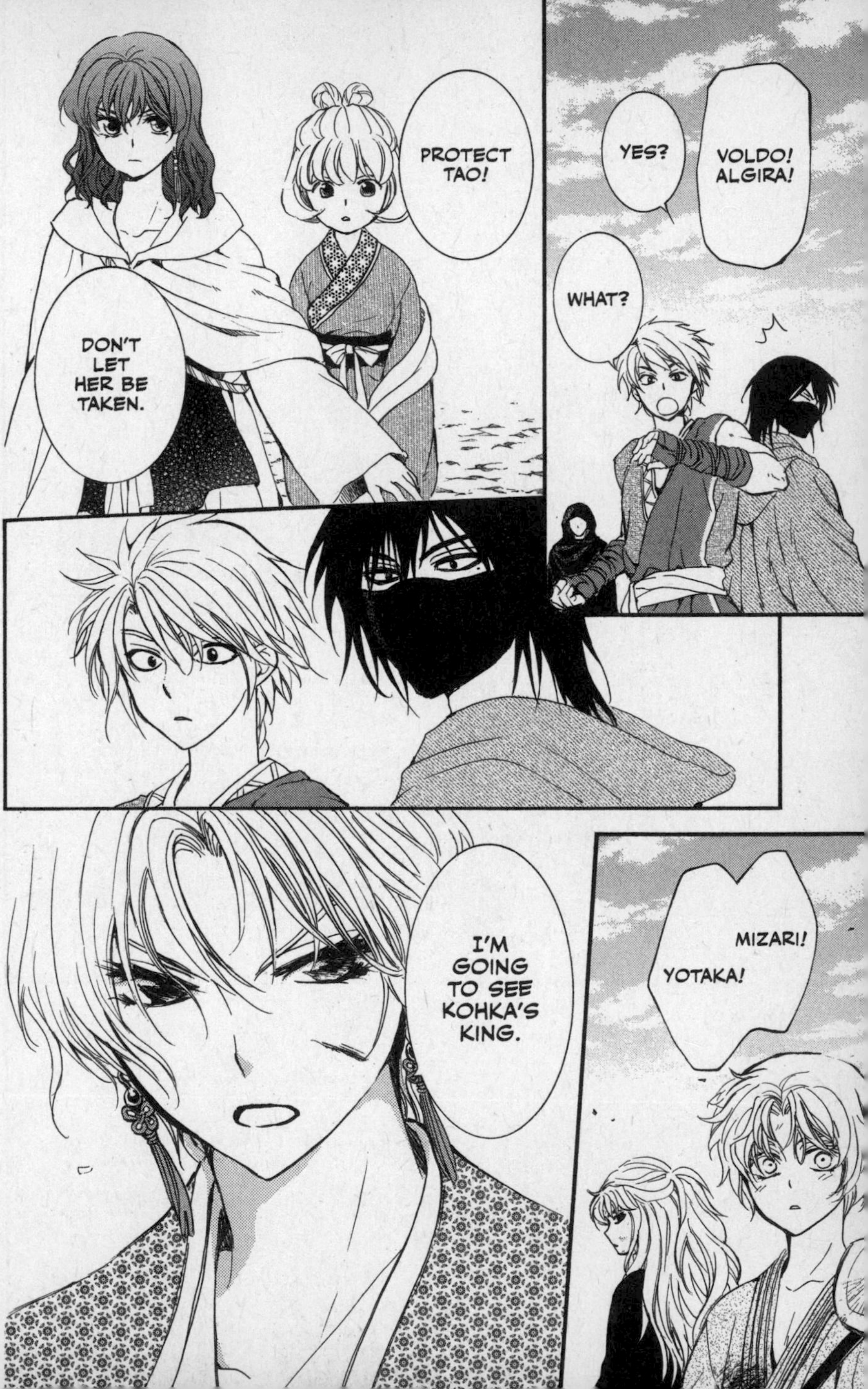
VOLDO! ALGIRA!
YES?
WHAT?
PROTECT TAO!
DON'T LET HER BE TAKEN.
MIZARI! YOTAKA!
I'M GOING TO SEE KOHKA'S KING.

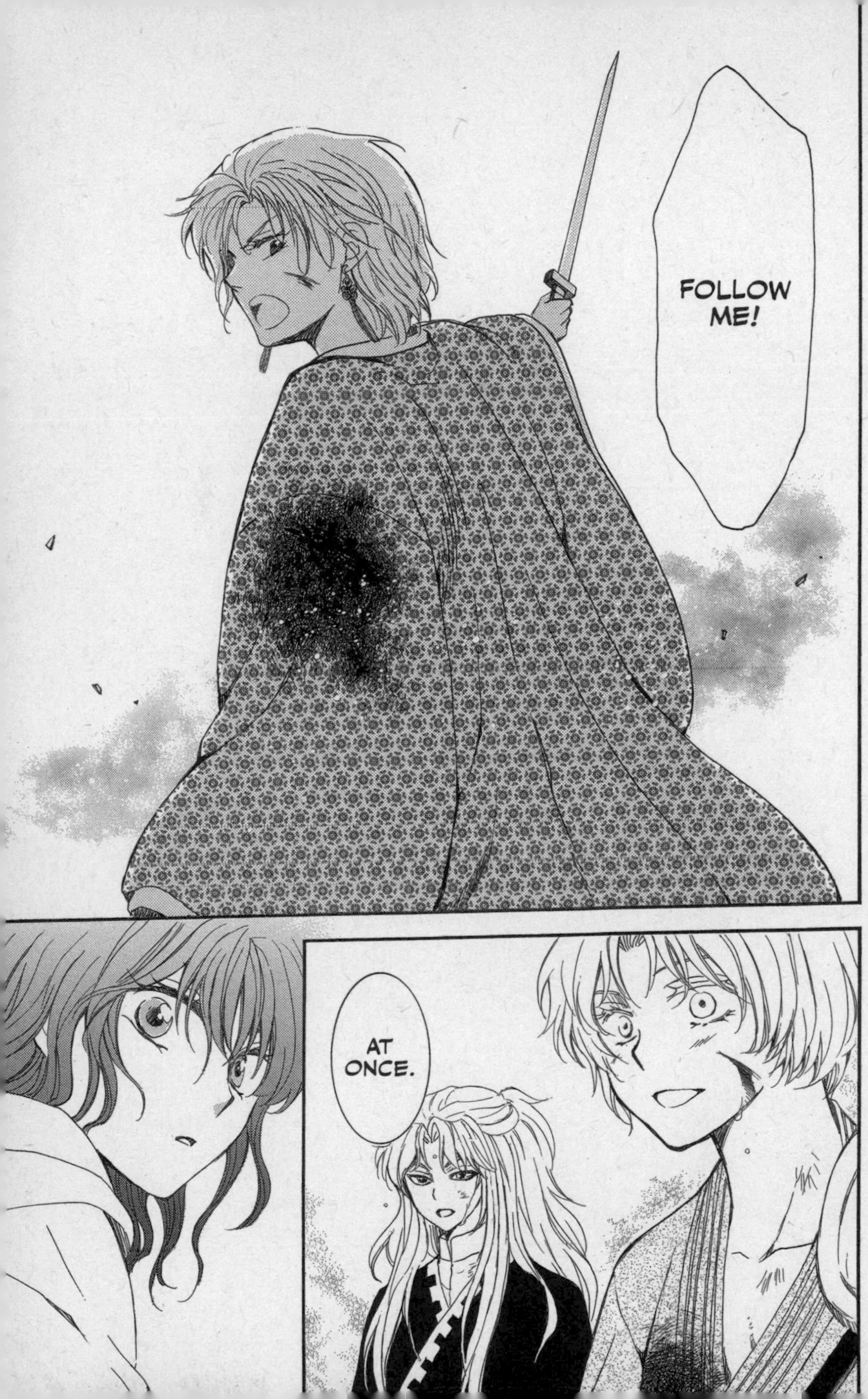
FOLLOW ME!
AT ONCE.

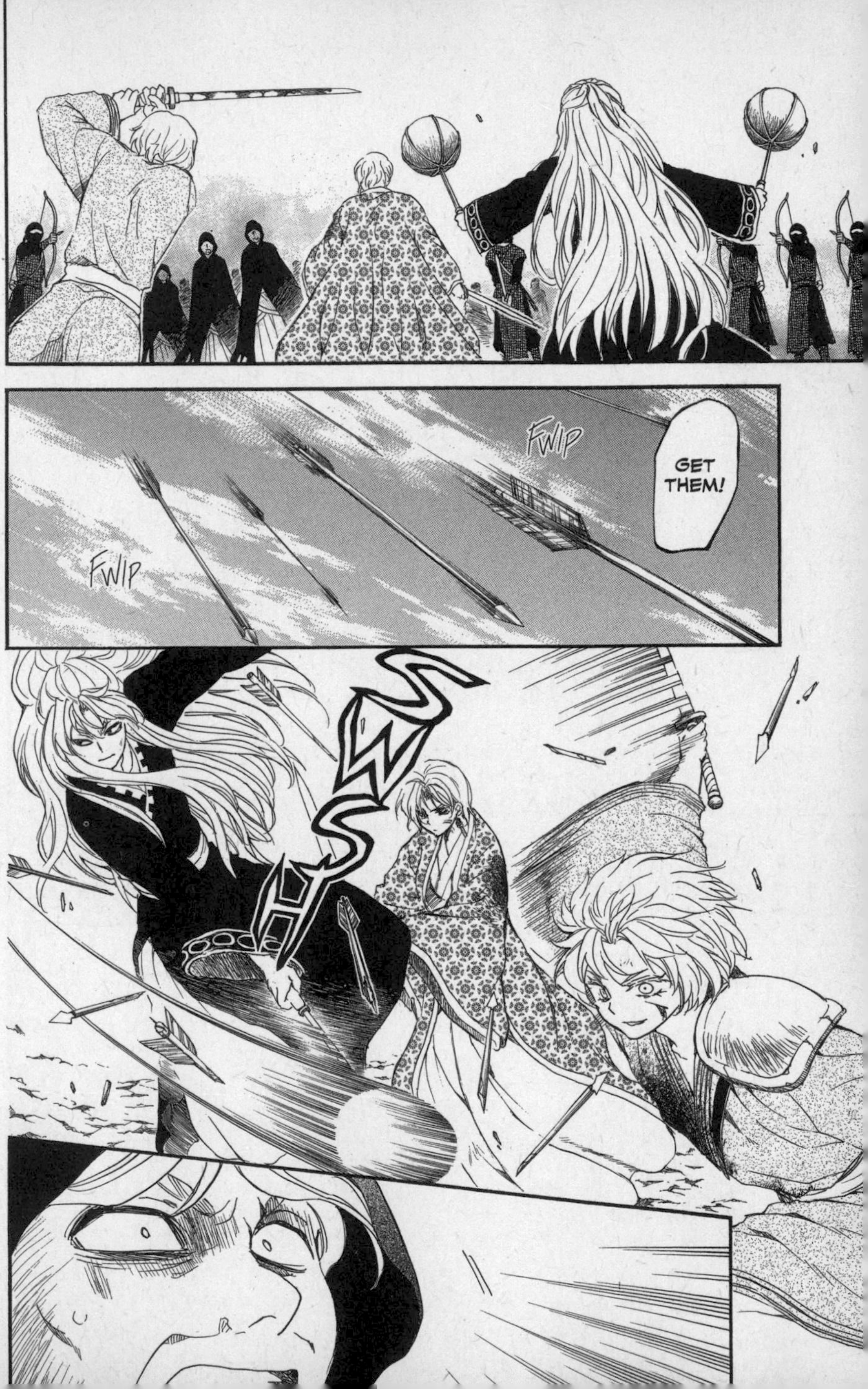
GET THEM!
FWIP
FWIP
SWISH

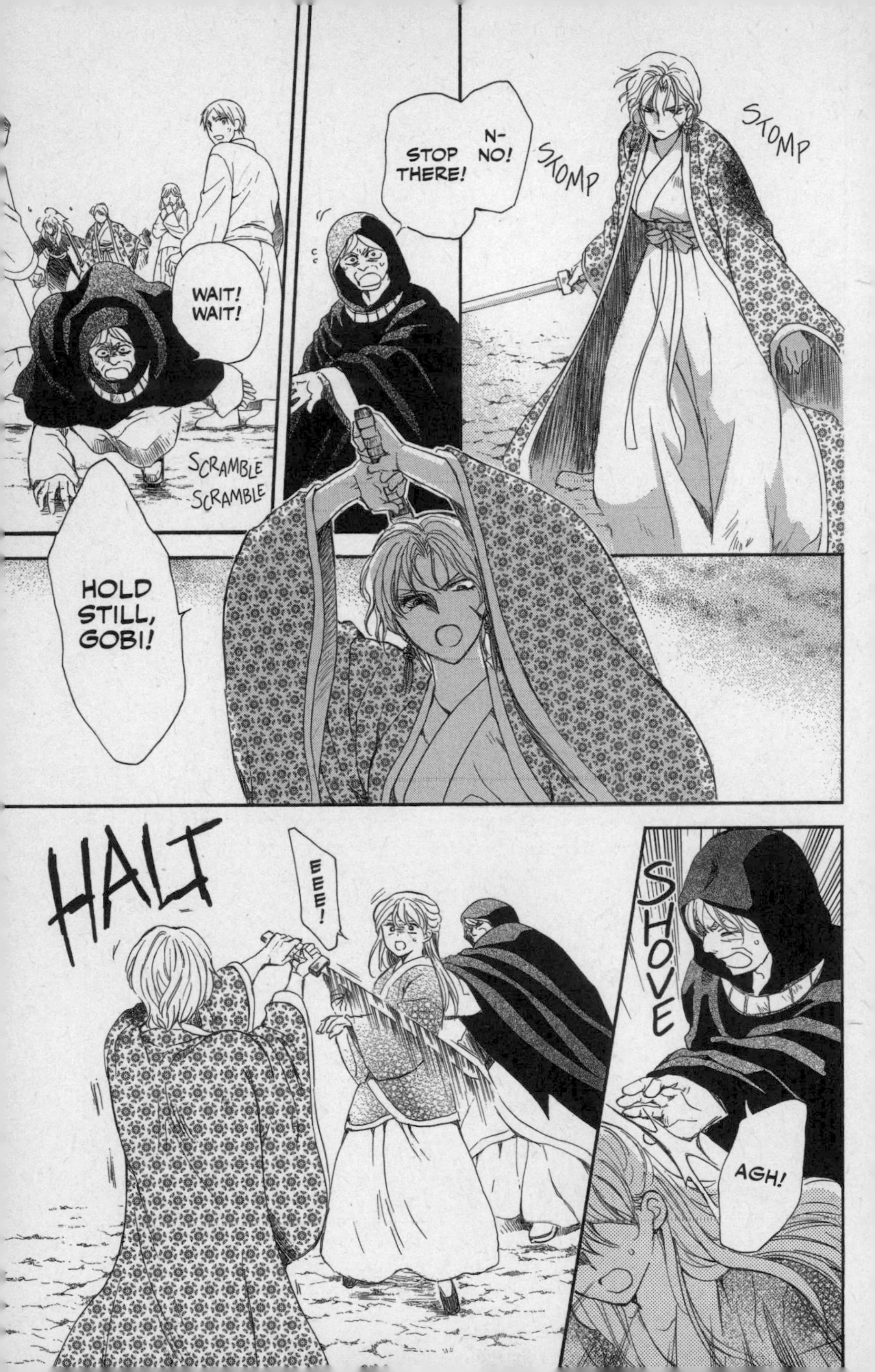
STOMP
STOMP
N-NO! STOP THERE!
WAIT! WAIT!
SCRAMBLE SCRAMBLE
HOLD STILL, GOBI!
SHOVE
AGH!
EEE!
HALT

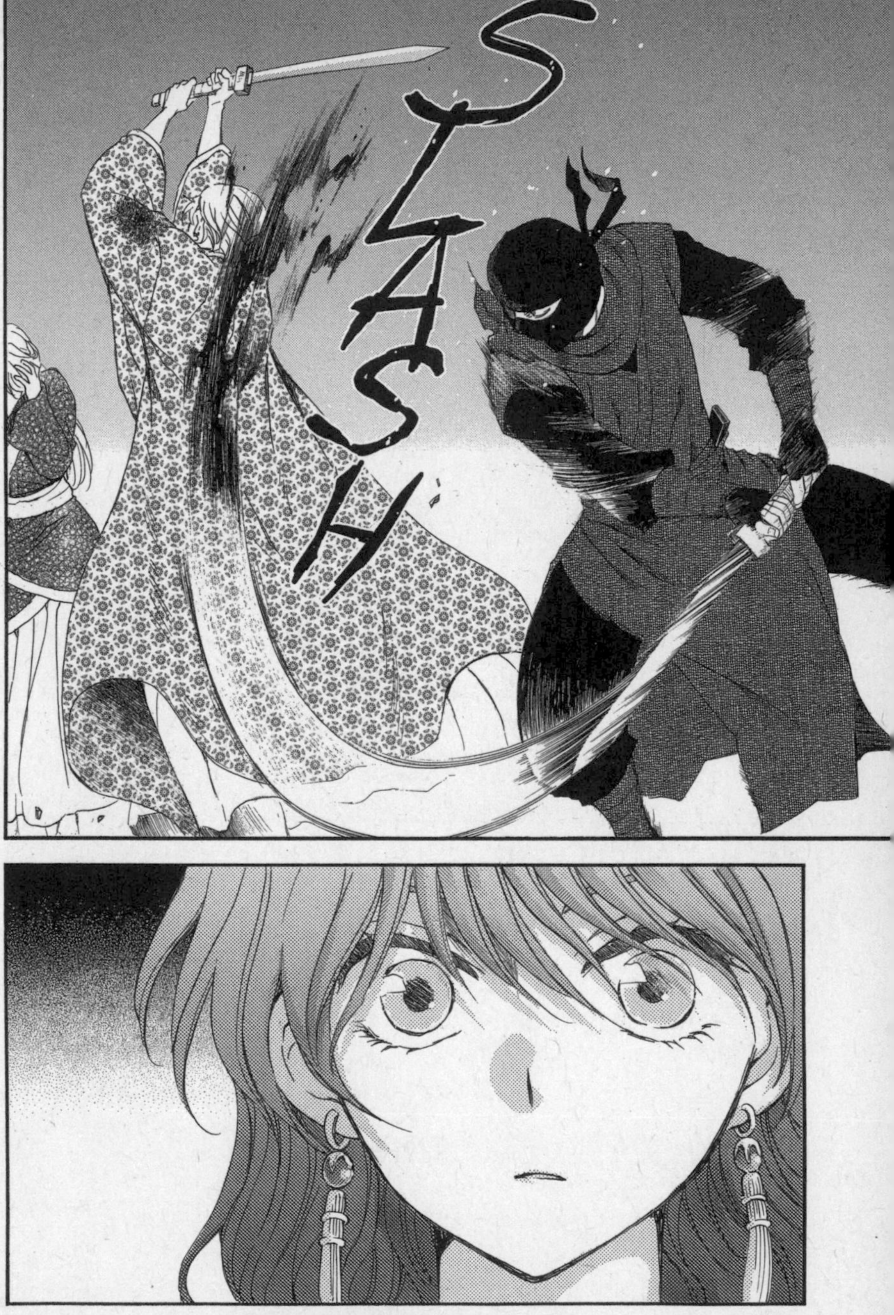
SLASH

CHAPTER 148 / THE END

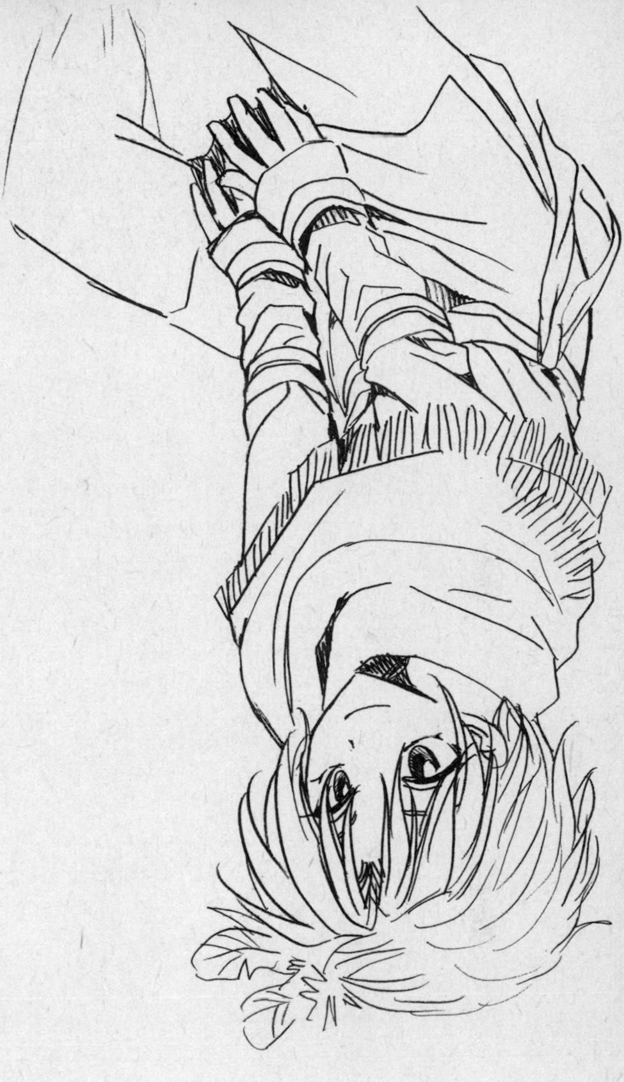

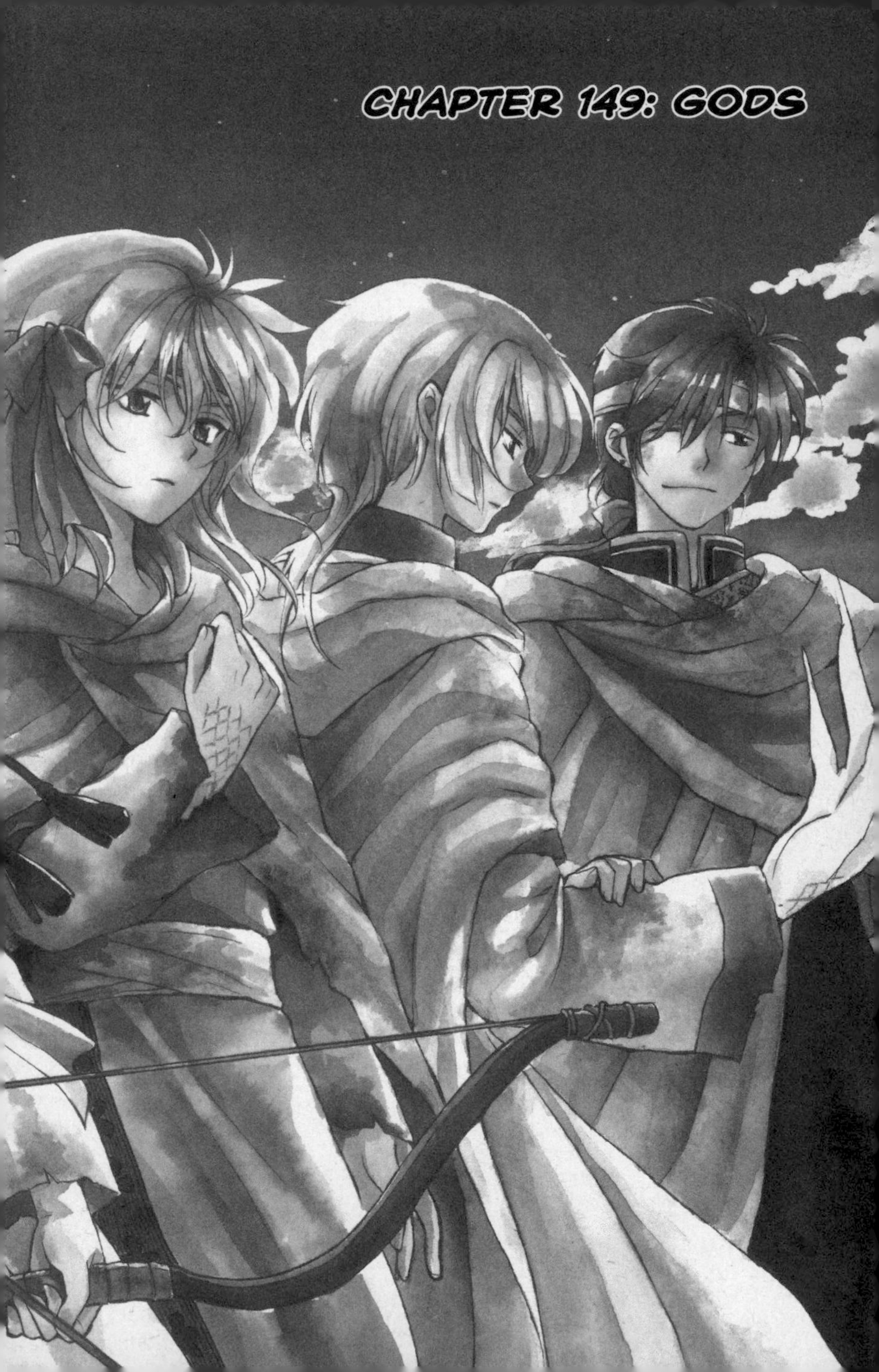
CHAPTER 149: GODS

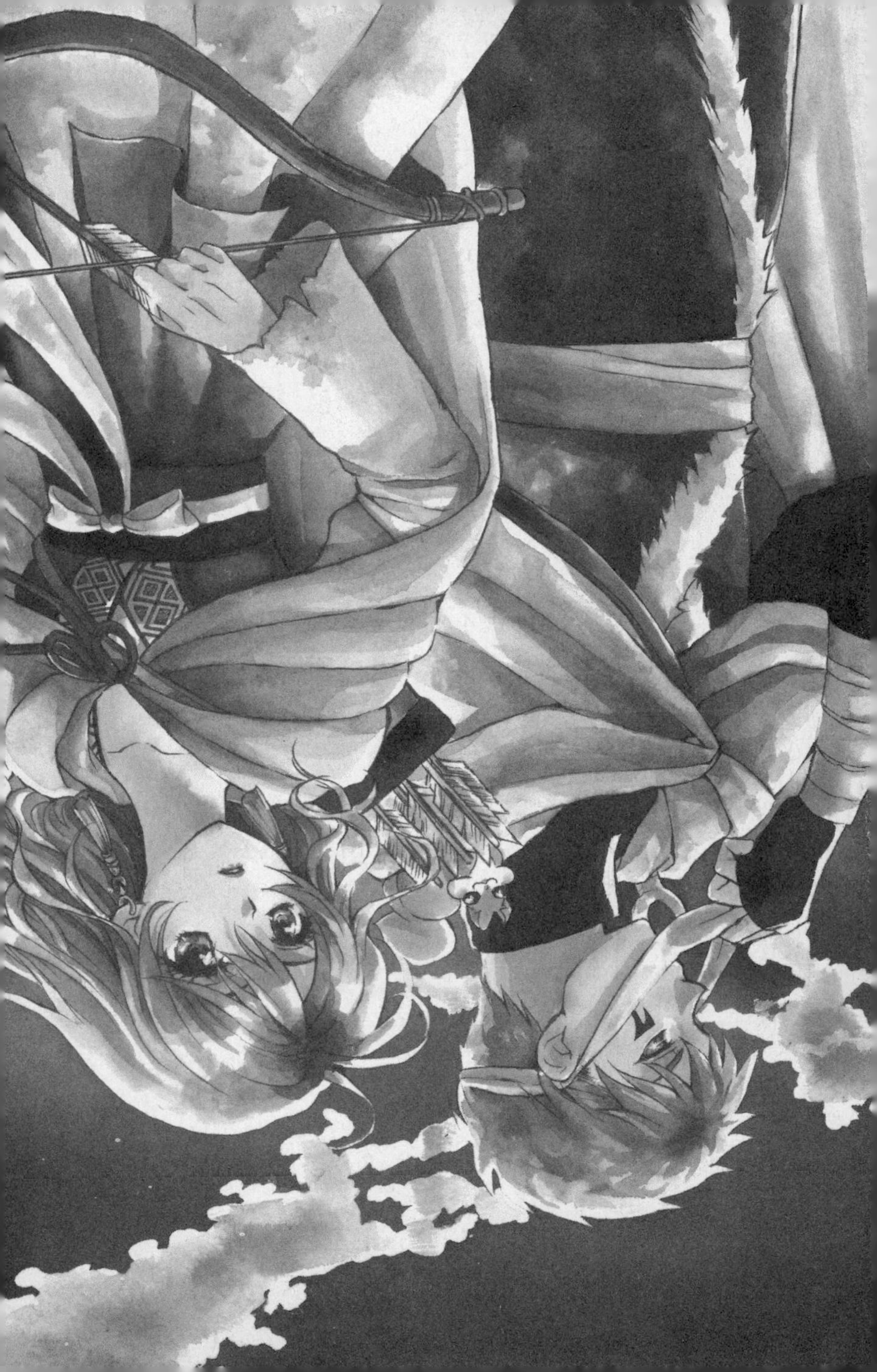

Hax kitty

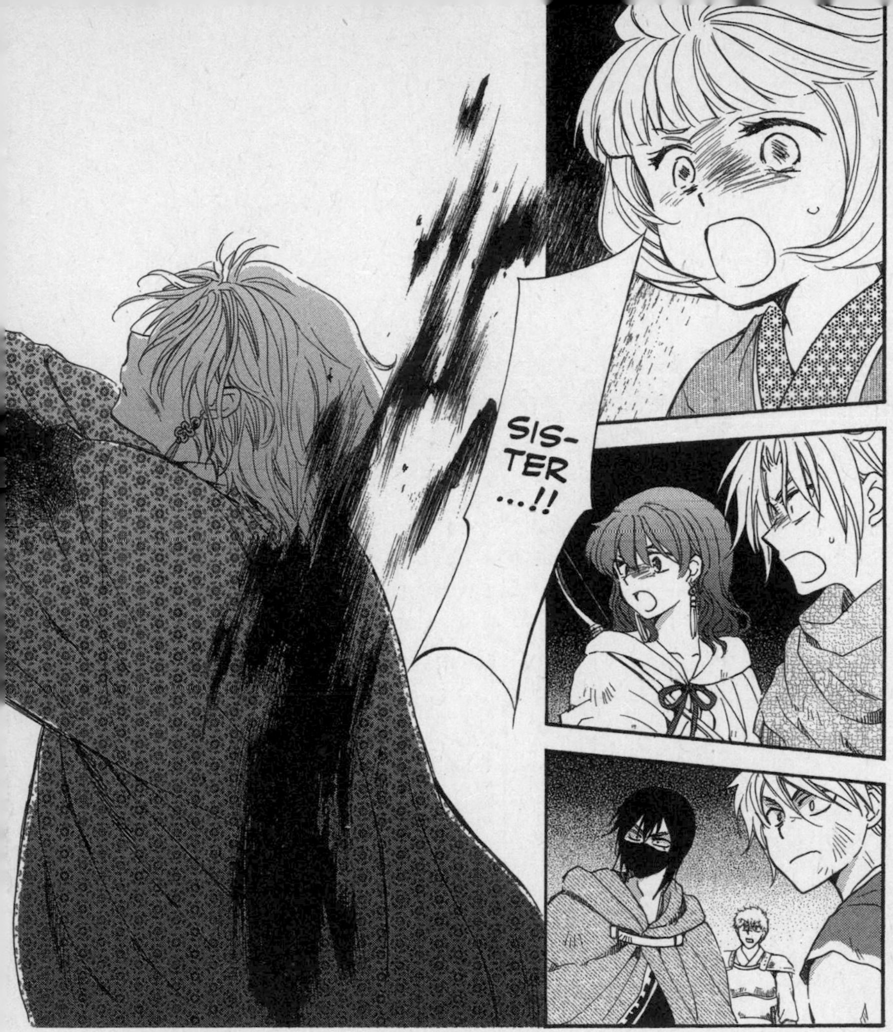
SIS-
TER
...!!

Yona
of the
Dawn

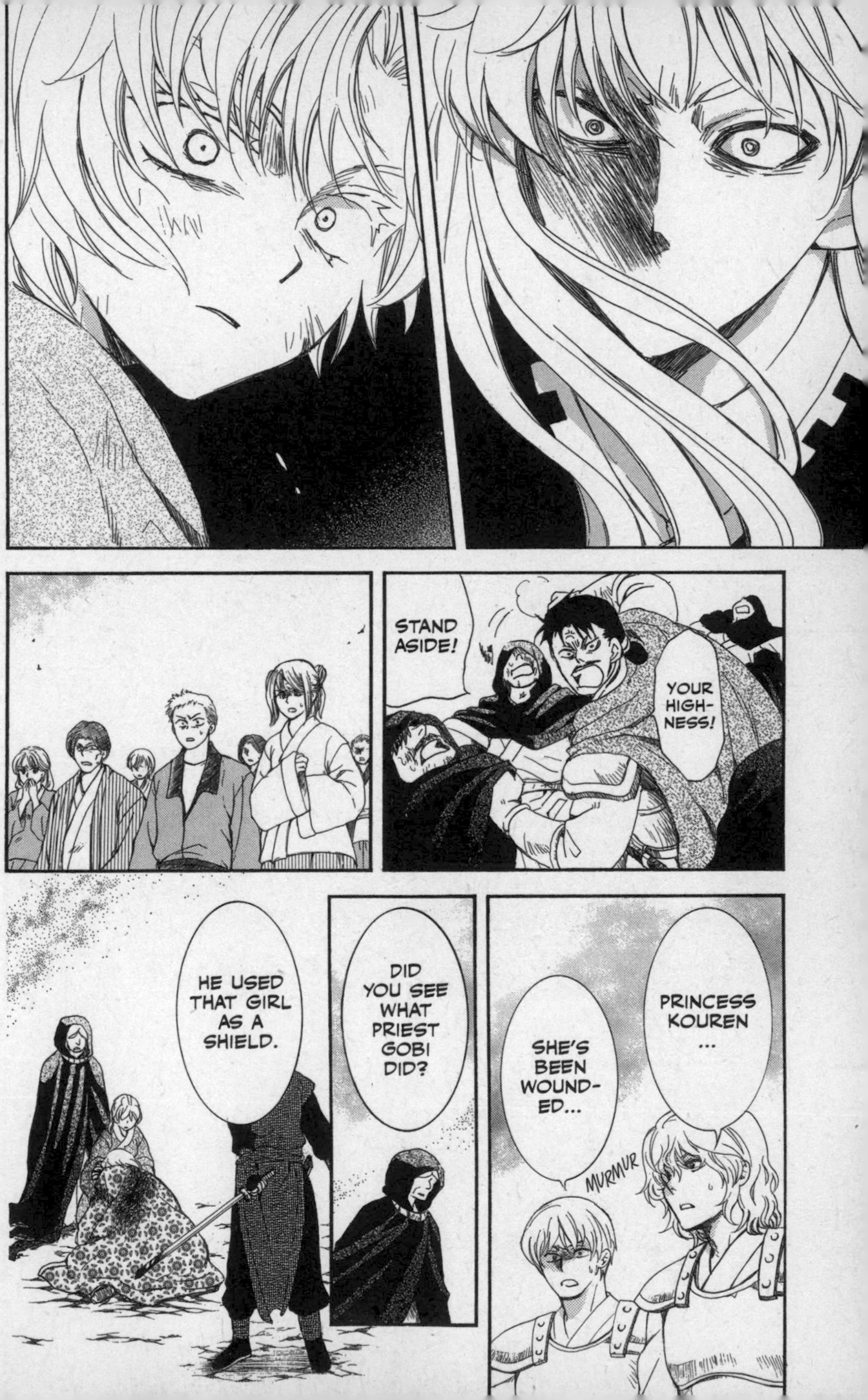
YOUR HIGH-NESS!
STAND ASIDE!
PRINCESS KOUREN ...
SHE'S BEEN WOUND-ED...
MURMUR
DID YOU SEE WHAT PRIEST GOBI DID?
HE USED THAT GIRL AS A SHIELD.

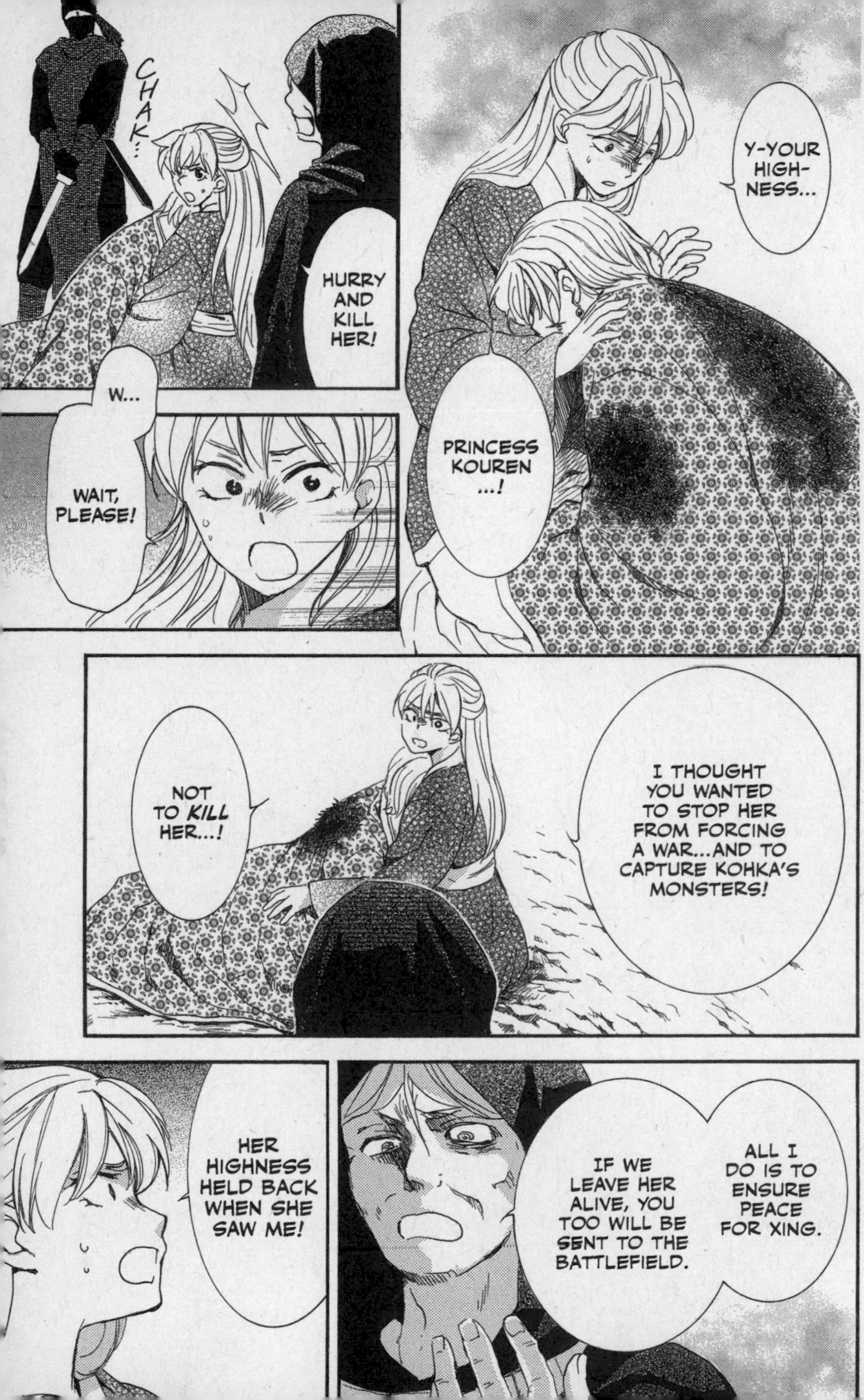
Y-YOUR HIGH-NESS...
PRINCESS KOUREN ...!
HURRY AND KILL HER!
CHAK...
W...
WAIT, PLEASE!
I THOUGHT YOU WANTED TO STOP HER FROM FORCING A WAR...AND TO CAPTURE KOHKA'S MONSTERS!
NOT TO KILL HER...!
ALL I DO IS TO ENSURE PEACE FOR XING.
IF WE LEAVE HER ALIVE, YOU TOO WILL BE SENT TO THE BATTLEFIELD.
HER HIGHNESS HELD BACK WHEN SHE SAW ME!

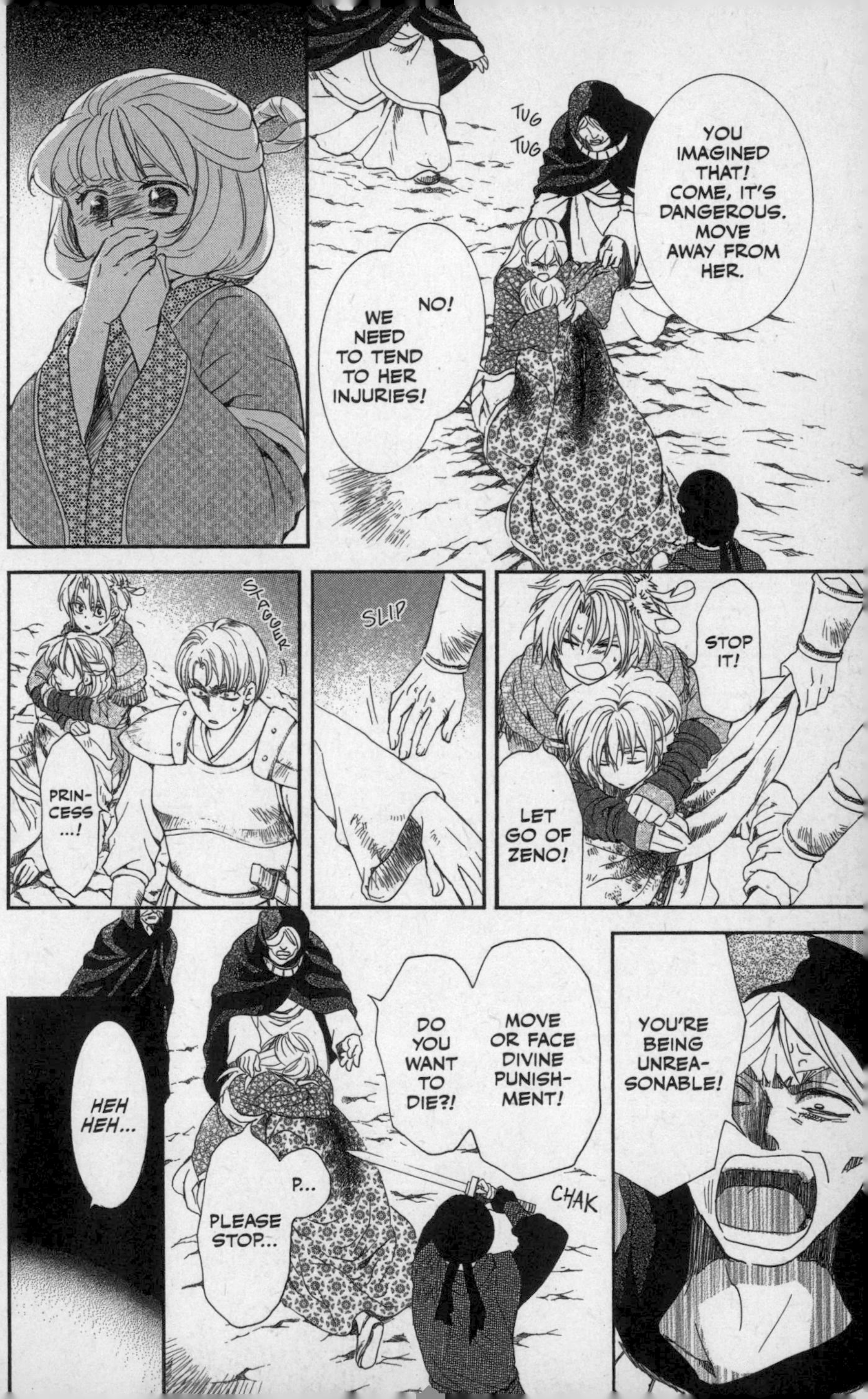
TUG
TUG
YOU IMAGINED THAT! COME, IT'S DANGEROUS. MOVE AWAY FROM HER.
NO!
WE NEED TO TEND TO HER INJURIES!
STOP IT!
LET GO OF ZENO!
SLIP
STAGGER
PRIN-CESS...!
YOU'RE BEING UNREA-SONABLE!
MOVE OR FACE DIVINE PUNISH-MENT!
DO YOU WANT TO DIE?!
CHAK
P...
PLEASE STOP...
HEH HEH...

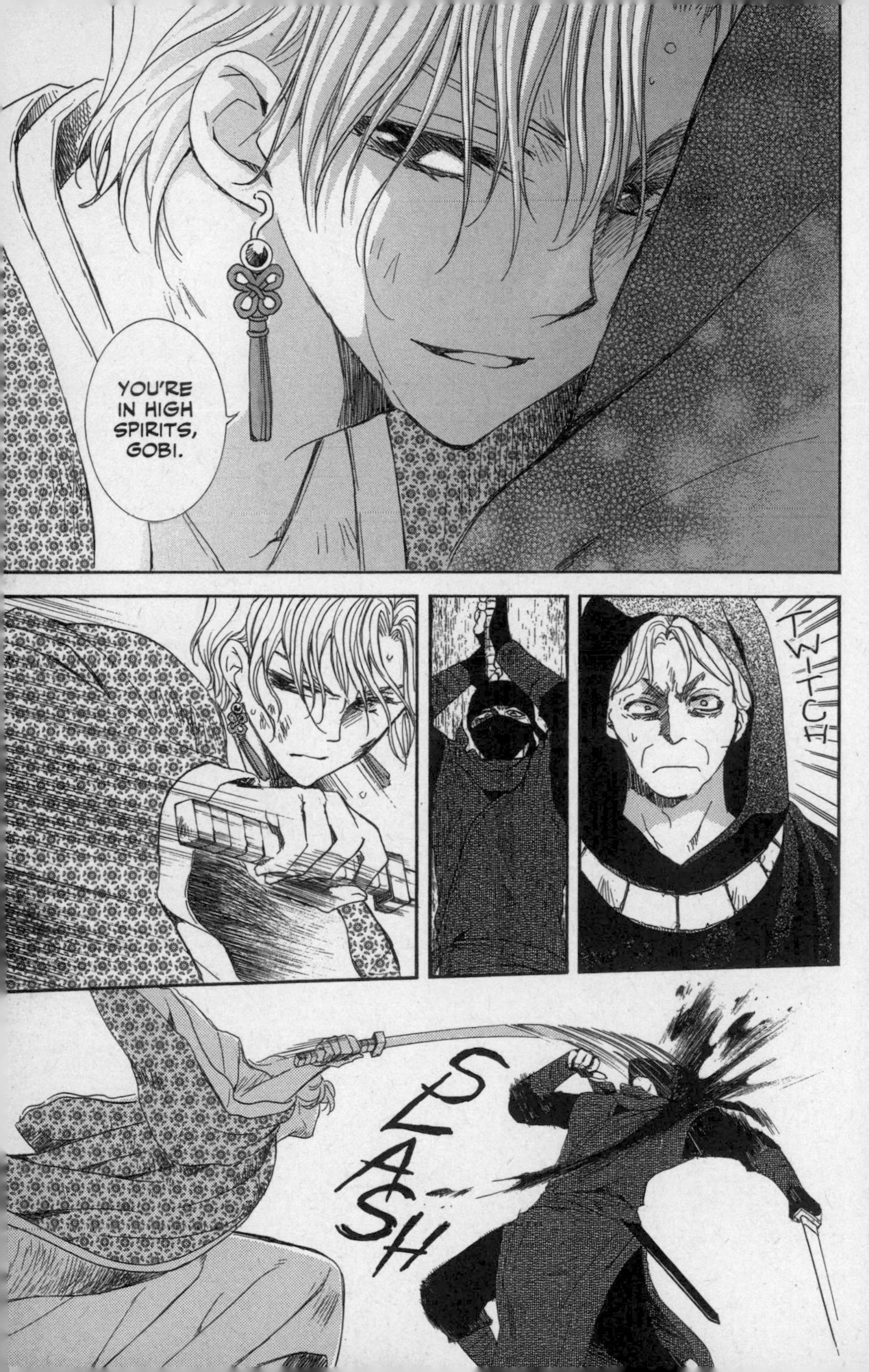
YOU'RE IN HIGH SPIRITS, GOBI.
TWITCH
SLASH

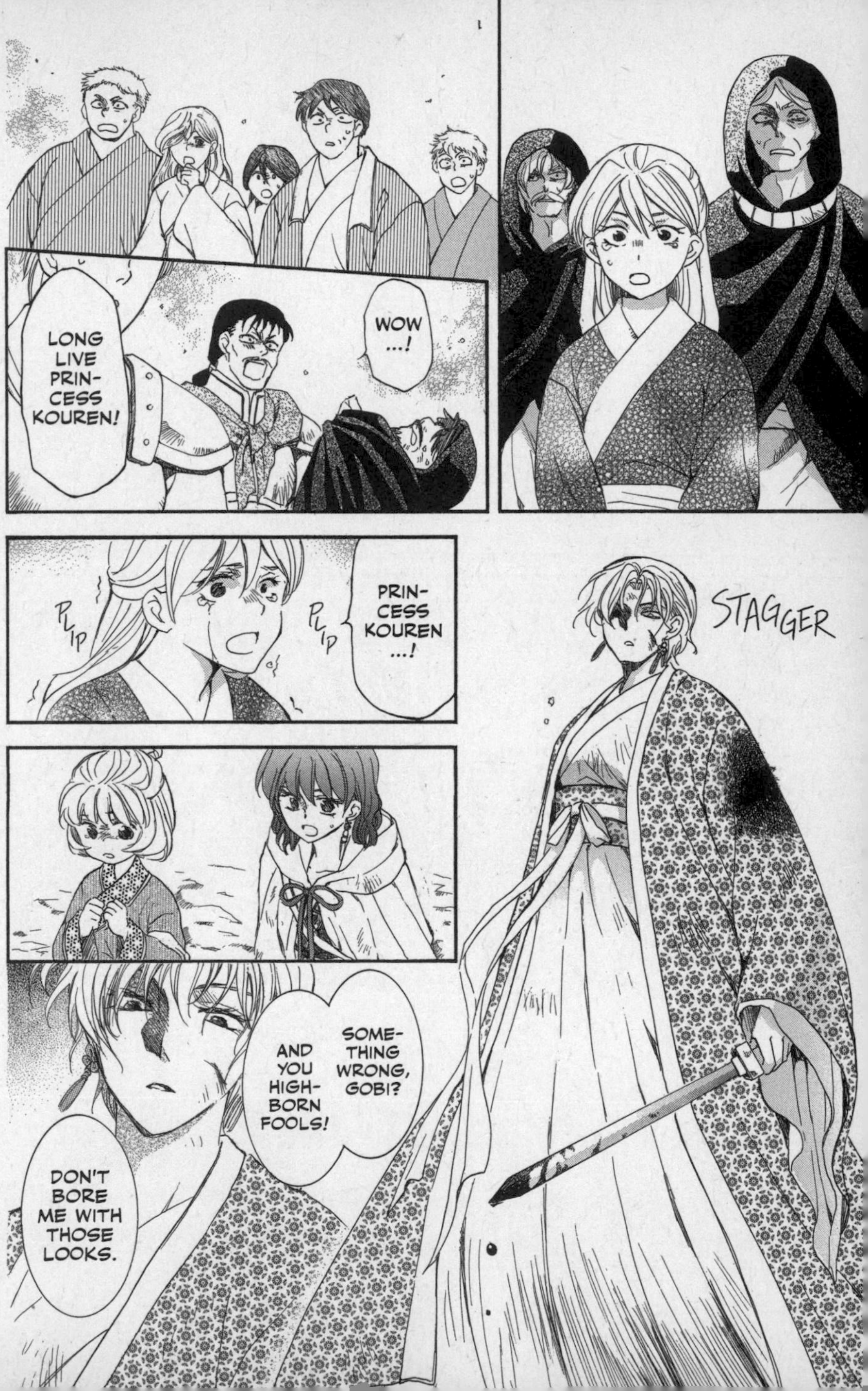
WOW ...!
LONG LIVE PRINCESS KOUREN!
STAGGER
PRINCESS KOUREN ...!
PLIP
PLIP
SOMETHING WRONG, GOBI?
AND YOU HIGHBORN FOOLS!
DON'T BORE ME WITH THOSE LOOKS.

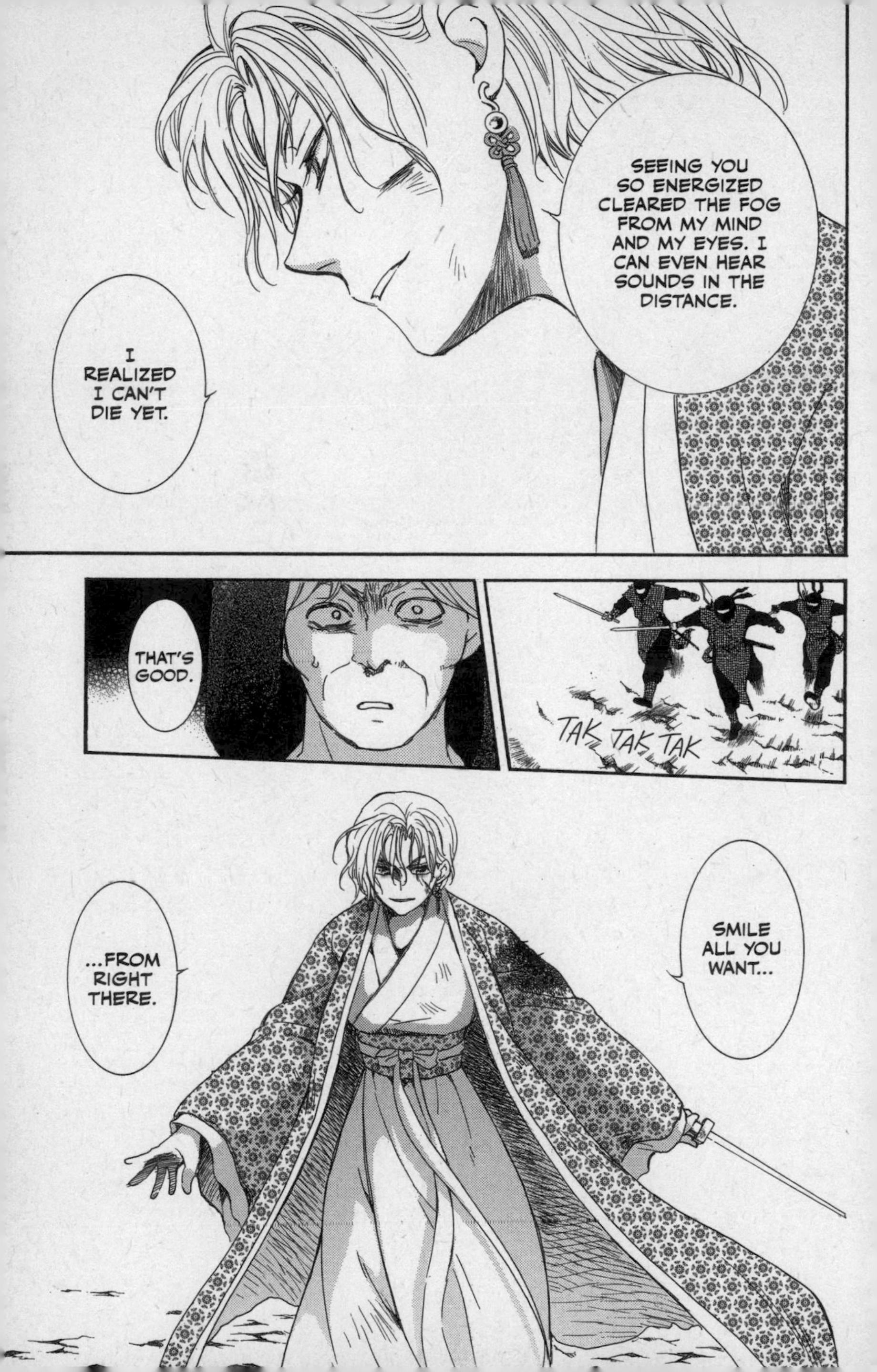
SEEING YOU SO ENERGIZED CLEARED THE FOG FROM MY MIND AND MY EYES. I CAN EVEN HEAR SOUNDS IN THE DISTANCE.
I REALIZED I CAN'T DIE YET.
TAK TAK TAK
THAT'S GOOD.
SMILE ALL YOU WANT...
...FROM RIGHT THERE.

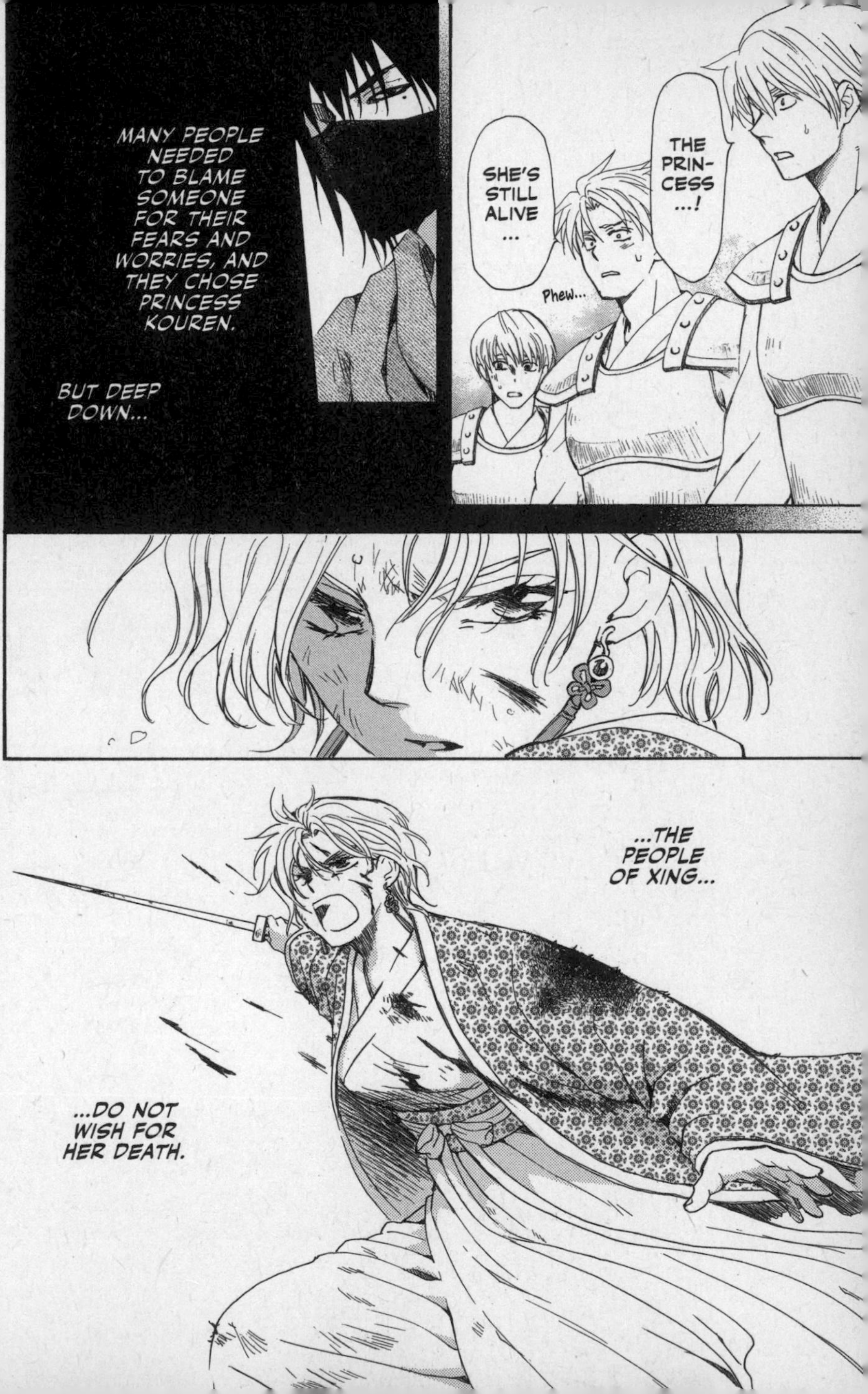
THE PRIN- CESS ...!
SHE'S STILL ALIVE ...
Phew...
MANY PEOPLE NEEDED TO BLAME SOMEONE FOR THEIR FEARS AND WORRIES, AND THEY CHOSE PRINCESS KOUREN.
BUT DEEP DOWN...
...THE PEOPLE OF XING...
...DO NOT WISH FOR HER DEATH.

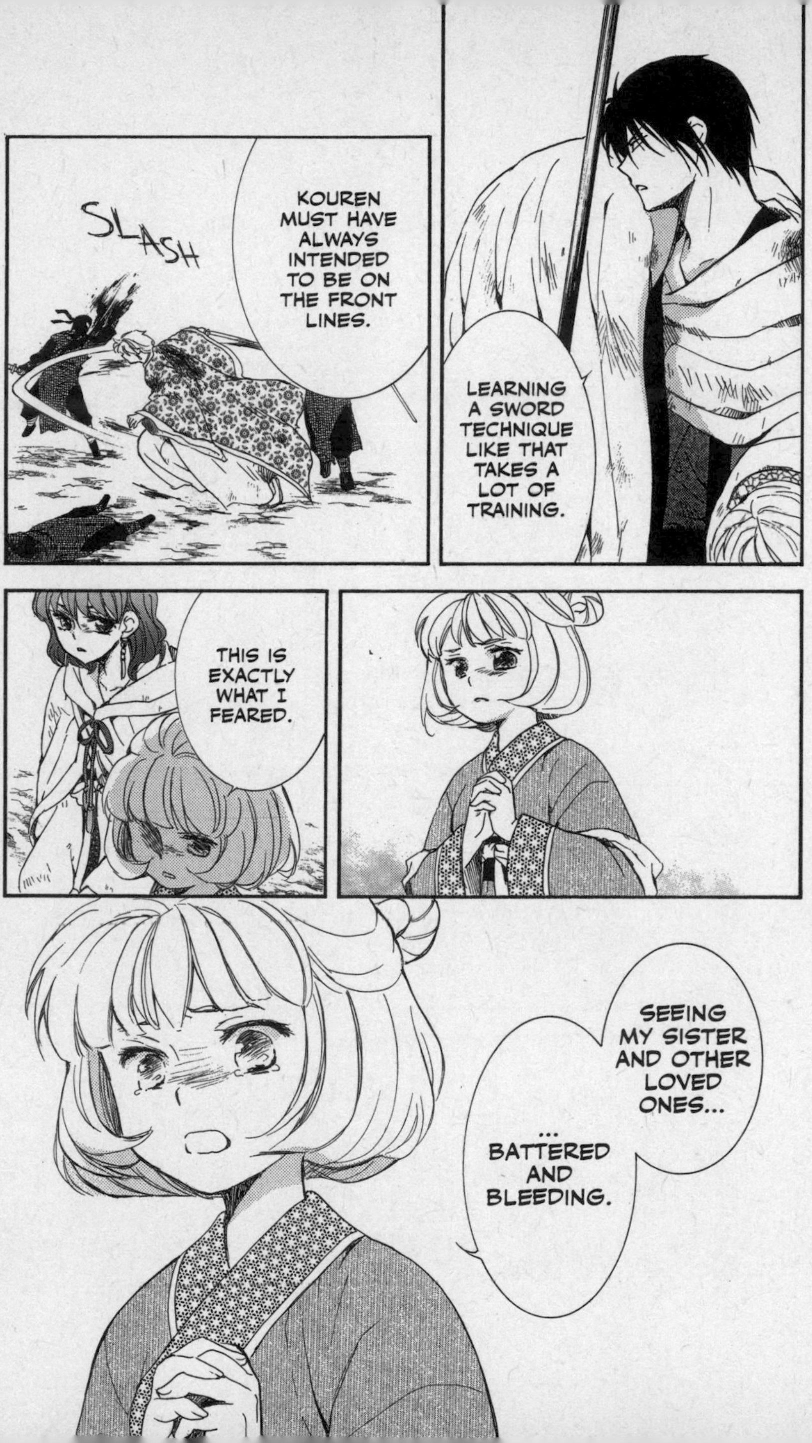
LEARNING A SWORD TECHNIQUE LIKE THAT TAKES A LOT OF TRAINING.
KOUREN MUST HAVE ALWAYS INTENDED TO BE ON THE FRONT LINES.
SLASH
THIS IS EXACTLY WHAT I FEARED.
SEEING MY SISTER AND OTHER LOVED ONES...
...BATTERED AND BLEEDING.

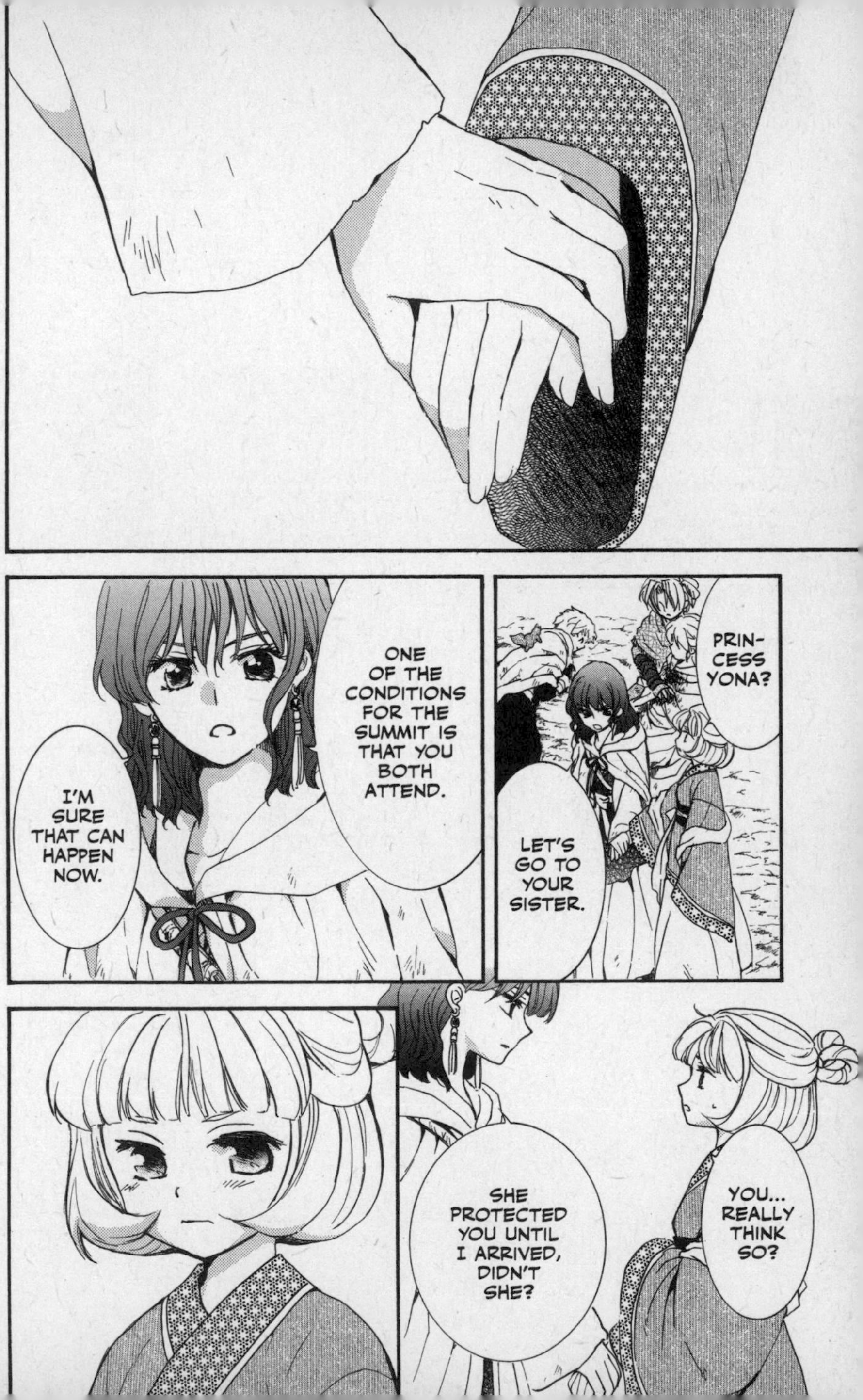
PRIN-CESS YONA?
LET'S GO TO YOUR SISTER.
ONE OF THE CONDITIONS FOR THE SUMMIT IS THAT YOU BOTH ATTEND.
I'M SURE THAT CAN HAPPEN NOW.
YOU... REALLY THINK SO?
SHE PROTECTED YOU UNTIL I ARRIVED, DIDN'T SHE?

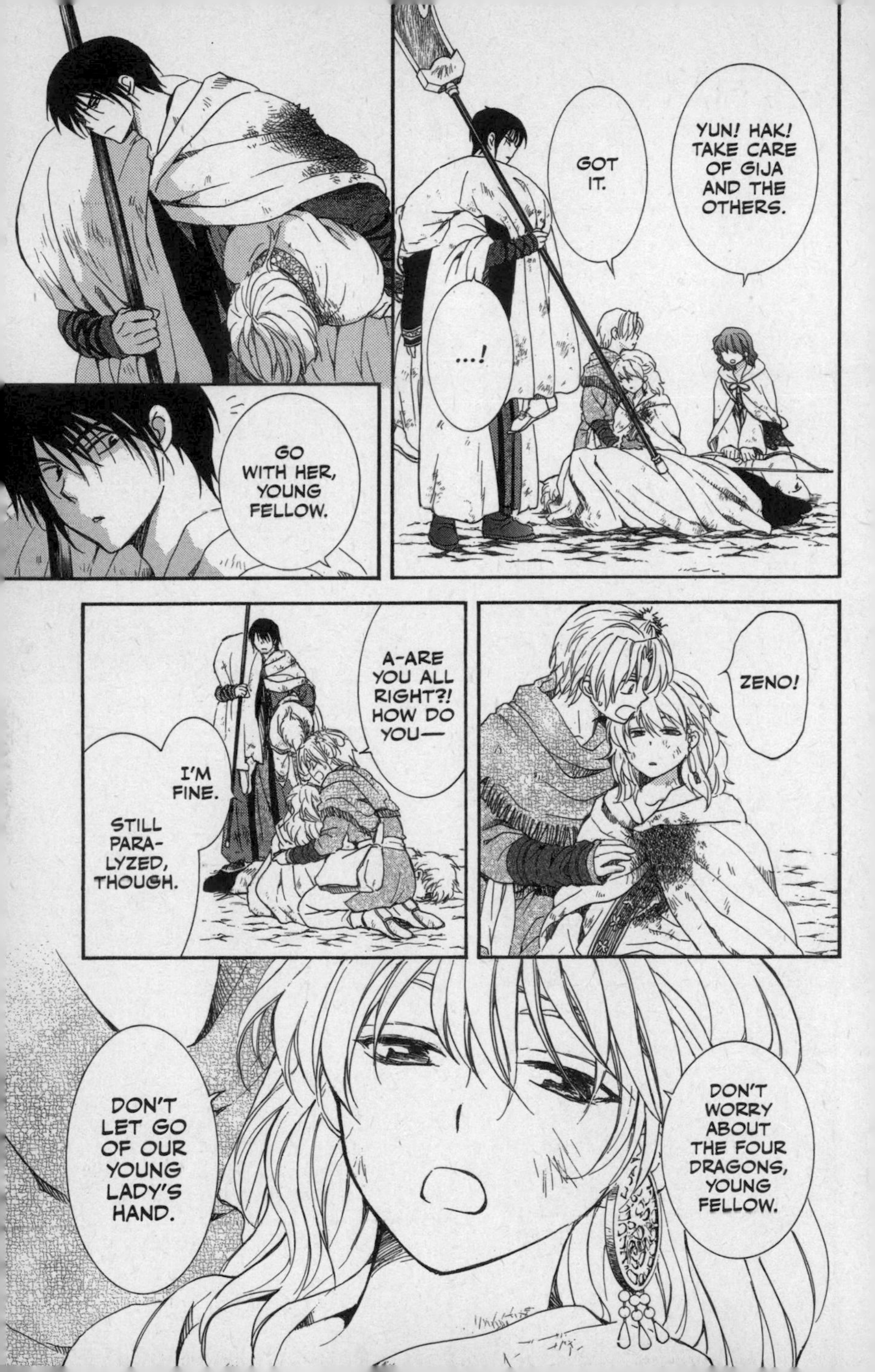
YUN! HAK! TAKE CARE OF GIJA AND THE OTHERS.
GOT IT.
...!
GO WITH HER, YOUNG FELLOW.
ZENO!
A-ARE YOU ALL RIGHT?! HOW DO YOU—
I'M FINE.
STILL PARA-LYZED, THOUGH.
DON'T WORRY ABOUT THE FOUR DRAGONS, YOUNG FELLOW.
DON'T LET GO OF OUR YOUNG LADY'S HAND.

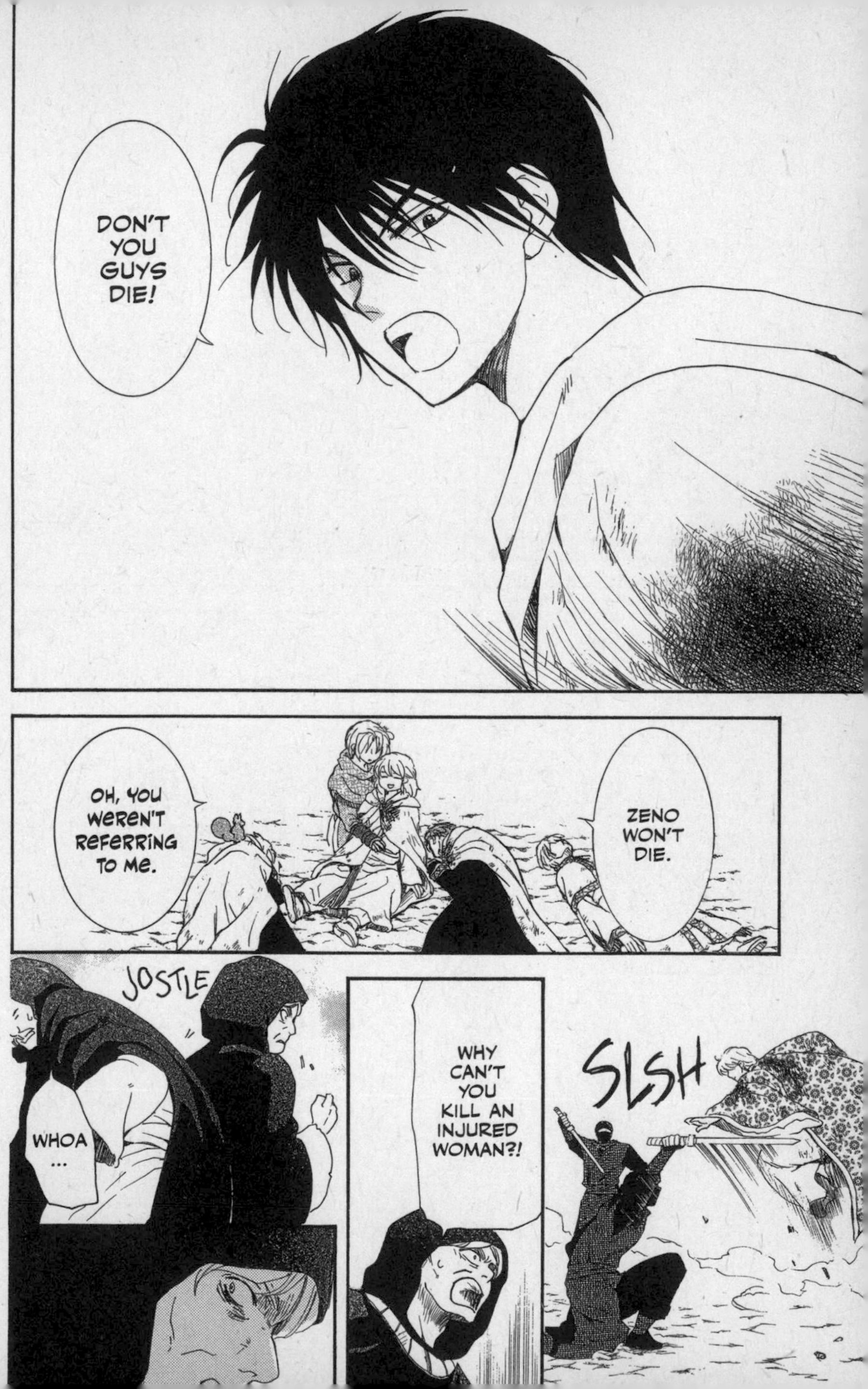
DON'T YOU GUYS DIE!
ZENO WON'T DIE.
OH, YOU WEREN'T REFERRING TO ME.
SLSH
WHY CAN'T YOU KILL AN INJURED WOMAN?!
JOSTLE
WHOA ...

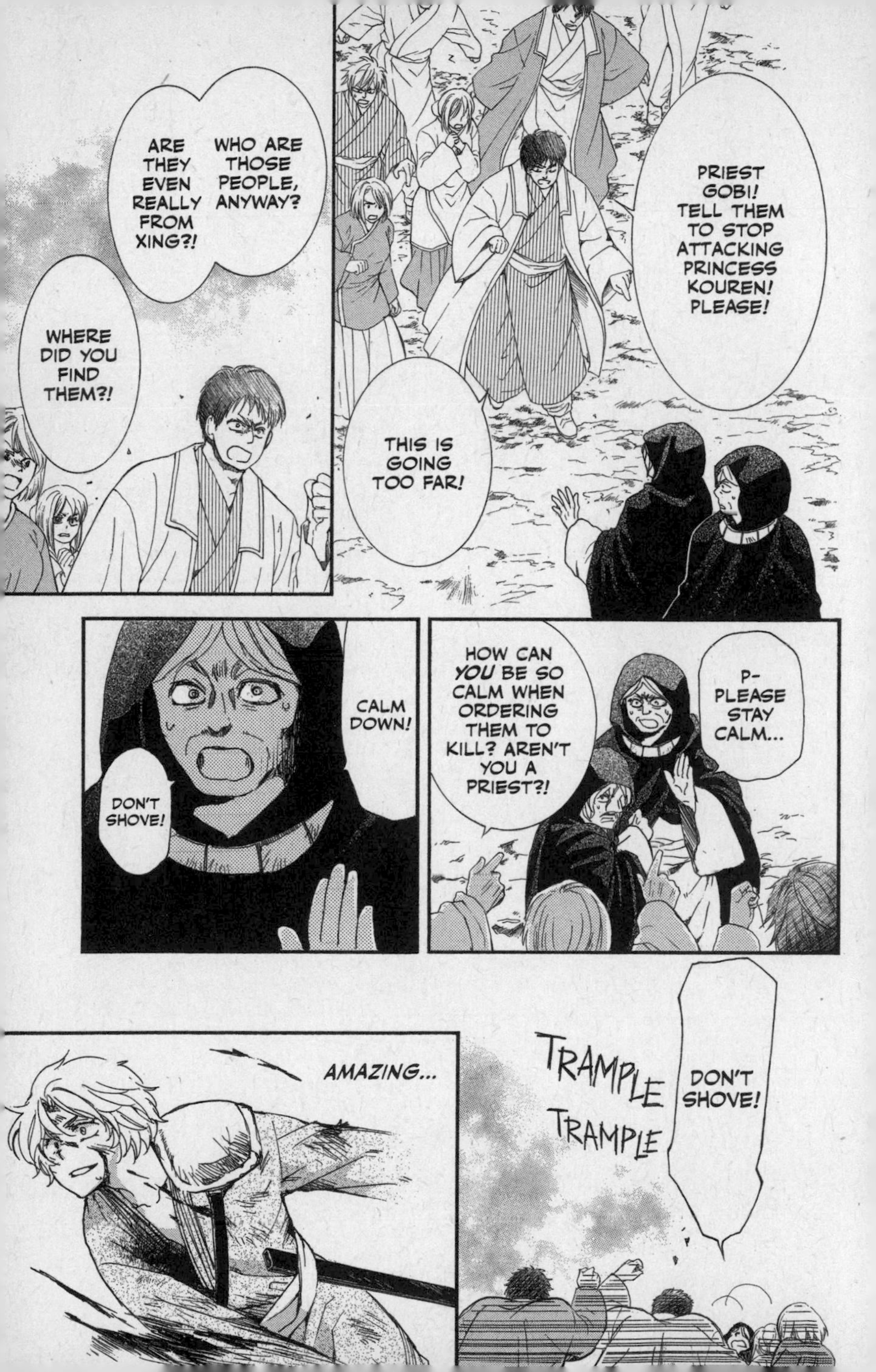
PRIEST GOBI! TELL THEM TO STOP ATTACKING PRINCESS KOUREN! PLEASE!
THIS IS GOING TOO FAR!
WHO ARE THOSE PEOPLE, ANYWAY?
ARE THEY EVEN REALLY FROM XING?!
WHERE DID YOU FIND THEM?!
P-PLEASE STAY CALM...
HOW CAN *YOU* BE SO CALM WHEN ORDERING THEM TO KILL? AREN'T YOU A PRIEST?!
CALM DOWN!
DON'T SHOVE!
DON'T SHOVE!
TRAMPLE
TRAMPLE
AMAZING...

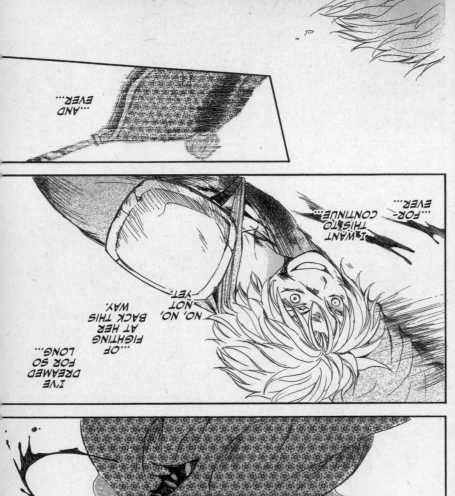

SHE'S SO AMAZING...!
THE PRINCESS IS GLORIOUS.
I'VE DREAMED FOR SO LONG...
...OF FIGHTING AT HER BACK THIS WAY.
NO, NO, NOT YET.
I WANT THIS TO CONTINUE...
...FOR-EVER...
...AND EVER...

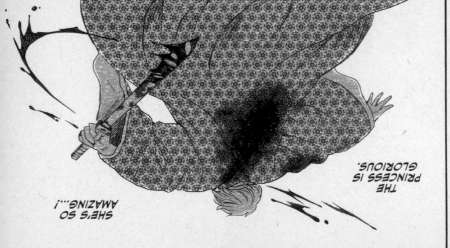

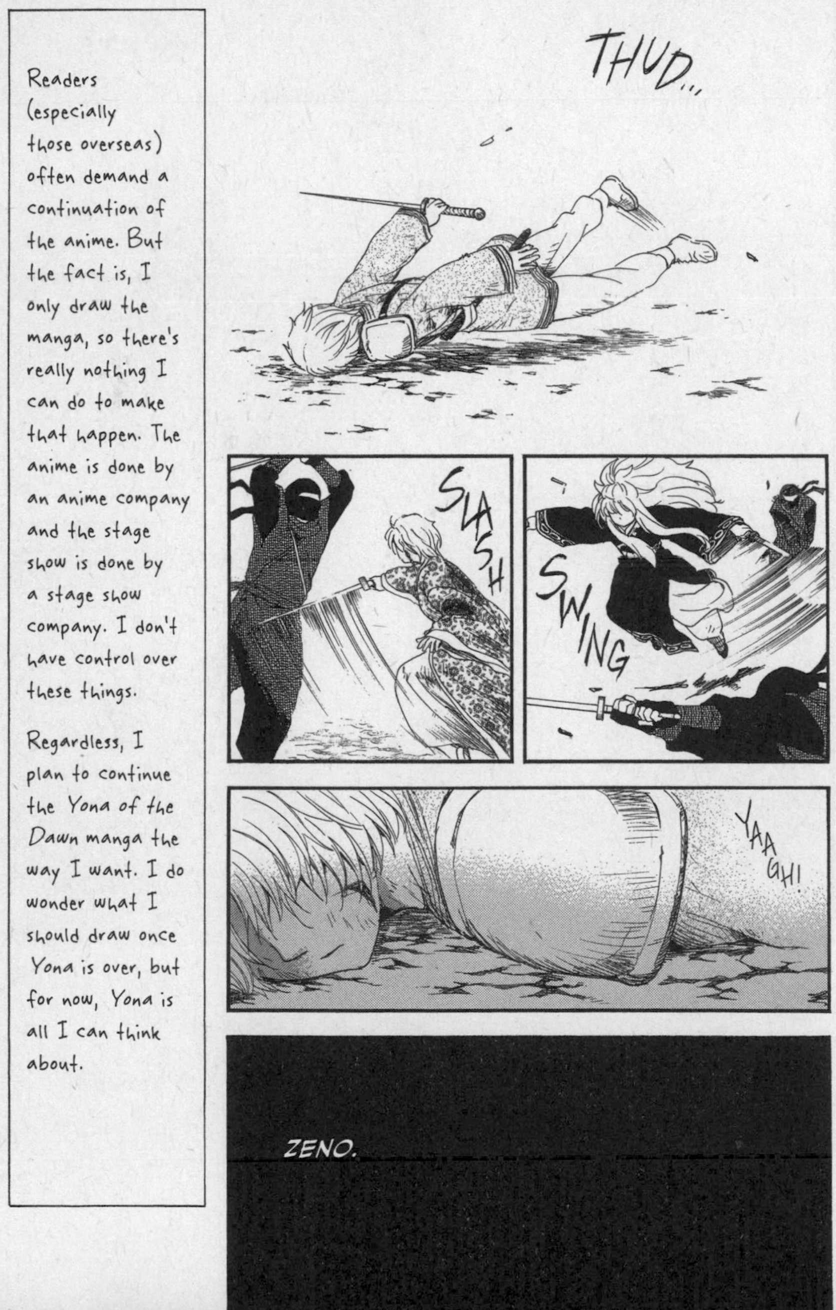
THUD...
SWING
SLASH
YAAGH!
ZENO.

Readers (especially those overseas) often demand a continuation of the anime. But the fact is, I only draw the manga, so there's really nothing I can do to make that happen. The anime is done by an anime company and the stage show is done by a stage show company. I don't have control over these things.

Regardless, I plan to continue the *Yona of the Dawn* manga the way I want. I do wonder what I should draw once *Yona* is over, but for now, *Yona* is all I can think about.

I WANT MORE TIME.
I WANT IT SO BADLY.
I WANT TO...
...SEE MORE OF WHAT SHE'LL ACCOMPLISH.
THIS TIME...
...I WANT TO BE ABLE TO HELP HER.
PRINCESS...
...KOUREN...
PRINCESS KOUREN...

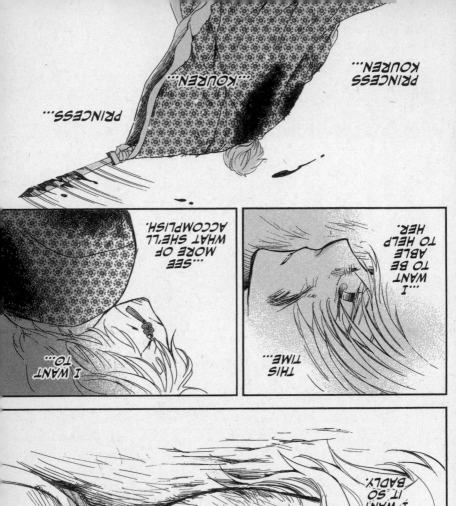

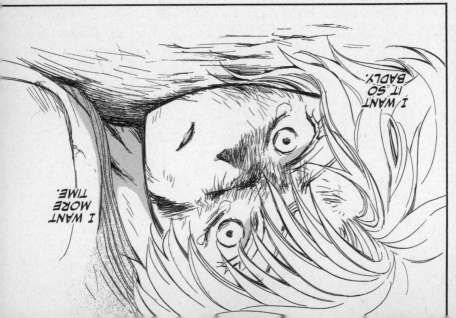

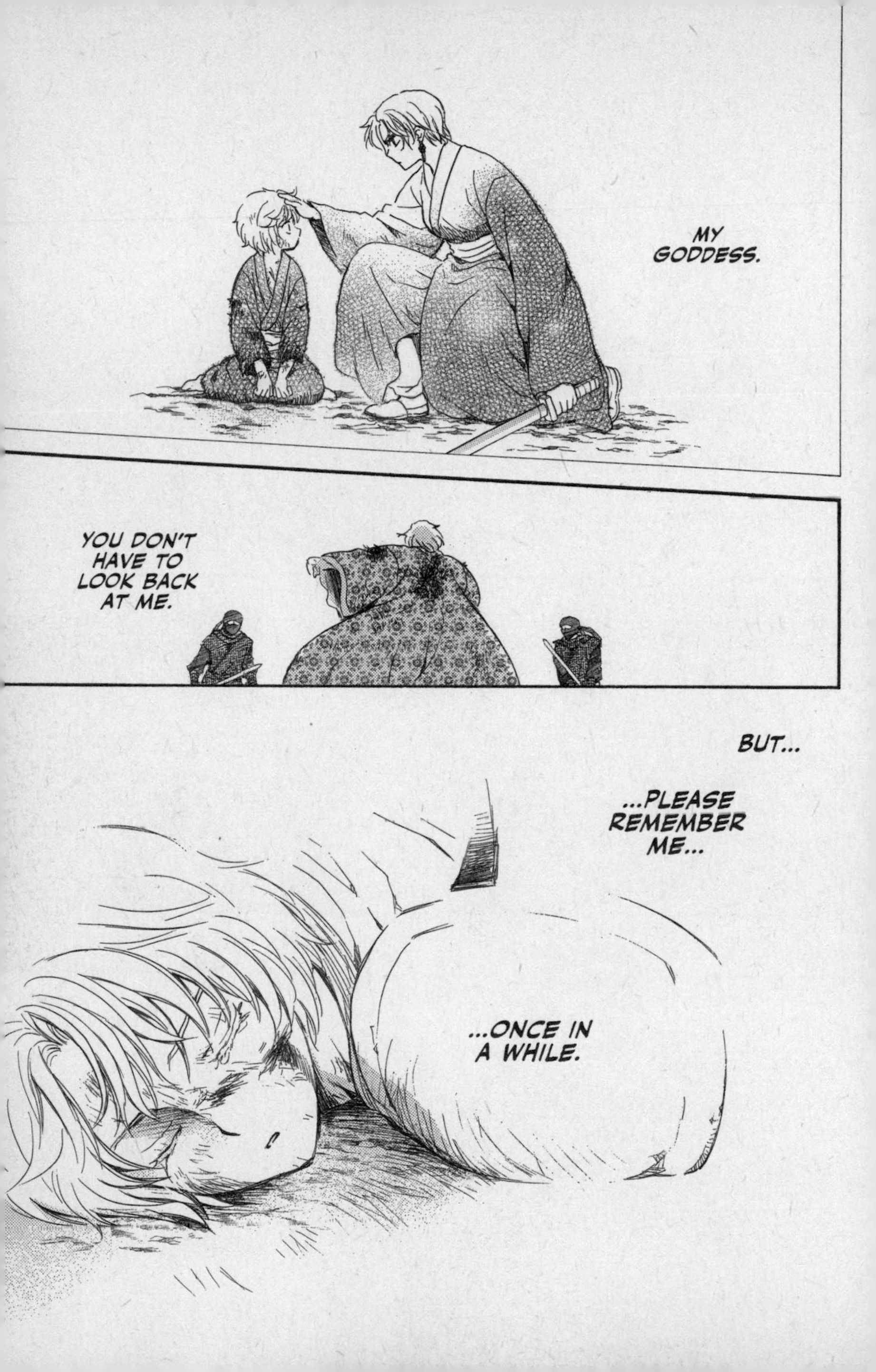
MY GODDESS.
YOU DON'T HAVE TO LOOK BACK AT ME.
BUT...
...PLEASE REMEMBER ME...
...ONCE IN A WHILE.

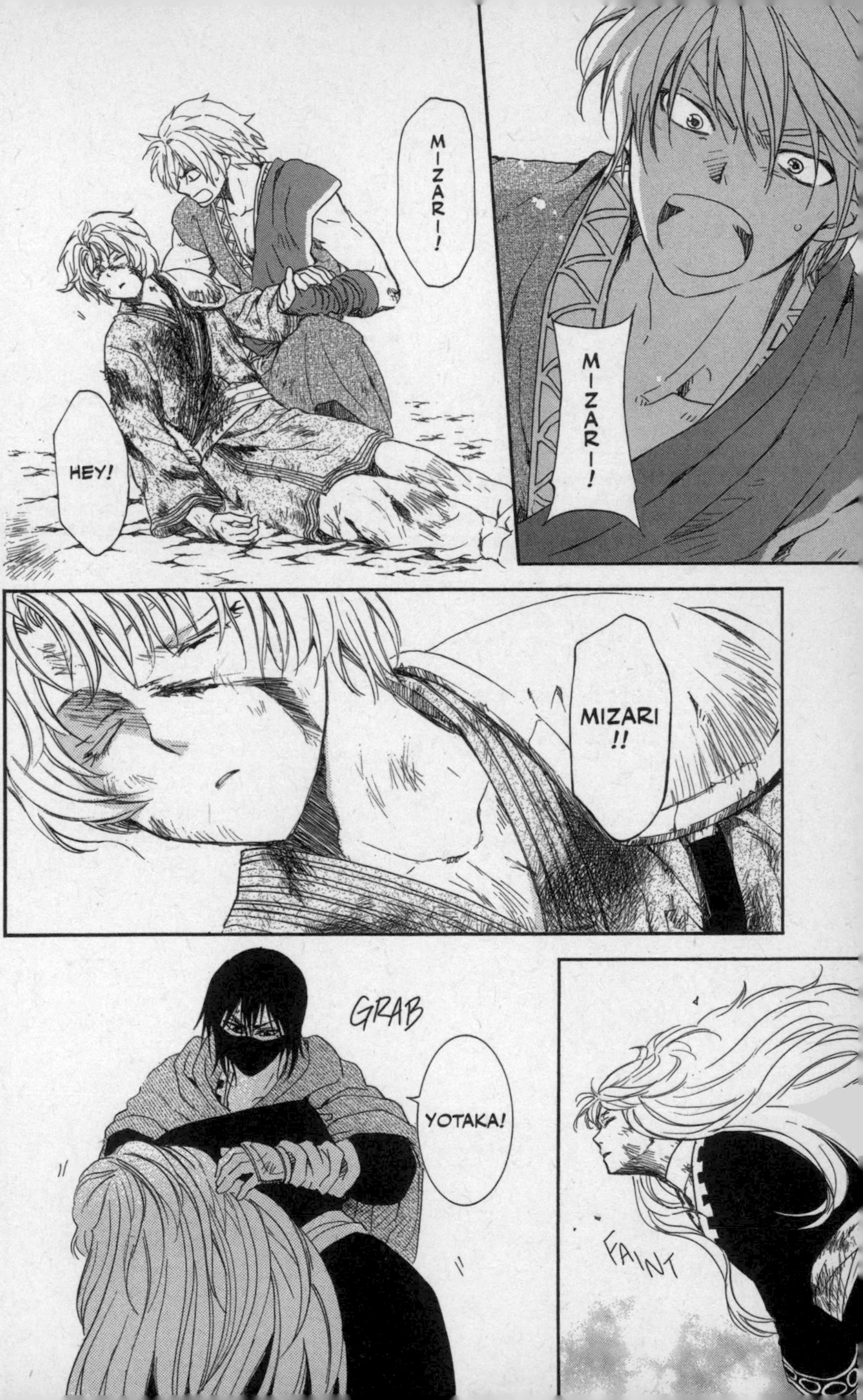
MIZARI!
MIZARI!
HEY!
MIZARI !!
FAINT
GRAB
YOTAKA!

SLASH
FWUD
Huff
Huff
GRAB
SISTER ...!

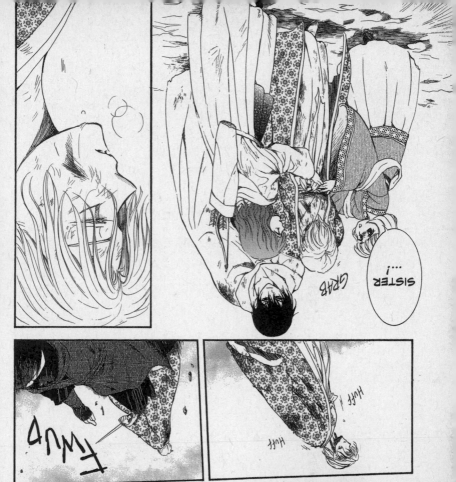

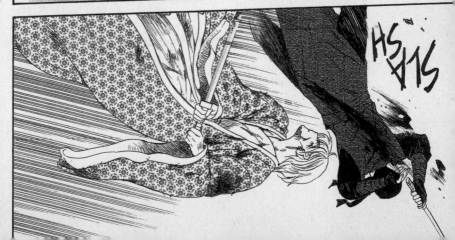

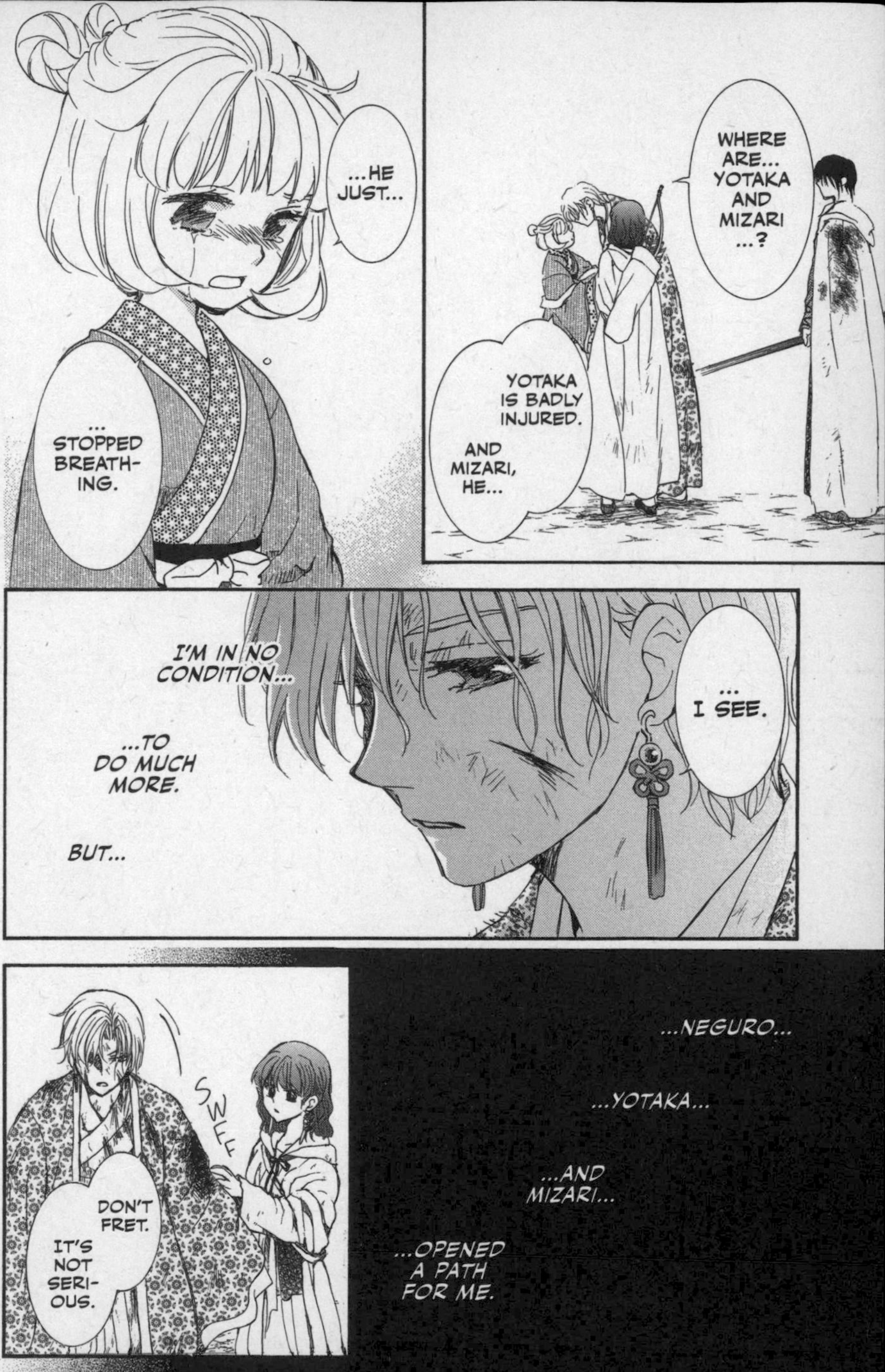
WHERE ARE... YOTAKA AND MIZARI ...?
YOTAKA IS BADLY INJURED.
AND MIZARI, HE...
...HE JUST...
... STOPPED BREATH-ING.
... I SEE.
I'M IN NO CONDITION...
...TO DO MUCH MORE.
BUT...
...NEGURO...
...YOTAKA...
...AND MIZARI...
...OPENED A PATH FOR ME.
SWEFF
DON'T FRET.
IT'S NOT SERI-OUS.

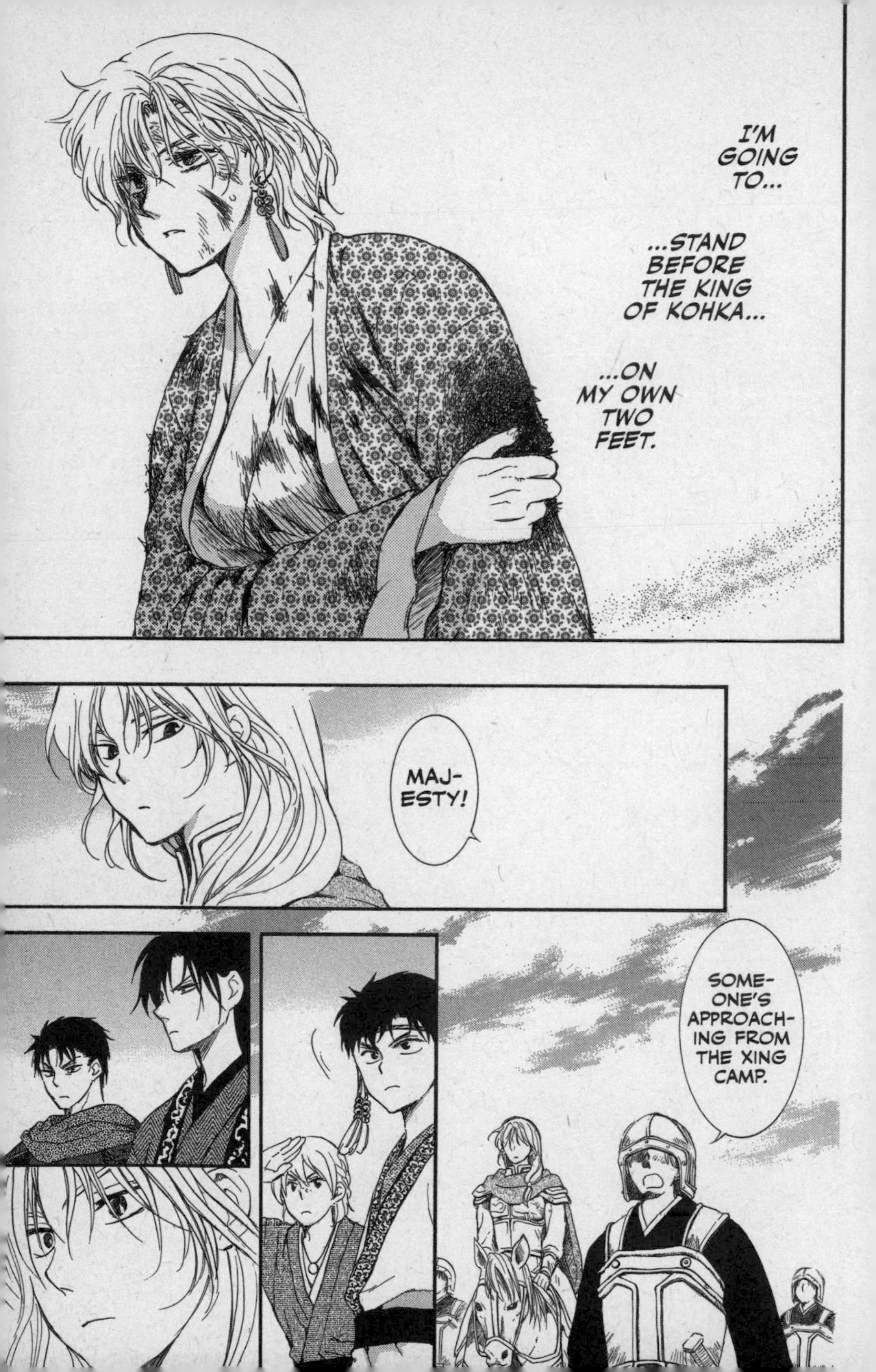
I'M GOING TO...
...STAND BEFORE THE KING OF KOHKA...
...ON MY OWN TWO FEET.
MAJ-ESTY!
SOME-ONE'S APPROACH-ING FROM THE XING CAMP.

HEY—
ISN'T THAT
GENERAL
HAK?

WSP

AND
PRINCESS
YONA...?
WHY ARE
THEY WITH
XING?

WSP

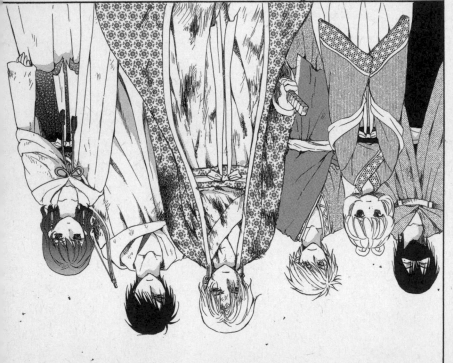

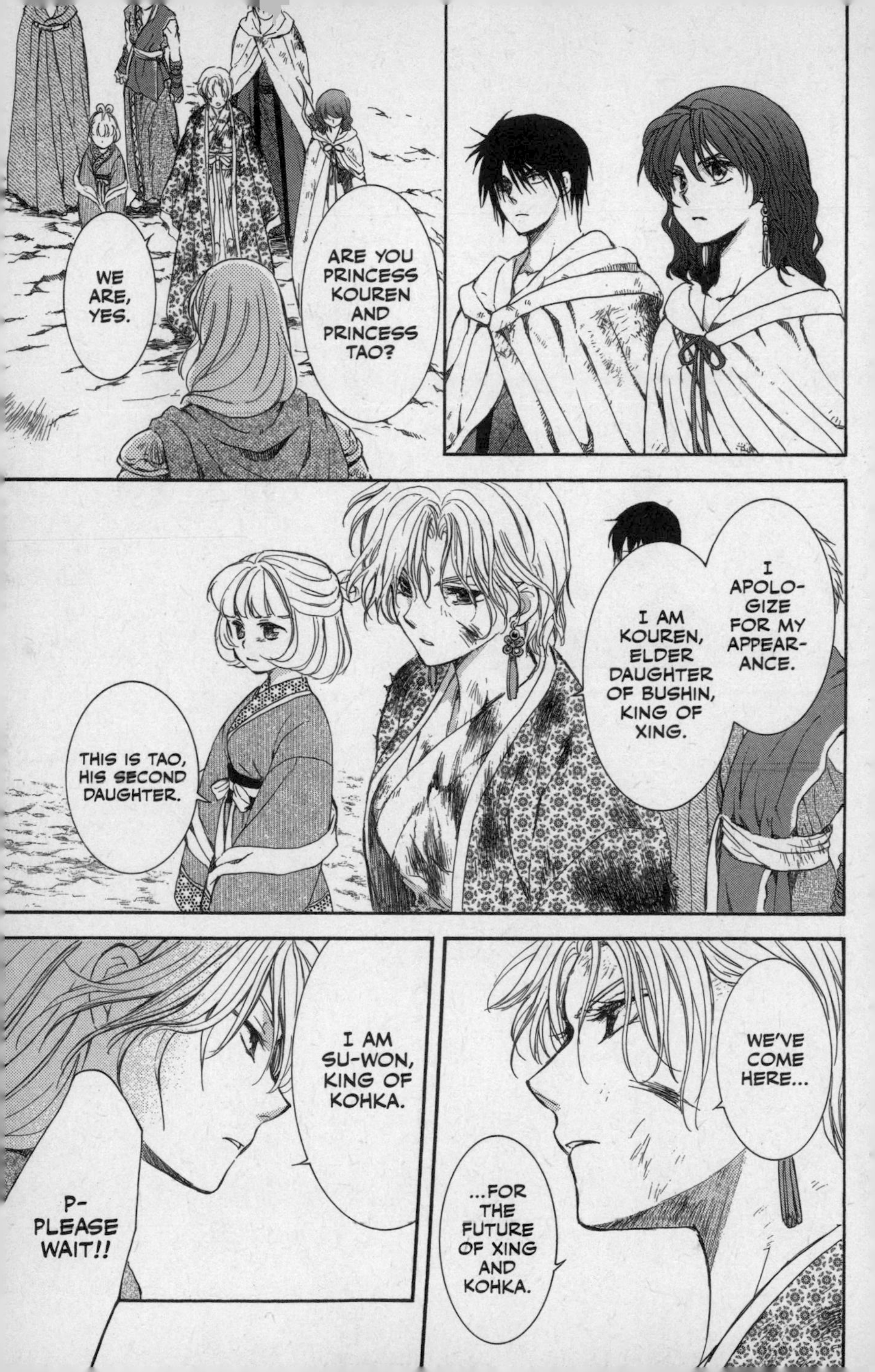
ARE YOU PRINCESS KOUREN AND PRINCESS TAO?
WE ARE, YES.
I APOLOGIZE FOR MY APPEARANCE.
I AM KOUREN, ELDER DAUGHTER OF BUSHIN, KING OF XING.
THIS IS TAO, HIS SECOND DAUGHTER.
WE'VE COME HERE...
...FOR THE FUTURE OF XING AND KOHKA.
I AM SU-WON, KING OF KOHKA.
P-PLEASE WAIT!!

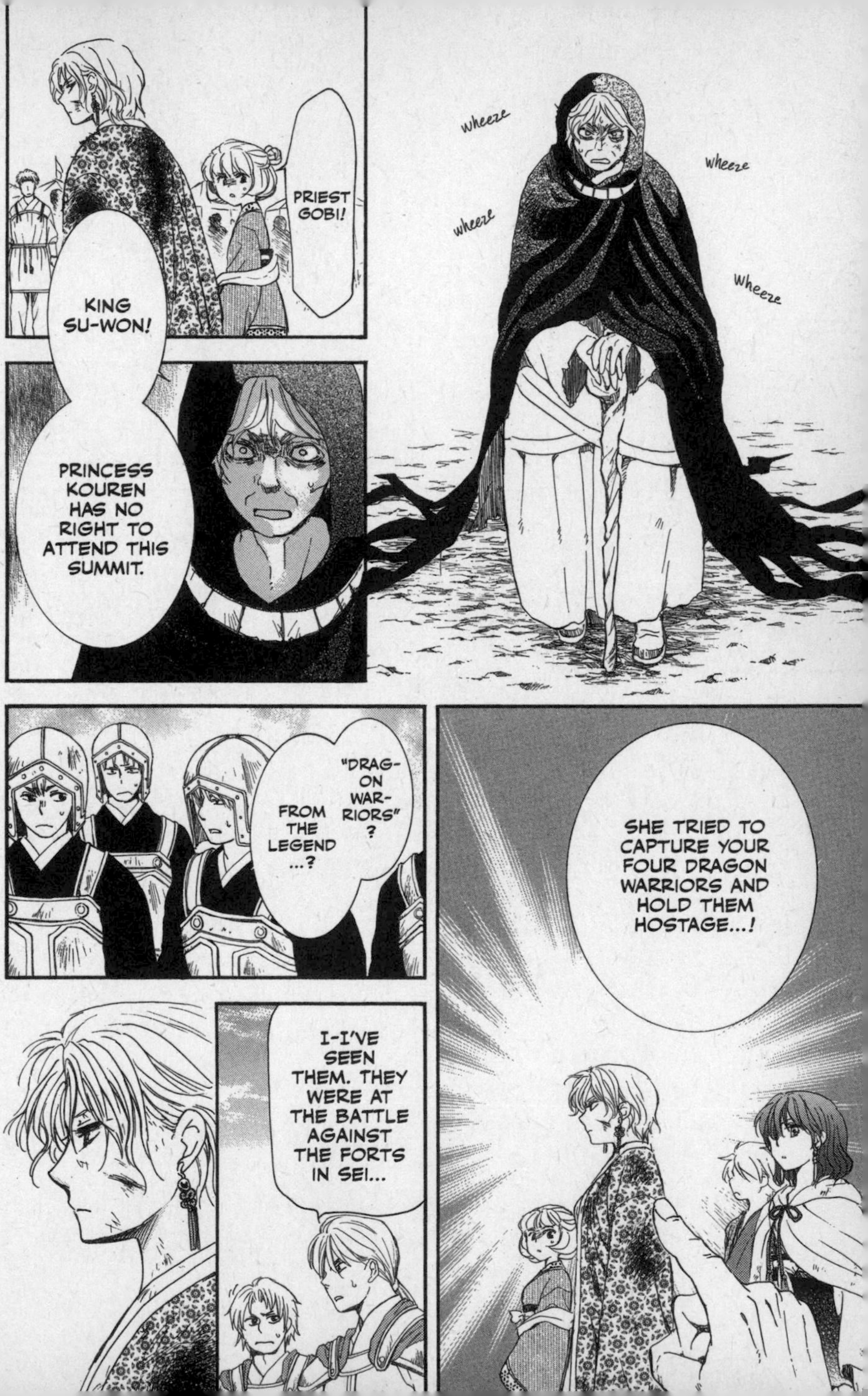
wheeze
wheeze
wheeze
wheeze
PRIEST GOBI!
KING SU-WON!
PRINCESS KOUREN HAS NO RIGHT TO ATTEND THIS SUMMIT.
SHE TRIED TO CAPTURE YOUR FOUR DRAGON WARRIORS AND HOLD THEM HOSTAGE...!
"DRAG-ON WAR-RIORS"?
FROM THE LEGEND...?
I-I'VE SEEN THEM. THEY WERE AT THE BATTLE AGAINST THE FORTS IN SEI...

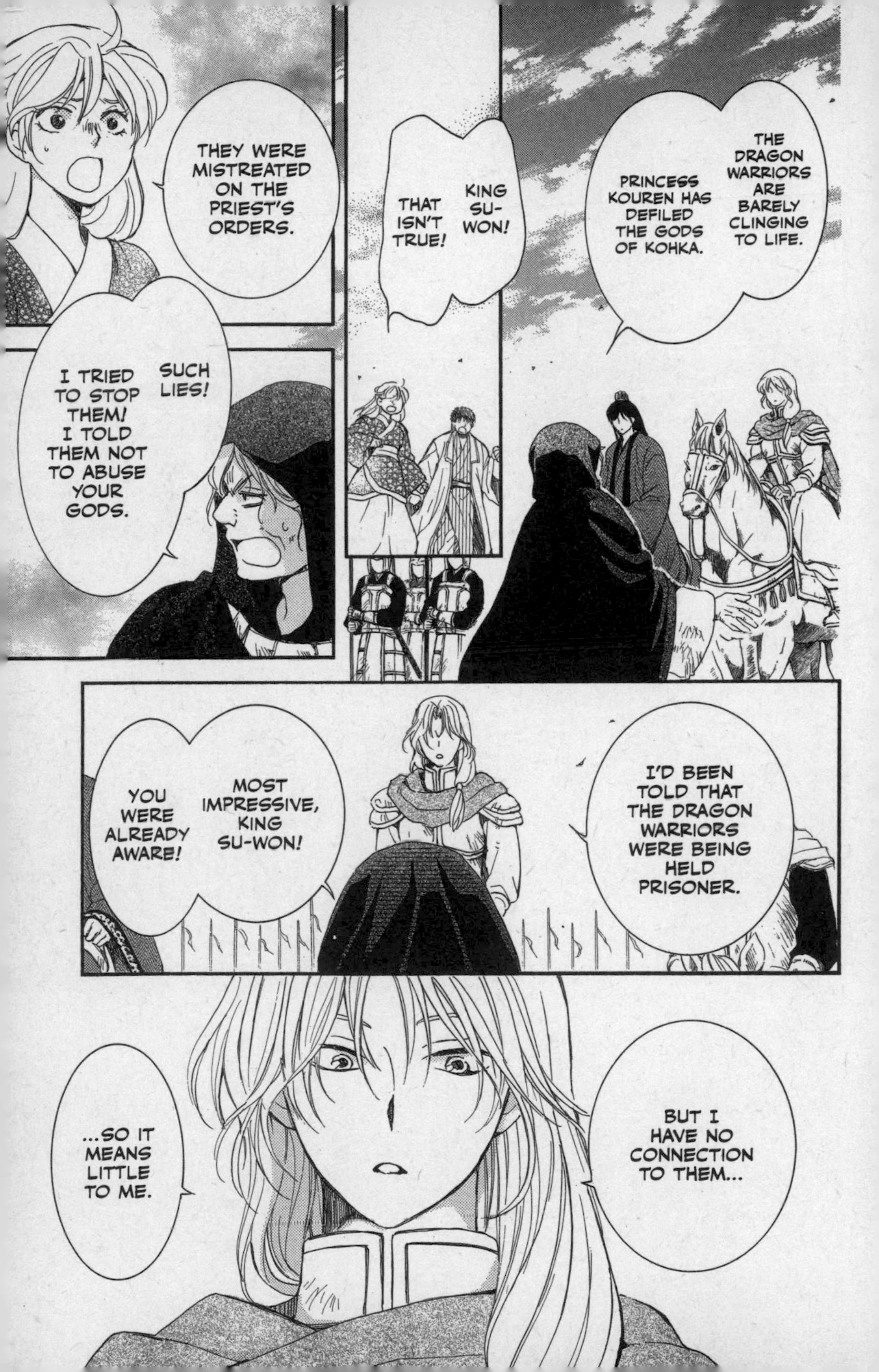
THE DRAGON WARRIORS ARE BARELY CLINGING TO LIFE.
PRINCESS KOUREN HAS DEFILED THE GODS OF KOHKA.
KING SU-WON!
THAT ISN'T TRUE!
THEY WERE MISTREATED ON THE PRIEST'S ORDERS.
SUCH LIES!
I TRIED TO STOP THEM! I TOLD THEM NOT TO ABUSE YOUR GODS.
I'D BEEN TOLD THAT THE DRAGON WARRIORS WERE BEING HELD PRISONER.
MOST IMPRESSIVE, KING SU-WON!
YOU WERE ALREADY AWARE!
BUT I HAVE NO CONNECTION TO THEM...
...SO IT MEANS LITTLE TO ME.

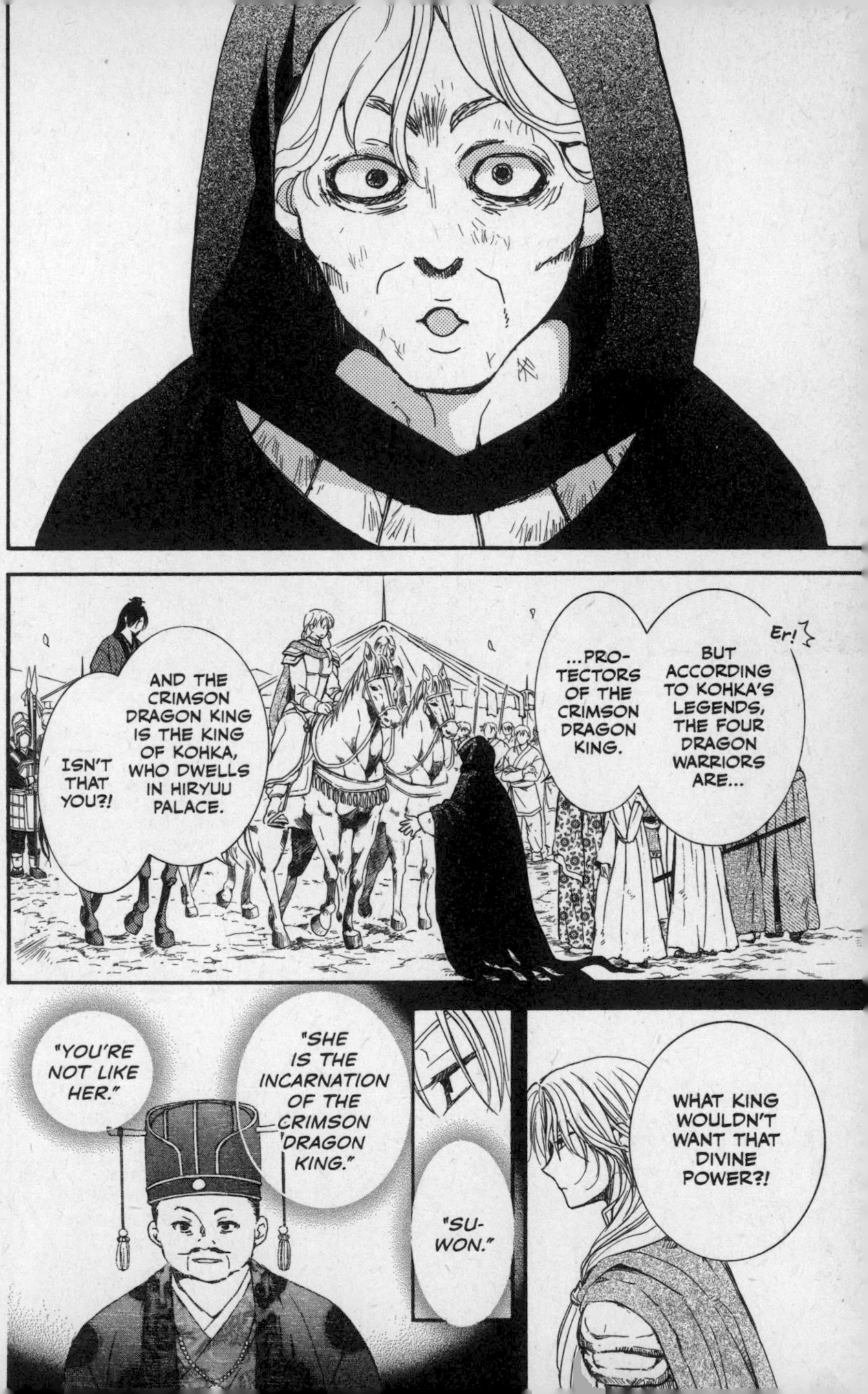
Er!
BUT ACCORDING TO KOHKA'S LEGENDS, THE FOUR DRAGON WARRIORS ARE...
...PRO-TECTORS OF THE CRIMSON DRAGON KING.
AND THE CRIMSON DRAGON KING IS THE KING OF KOHKA, WHO DWELLS IN HIRYUU PALACE.
ISN'T THAT YOU?!
WHAT KING WOULDN'T WANT THAT DIVINE POWER?!
"SU-WON."
"SHE IS THE INCARNATION OF THE CRIMSON DRAGON KING."
"YOU'RE NOT LIKE HER."

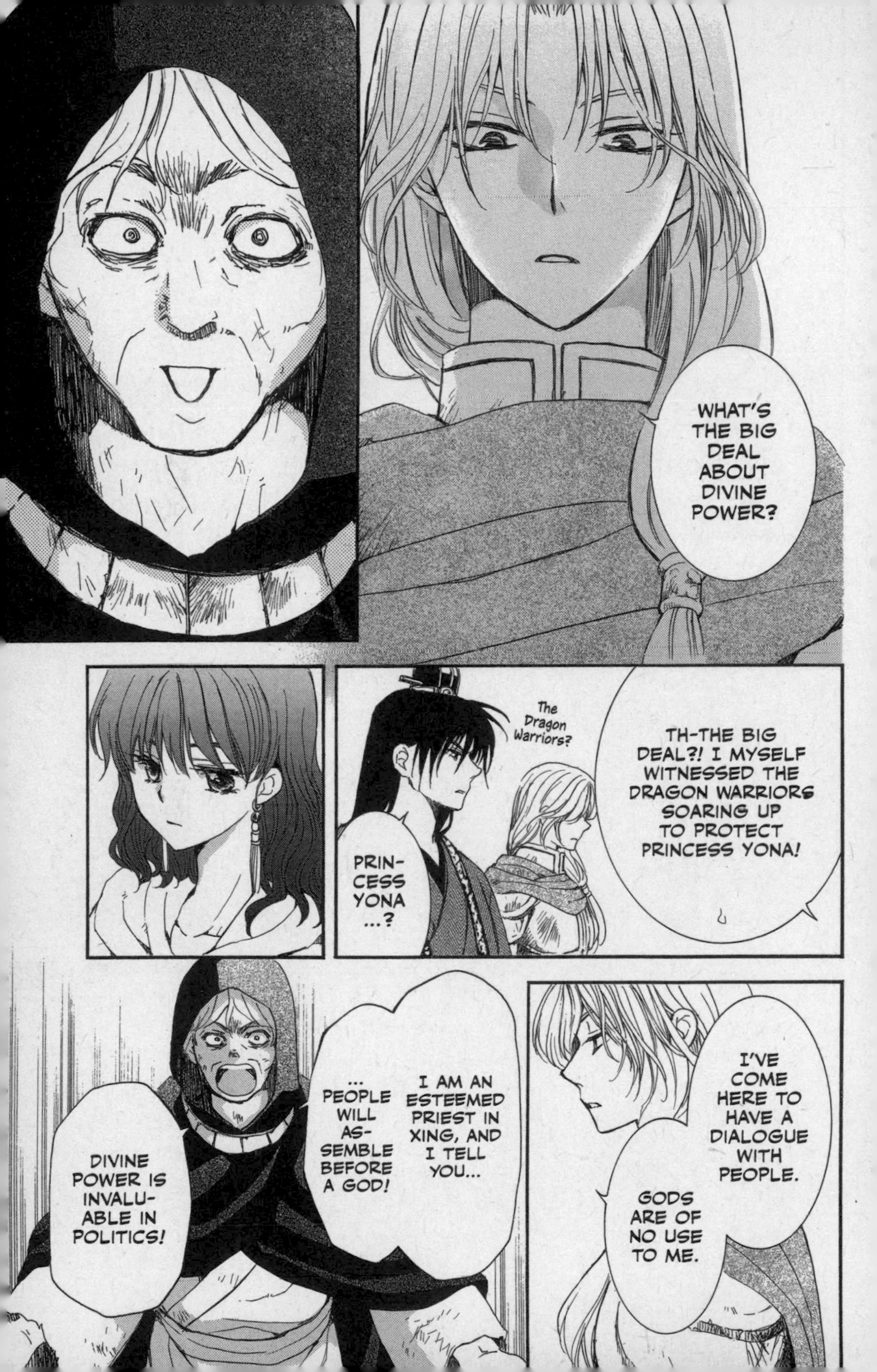
WHAT'S THE BIG DEAL ABOUT DIVINE POWER?
TH-THE BIG DEAL?! I MYSELF WITNESSED THE DRAGON WARRIORS SOARING UP TO PROTECT PRINCESS YONA!
The Dragon Warriors?
PRINCESS YONA ...?
I AM AN ESTEEMED PRIEST IN XING, AND I TELL YOU...
... PEOPLE WILL ASSEMBLE BEFORE A GOD!
DIVINE POWER IS INVALUABLE IN POLITICS!
I'VE COME HERE TO HAVE A DIALOGUE WITH PEOPLE.
GODS ARE OF NO USE TO ME.

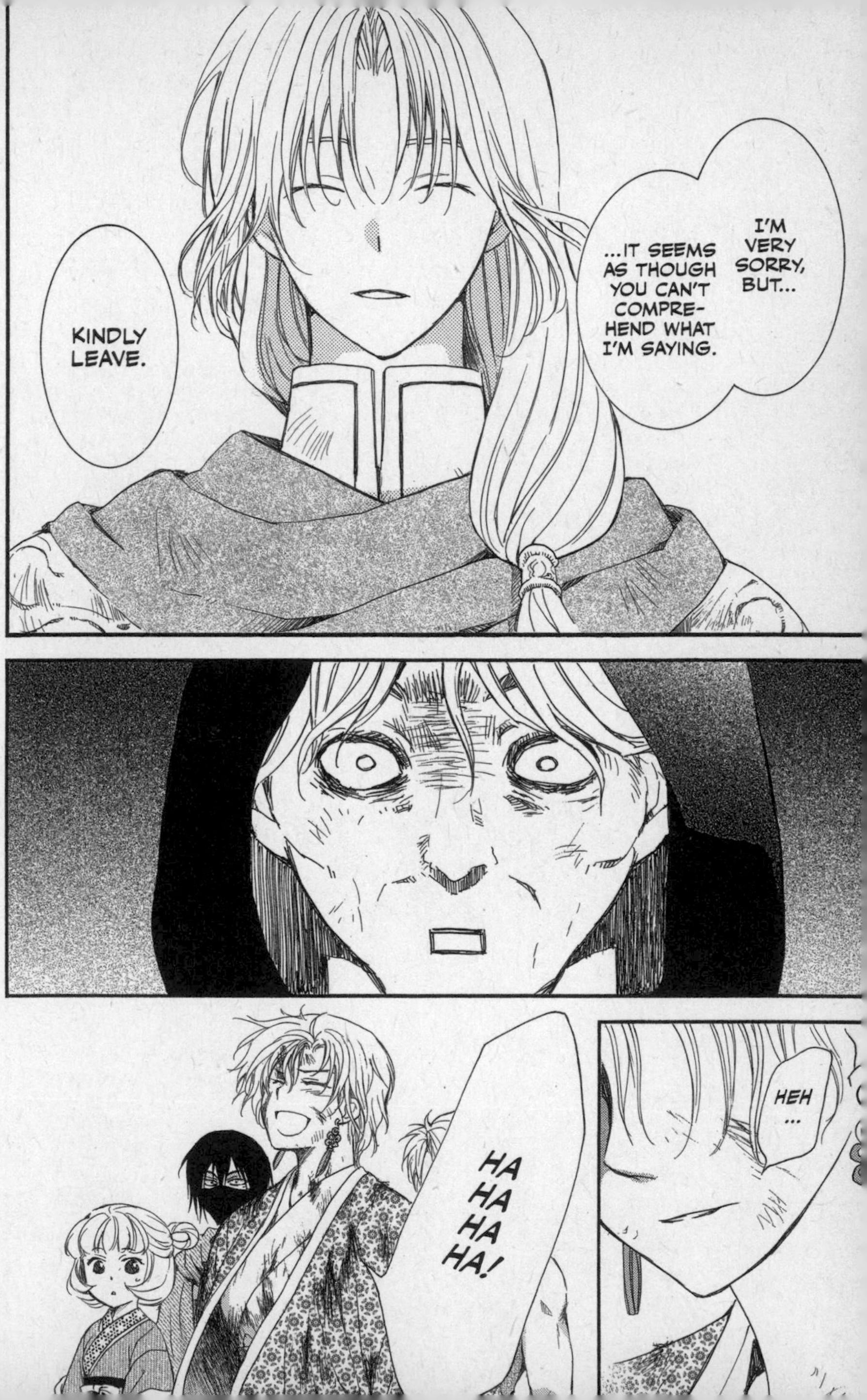
I'M VERY SORRY, BUT...
...IT SEEMS AS THOUGH YOU CAN'T COMPRE-HEND WHAT I'M SAYING.
KINDLY LEAVE.
HEH ...
HA HA HA HA!

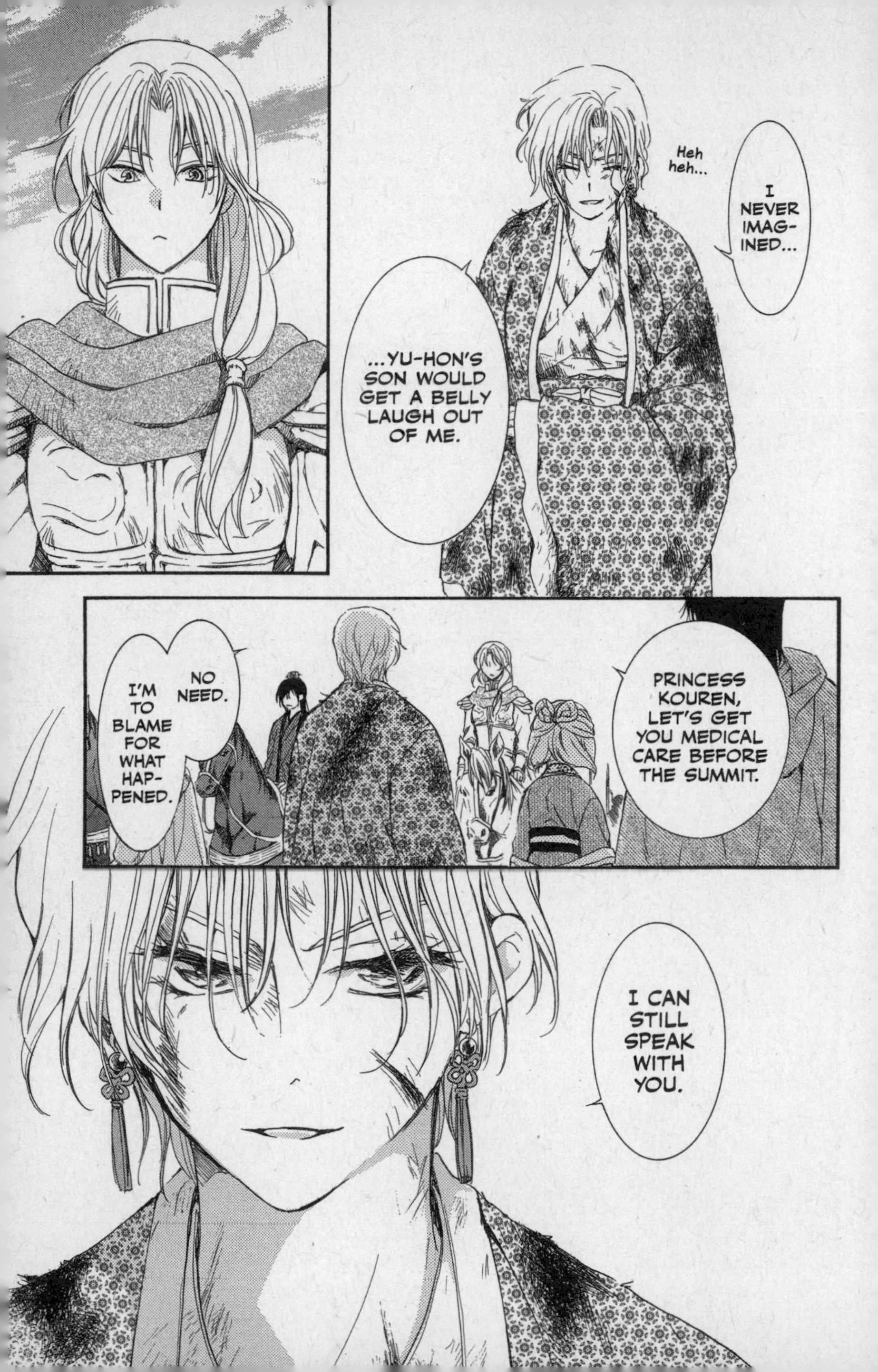
I NEVER IMAG-INED...
Heh heh...
...YU-HON'S SON WOULD GET A BELLY LAUGH OUT OF ME.
PRINCESS KOUREN, LET'S GET YOU MEDICAL CARE BEFORE THE SUMMIT.
NO NEED.
I'M TO BLAME FOR WHAT HAP-PENED.
I CAN STILL SPEAK WITH YOU.

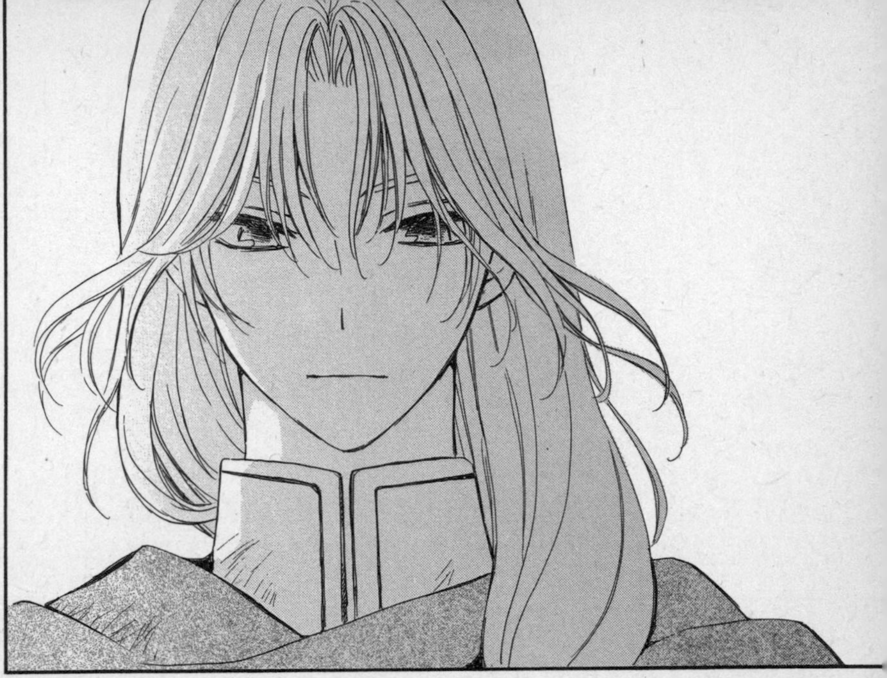

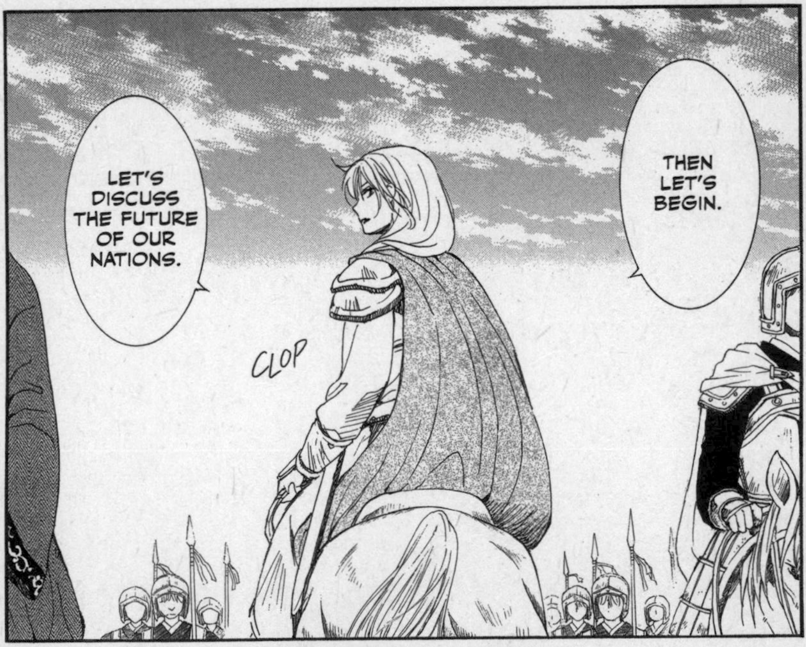
THEN LET'S BEGIN.
LET'S DISCUSS THE FUTURE OF OUR NATIONS.
CLOP

CHAPTER 149 / THE END

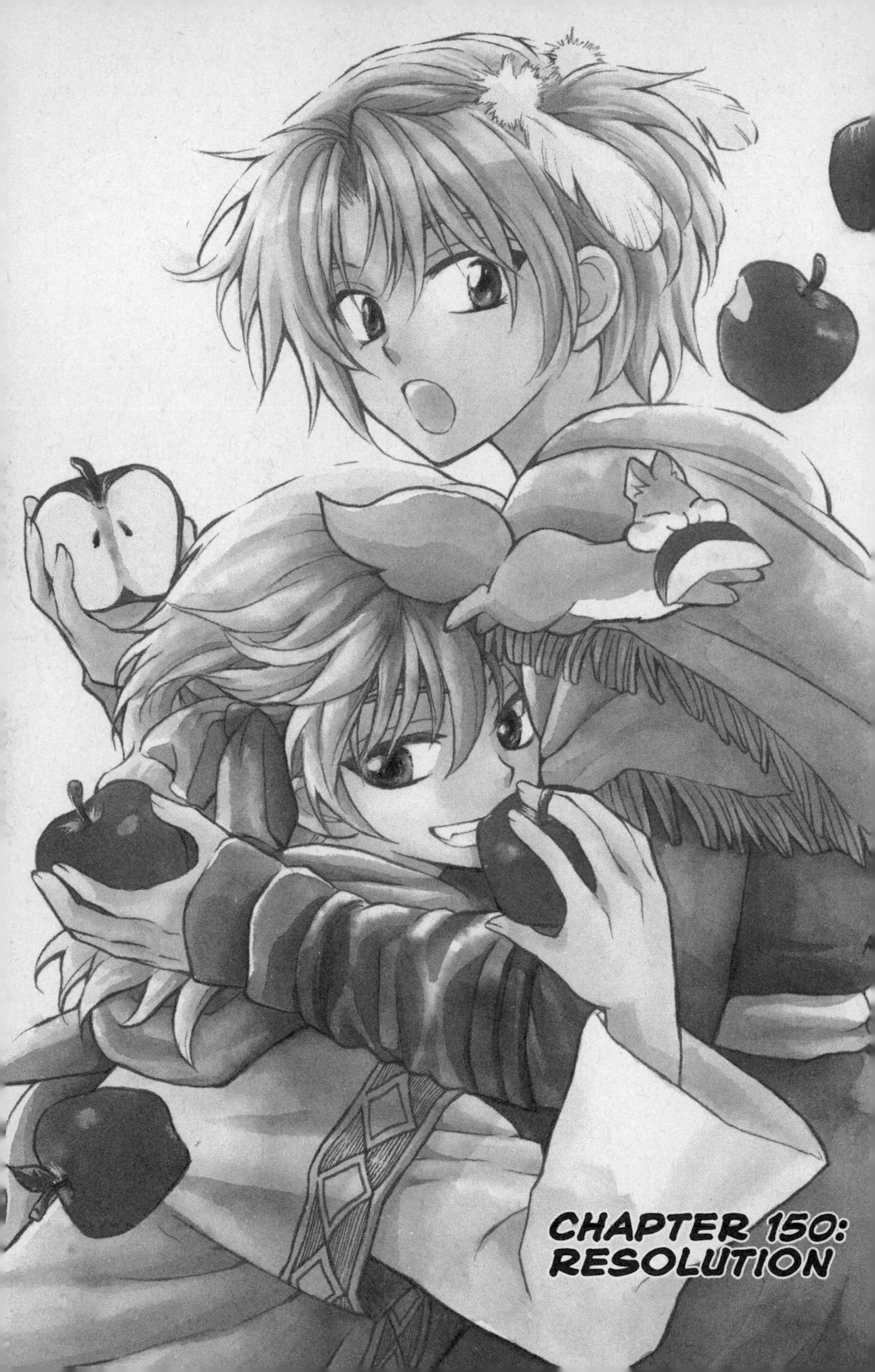
CHAPTER 150:
RESOLUTION

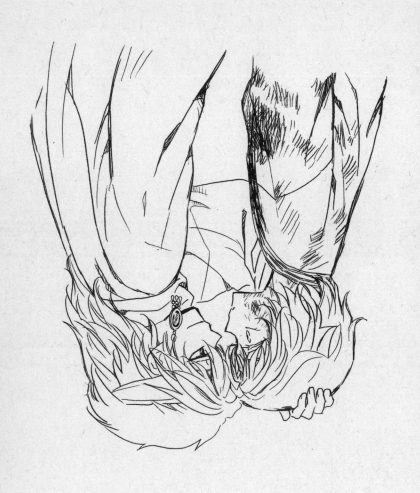

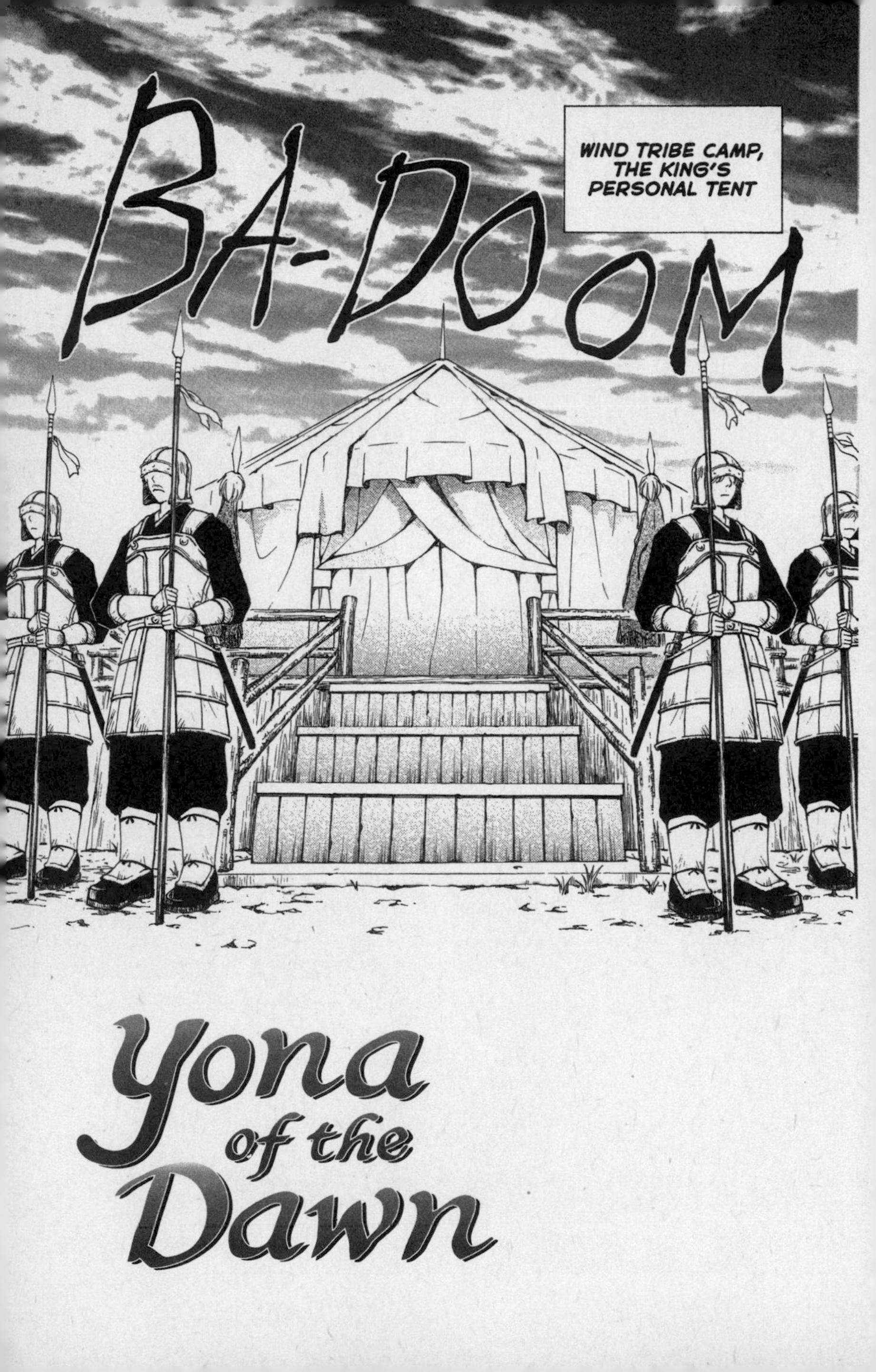
WIND TRIBE CAMP, THE KING'S PERSONAL TENT
BA-DOOM
Yona of the Dawn

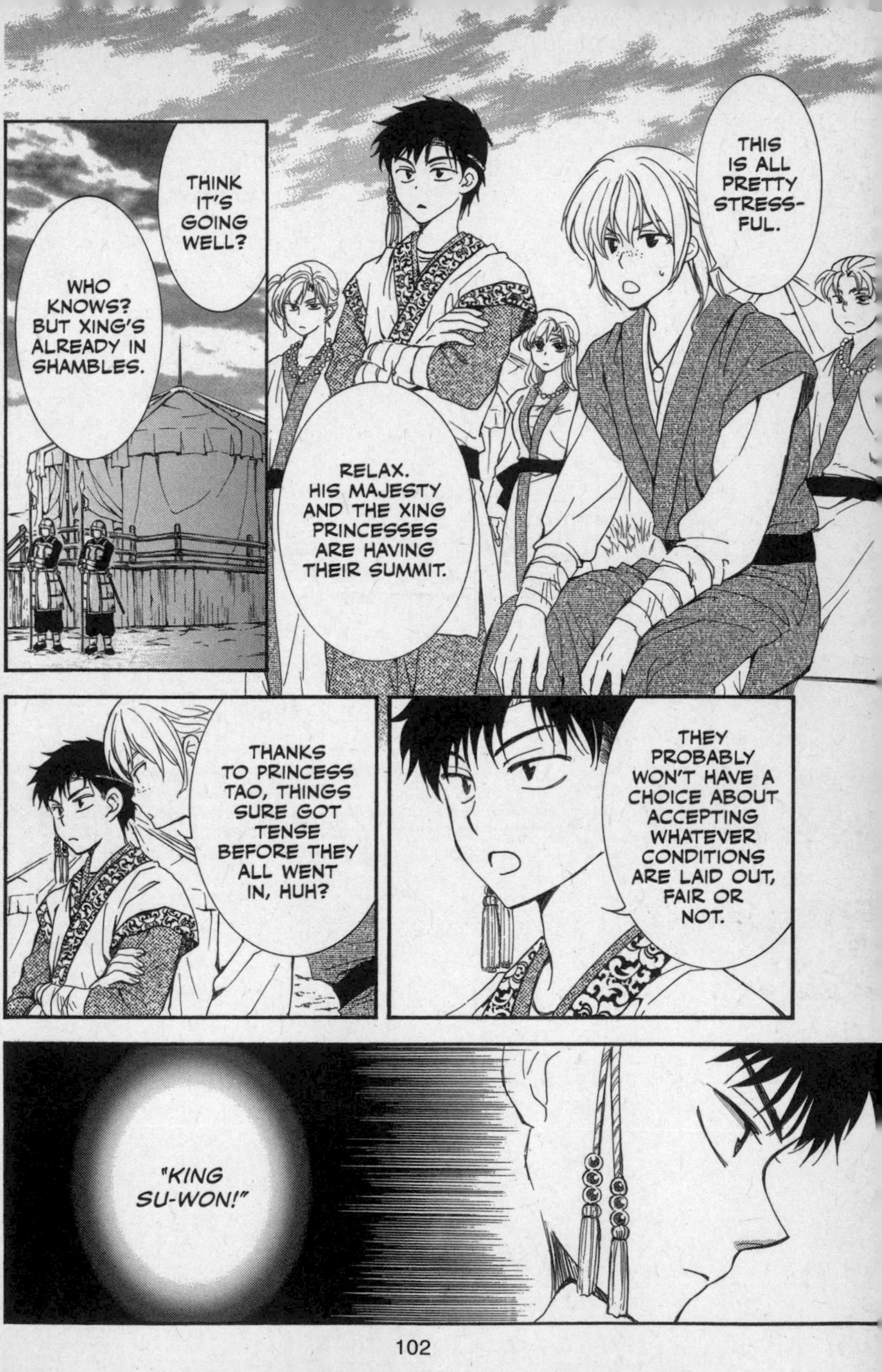
THIS IS ALL PRETTY STRESS-FUL.
RELAX. HIS MAJESTY AND THE XING PRINCESSES ARE HAVING THEIR SUMMIT.
THINK IT'S GOING WELL?
WHO KNOWS? BUT XING'S ALREADY IN SHAMBLES.
THEY PROBABLY WON'T HAVE A CHOICE ABOUT ACCEPTING WHATEVER CONDITIONS ARE LAID OUT, FAIR OR NOT.
THANKS TO PRINCESS TAO, THINGS SURE GOT TENSE BEFORE THEY ALL WENT IN, HUH?
"KING SU-WON!"

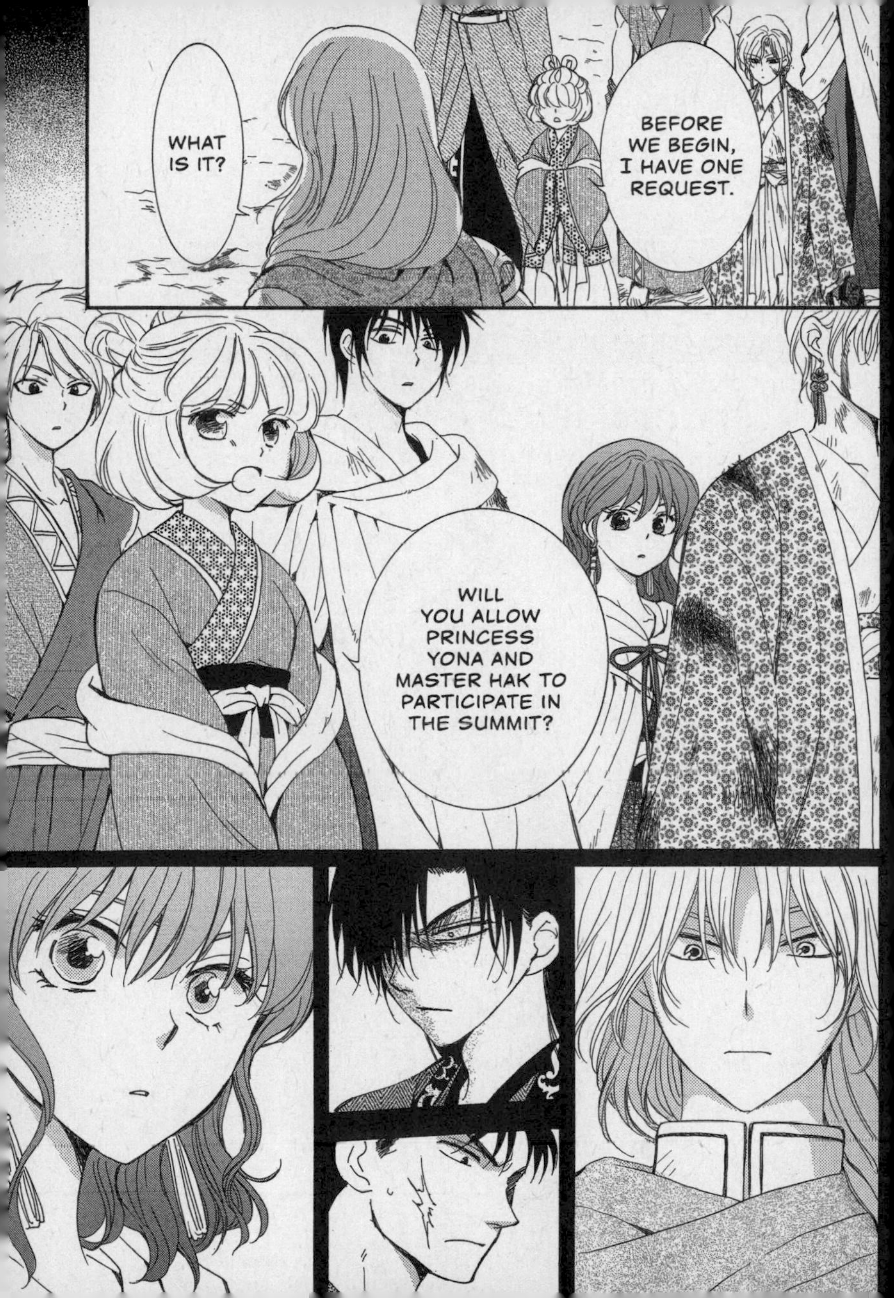
BEFORE WE BEGIN, I HAVE ONE REQUEST.
WHAT IS IT?
WILL YOU ALLOW PRINCESS YONA AND MASTER HAK TO PARTICIPATE IN THE SUMMIT?

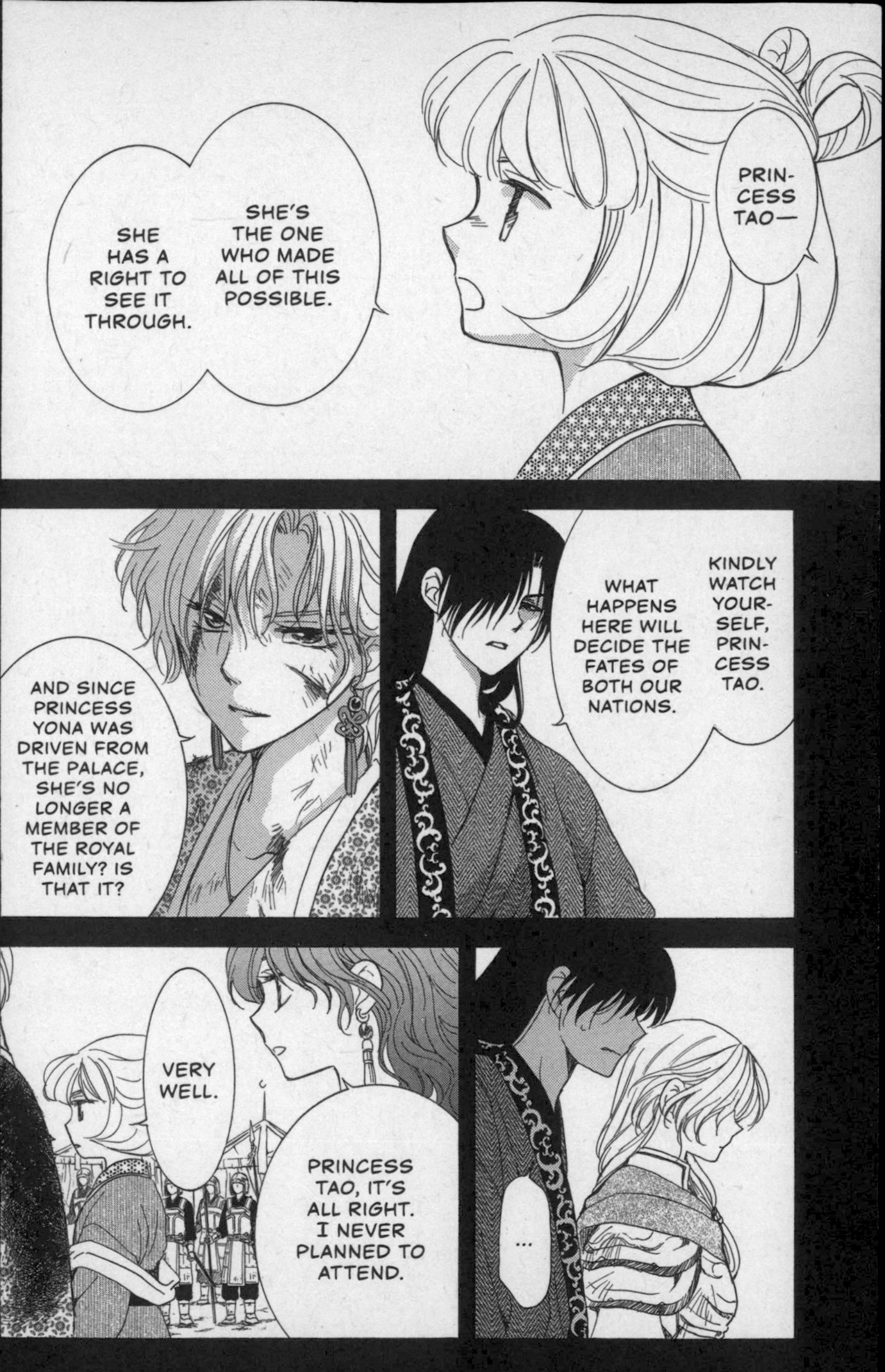
PRIN-CESS TAO—
SHE'S THE ONE WHO MADE ALL OF THIS POSSIBLE.
SHE HAS A RIGHT TO SEE IT THROUGH.
KINDLY WATCH YOUR-SELF, PRIN-CESS TAO.
WHAT HAPPENS HERE WILL DECIDE THE FATES OF BOTH OUR NATIONS.
AND SINCE PRINCESS YONA WAS DRIVEN FROM THE PALACE, SHE'S NO LONGER A MEMBER OF THE ROYAL FAMILY? IS THAT IT?
...
PRINCESS TAO, IT'S ALL RIGHT. I NEVER PLANNED TO ATTEND.
VERY WELL.

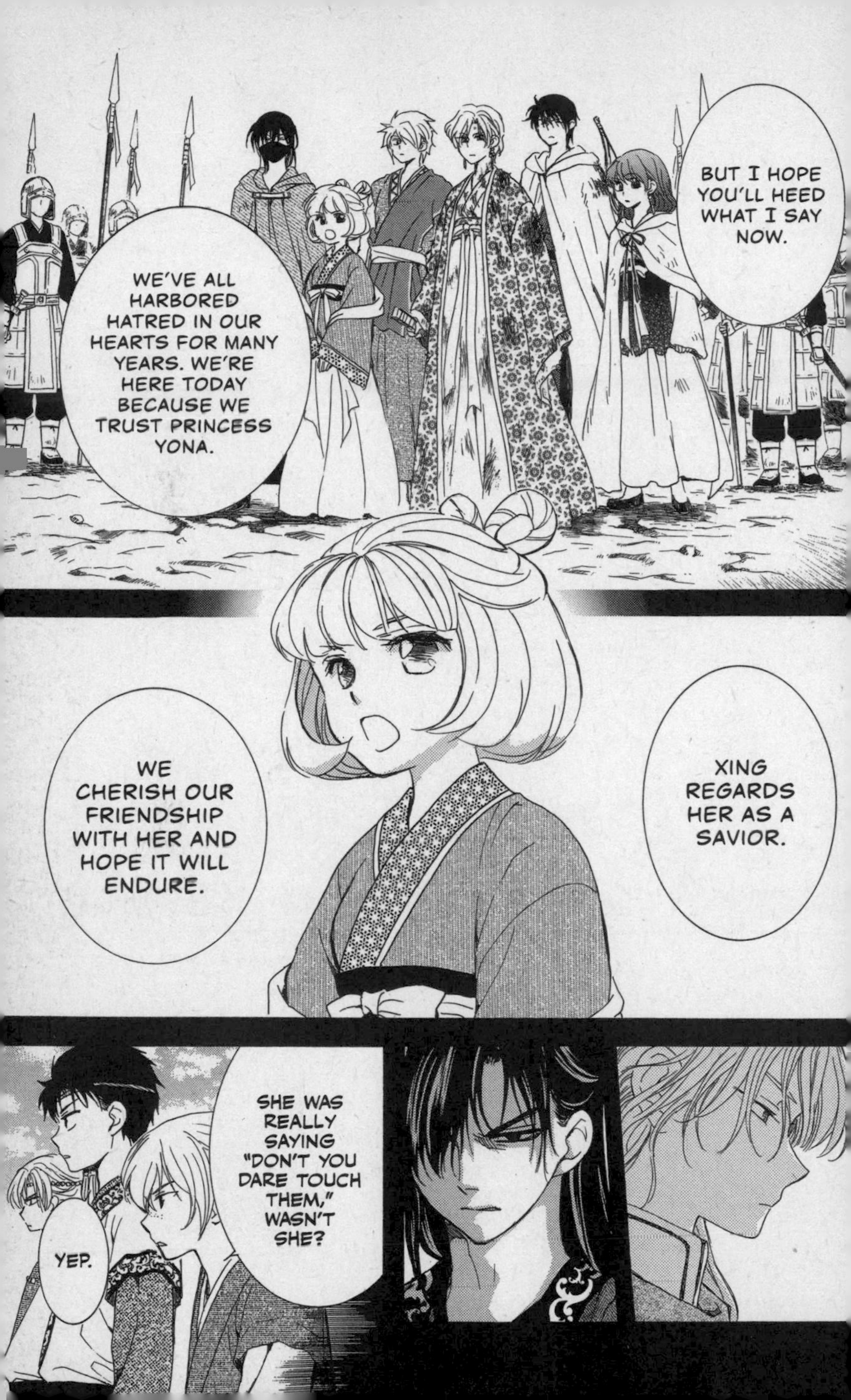
BUT I HOPE YOU'LL HEED WHAT I SAY NOW.
WE'VE ALL HARBORED HATRED IN OUR HEARTS FOR MANY YEARS. WE'RE HERE TODAY BECAUSE WE TRUST PRINCESS YONA.
XING REGARDS HER AS A SAVIOR.
WE CHERISH OUR FRIENDSHIP WITH HER AND HOPE IT WILL ENDURE.
SHE WAS REALLY SAYING "DON'T YOU DARE TOUCH THEM," WASN'T SHE?
YEP.

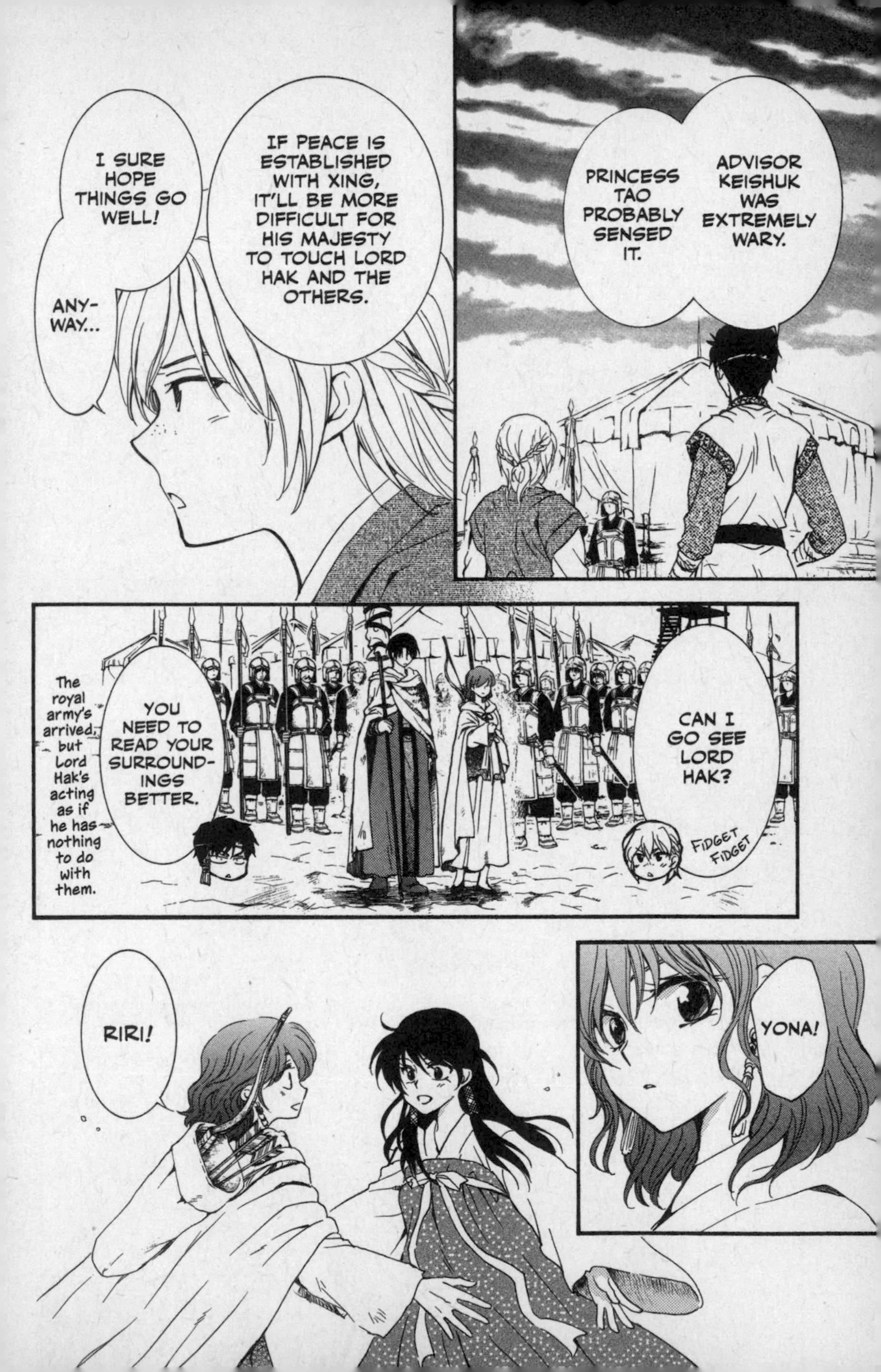
ADVISOR KEISHUK WAS EXTREMELY WARY.
PRINCESS TAO PROBABLY SENSED IT.
IF PEACE IS ESTABLISHED WITH XING, IT'LL BE MORE DIFFICULT FOR HIS MAJESTY TO TOUCH LORD HAK AND THE OTHERS.
I SURE HOPE THINGS GO WELL!
ANY-WAY...
CAN I GO SEE LORD HAK?
FIDGET FIDGET
YOU NEED TO READ YOUR SURROUND-INGS BETTER.
The royal army's arrived, but Lord Hak's acting as if he has nothing to do with them.
YONA!
RIRI!

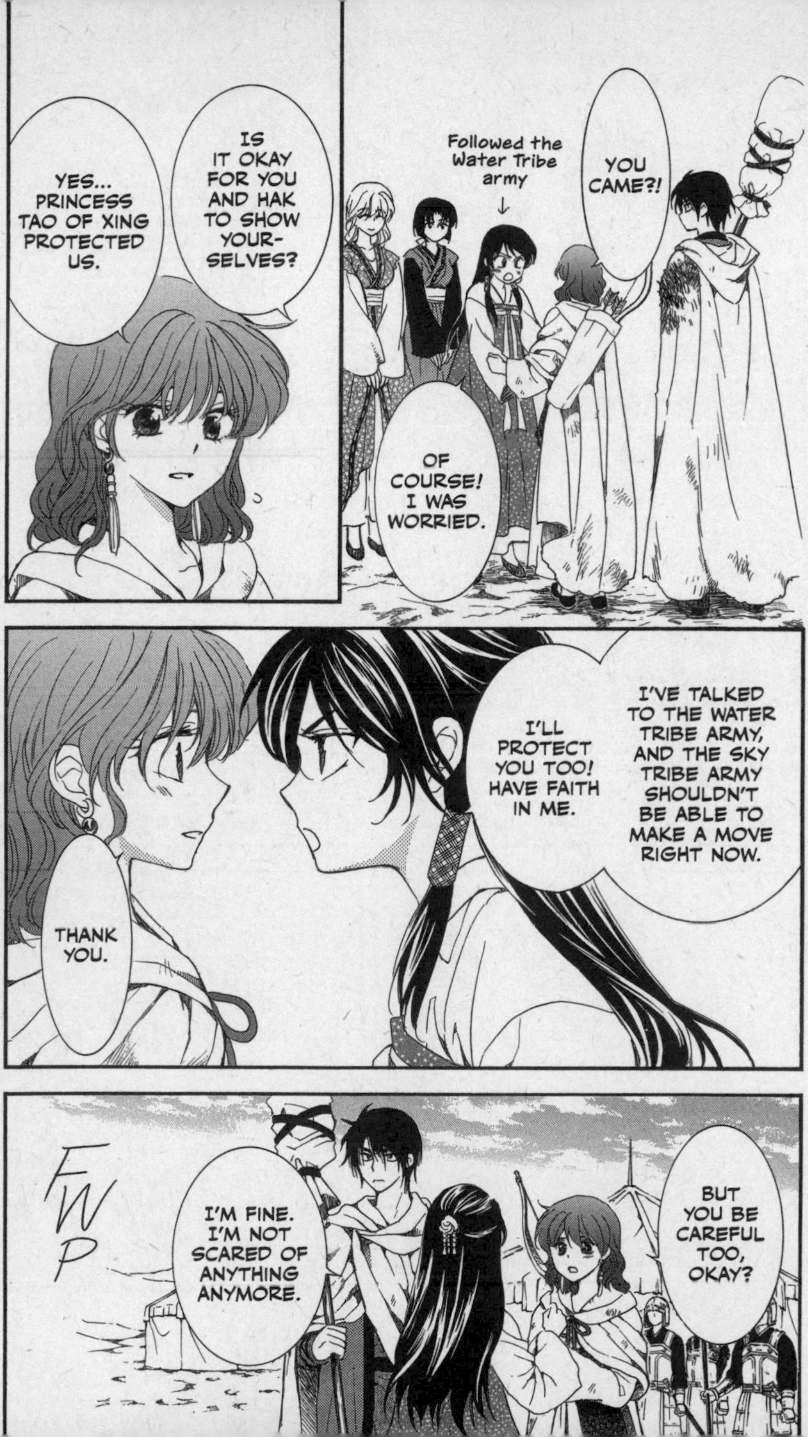
YOU CAME?!
Followed the Water Tribe army
OF COURSE! I WAS WORRIED.
IS IT OKAY FOR YOU AND HAK TO SHOW YOUR-SELVES?
YES... PRINCESS TAO OF XING PROTECTED US.
I'VE TALKED TO THE WATER TRIBE ARMY, AND THE SKY TRIBE ARMY SHOULDN'T BE ABLE TO MAKE A MOVE RIGHT NOW.
I'LL PROTECT YOU TOO! HAVE FAITH IN ME.
THANK YOU.
BUT YOU BE CAREFUL TOO, OKAY?
I'M FINE. I'M NOT SCARED OF ANYTHING ANYMORE.
FWP

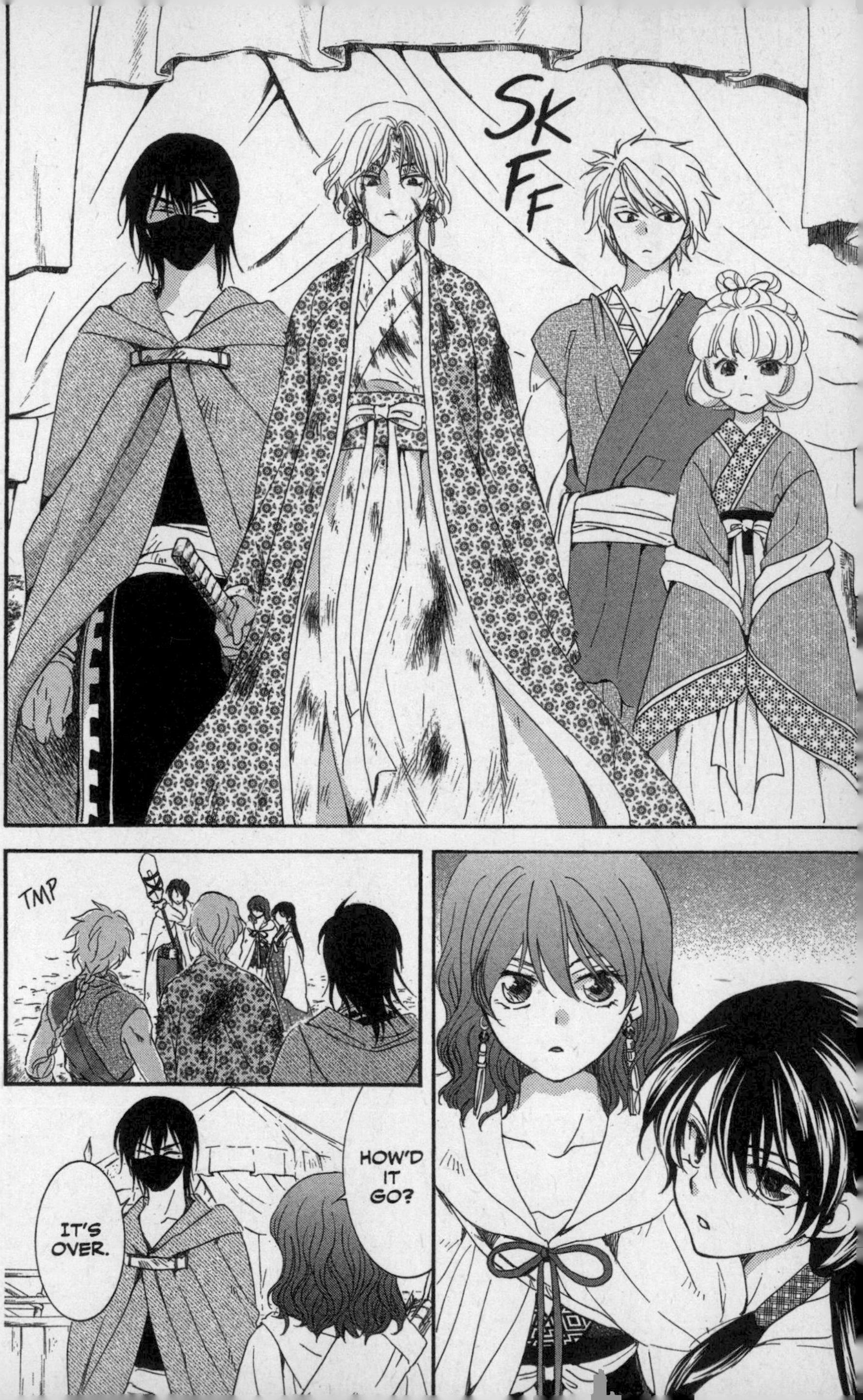
SKFF
TMP
HOW'D IT GO?
IT'S OVER.

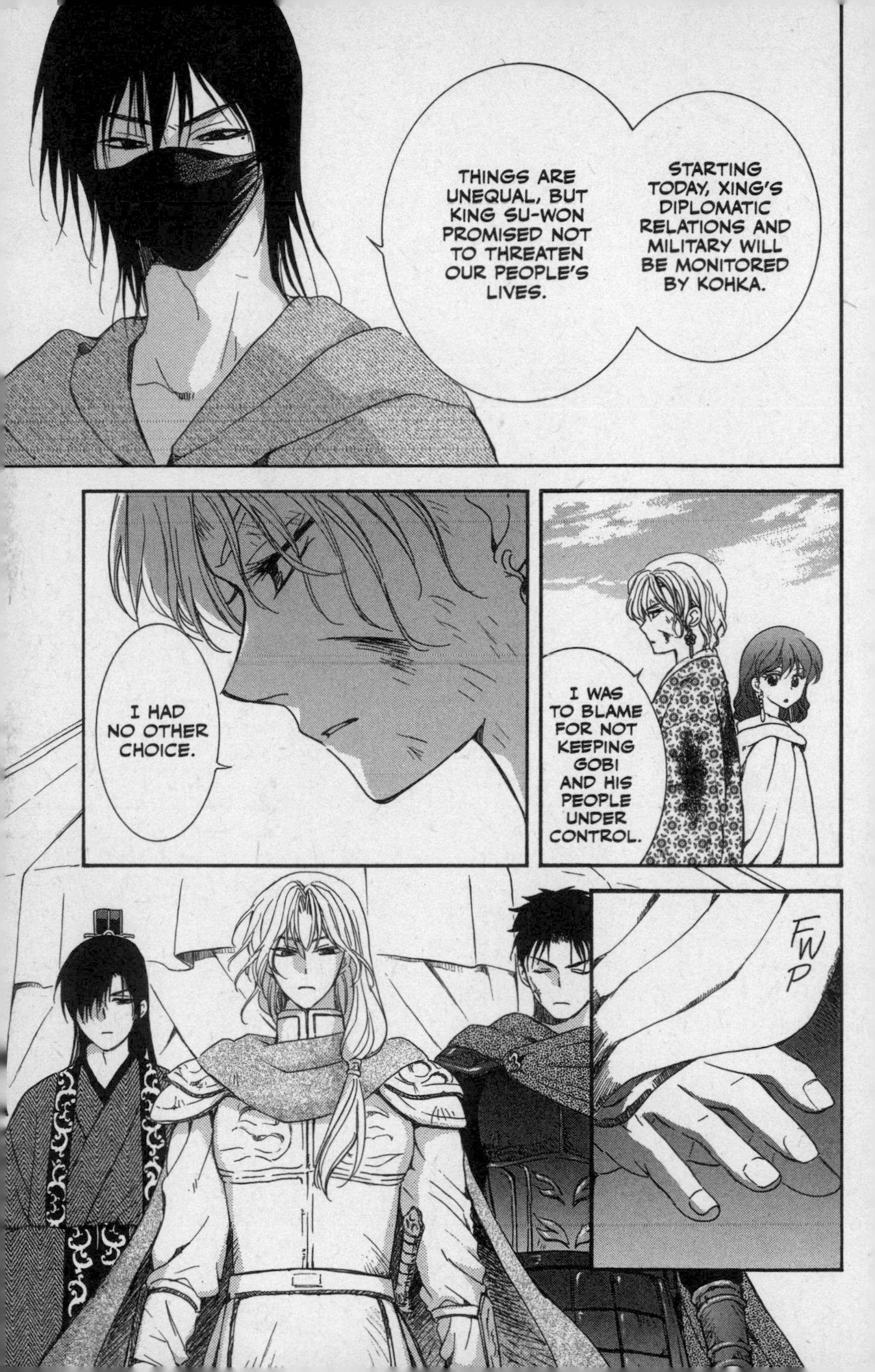
STARTING TODAY, XING'S DIPLOMATIC RELATIONS AND MILITARY WILL BE MONITORED BY KOHKA.
THINGS ARE UNEQUAL, BUT KING SU-WON PROMISED NOT TO THREATEN OUR PEOPLE'S LIVES.
I WAS TO BLAME FOR NOT KEEPING GOBI AND HIS PEOPLE UNDER CONTROL.
I HAD NO OTHER CHOICE.
FWP

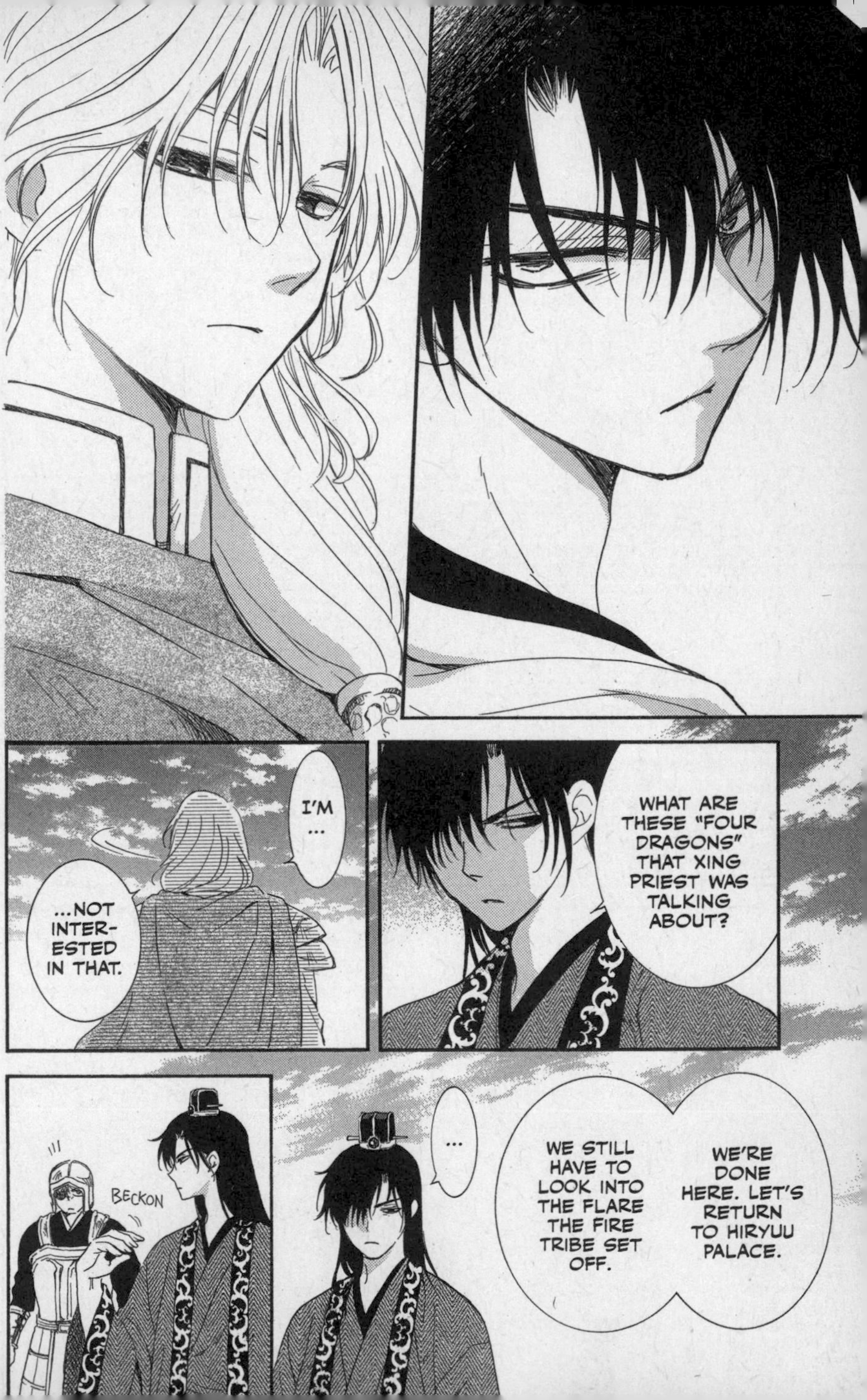
WHAT ARE THESE "FOUR DRAGONS" THAT XING PRIEST WAS TALKING ABOUT?
I'M ...
...NOT INTER-ESTED IN THAT.
WE'RE DONE HERE. LET'S RETURN TO HIRYUU PALACE.
WE STILL HAVE TO LOOK INTO THE FLARE THE FIRE TRIBE SET OFF.
...
BECKON

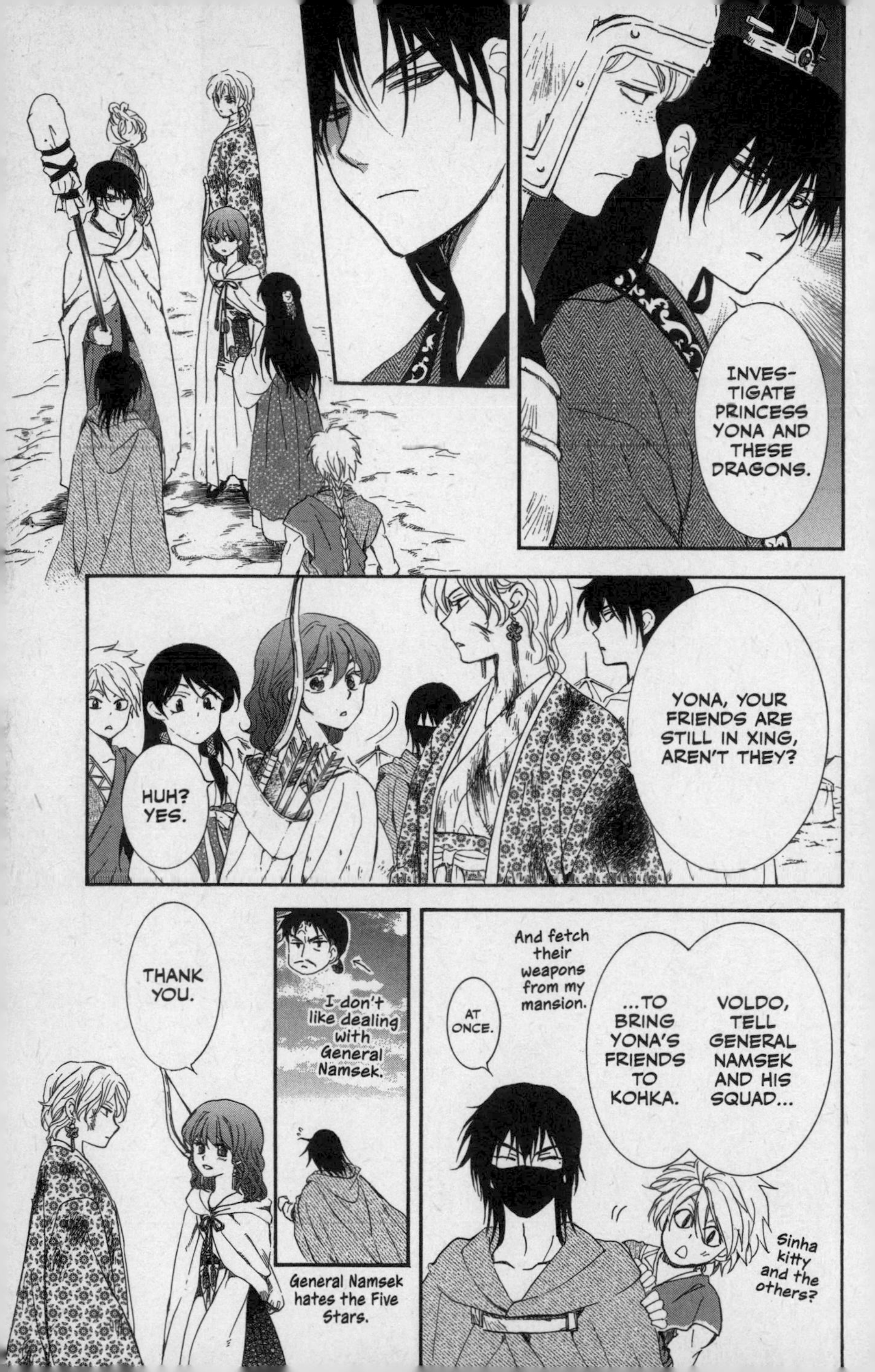
INVES-TIGATE PRINCESS YONA AND THESE DRAGONS.
YONA, YOUR FRIENDS ARE STILL IN XING, AREN'T THEY?
HUH? YES.
VOLDO, TELL GENERAL NAMSEK AND HIS SQUAD...
...TO BRING YONA'S FRIENDS TO KOHKA.
And fetch their weapons from my mansion.
AT ONCE.
Sinha kitty and the others?
I don't like dealing with General Namsek.
General Namsek hates the Five Stars.
THANK YOU.

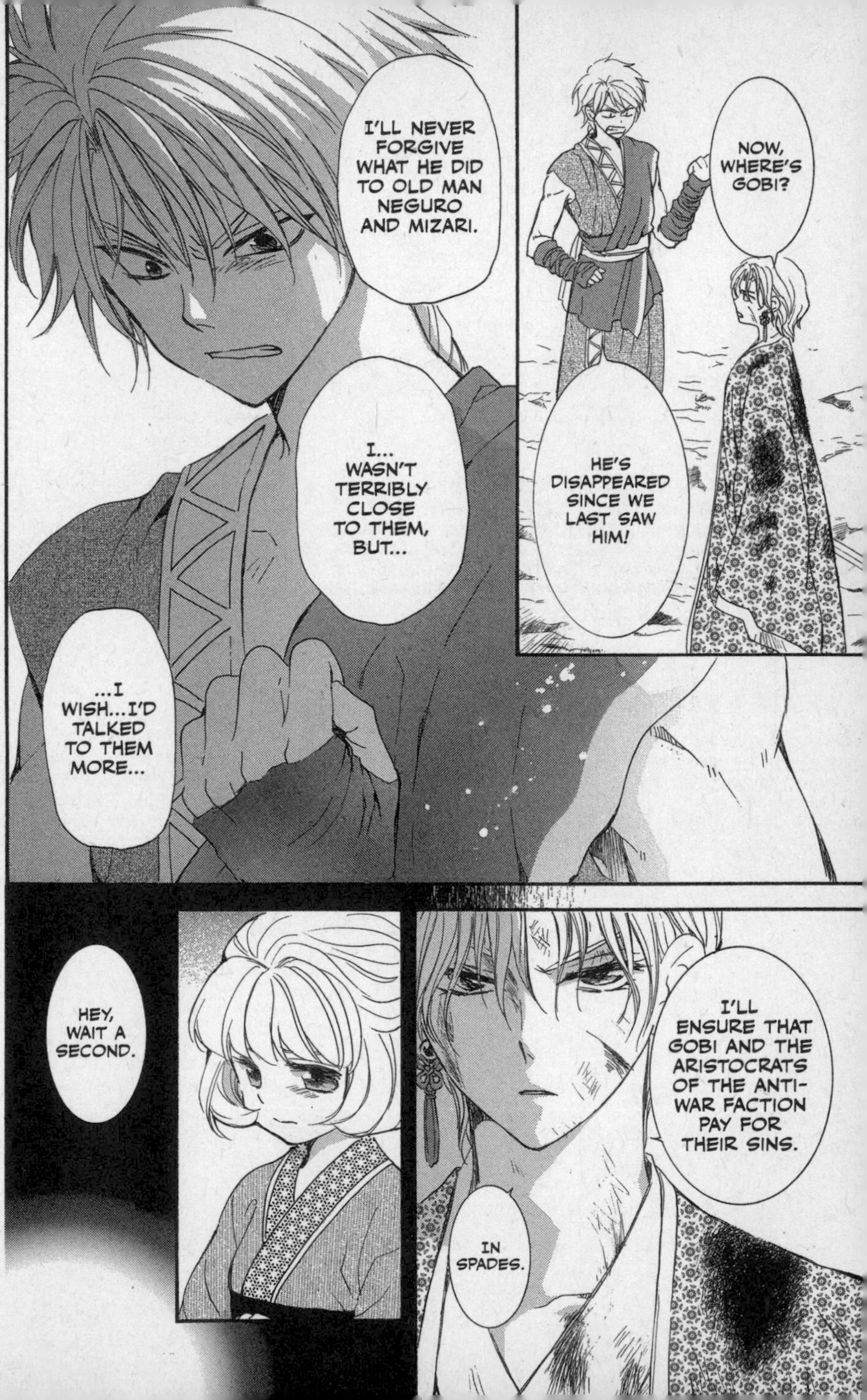
NOW, WHERE'S GOBI?
HE'S DISAPPEARED SINCE WE LAST SAW HIM!
I'LL NEVER FORGIVE WHAT HE DID TO OLD MAN NEGURO AND MIZARI.
I... WASN'T TERRIBLY CLOSE TO THEM, BUT...
...I WISH...I'D TALKED TO THEM MORE...
I'LL ENSURE THAT GOBI AND THE ARISTOCRATS OF THE ANTI-WAR FACTION PAY FOR THEIR SINS.
IN SPADES.
HEY, WAIT A SECOND.

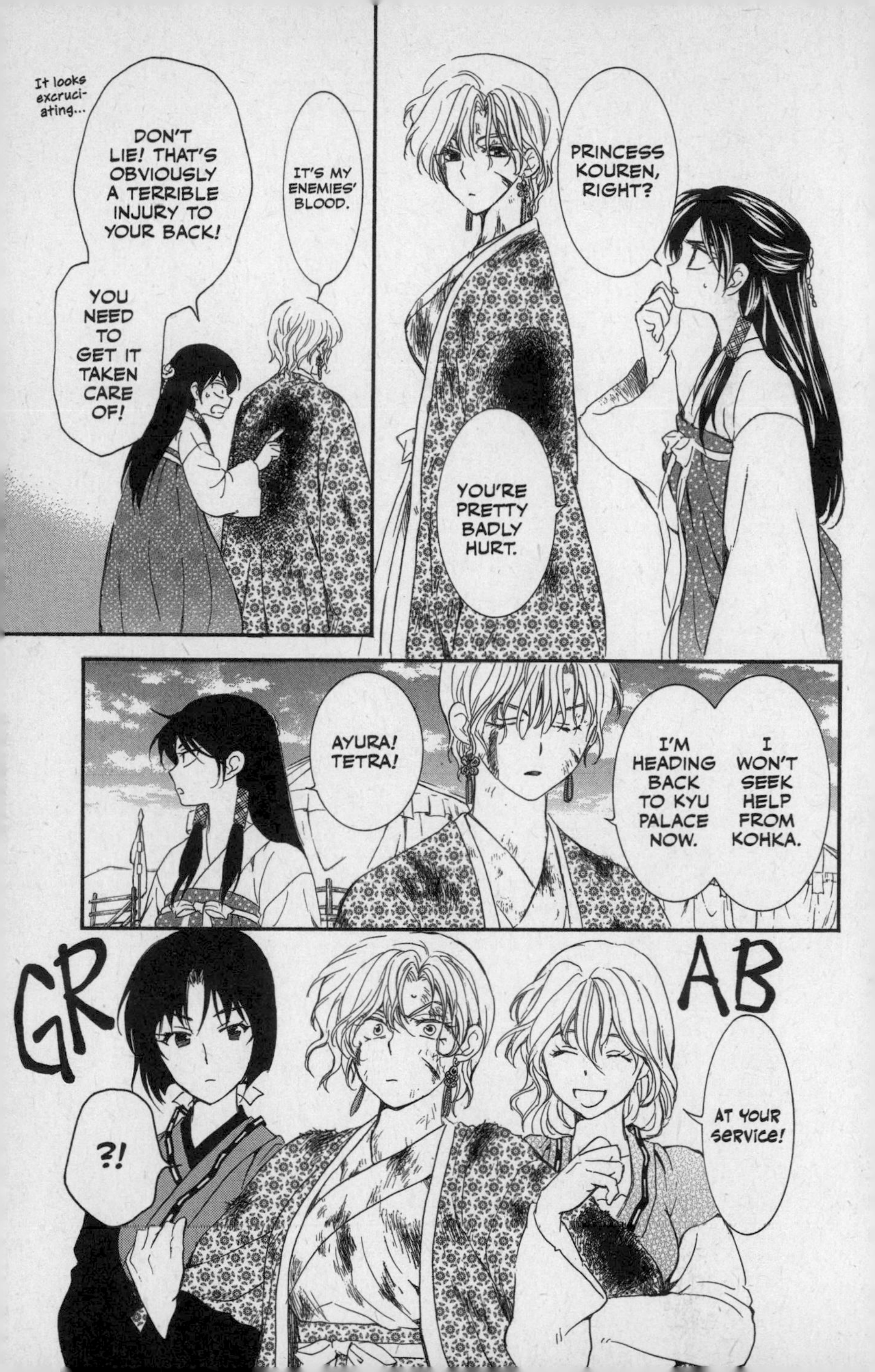
PRINCESS KOUREN, RIGHT?
YOU'RE PRETTY BADLY HURT.
IT'S MY ENEMIES' BLOOD.
DON'T LIE! THAT'S OBVIOUSLY A TERRIBLE INJURY TO YOUR BACK!
YOU NEED TO GET IT TAKEN CARE OF!
It looks excruciating...
I WON'T SEEK HELP FROM KOHKA.
I'M HEADING BACK TO KYU PALACE NOW.
AYURA! TETRA!
AB
AT YOUR SERVICE!
GR
?!

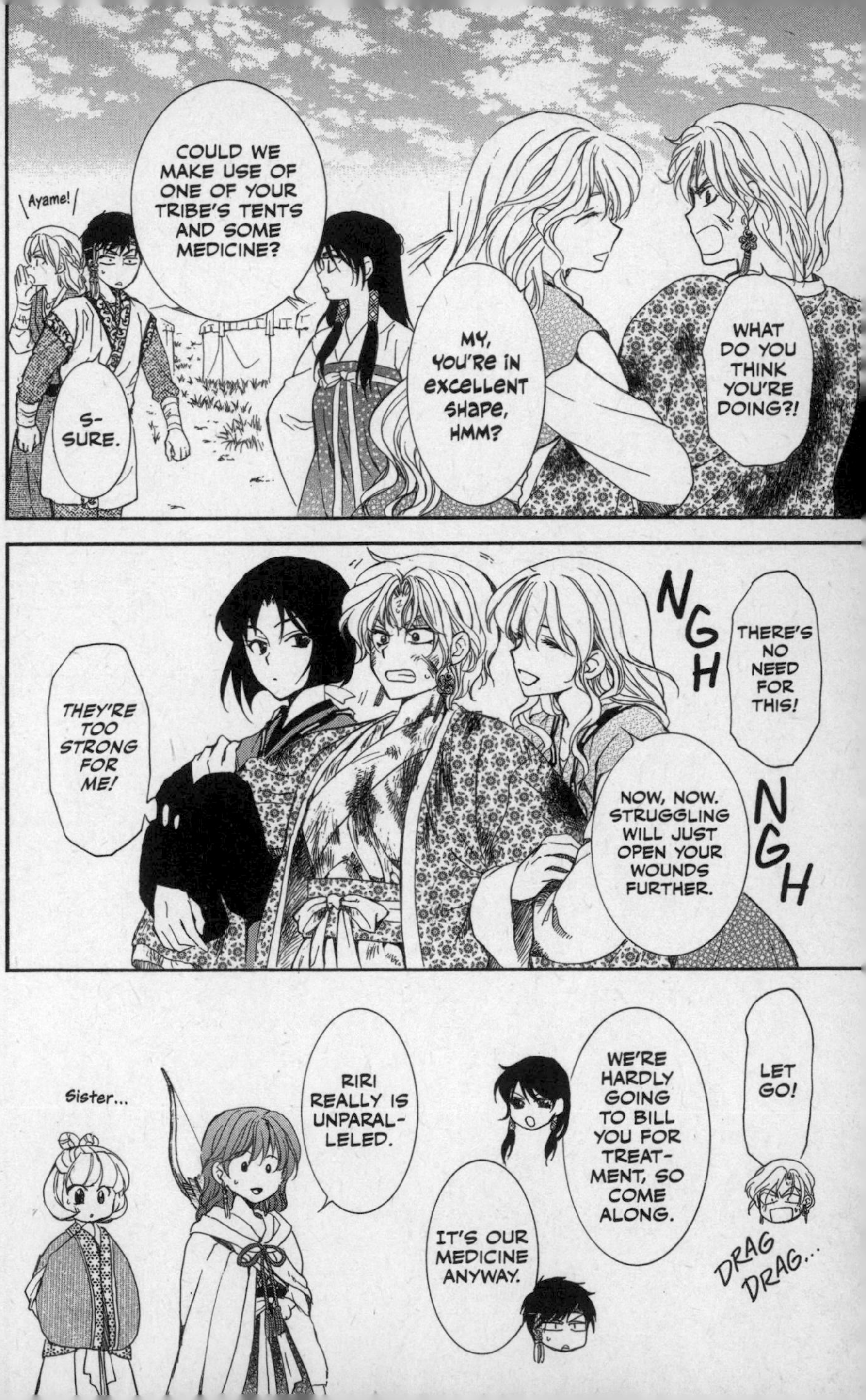
WHAT DO YOU THINK YOU'RE DOING?!
MY, YOU'RE IN EXCELLENT SHAPE, HMM?
COULD WE MAKE USE OF ONE OF YOUR TRIBE'S TENTS AND SOME MEDICINE?
Ayame!
S-SURE.
THERE'S NO NEED FOR THIS!
NGH
NGH
NOW, NOW. STRUGGLING WILL JUST OPEN YOUR WOUNDS FURTHER.
THEY'RE TOO STRONG FOR ME!
LET GO!
DRAG DRAG...
WE'RE HARDLY GOING TO BILL YOU FOR TREATMENT, SO COME ALONG.
IT'S OUR MEDICINE ANYWAY.
RIRI REALLY IS UNPARALLELED.
Sister...

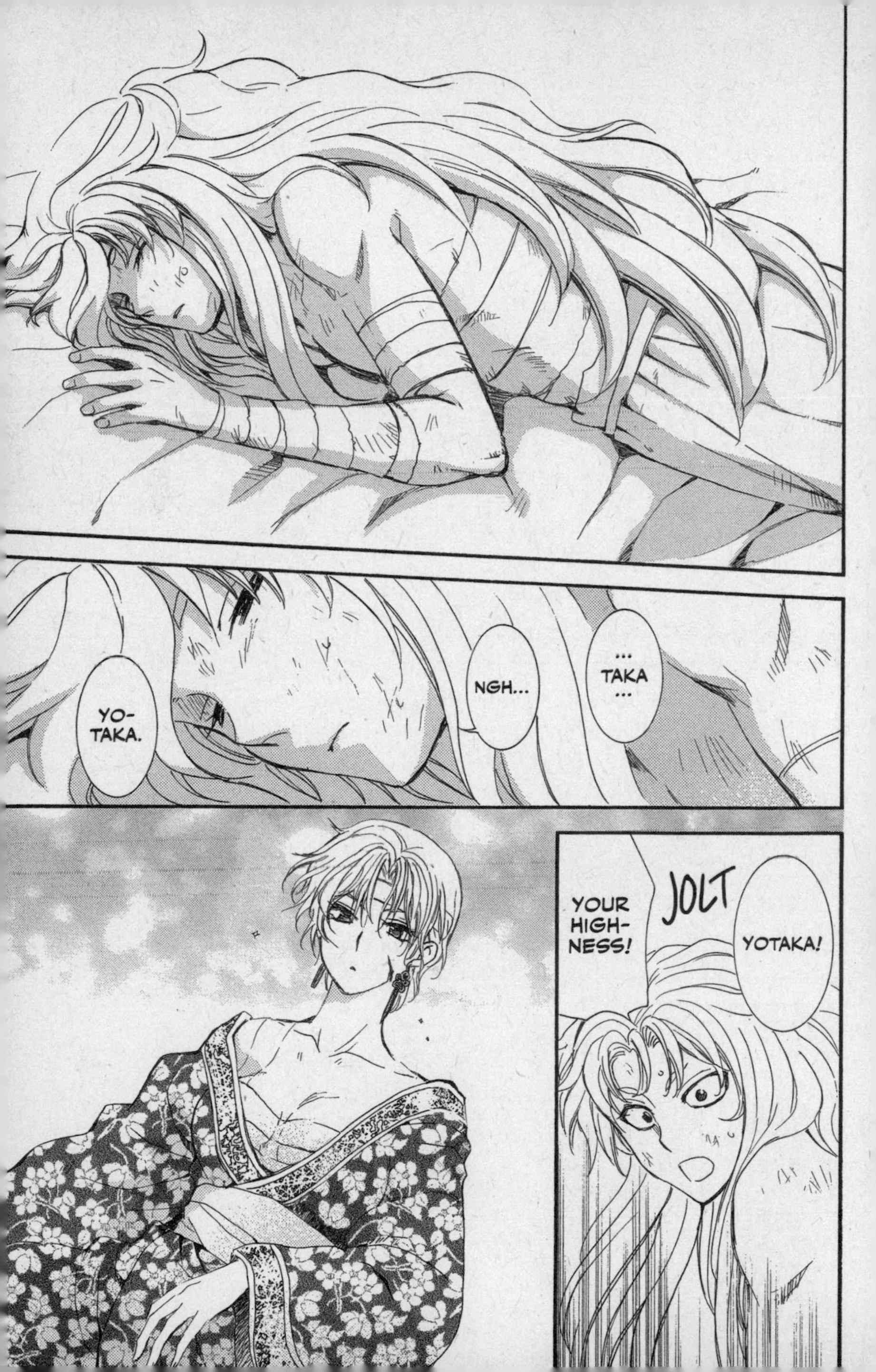
...TAKA...
NGH...
YO-TAKA.
YOTAKA!
JOLT
YOUR HIGH-NESS!

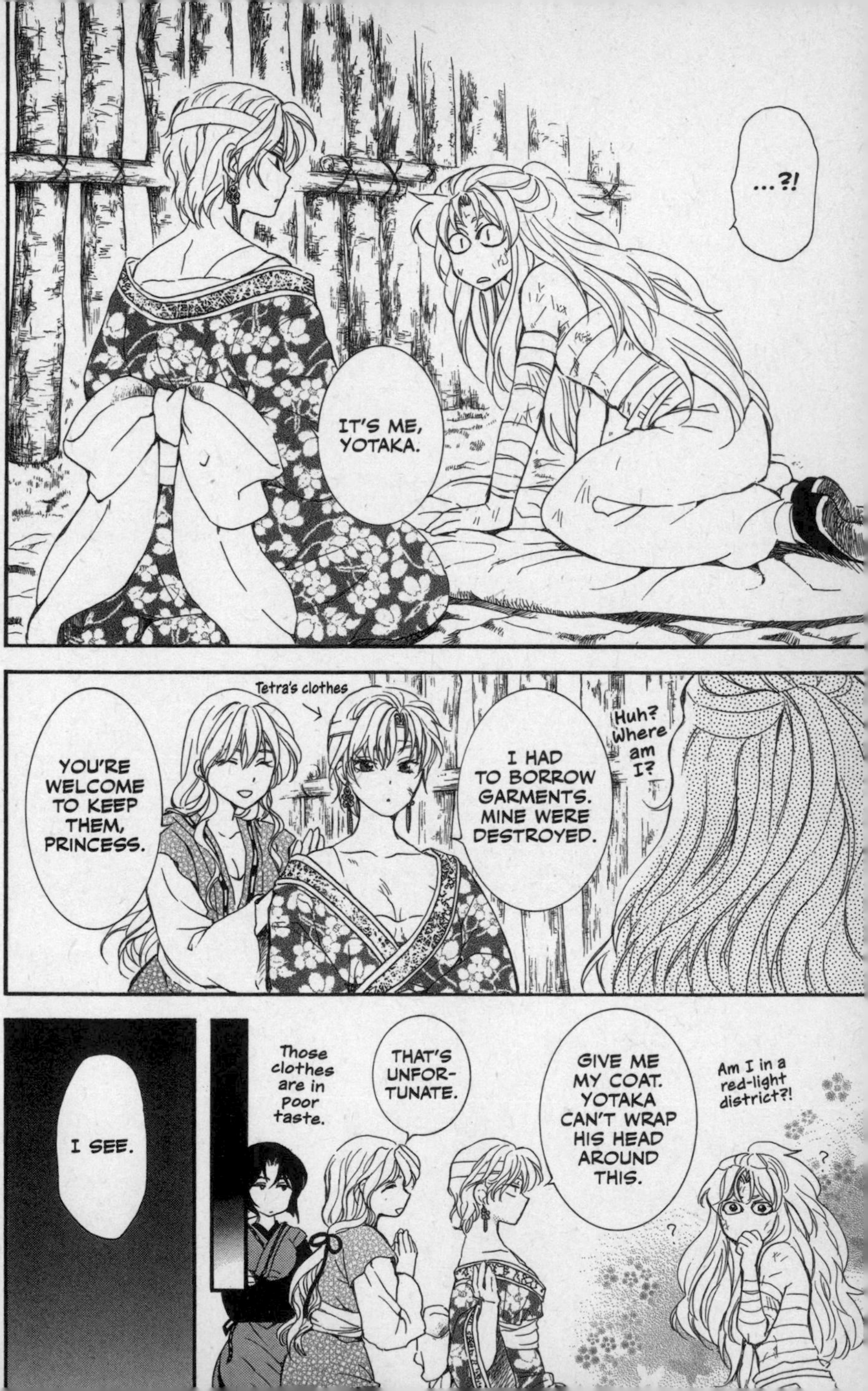
...?!
IT'S ME, YOTAKA.
Huh? Where am I?
I HAD TO BORROW GARMENTS. MINE WERE DESTROYED.
Tetra's clothes
YOU'RE WELCOME TO KEEP THEM, PRINCESS.
Am I in a red-light district?!
GIVE ME MY COAT. YOTAKA CAN'T WRAP HIS HEAD AROUND THIS.
THAT'S UNFORTUNATE.
Those clothes are in poor taste.
I SEE.

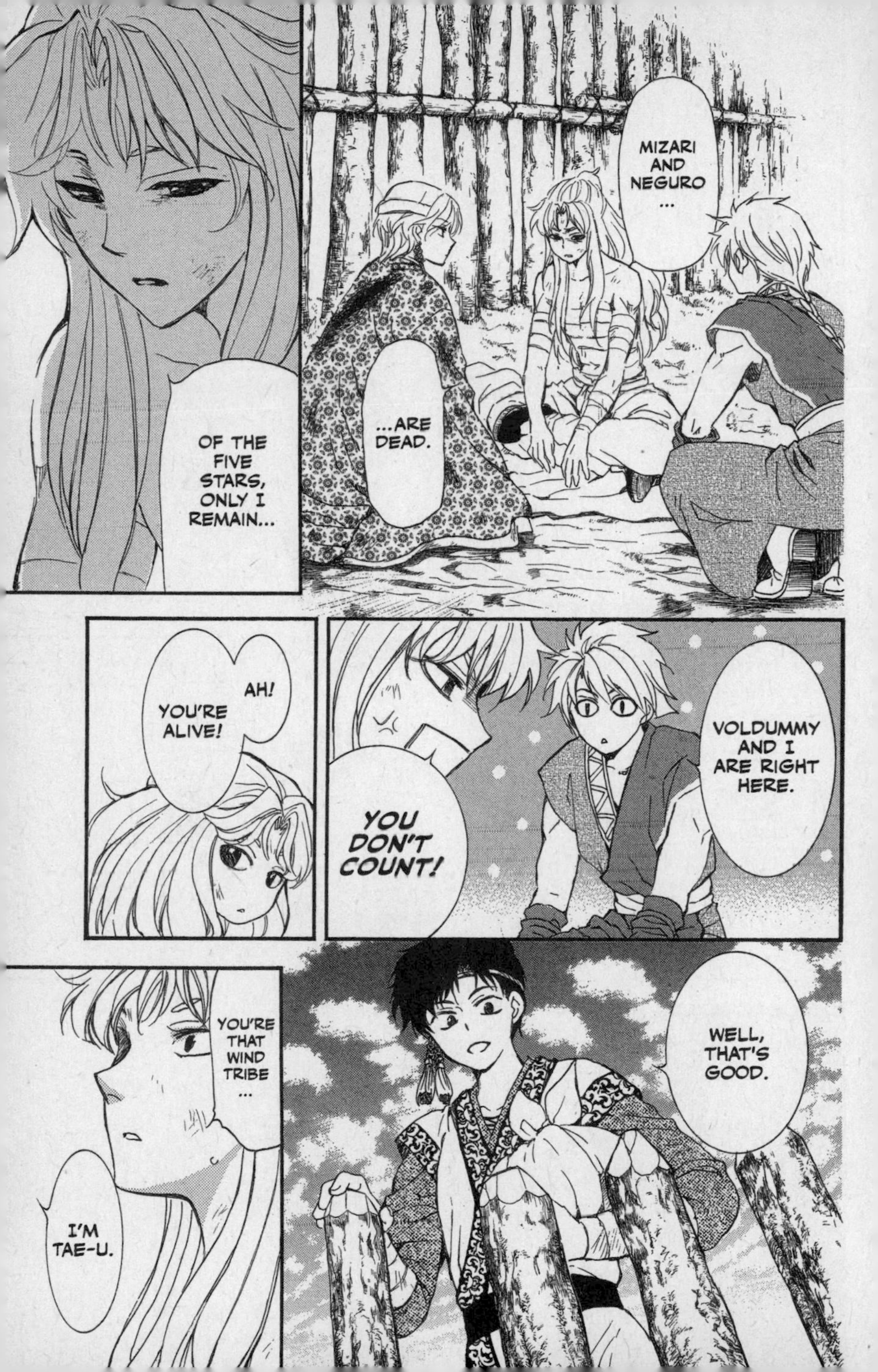
MIZARI AND NEGURO ...
...ARE DEAD.
OF THE FIVE STARS, ONLY I REMAIN...
VOLDUMMY AND I ARE RIGHT HERE.
YOU DON'T COUNT!
AH! YOU'RE ALIVE!
WELL, THAT'S GOOD.
YOU'RE THAT WIND TRIBE ...
I'M TAE-U.

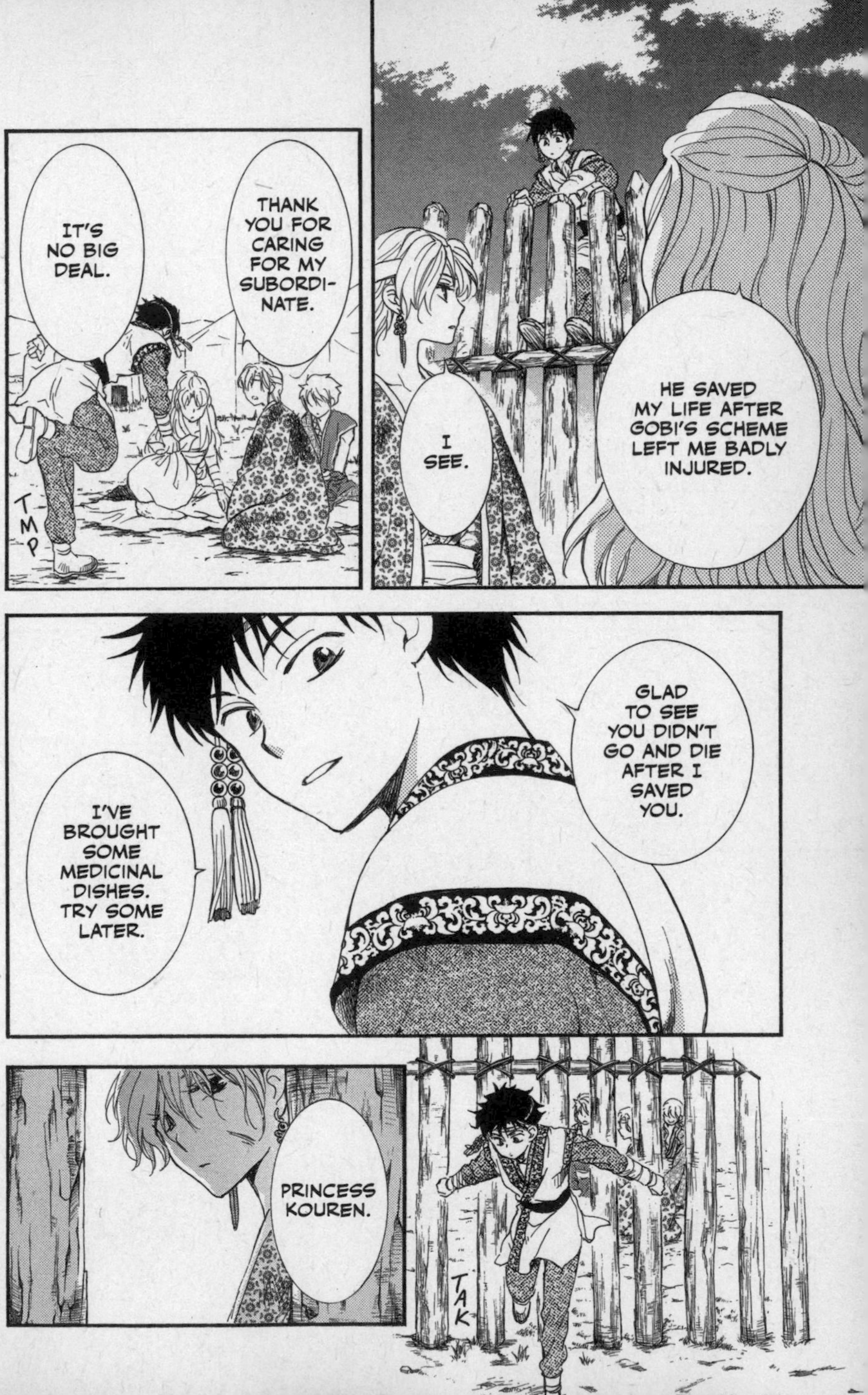
HE SAVED MY LIFE AFTER GOBI'S SCHEME LEFT ME BADLY INJURED.
I SEE.
THANK YOU FOR CARING FOR MY SUBORDI-NATE.
IT'S NO BIG DEAL.
TMP
GLAD TO SEE YOU DIDN'T GO AND DIE AFTER I SAVED YOU.
I'VE BROUGHT SOME MEDICINAL DISHES. TRY SOME LATER.
TAK
PRINCESS KOUREN.

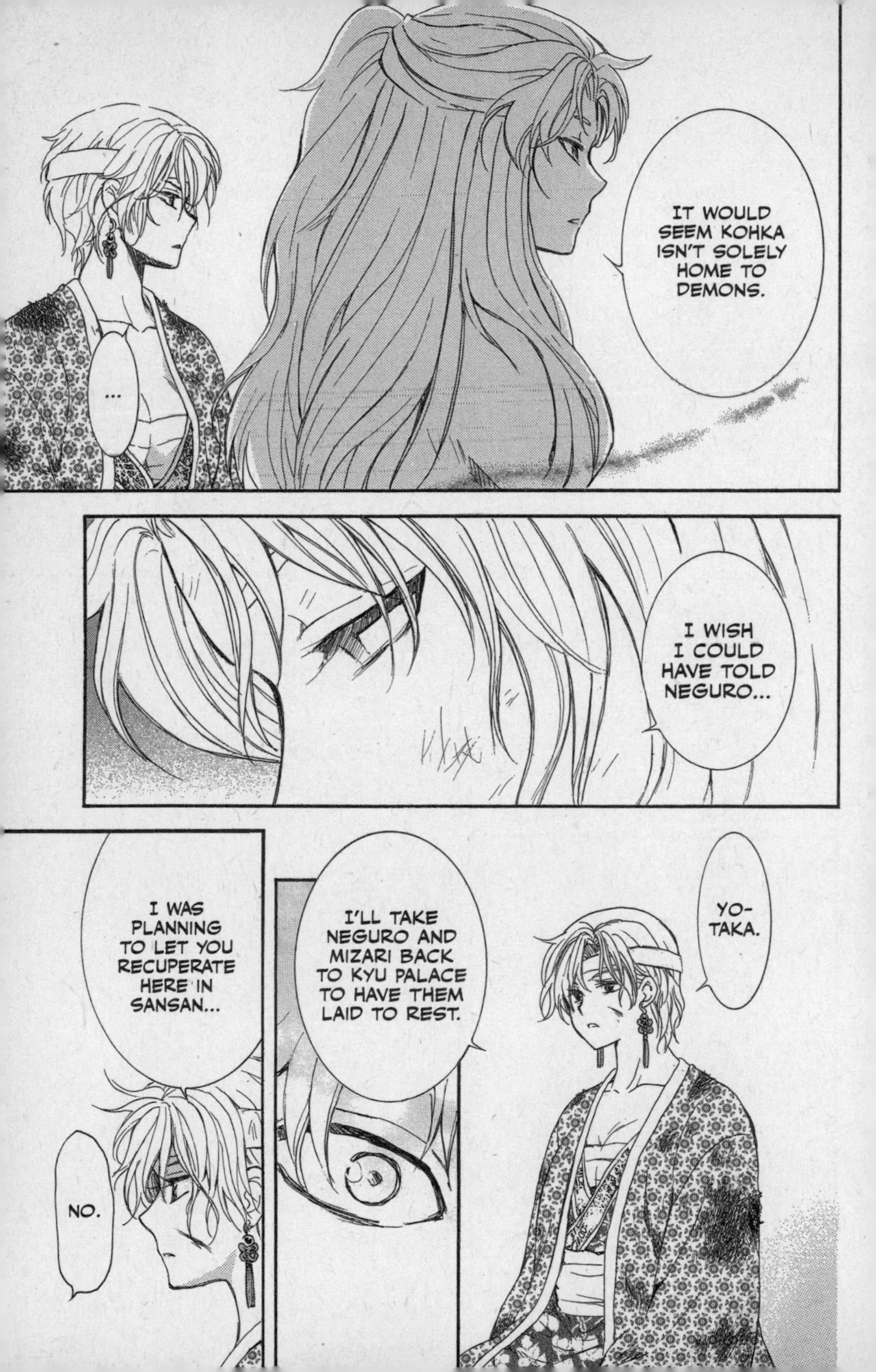
IT WOULD SEEM KOHKA ISN'T SOLELY HOME TO DEMONS.
...
I WISH I COULD HAVE TOLD NEGURO...
YO-TAKA.
I'LL TAKE NEGURO AND MIZARI BACK TO KYU PALACE TO HAVE THEM LAID TO REST.
I WAS PLANNING TO LET YOU RECUPERATE HERE IN SANSAN...
NO.

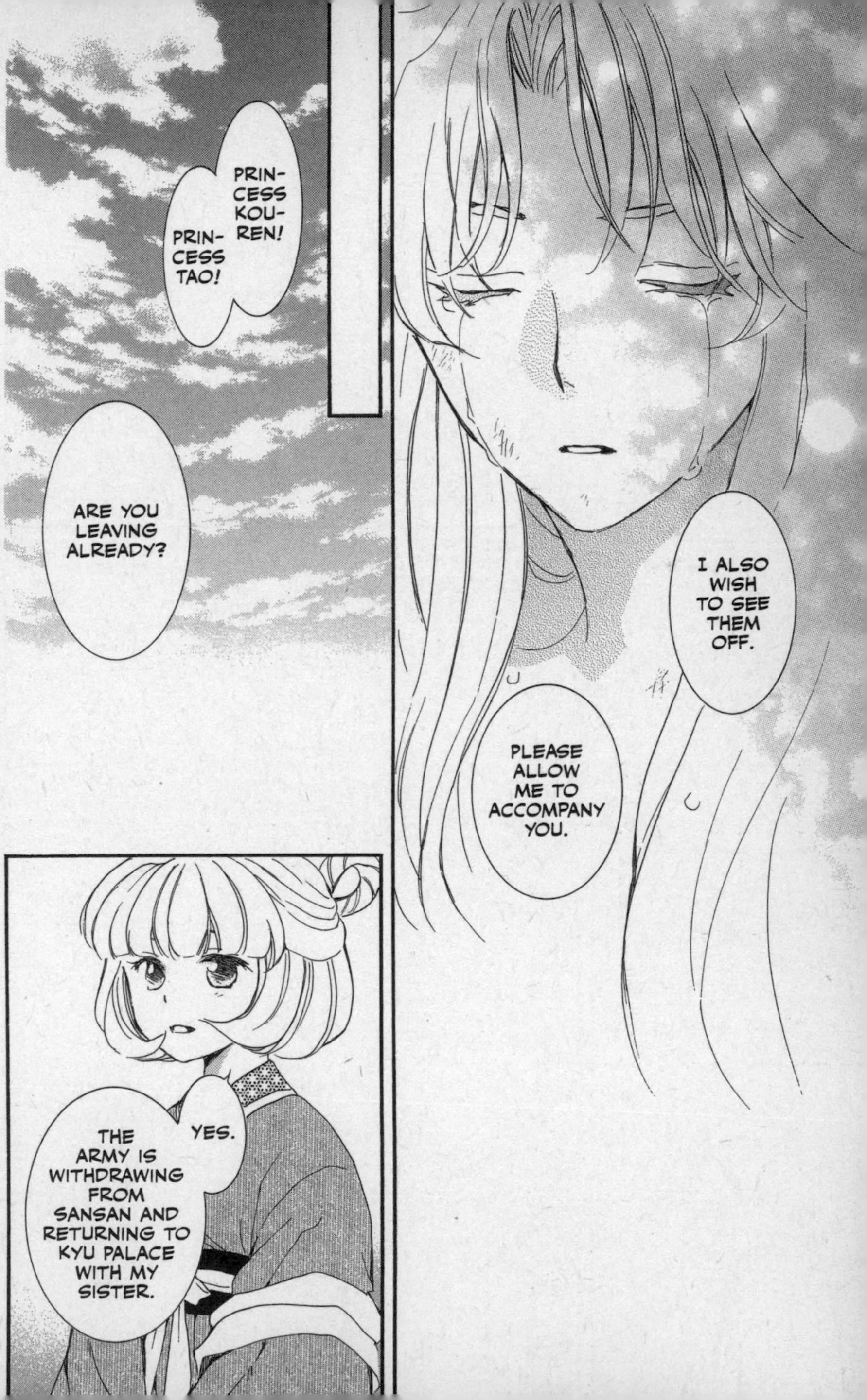
I ALSO WISH TO SEE THEM OFF.
PLEASE ALLOW ME TO ACCOMPANY YOU.
PRIN-CESS KOU-REN!
PRIN-CESS TAO!
ARE YOU LEAVING ALREADY?
YES.
THE ARMY IS WITHDRAWING FROM SANSAN AND RETURNING TO KYU PALACE WITH MY SISTER.

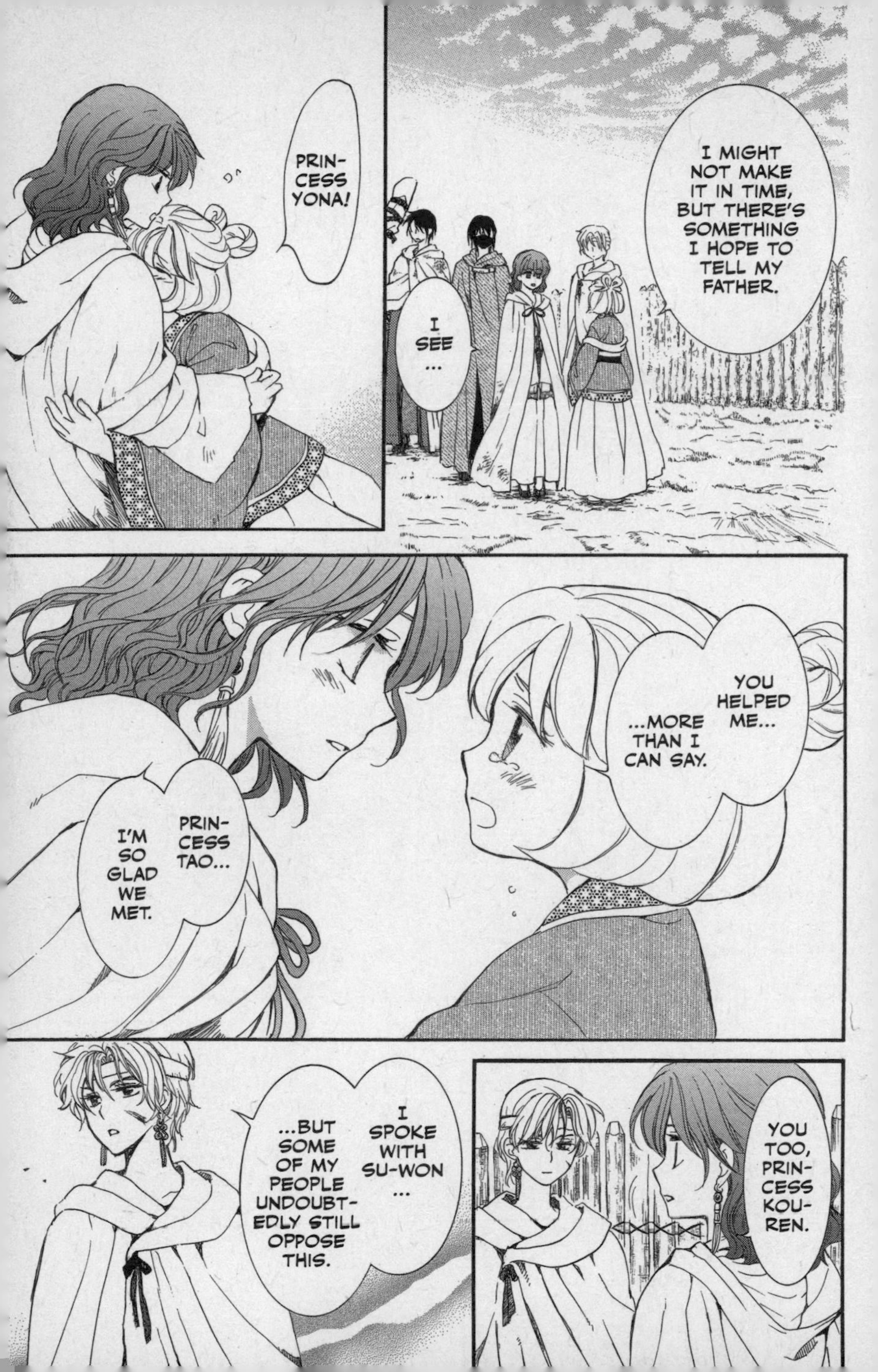
I MIGHT NOT MAKE IT IN TIME, BUT THERE'S SOMETHING I HOPE TO TELL MY FATHER.
I SEE...
PRINCESS YONA!
YOU HELPED ME...
...MORE THAN I CAN SAY.
PRINCESS TAO...
I'M SO GLAD WE MET.
YOU TOO, PRINCESS KOUREN.
I SPOKE WITH SU-WON...
...BUT SOME OF MY PEOPLE UNDOUBTEDLY STILL OPPOSE THIS.

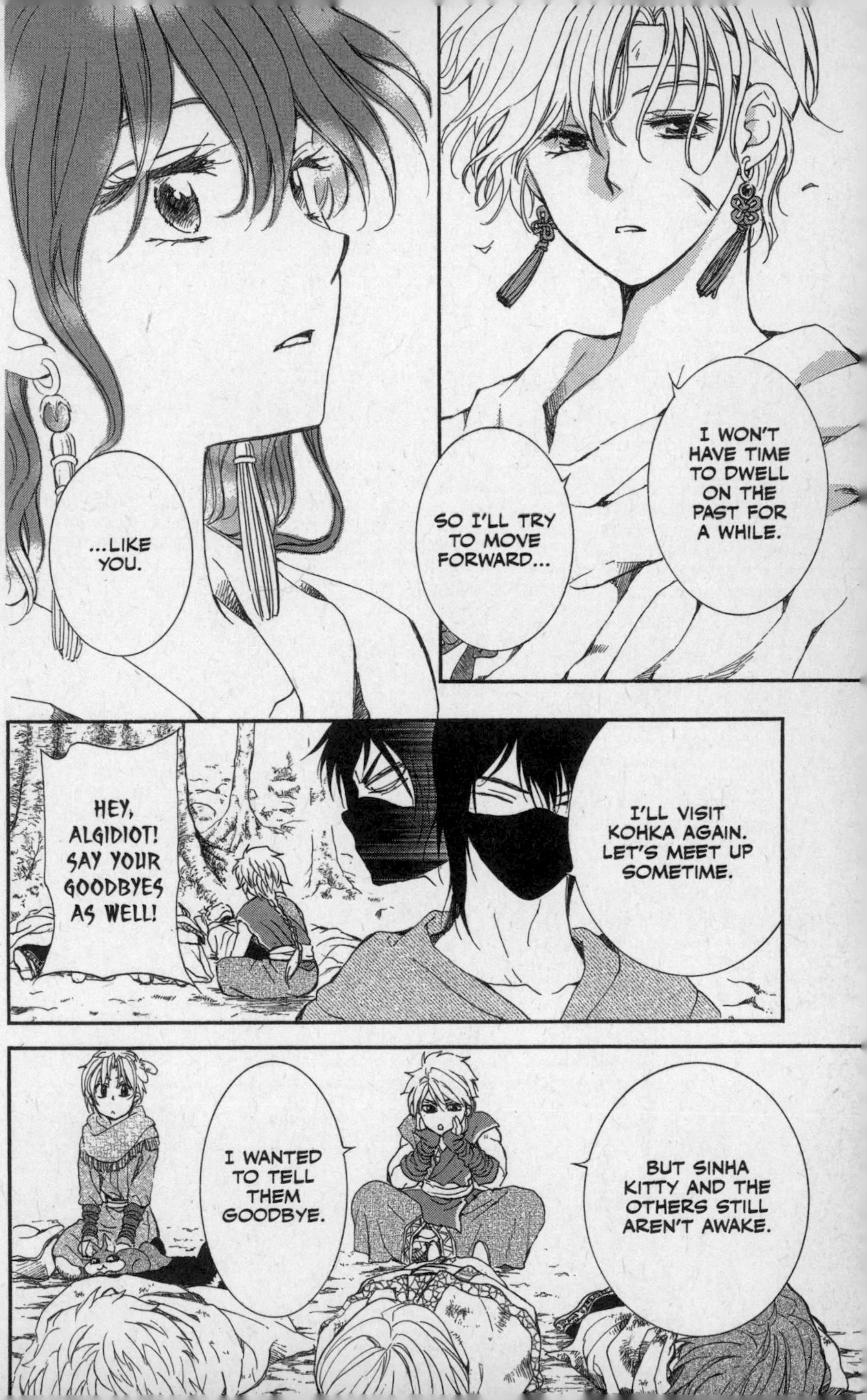
I WON'T HAVE TIME TO DWELL ON THE PAST FOR A WHILE.
SO I'LL TRY TO MOVE FORWARD...
...LIKE YOU.
I'LL VISIT KOHKA AGAIN. LET'S MEET UP SOMETIME.
HEY, ALGIDIOT! SAY YOUR GOODBYES AS WELL!
BUT SINHA KITTY AND THE OTHERS STILL AREN'T AWAKE.
I WANTED TO TELL THEM GOODBYE.

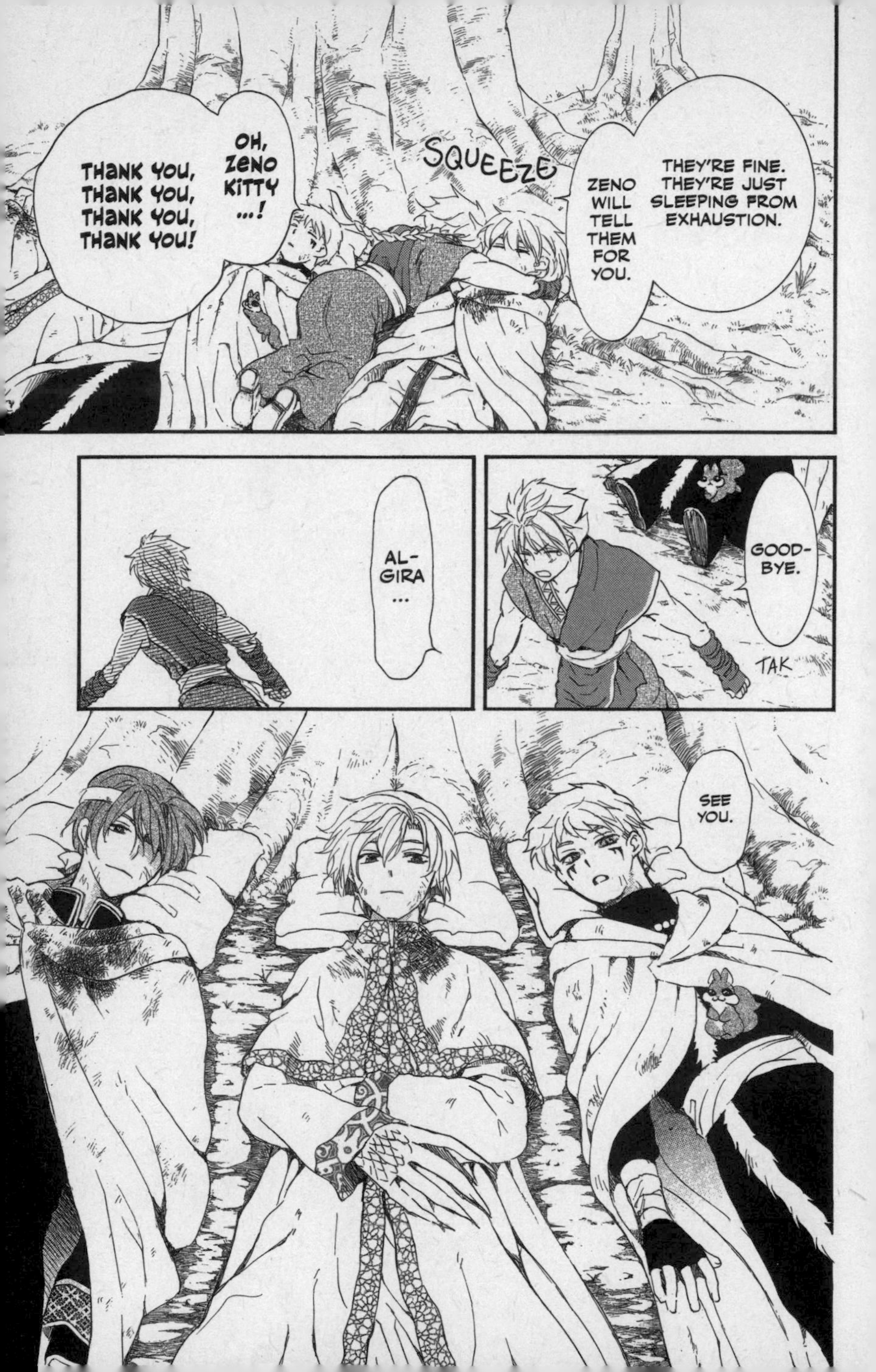
THEY'RE FINE. THEY'RE JUST SLEEPING FROM EXHAUSTION.
ZENO WILL TELL THEM FOR YOU.
SQUEEZE
OH, ZENO KITTY ...!
THANK YOU, THANK YOU, THANK YOU, THANK YOU!
GOOD-BYE.
TAK
AL-GIRA ...
SEE YOU.

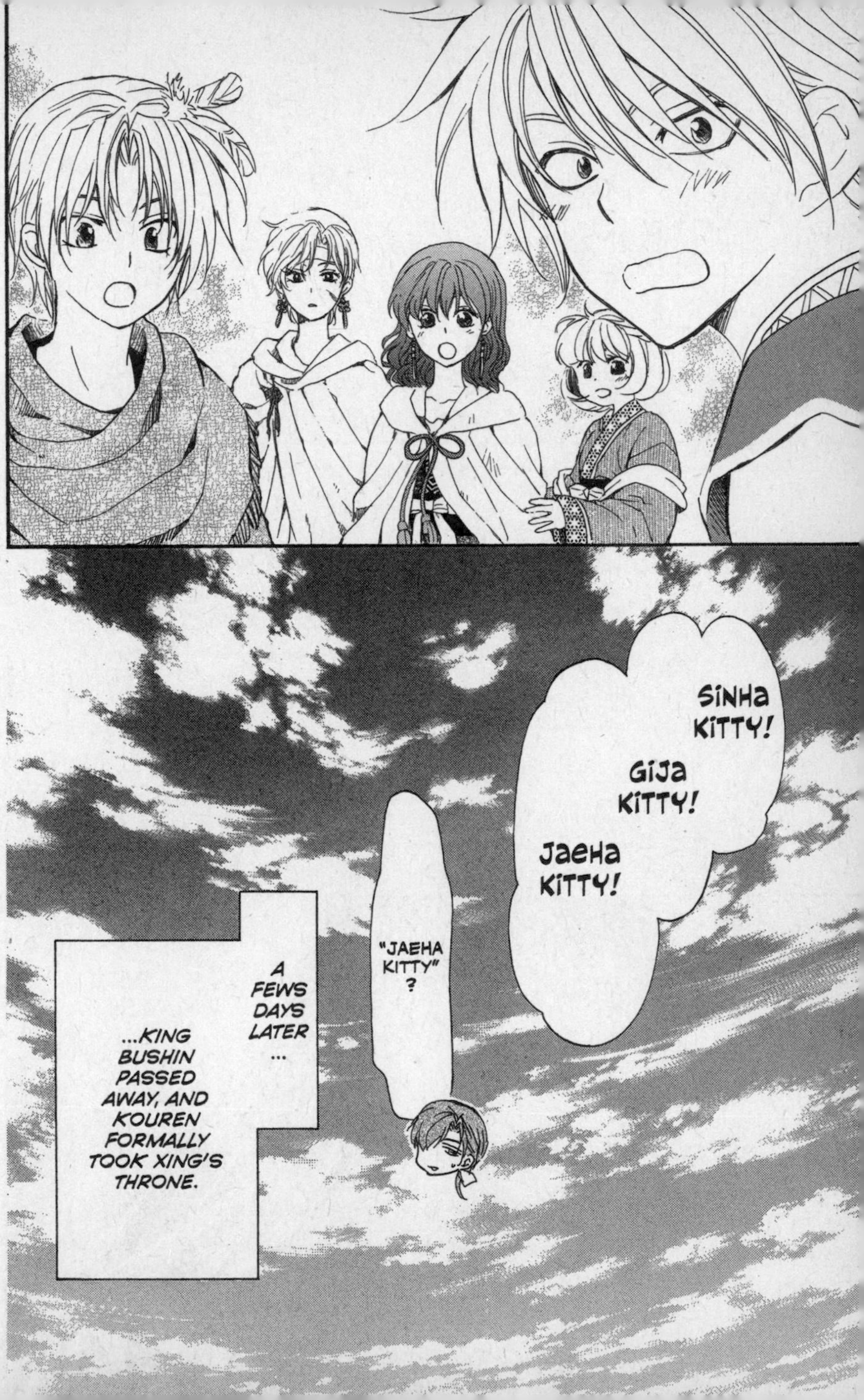
Sinha kitty! Gija kitty! Jaeha kitty!
"Jaeha kitty"?
A fews days later...
...King Bushin passed away, and Kouren formally took Xing's throne.

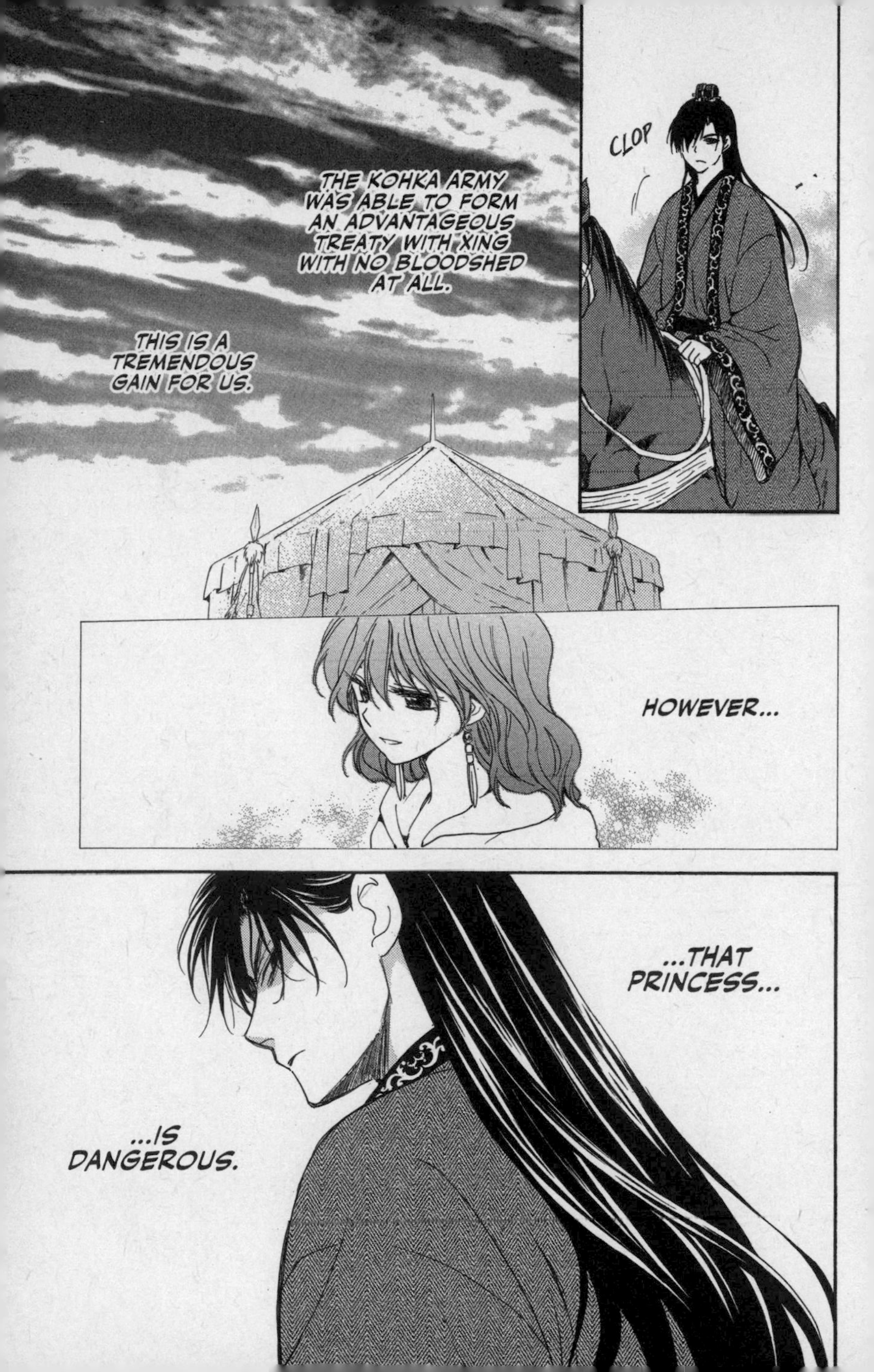
CLOP
THE KOHKA ARMY WAS ABLE TO FORM AN ADVANTAGEOUS TREATY WITH XING WITH NO BLOODSHED AT ALL.
THIS IS A TREMENDOUS GAIN FOR US.
HOWEVER...
...THAT PRINCESS...
...IS DANGEROUS.

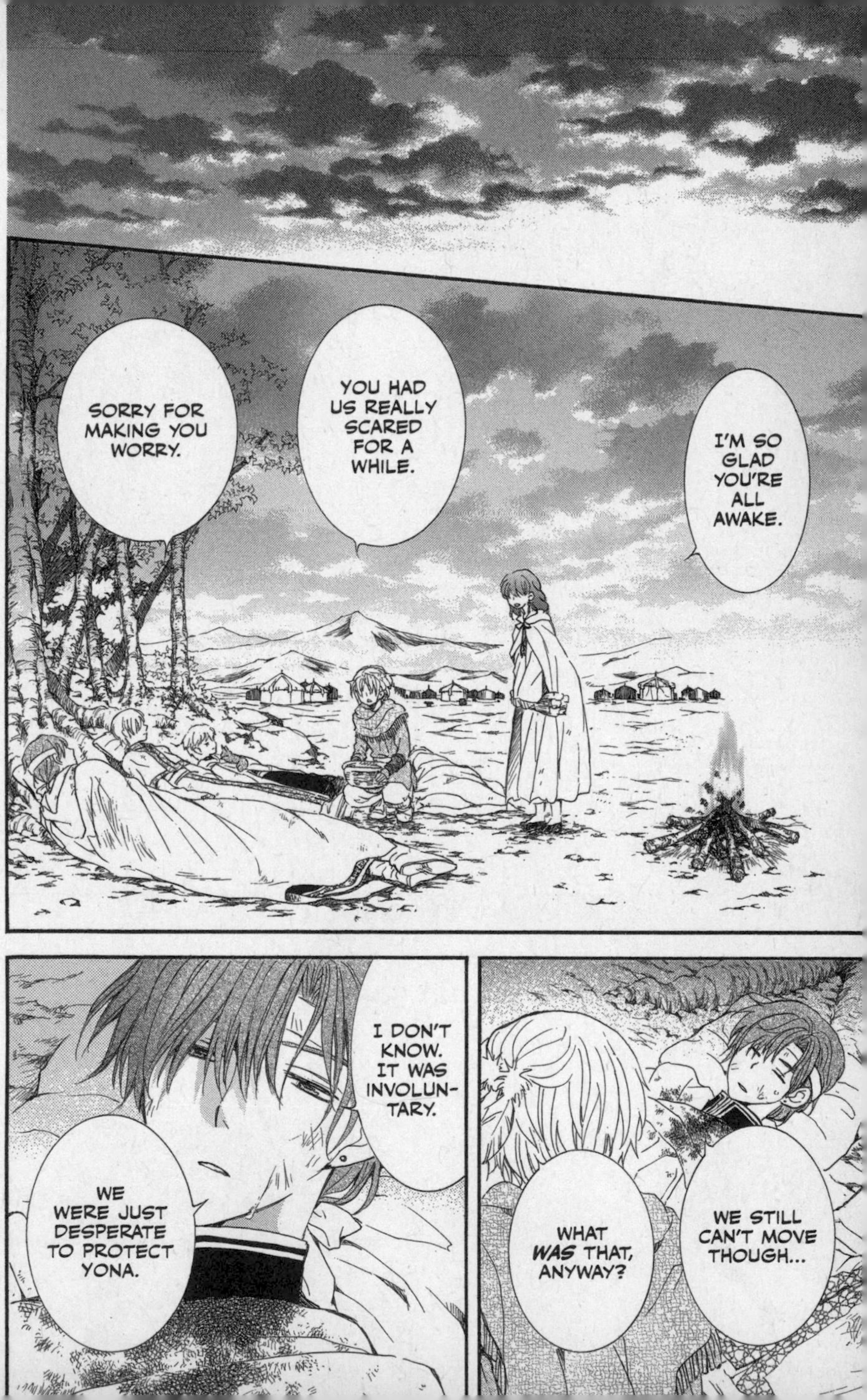
I'M SO GLAD YOU'RE ALL AWAKE.
YOU HAD US REALLY SCARED FOR A WHILE.
SORRY FOR MAKING YOU WORRY.
WE STILL CAN'T MOVE THOUGH...
WHAT *WAS* THAT, ANYWAY?
I DON'T KNOW. IT WAS INVOLUNTARY.
WE WERE JUST DESPERATE TO PROTECT YONA.

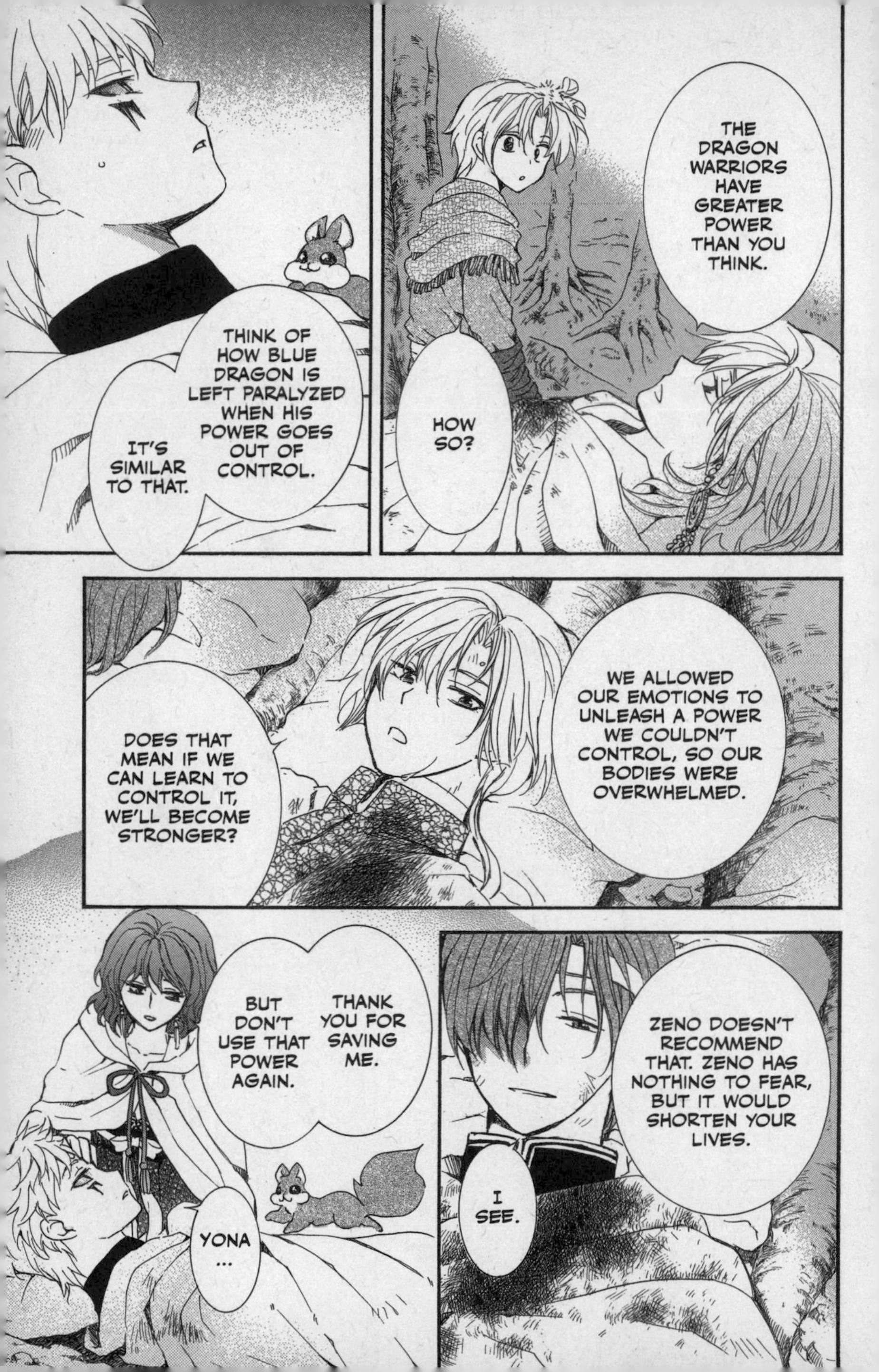
THE DRAGON WARRIORS HAVE GREATER POWER THAN YOU THINK.
HOW SO?
THINK OF HOW BLUE DRAGON IS LEFT PARALYZED WHEN HIS POWER GOES OUT OF CONTROL.
IT'S SIMILAR TO THAT.
WE ALLOWED OUR EMOTIONS TO UNLEASH A POWER WE COULDN'T CONTROL, SO OUR BODIES WERE OVERWHELMED.
DOES THAT MEAN IF WE CAN LEARN TO CONTROL IT, WE'LL BECOME STRONGER?
ZENO DOESN'T RECOMMEND THAT. ZENO HAS NOTHING TO FEAR, BUT IT WOULD SHORTEN YOUR LIVES.
I SEE.
THANK YOU FOR SAVING ME.
BUT DON'T USE THAT POWER AGAIN.
YONA ...

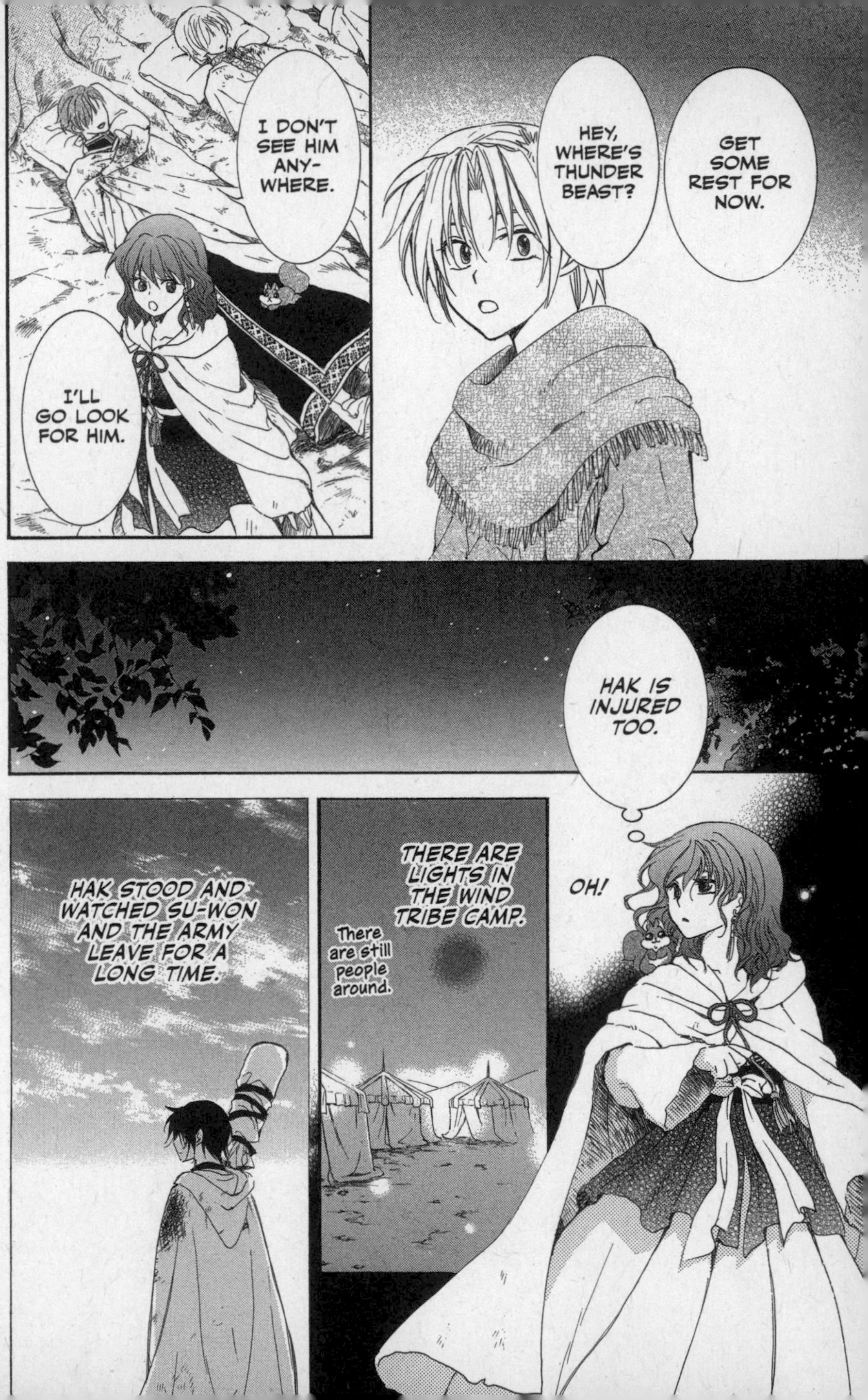
GET SOME REST FOR NOW.
HEY, WHERE'S THUNDER BEAST?
I DON'T SEE HIM ANY-WHERE.
I'LL GO LOOK FOR HIM.
HAK IS INJURED TOO.
OH!
THERE ARE LIGHTS IN THE WIND TRIBE CAMP.
There are still people around.
HAK STOOD AND WATCHED SU-WON AND THE ARMY LEAVE FOR A LONG TIME.

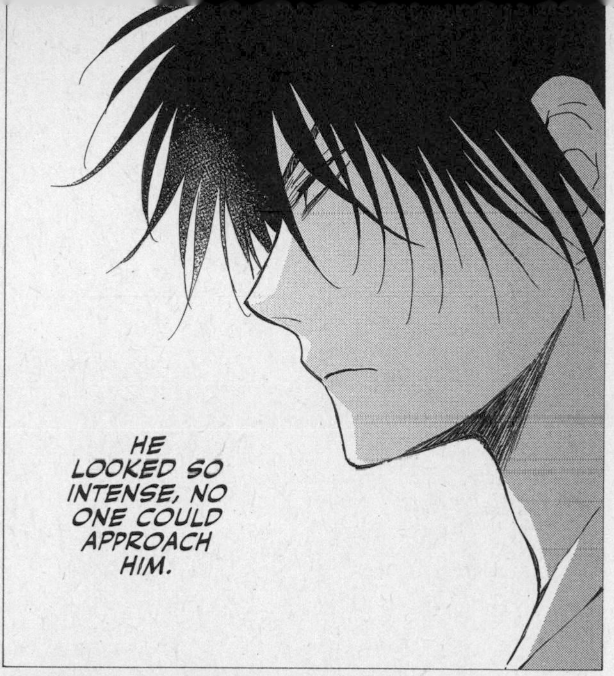
HE LOOKED SO INTENSE, NO ONE COULD APPROACH HIM.
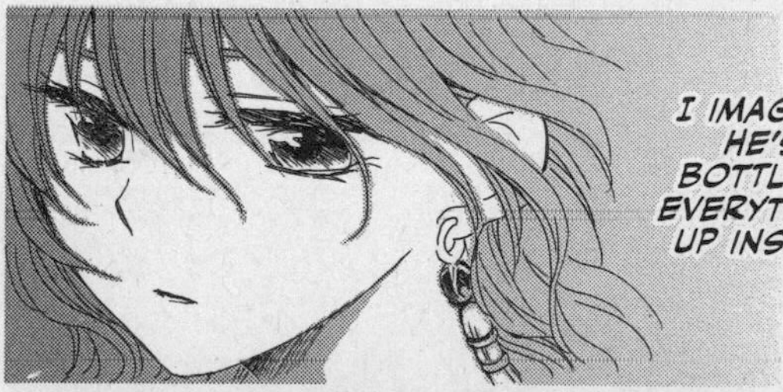
I IMAGINE HE'S BOTTLING EVERYTHING UP INSIDE.
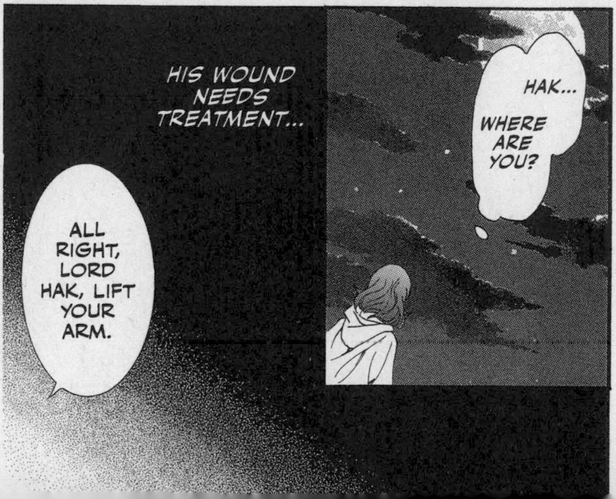
HAK... WHERE ARE YOU?
HIS WOUND NEEDS TREATMENT...
ALL RIGHT, LORD HAK, LIFT YOUR ARM.
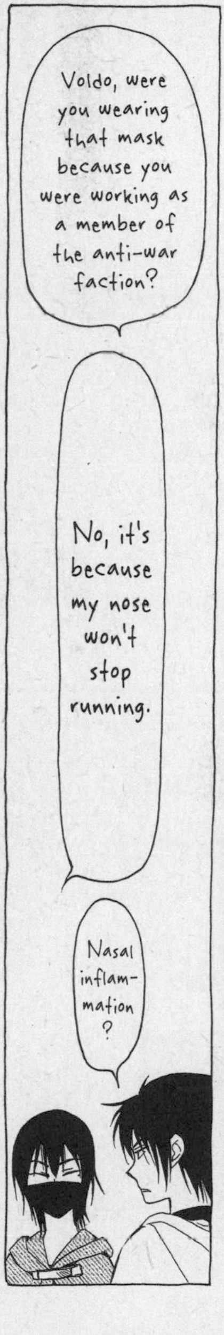
Voldo, were you wearing that mask because you were working as a member of the anti-war faction?
No, it's because my nose won't stop running.
Nasal inflam-mation?

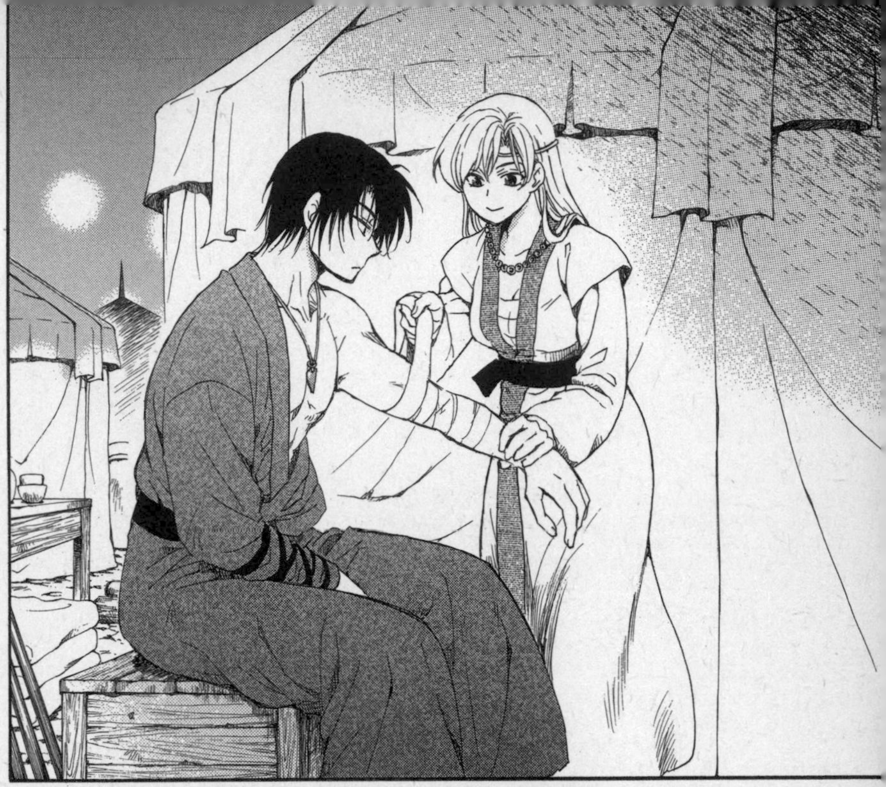
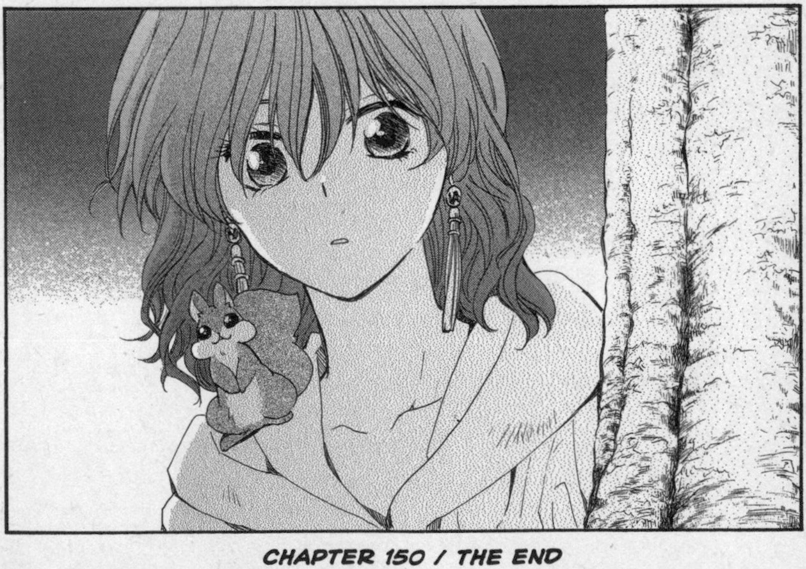

CHAPTER 150 / THE END

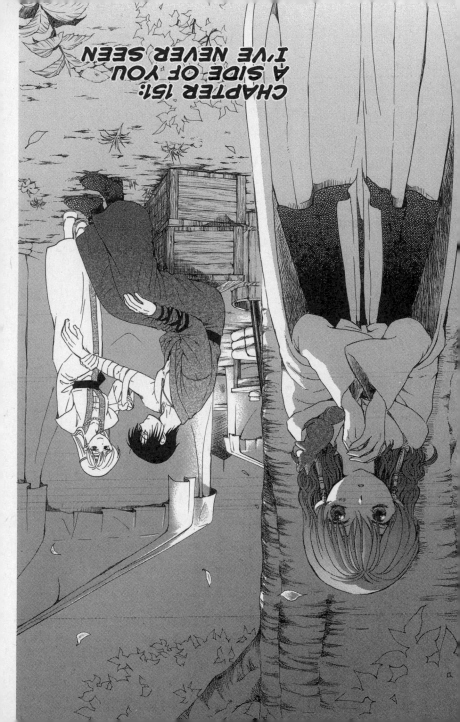

CHAPTER 151:
A SIDE OF YOU
I'VE NEVER SEEN

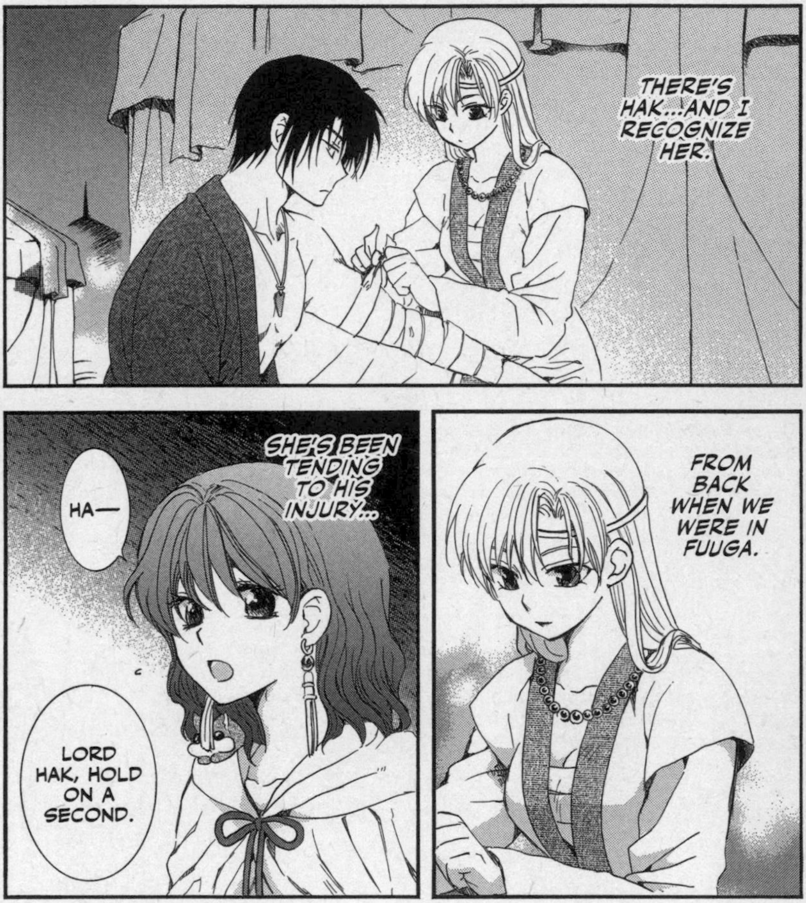
THERE'S HAK...AND I RECOGNIZE HER.
FROM BACK WHEN WE WERE IN FUUGA.
SHE'S BEEN TENDING TO HIS INJURY...
HA—
LORD HAK, HOLD ON A SECOND.

A special thanks! ♥♥
My assistants who are always helping me → Mikorun, C.F., Ryo Sakura, Ryo, Awafuji, Oka, Eika and my little sister...
My editors who are always helping me → Tokushige, my previous editors and the *Hana to Yume* editorial office...
Everyone who's involved in creating and selling *Yona*-related merchandise...
My family, friends and readers who have given me tons of support and the environment to draw.
My ideas and drawings don't always go the way I want them to, but I'll do my best to carefully lead my characters to a good place.

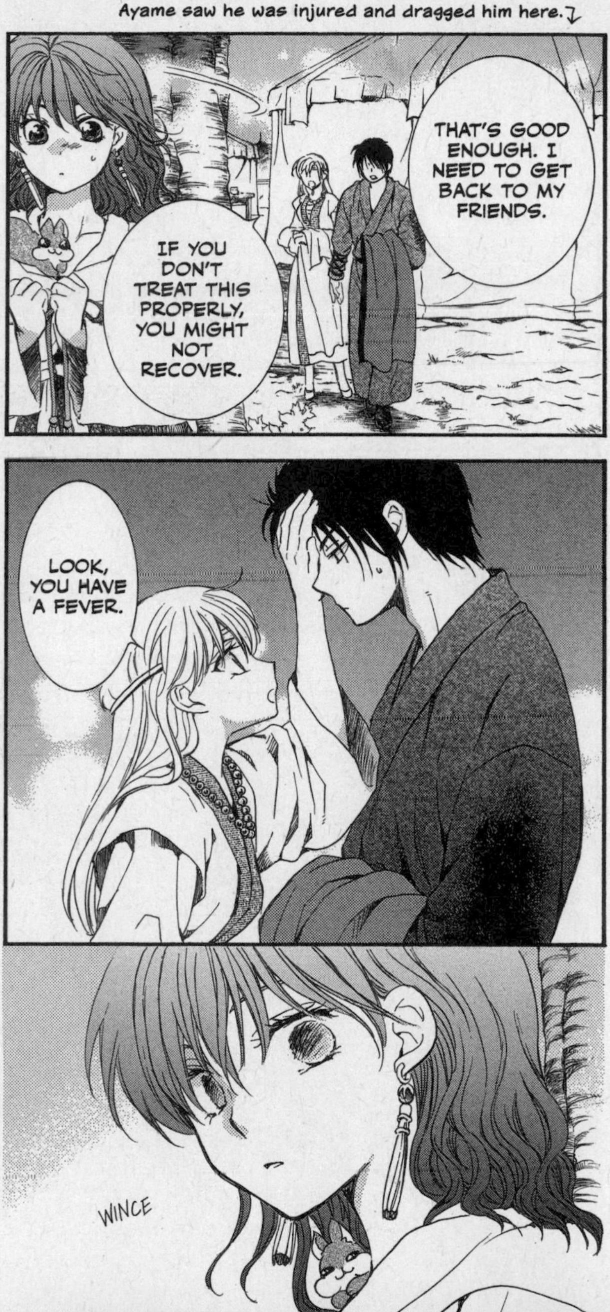
Ayame saw he was injured and dragged him here.
THAT'S GOOD ENOUGH. I NEED TO GET BACK TO MY FRIENDS.
IF YOU DON'T TREAT THIS PROPERLY, YOU MIGHT NOT RECOVER.
LOOK, YOU HAVE A FEVER.
WINCE

About the Nation of Xing arc... This arc involves so many people that it was difficult to choose what to draw. And Xing arc or not, Yona is the protagonist, so I tried to not spend too much time on the backstories of the Xing characters.

I wanted to draw more of Mizari (which I enjoyed). Visually, I liked Yotaka. My readers disliked Mizari (*Ha ha*), but I'm sad I can't draw him anymore. People tend to hate wicked characters, but I quite enjoy drawing them. For example, a lot of people dislike Keishuk, but I have fun drawing him.

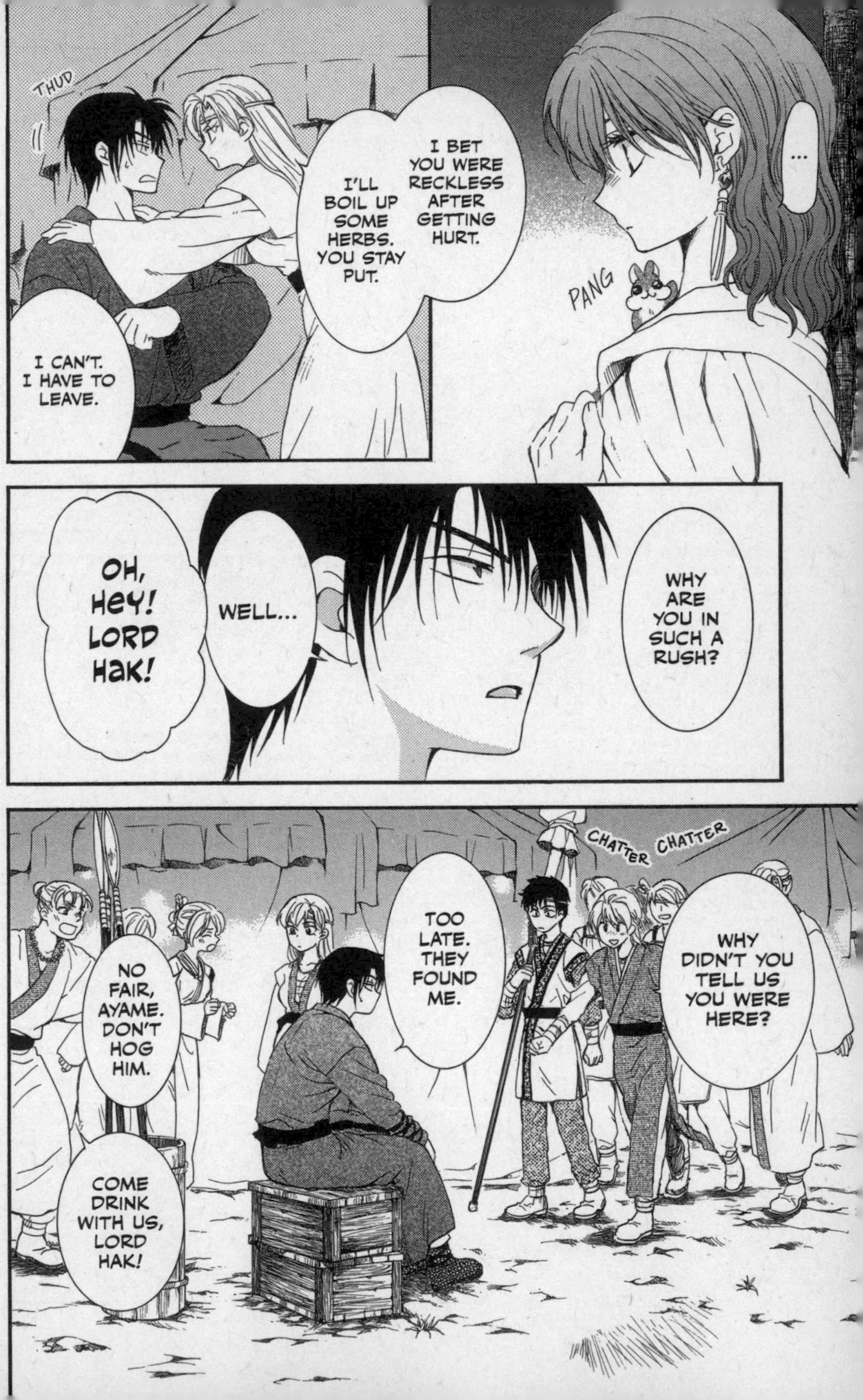
...
PANG
I BET YOU WERE RECKLESS AFTER GETTING HURT.
I'LL BOIL UP SOME HERBS. YOU STAY PUT.
THUD
I CAN'T. I HAVE TO LEAVE.
WHY ARE YOU IN SUCH A RUSH?
WELL...
OH, HEY! LORD HAK!
CHATTER CHATTER
WHY DIDN'T YOU TELL US YOU WERE HERE?
TOO LATE. THEY FOUND ME.
NO FAIR, AYAME. DON'T HOG HIM.
COME DRINK WITH US, LORD HAK!

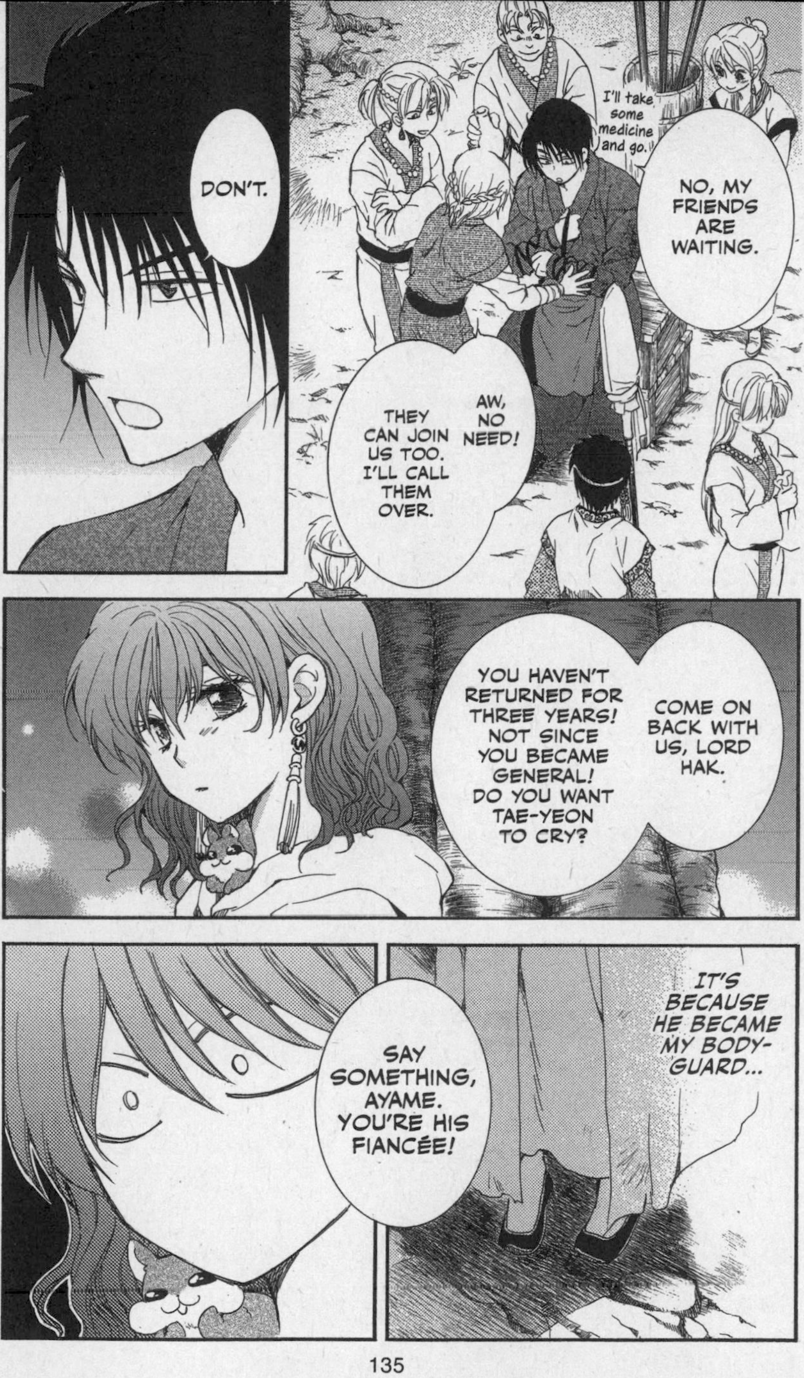
I'll take some medicine and go.
NO, MY FRIENDS ARE WAITING.
AW, NO NEED!
THEY CAN JOIN US TOO. I'LL CALL THEM OVER.
DON'T.
COME ON BACK WITH US, LORD HAK.
YOU HAVEN'T RETURNED FOR THREE YEARS! NOT SINCE YOU BECAME GENERAL! DO YOU WANT TAE-YEON TO CRY?
IT'S BECAUSE HE BECAME MY BODY-GUARD...
SAY SOMETHING, AYAME. YOU'RE HIS FIANCÉE!

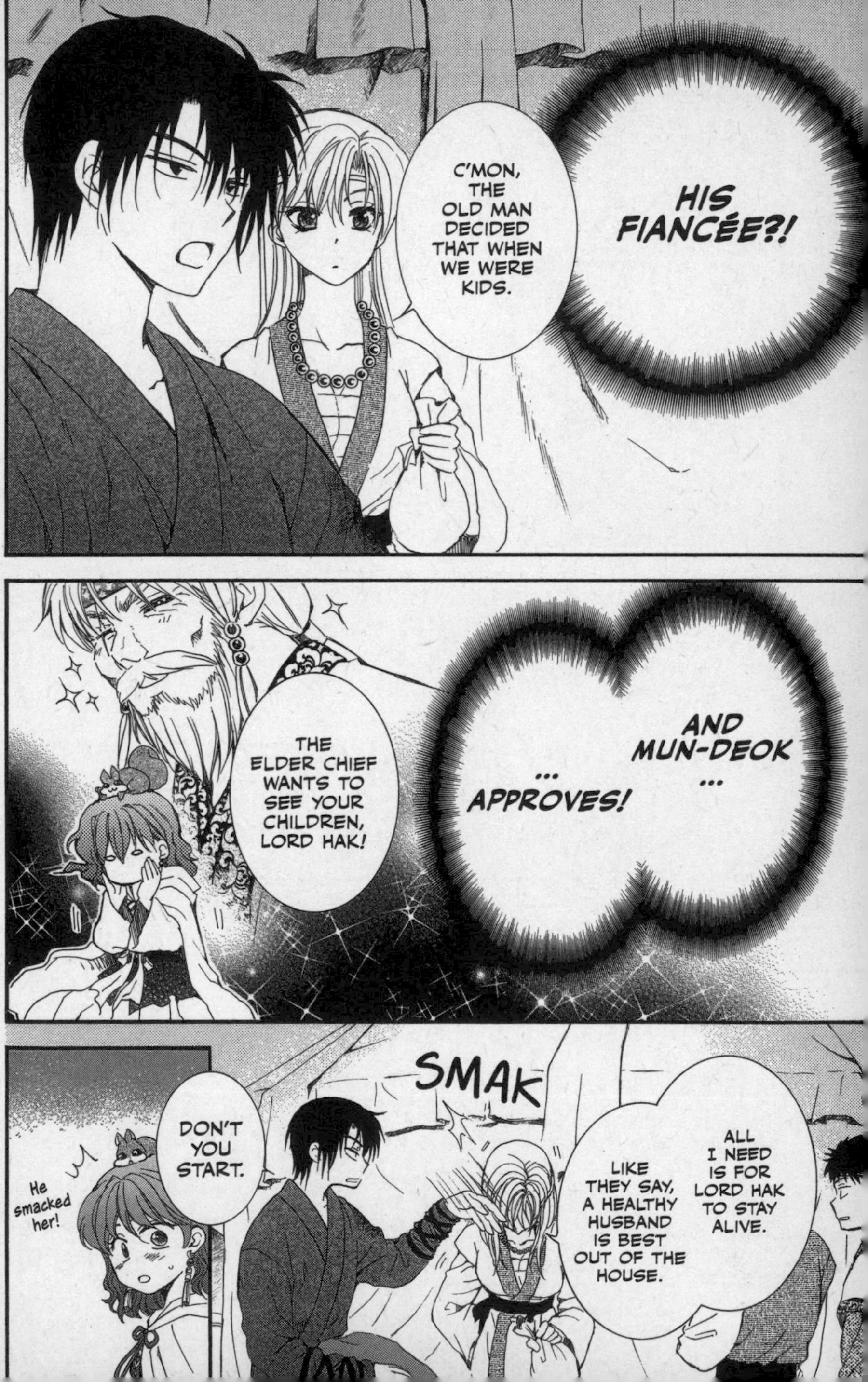
HIS FIANCÉE?!
C'MON, THE OLD MAN DECIDED THAT WHEN WE WERE KIDS.
AND MUN-DEOK ...
... APPROVES!
THE ELDER CHIEF WANTS TO SEE YOUR CHILDREN, LORD HAK!
ALL I NEED IS FOR LORD HAK TO STAY ALIVE.
LIKE THEY SAY, A HEALTHY HUSBAND IS BEST OUT OF THE HOUSE.
SMAK
DON'T YOU START.
He smacked her!

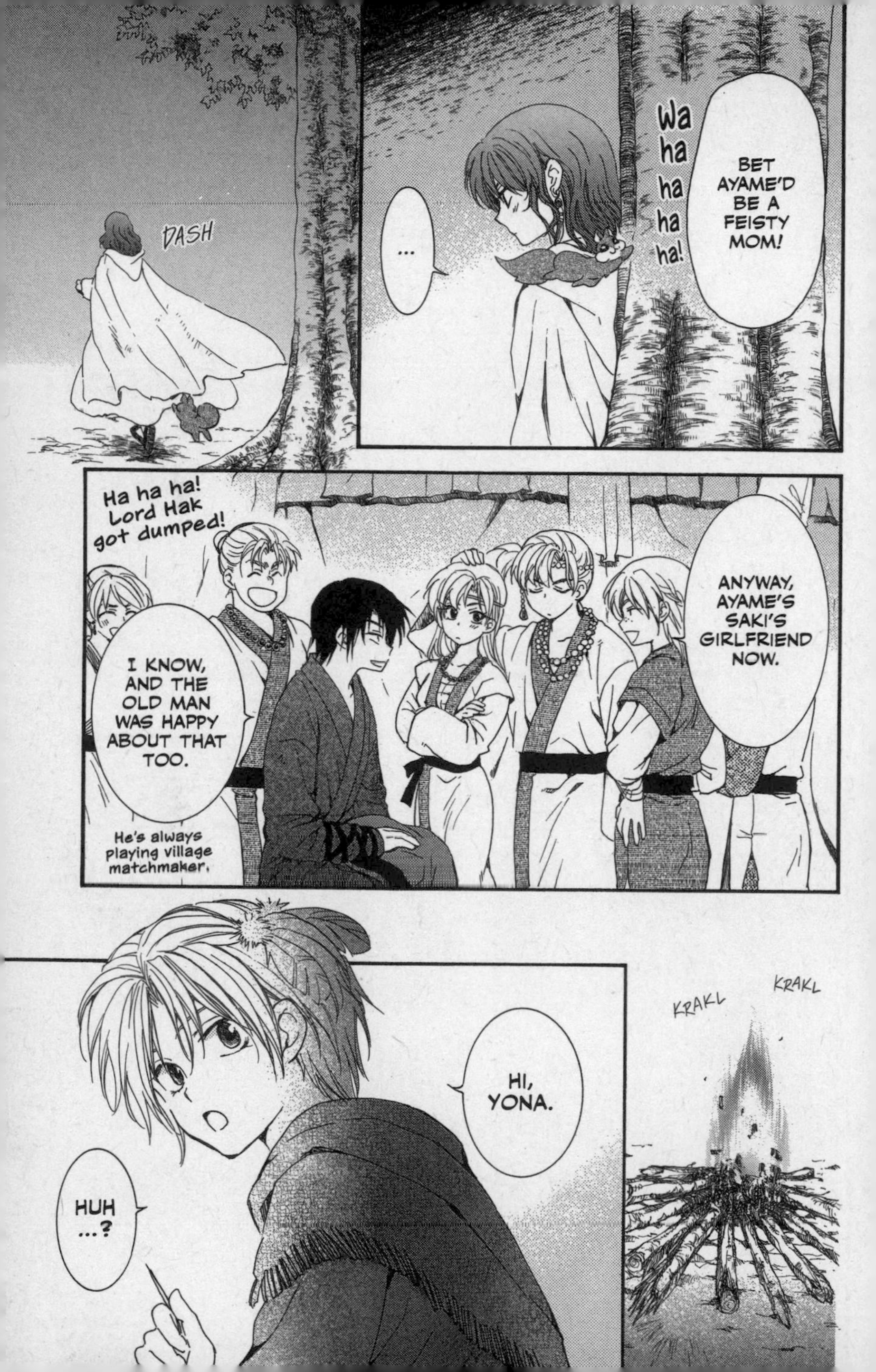
BET AYAME'D BE A FEISTY MOM!
Wa ha ha ha ha!
...
DASH
ANYWAY, AYAME'S SAKI'S GIRLFRIEND NOW.
Ha ha ha! Lord Hak got dumped!
I KNOW, AND THE OLD MAN WAS HAPPY ABOUT THAT TOO.
He's always playing village matchmaker.
KRAKL
KRAKL
HI, YONA.
HUH ...?

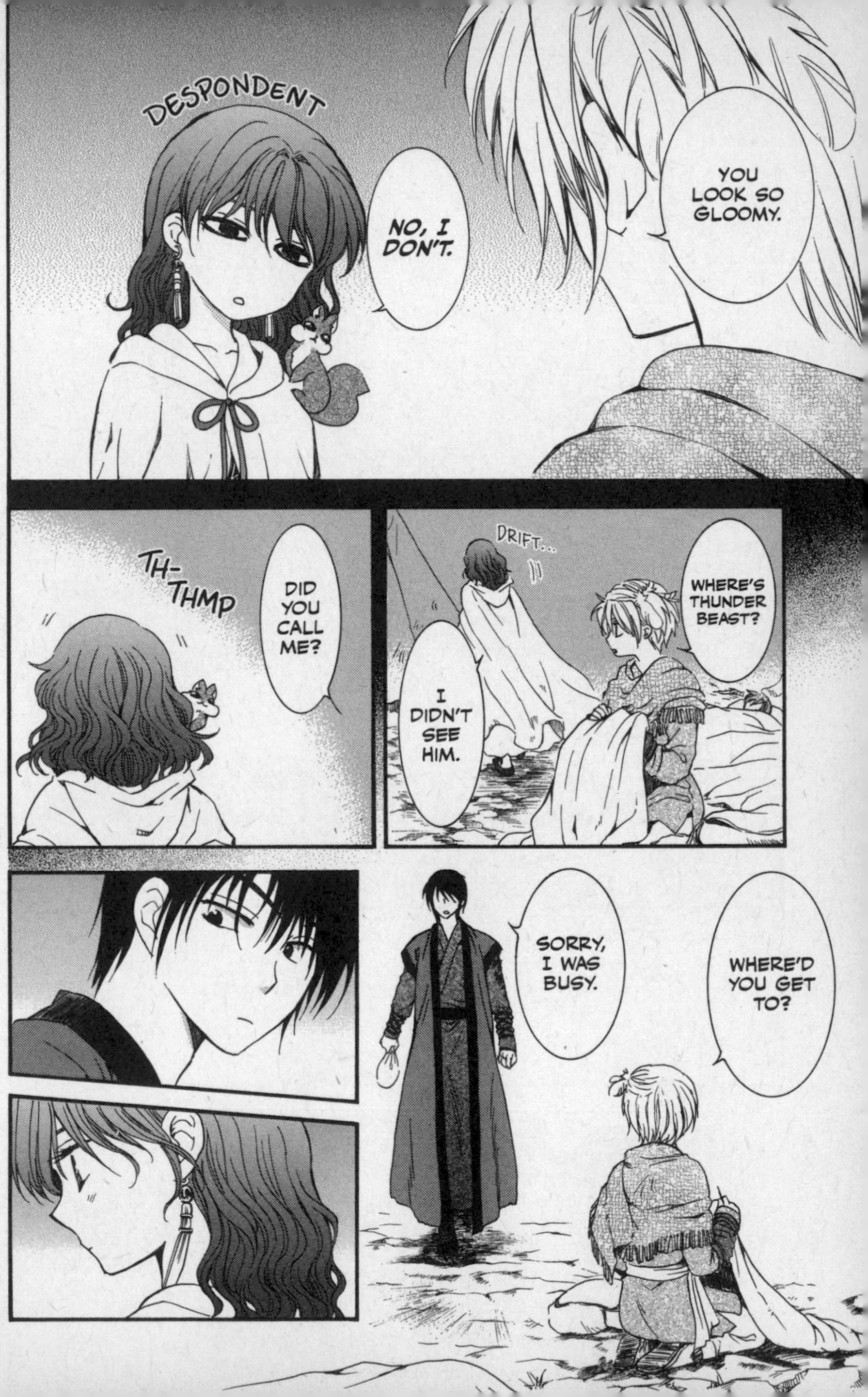
YOU LOOK SO GLOOMY.
NO, I DON'T.
DESPONDENT
WHERE'S THUNDER BEAST?
I DIDN'T SEE HIM.
DRIFT...
DID YOU CALL ME?
TH-THMP
WHERE'D YOU GET TO?
SORRY, I WAS BUSY.

WHAT'S THE MATTER, YOUR HIGHNESS?
HOW ARE YOU FEELING ?
FINE. THERE'S NOTHING WRONG.
SHE SAID HE HAD A FEVER. I WONDER IF HE GOT ANY MEDICINE...
I HOPE SO. I WANT HIM TO GET WELL QUICKLY.
SIGH...
??

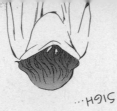

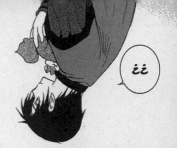

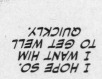

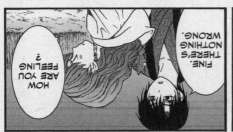

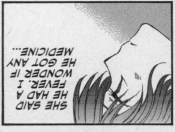

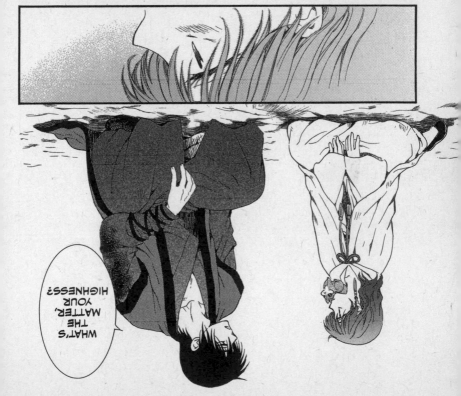

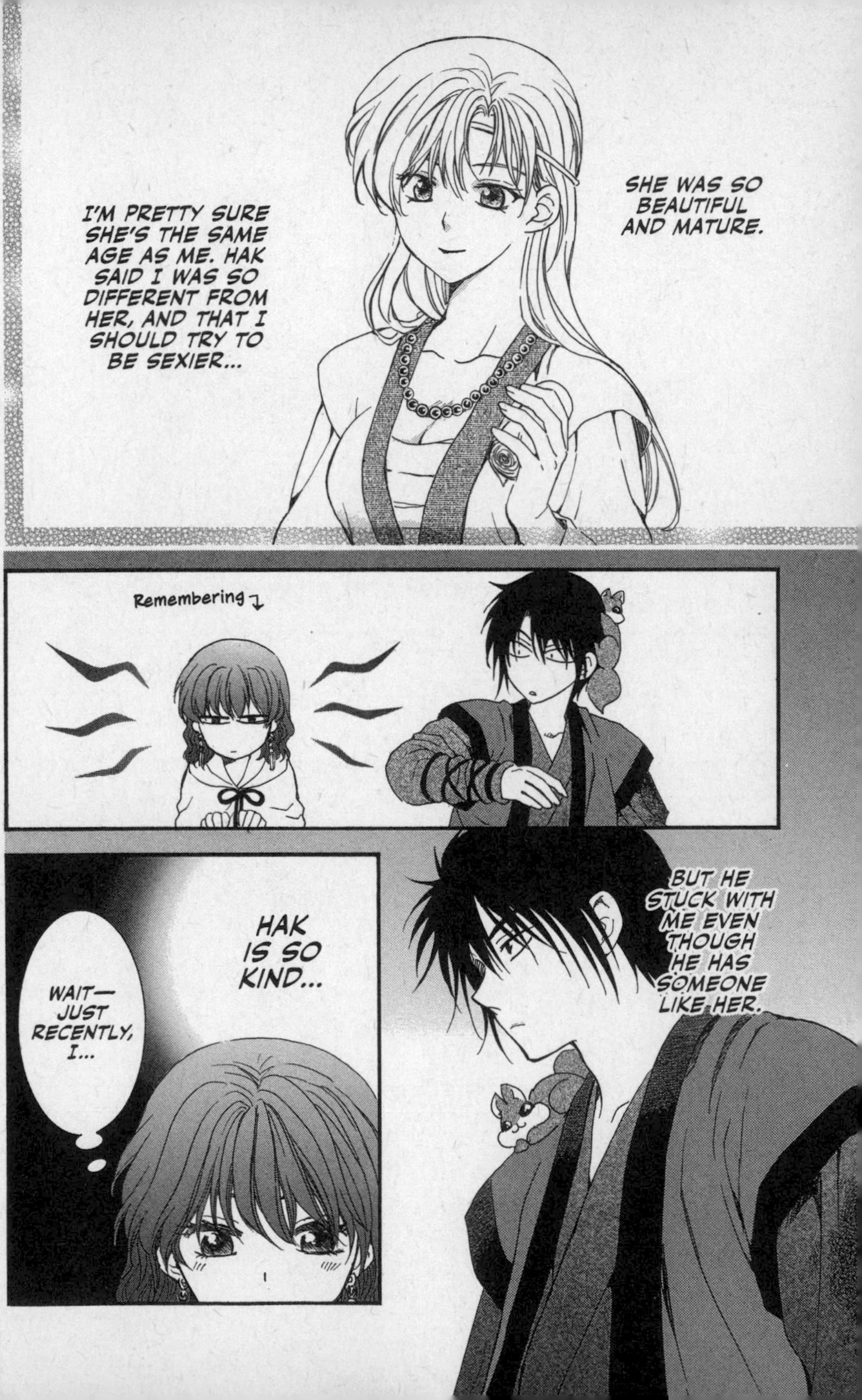
SHE WAS SO BEAUTIFUL AND MATURE.
I'M PRETTY SURE SHE'S THE SAME AGE AS ME. HAK SAID I WAS SO DIFFERENT FROM HER, AND THAT I SHOULD TRY TO BE SEXIER...
Remembering
BUT HE STUCK WITH ME EVEN THOUGH HE HAS SOMEONE LIKE HER.
HAK IS SO KIND...
WAIT— JUST RECENTLY, I...

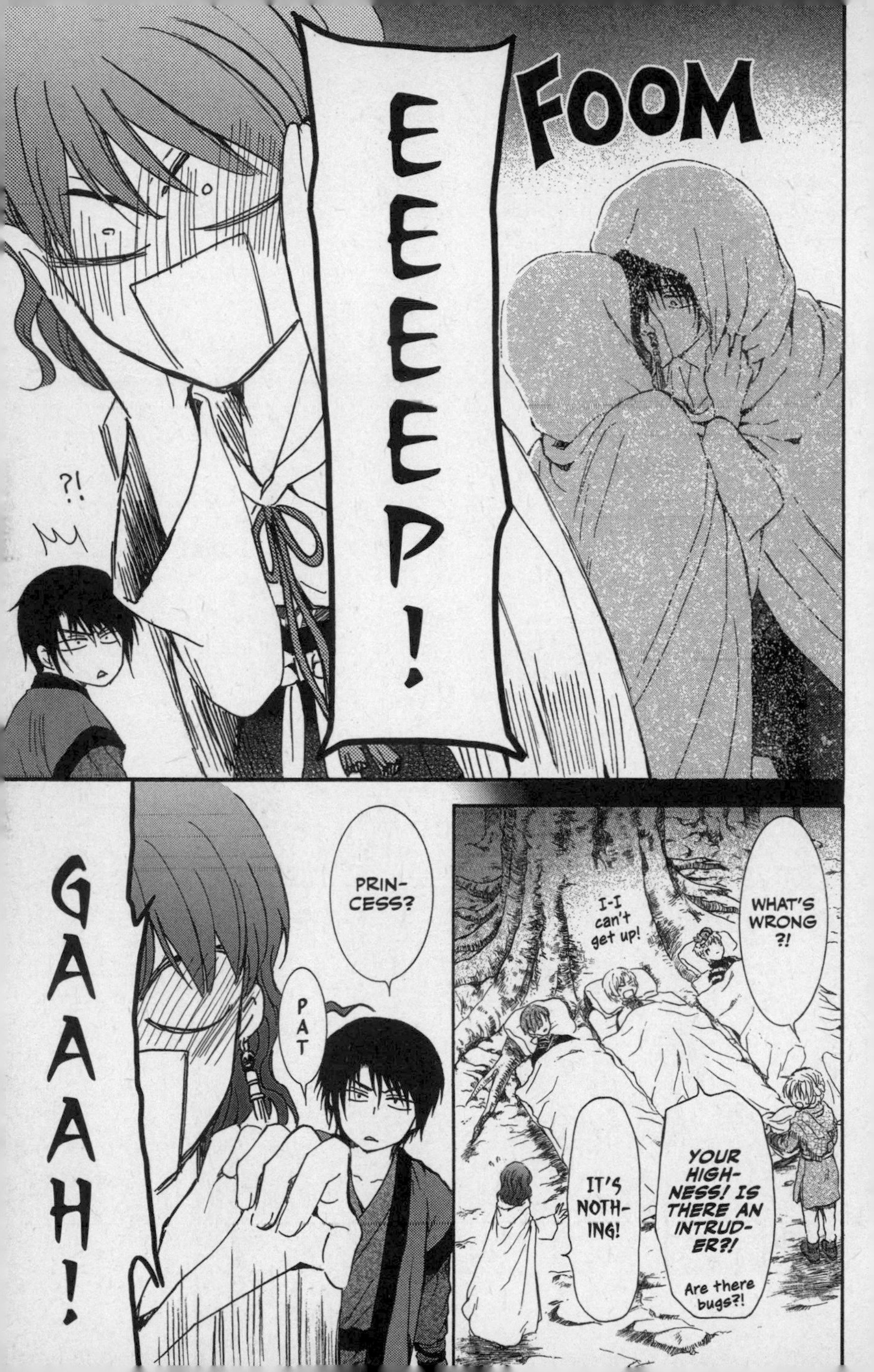
FOOM
EEEEP!
?!
WHAT'S WRONG ?!
I-I can't get up!
YOUR HIGH-NESS! IS THERE AN INTRUD-ER?!
Are there bugs?!
IT'S NOTH-ING!
PRIN-CESS?
PAT
GAAAH!

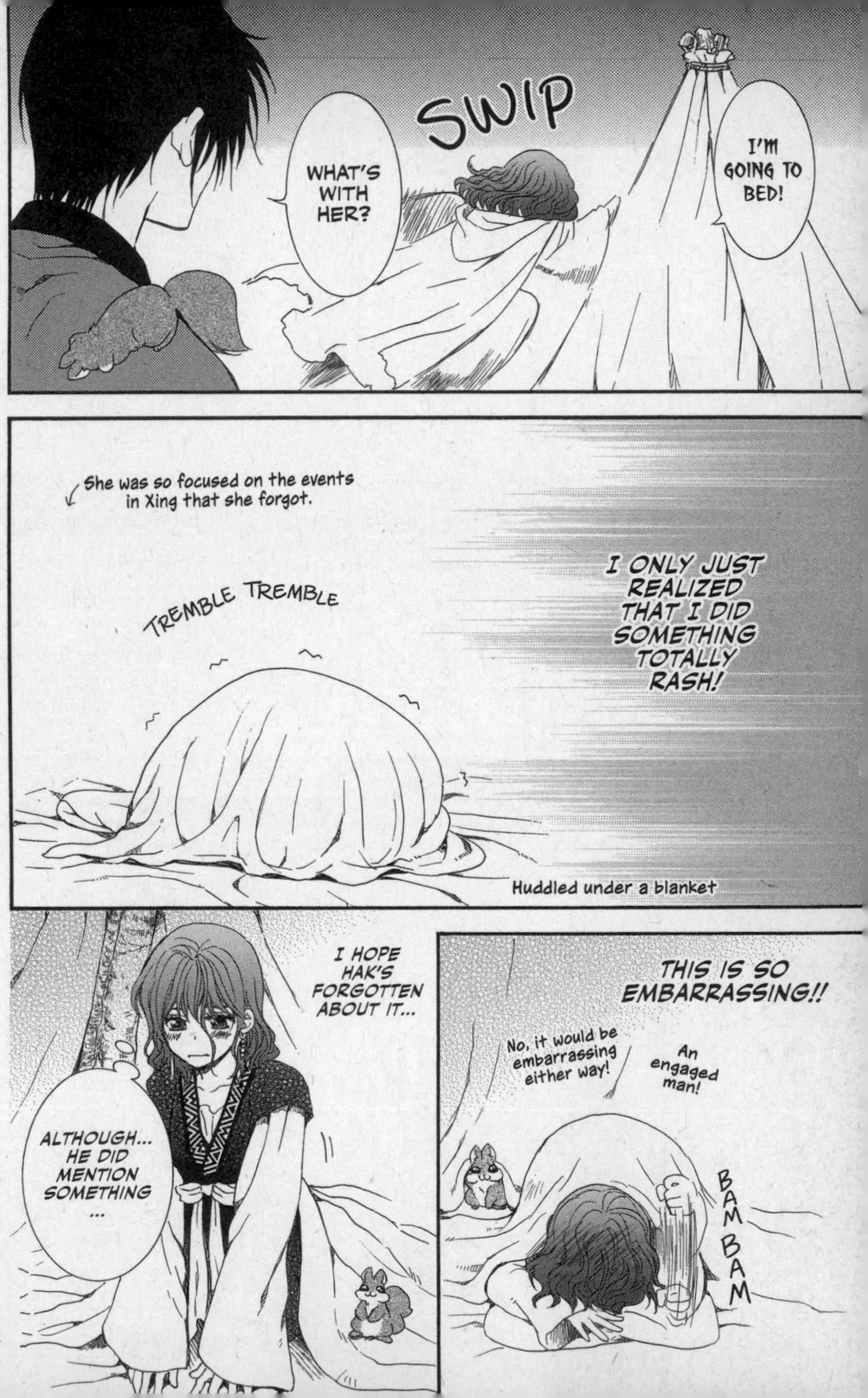
I'M GOING TO BED!
SWIP
WHAT'S WITH HER?
I ONLY JUST REALIZED THAT I DID SOMETHING TOTALLY RASH!
TREMBLE TREMBLE
She was so focused on the events in Xing that she forgot.
Huddled under a blanket
THIS IS SO EMBARRASSING!!
An engaged man!
No, it would be embarrassing either way!
BAM BAM
I HOPE HAK'S FORGOTTEN ABOUT IT...
ALTHOUGH... HE DID MENTION SOMETHING ...

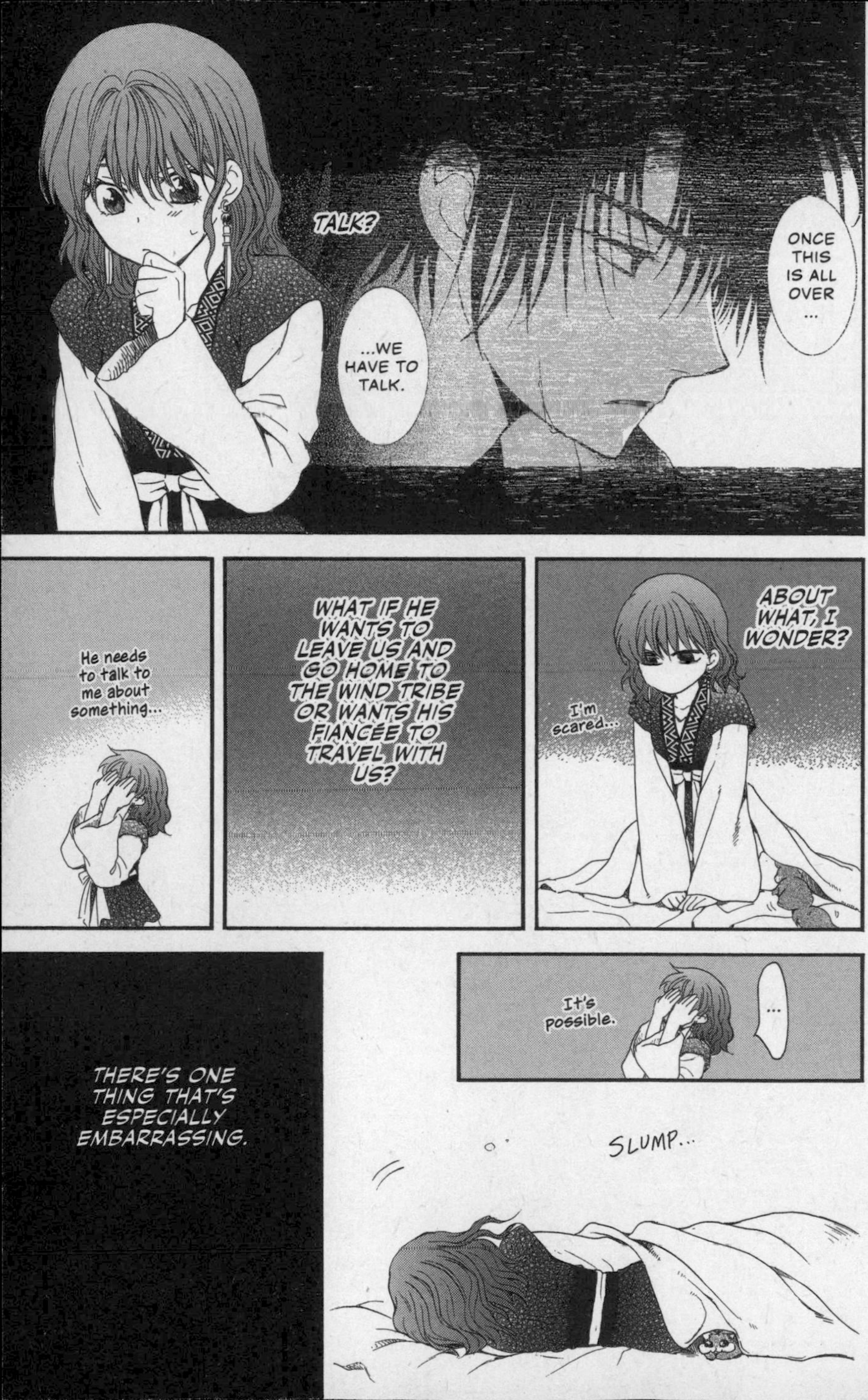
ONCE THIS IS ALL OVER ...
...WE HAVE TO TALK.
TALK?
ABOUT WHAT, I WONDER?
I'm scared...
WHAT IF HE WANTS TO LEAVE US AND GO HOME TO THE WIND TRIBE OR WANTS HIS FIANCÉE TO TRAVEL WITH US?
He needs to talk to me about something...
...
It's possible.
SLUMP...
THERE'S ONE THING THAT'S ESPECIALLY EMBARRASSING.

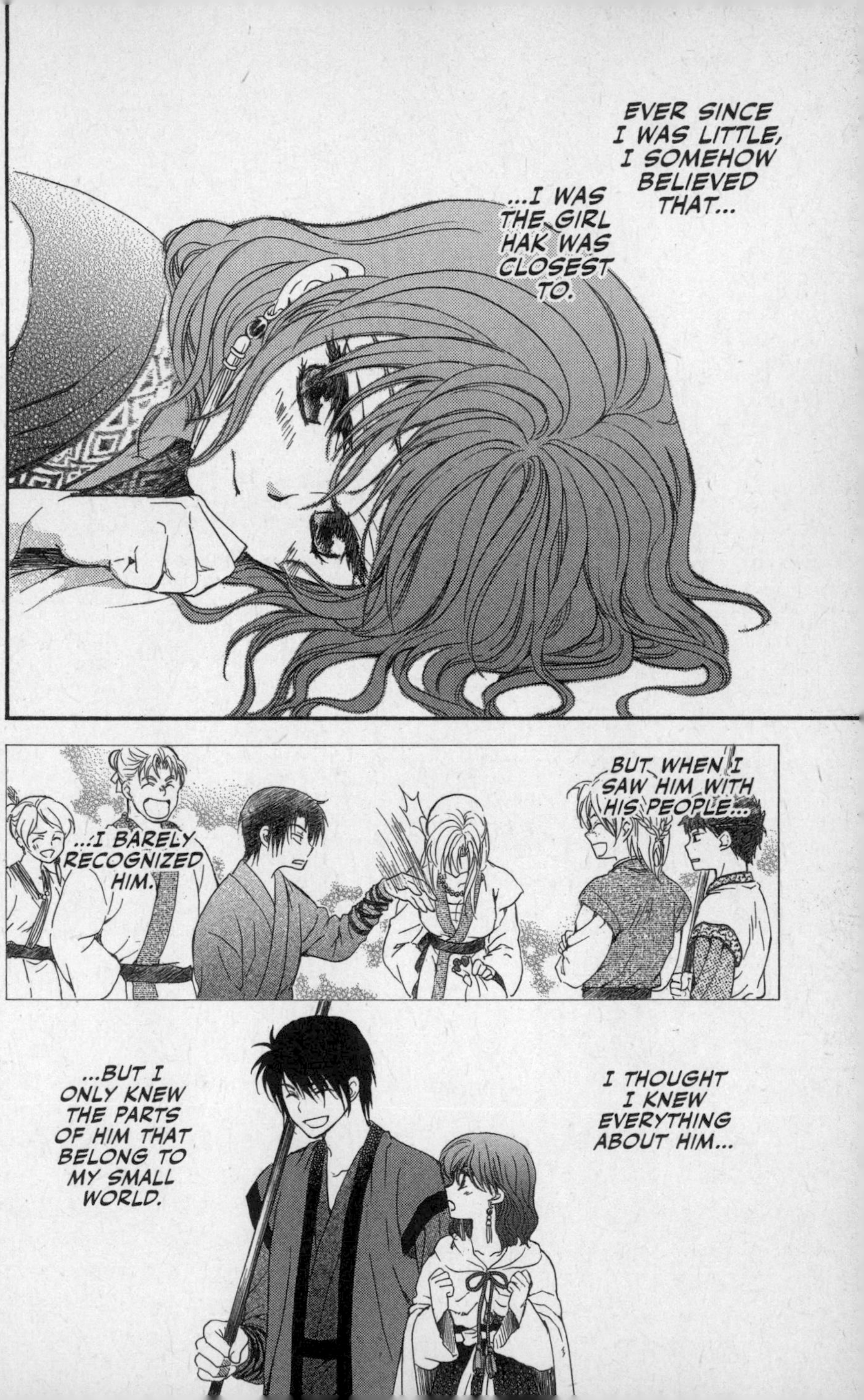
EVER SINCE I WAS LITTLE, I SOMEHOW BELIEVED THAT...
...I WAS THE GIRL HAK WAS CLOSEST TO.
BUT WHEN I SAW HIM WITH HIS PEOPLE...
...I BARELY RECOGNIZED HIM.
I THOUGHT I KNEW EVERYTHING ABOUT HIM...
...BUT I ONLY KNEW THE PARTS OF HIM THAT BELONG TO MY SMALL WORLD.

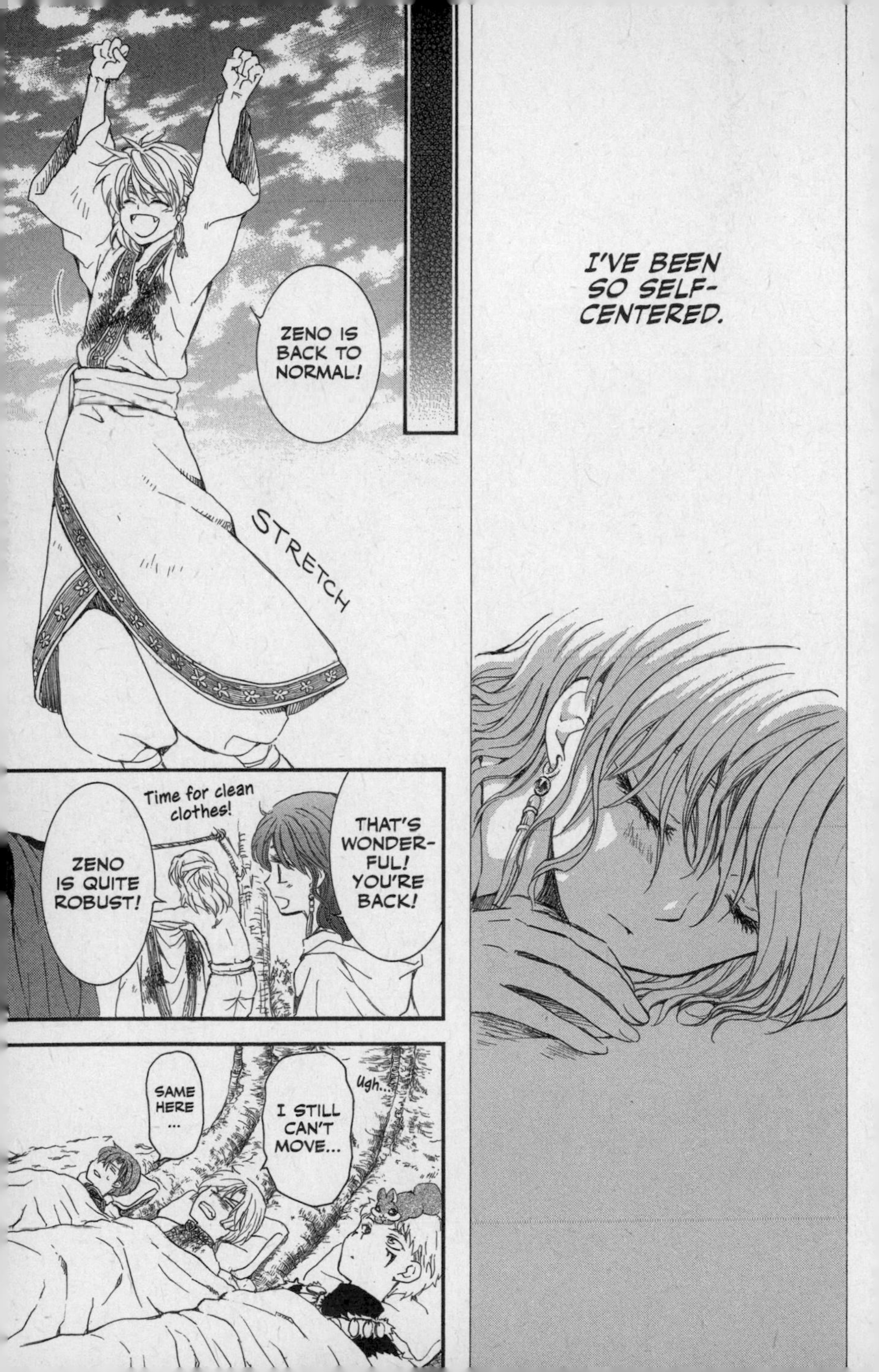
I'VE BEEN SO SELF-CENTERED.
ZENO IS BACK TO NORMAL!
STRETCH
THAT'S WONDERFUL! YOU'RE BACK!
Time for clean clothes!
ZENO IS QUITE ROBUST!
Ugh...
I STILL CAN'T MOVE...
SAME HERE ...

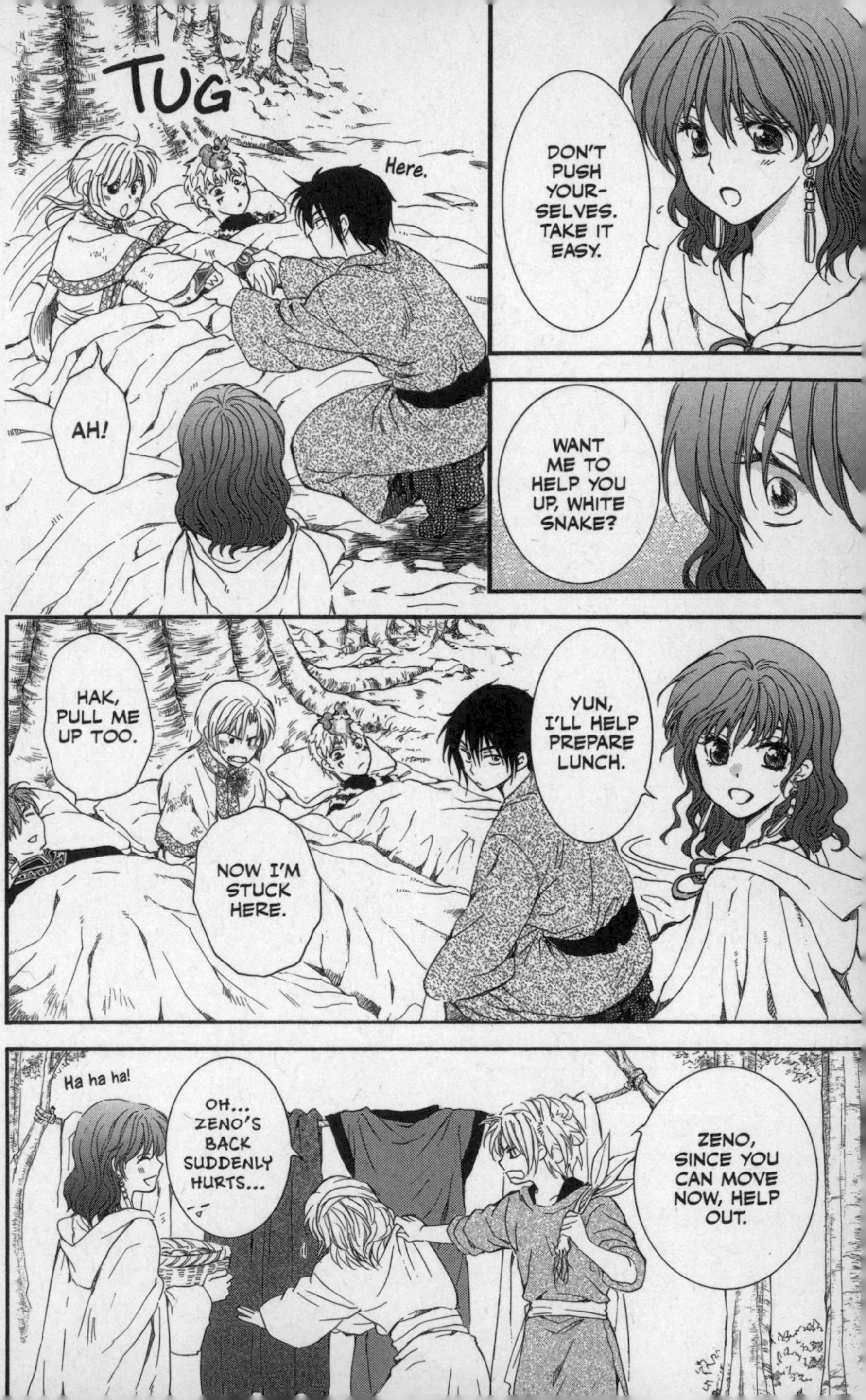
DON'T PUSH YOURSELVES. TAKE IT EASY.
TUG
Here.
WANT ME TO HELP YOU UP, WHITE SNAKE?
AH!
YUN, I'LL HELP PREPARE LUNCH.
HAK, PULL ME UP TOO.
NOW I'M STUCK HERE.
ZENO, SINCE YOU CAN MOVE NOW, HELP OUT.
OH... ZENO'S BACK SUDDENLY HURTS...
Ha ha ha!

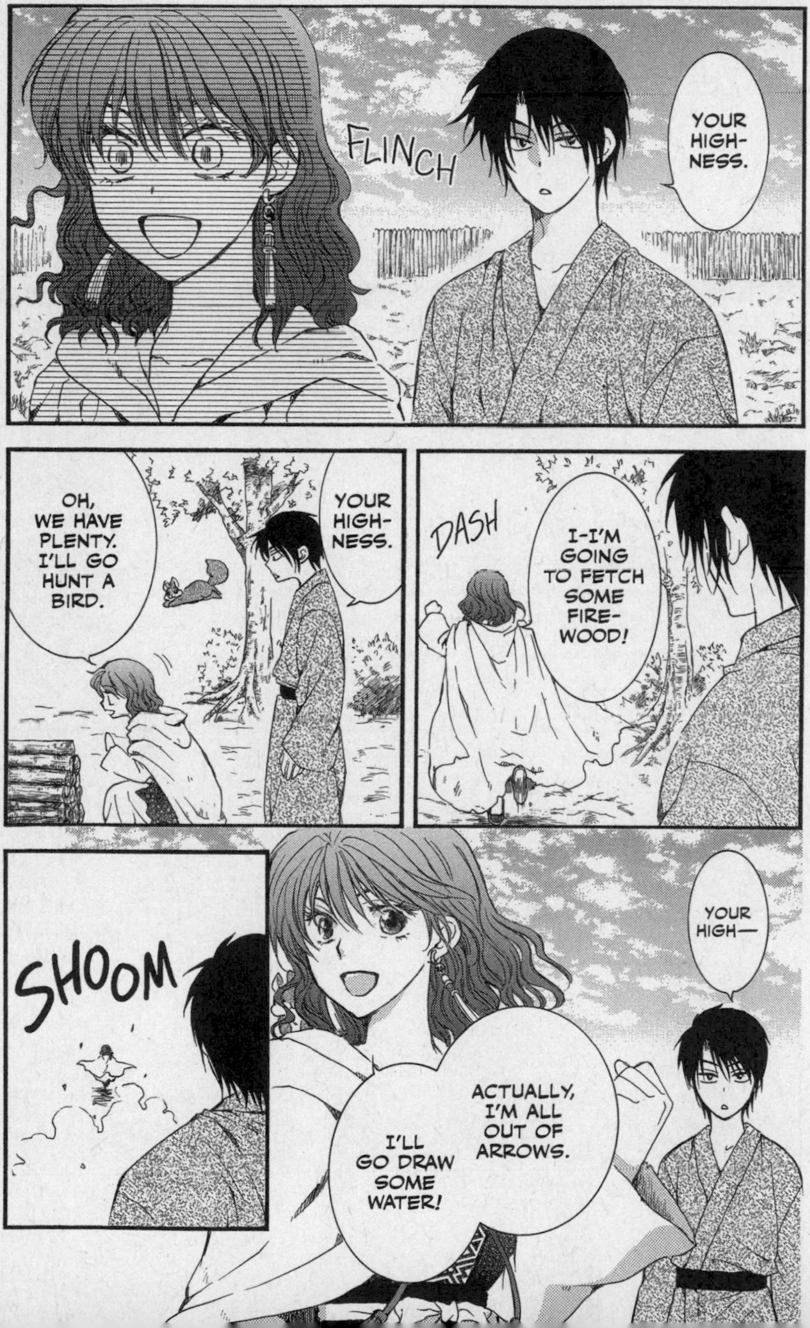
YOUR HIGH-NESS.
FLINCH
I-I'M GOING TO FETCH SOME FIRE-WOOD!
DASH
YOUR HIGH-NESS.
OH, WE HAVE PLENTY. I'LL GO HUNT A BIRD.
YOUR HIGH—
ACTUALLY, I'M ALL OUT OF ARROWS.
I'LL GO DRAW SOME WATER!
SHOOM

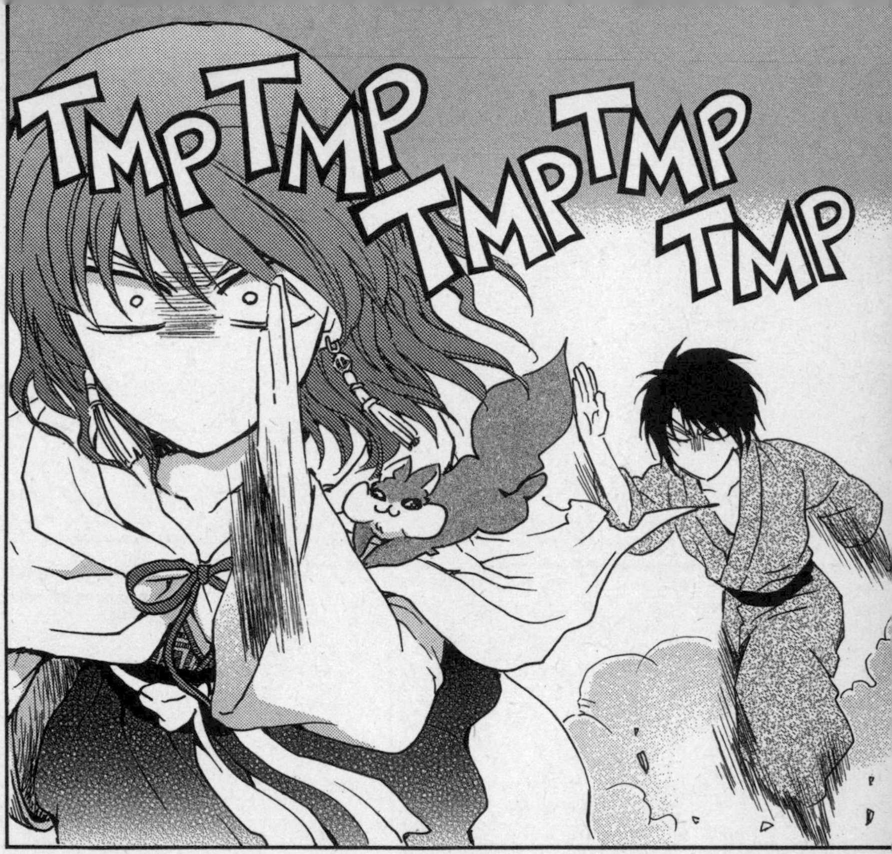
TMP TMP
TMP TMP
TMP
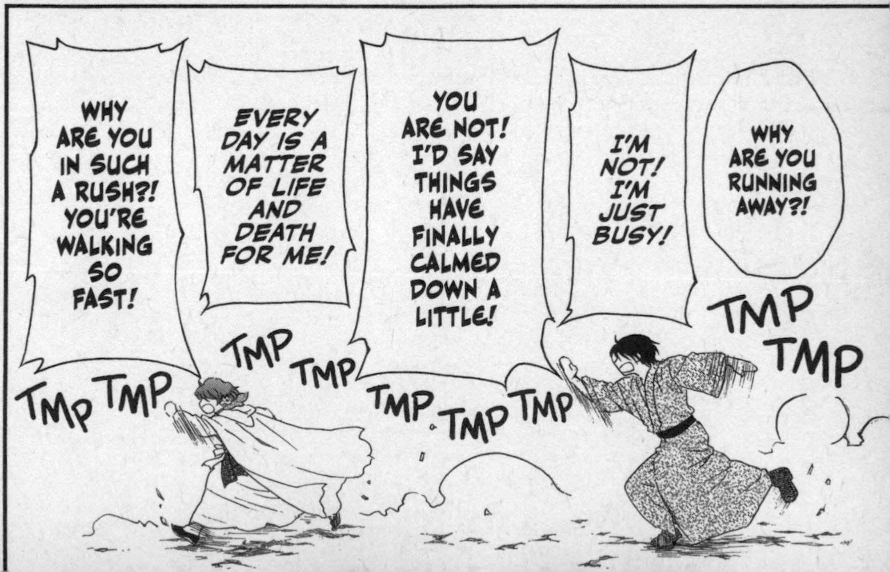
WHY ARE YOU IN SUCH A RUSH?! YOU'RE WALKING SO FAST!
EVERY DAY IS A MATTER OF LIFE AND DEATH FOR ME!
YOU ARE NOT! I'D SAY THINGS HAVE FINALLY CALMED DOWN A LITTLE!
I'M NOT! I'M JUST BUSY!
WHY ARE YOU RUNNING AWAY?!
TMP TMP
TMP TMP
TMP TMP TMP TMP
TMP TMP

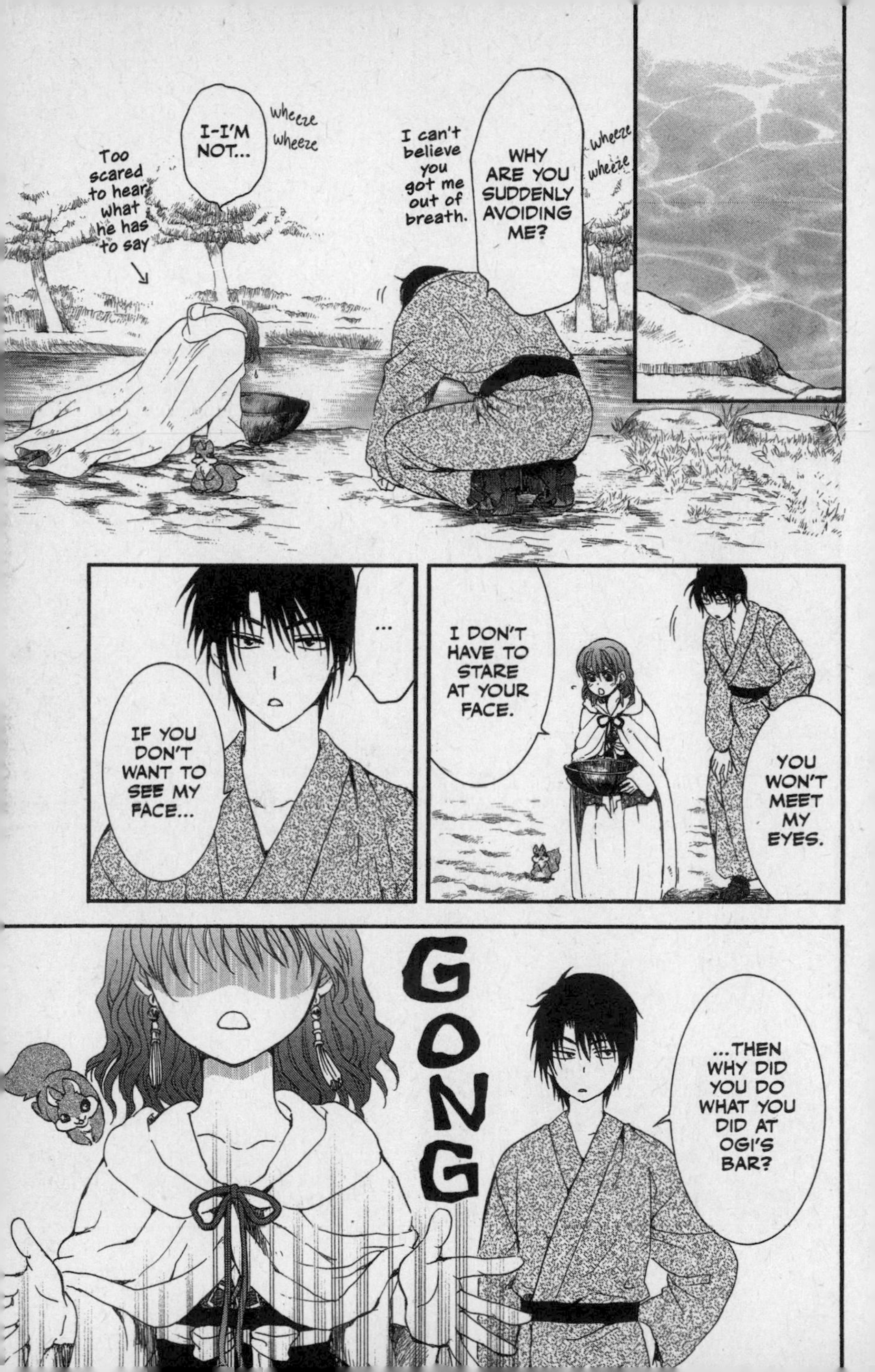
wheeze
wheeze
WHY ARE YOU SUDDENLY AVOIDING ME?
I can't believe you got me out of breath.
wheeze
wheeze
I-I'M NOT...
Too scared to hear what he has to say
YOU WON'T MEET MY EYES.
I DON'T HAVE TO STARE AT YOUR FACE.
...
IF YOU DON'T WANT TO SEE MY FACE...
...THEN WHY DID YOU DO WHAT YOU DID AT OGI'S BAR?
GONG

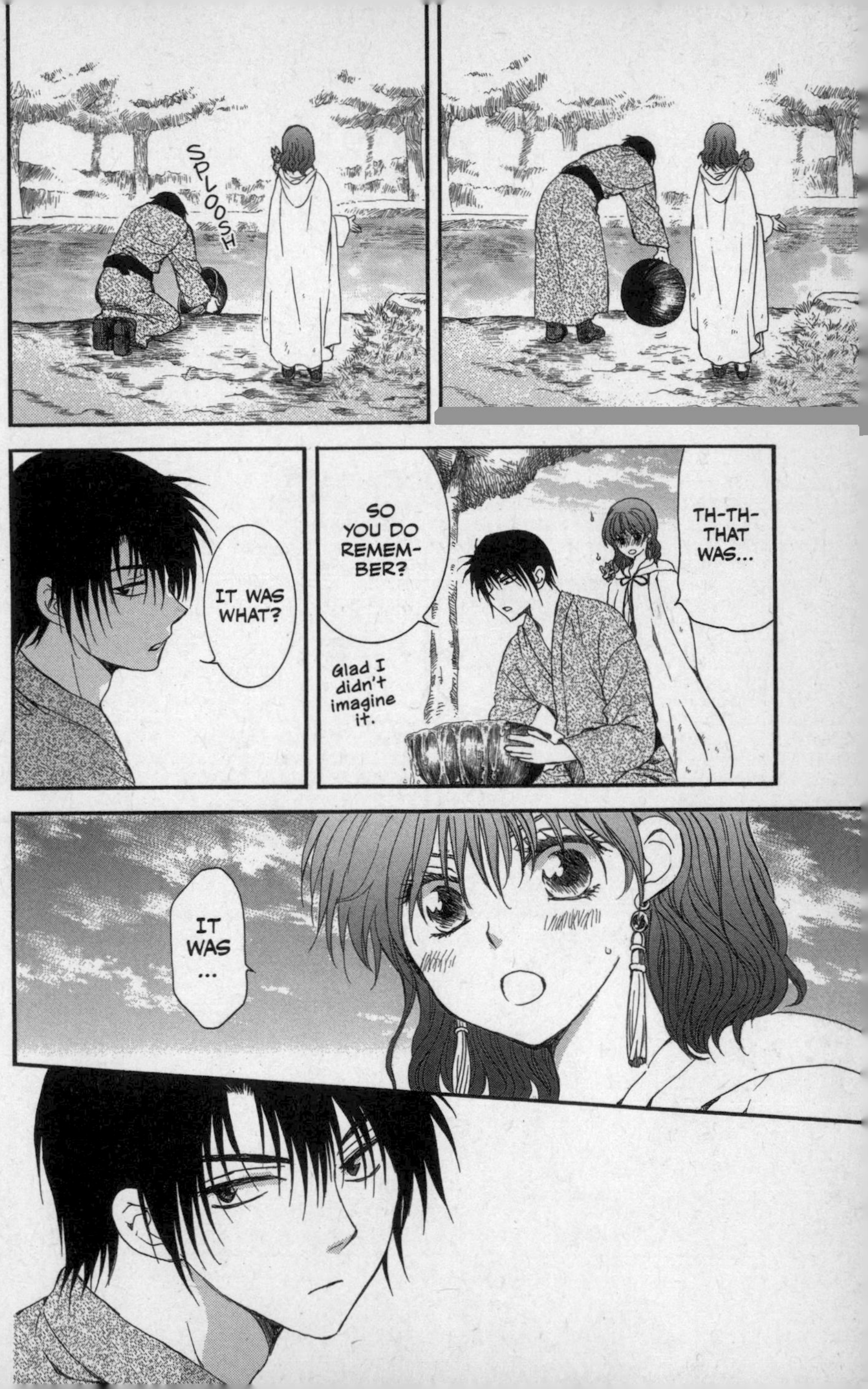
SPLOOSH
TH-TH-THAT WAS...
SO YOU DO REMEMBER?
Glad I didn't imagine it.
IT WAS WHAT?
IT WAS ...

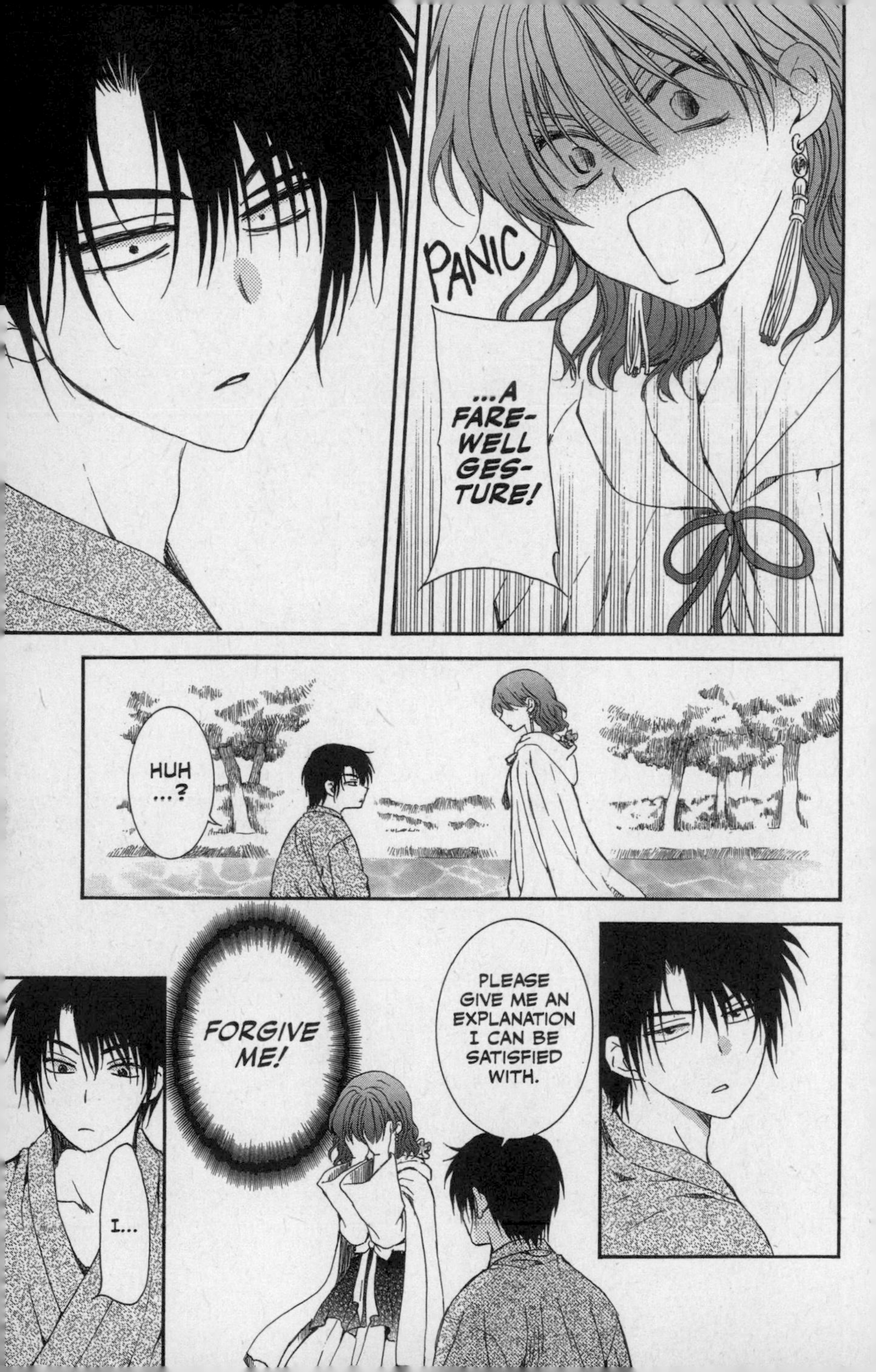
PANIC
...A FARE-WELL GES-TURE!
HUH ...?
PLEASE GIVE ME AN EXPLANATION I CAN BE SATISFIED WITH.
FORGIVE ME!
I...

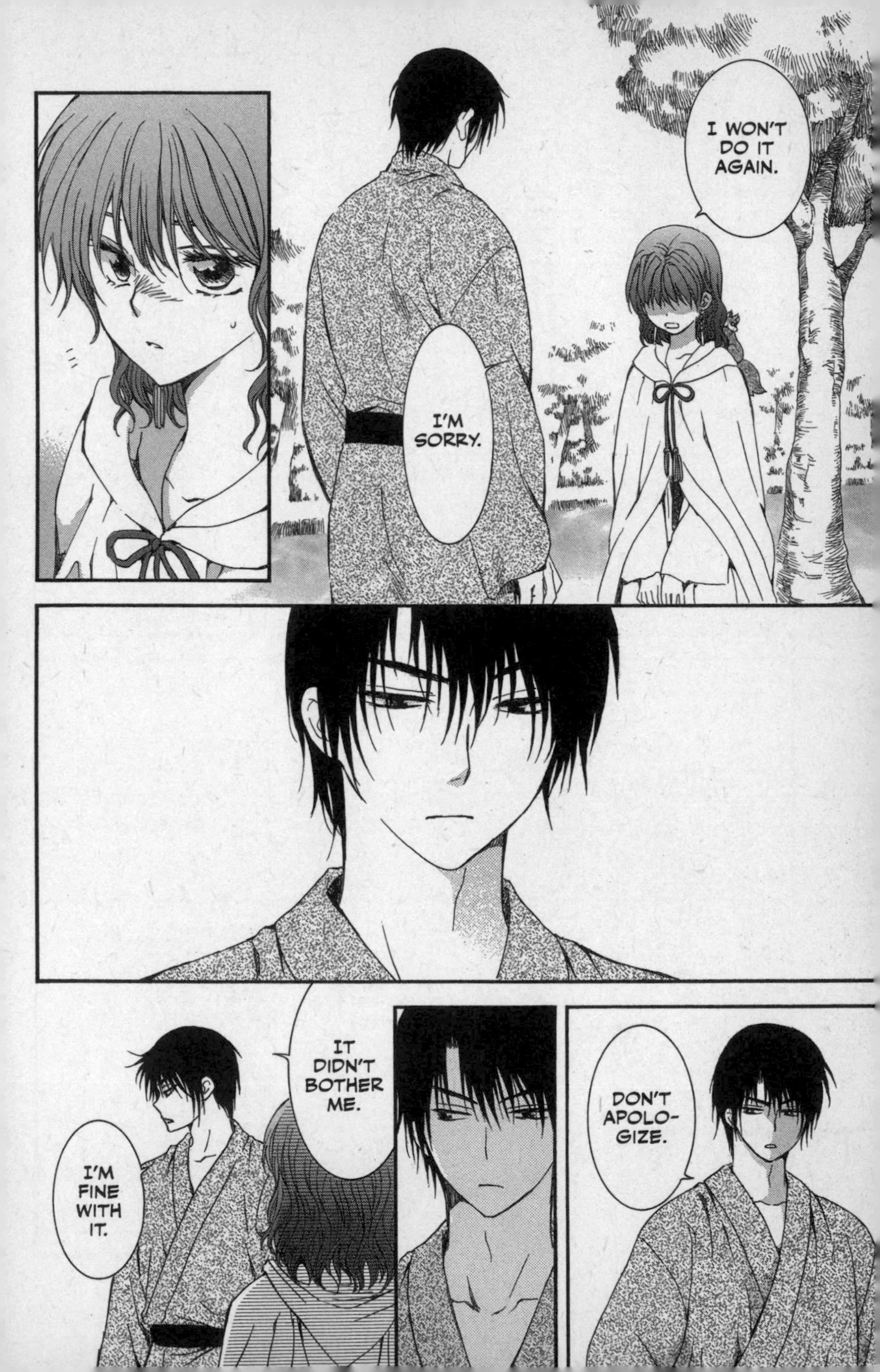
I WON'T DO IT AGAIN.
I'M SORRY.
DON'T APOLOGIZE.
IT DIDN'T BOTHER ME.
I'M FINE WITH IT.

R-RIGHT. IT'S NOT ONLY ABOUT ME. I NEED TO FIND OUT WHAT HE WANTED TO TALK ABOUT.
I HAVE TO ACCEPT WHATEVER HE SAYS.
HAK, UM...
YOU WANTED TO TALK TO ME?
DID I?
YOU KNOW, WHEN WE WERE ESCAPING THE ASSASSINS IN XING...
OH.
THAT.

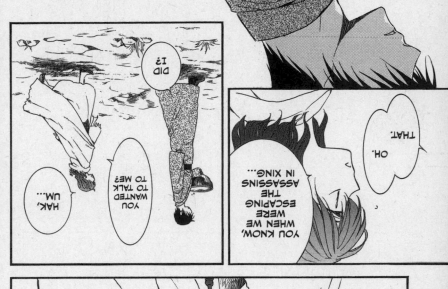

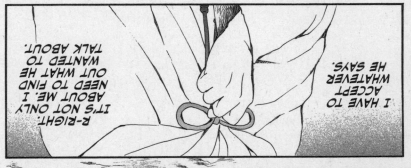

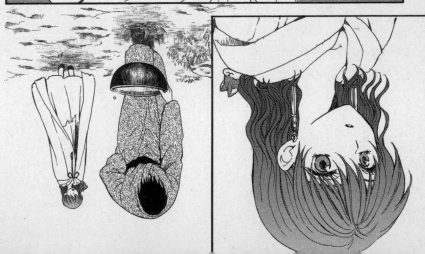

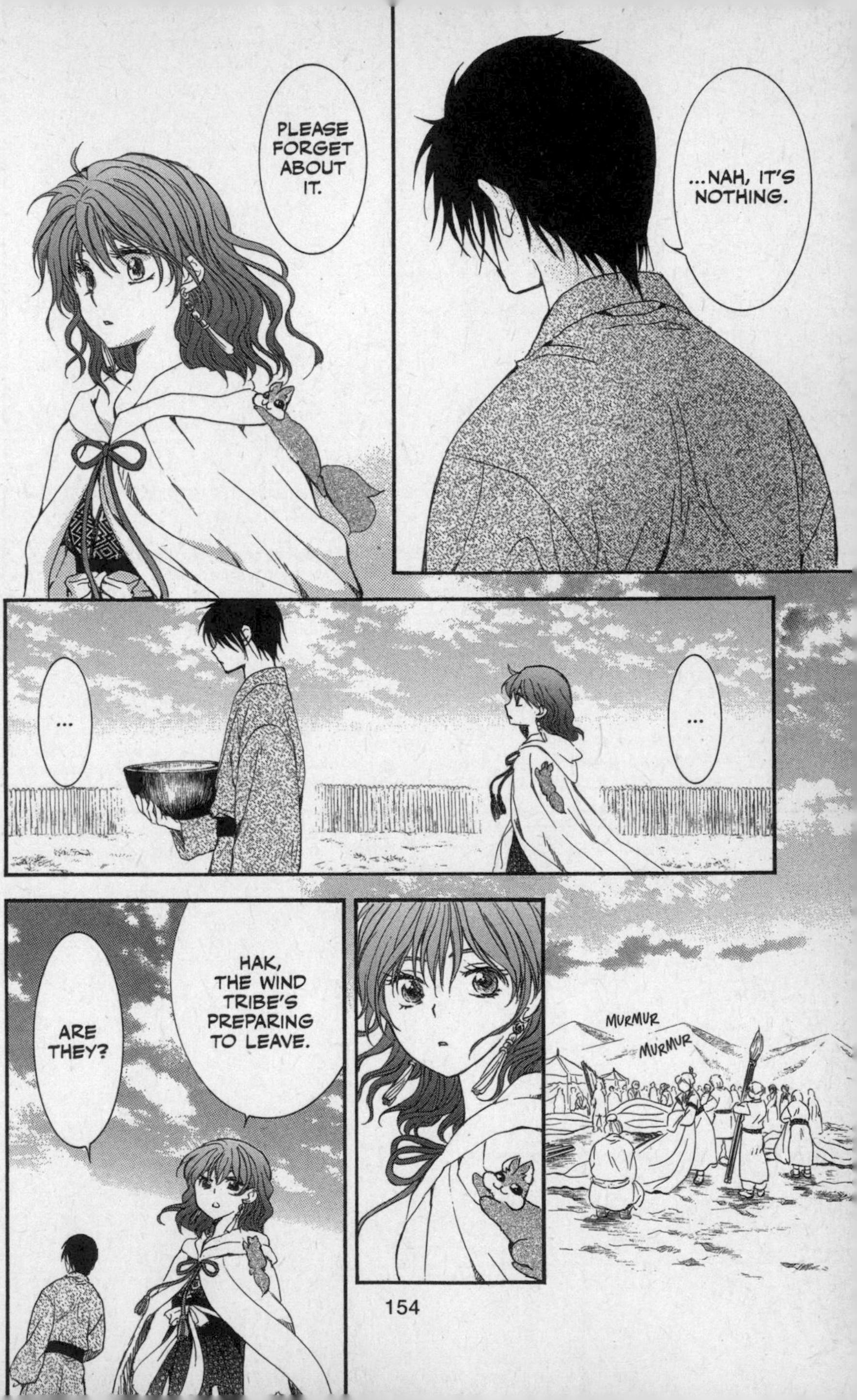
...NAH, IT'S NOTHING.
PLEASE FORGET ABOUT IT.
...
...
MURMUR
MURMUR
HAK, THE WIND TRIBE'S PREPARING TO LEAVE.
ARE THEY?

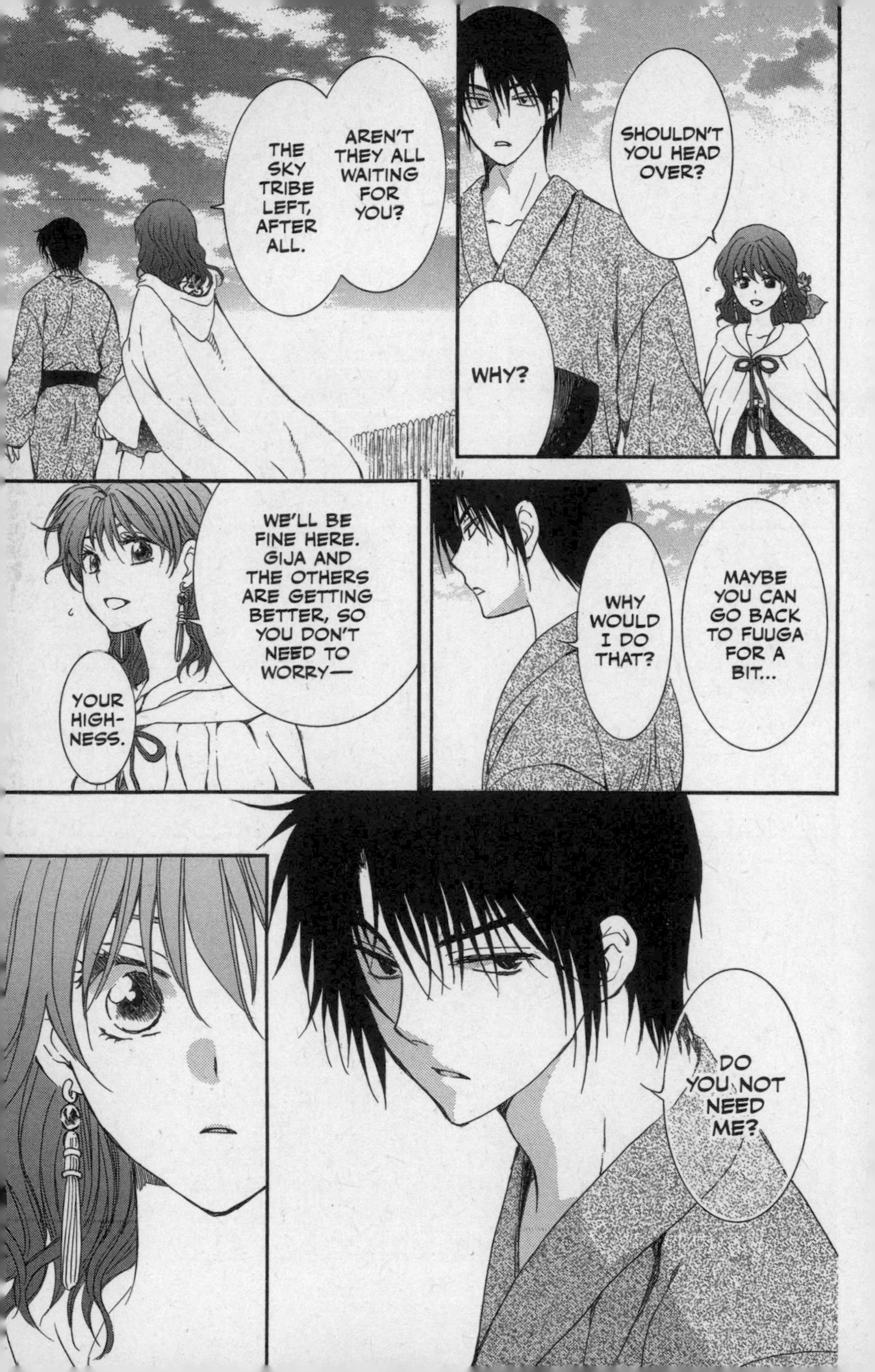
SHOULDN'T YOU HEAD OVER?
WHY?
AREN'T THEY ALL WAITING FOR YOU?
THE SKY TRIBE LEFT, AFTER ALL.
MAYBE YOU CAN GO BACK TO FUUGA FOR A BIT...
WHY WOULD I DO THAT?
WE'LL BE FINE HERE. GIJA AND THE OTHERS ARE GETTING BETTER, SO YOU DON'T NEED TO WORRY—
YOUR HIGH-NESS.
DO YOU NOT NEED ME?

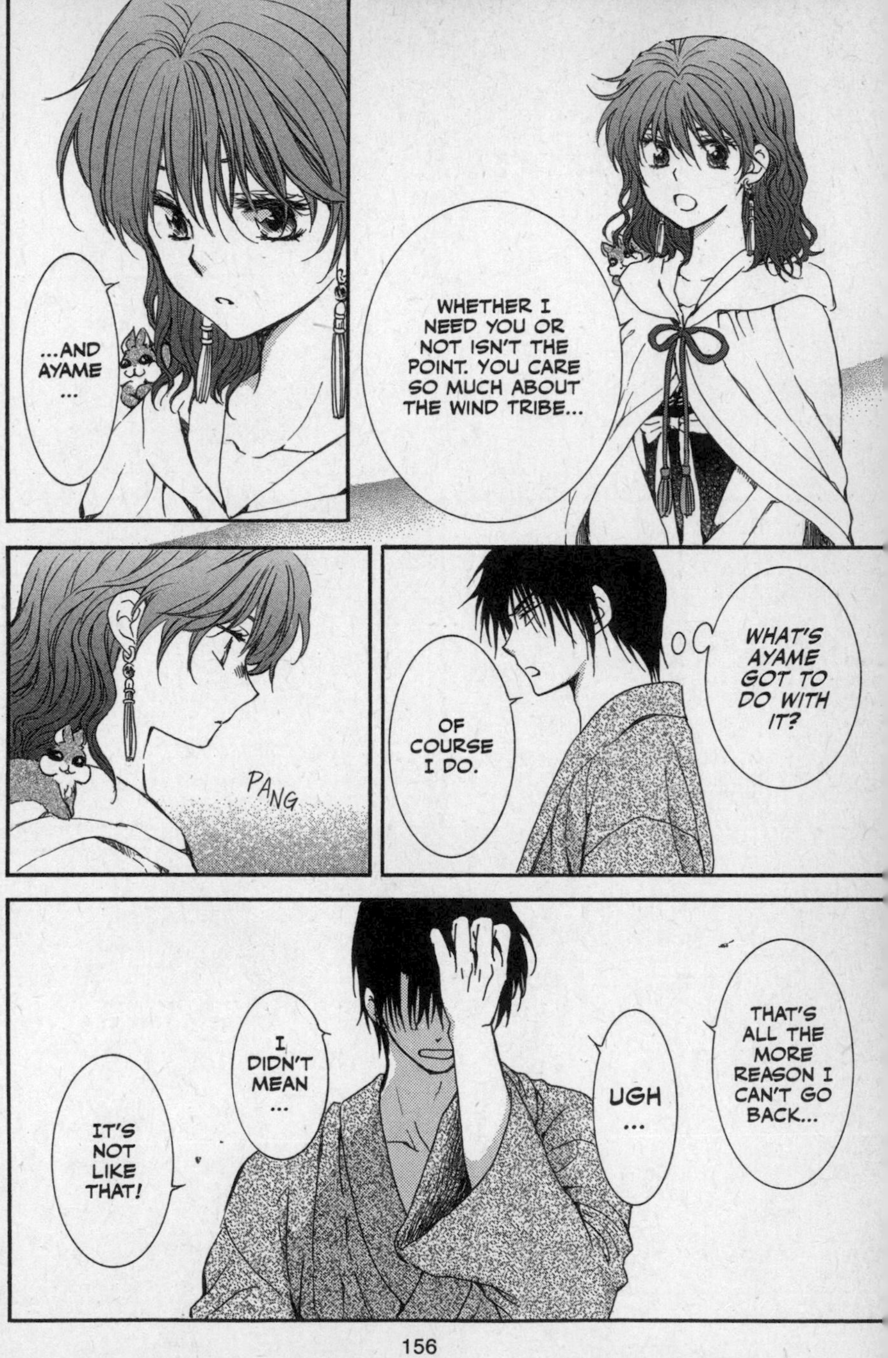
WHETHER I NEED YOU OR NOT ISN'T THE POINT. YOU CARE SO MUCH ABOUT THE WIND TRIBE...
...AND AYAME ...
WHAT'S AYAME GOT TO DO WITH IT?
OF COURSE I DO.
PANG
THAT'S ALL THE MORE REASON I CAN'T GO BACK...
UGH ...
I DIDN'T MEAN ...
IT'S NOT LIKE THAT!

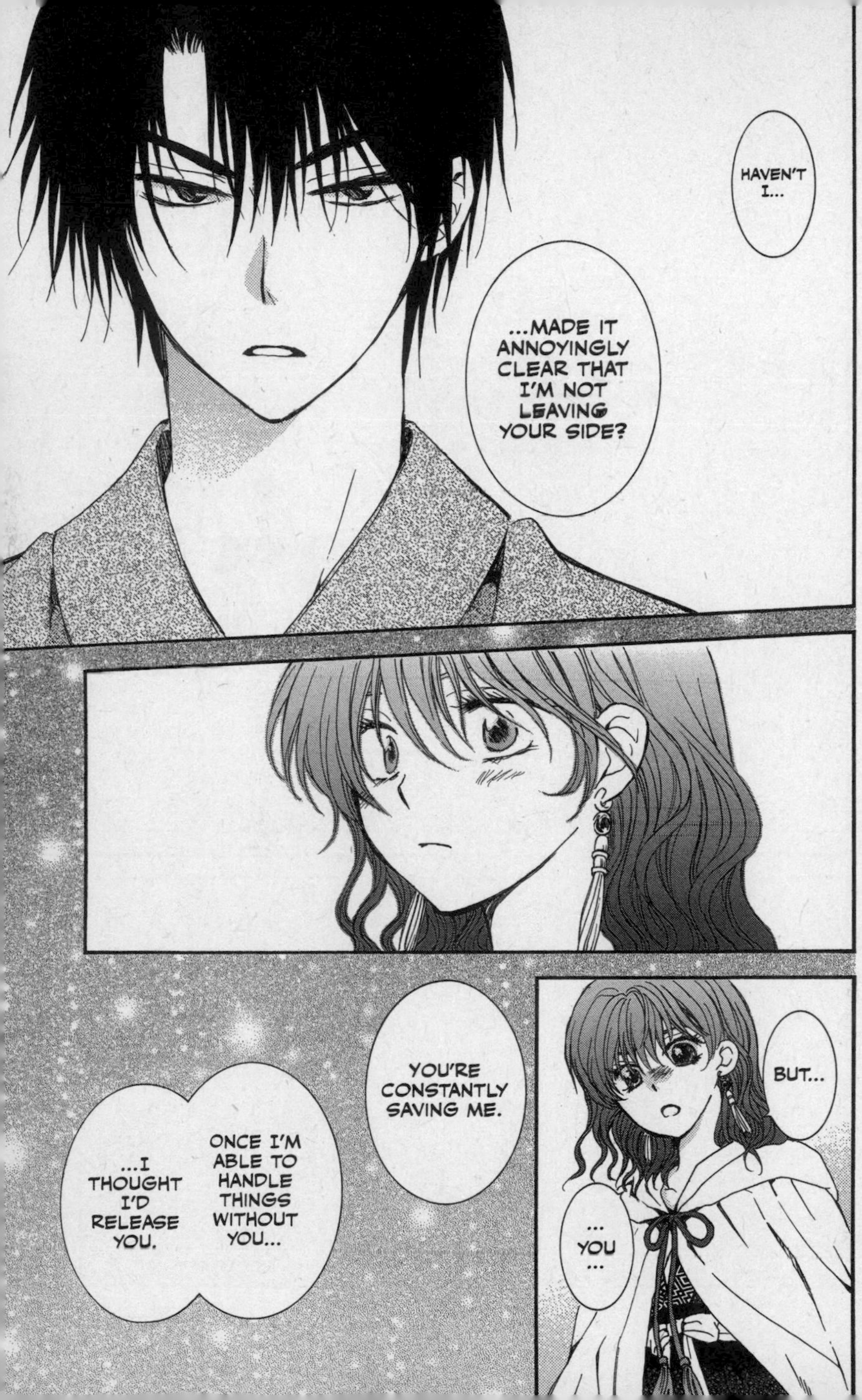
HAVEN'T I...
...MADE IT ANNOYINGLY CLEAR THAT I'M NOT LEAVING YOUR SIDE?
BUT...
...YOU...
YOU'RE CONSTANTLY SAVING ME.
ONCE I'M ABLE TO HANDLE THINGS WITHOUT YOU...
...I THOUGHT I'D RELEASE YOU.

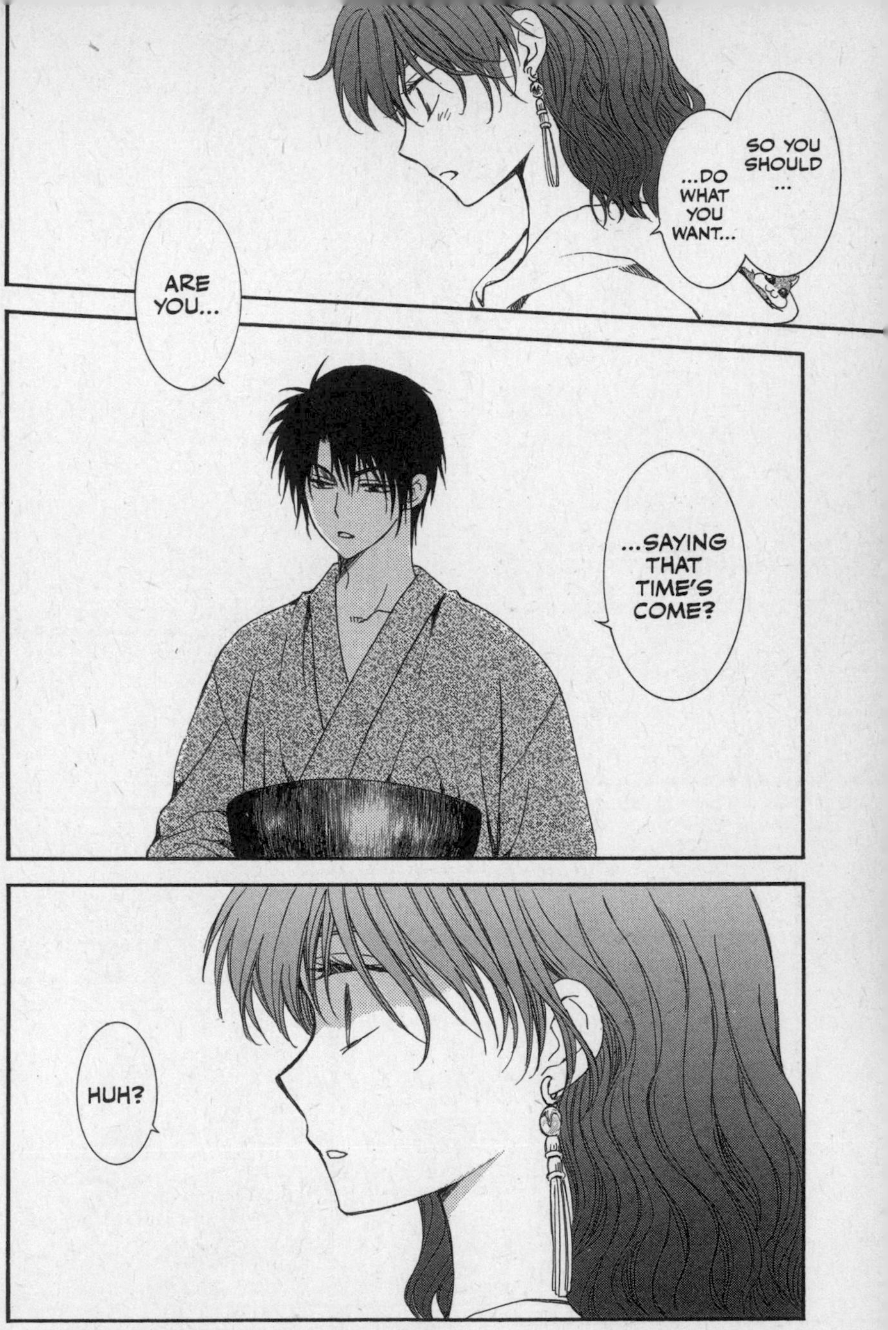
SO YOU SHOULD ...
...DO WHAT YOU WANT...
ARE YOU...
...SAYING THAT TIME'S COME?
HUH?

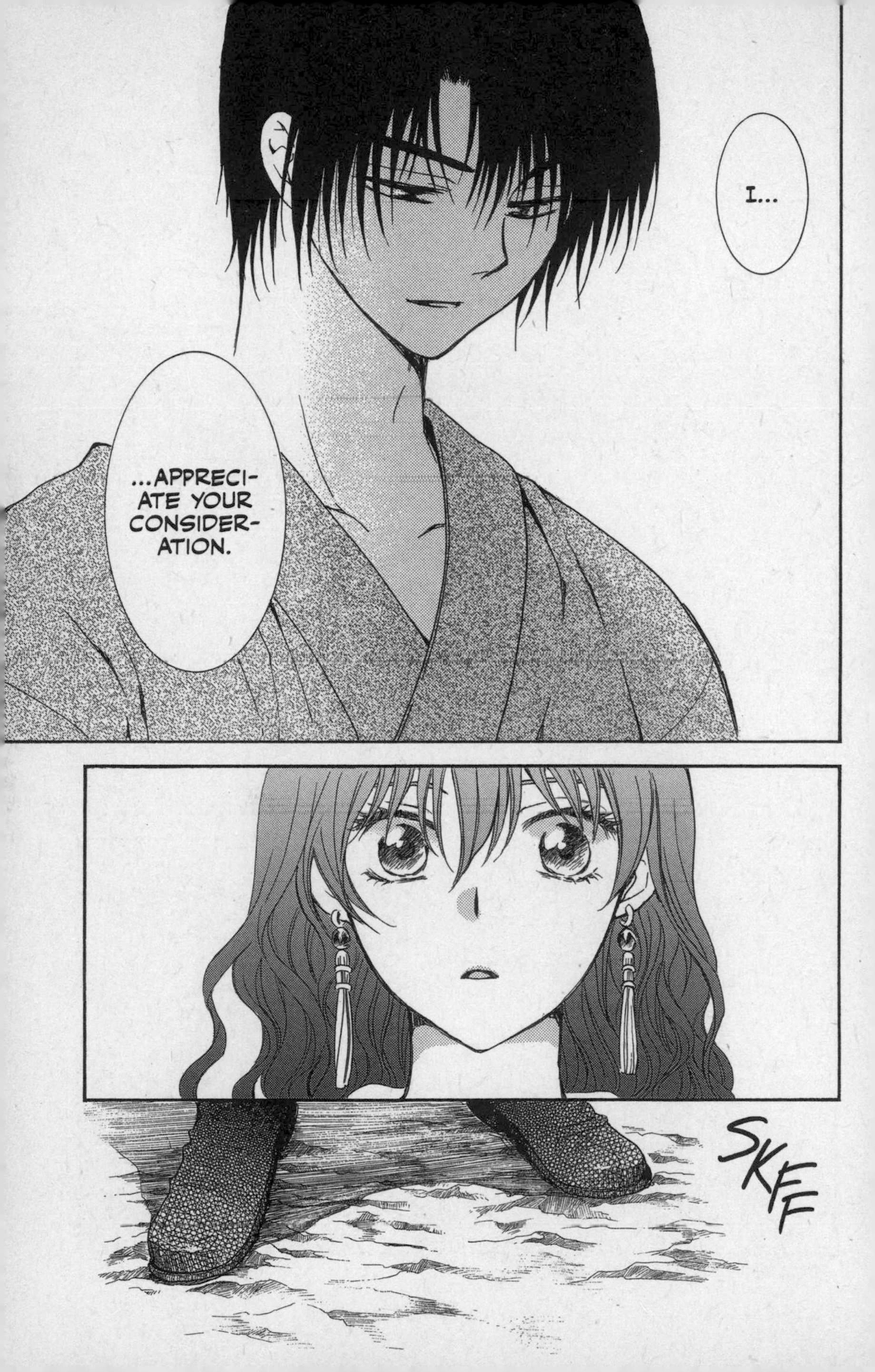
I...
...APPRECI-ATE YOUR CONSIDER-ATION.
SKFF

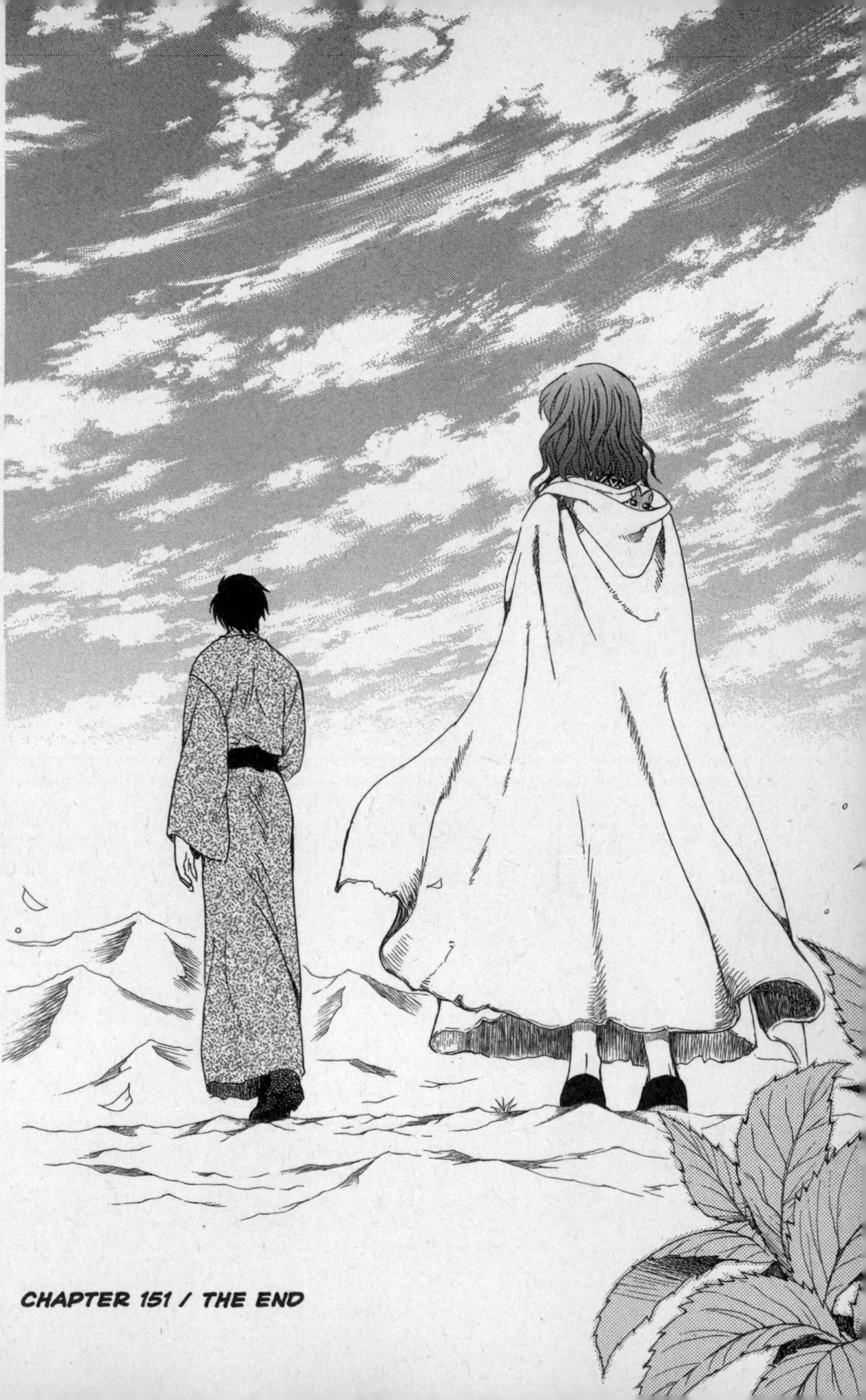
CHAPTER 151 / THE END

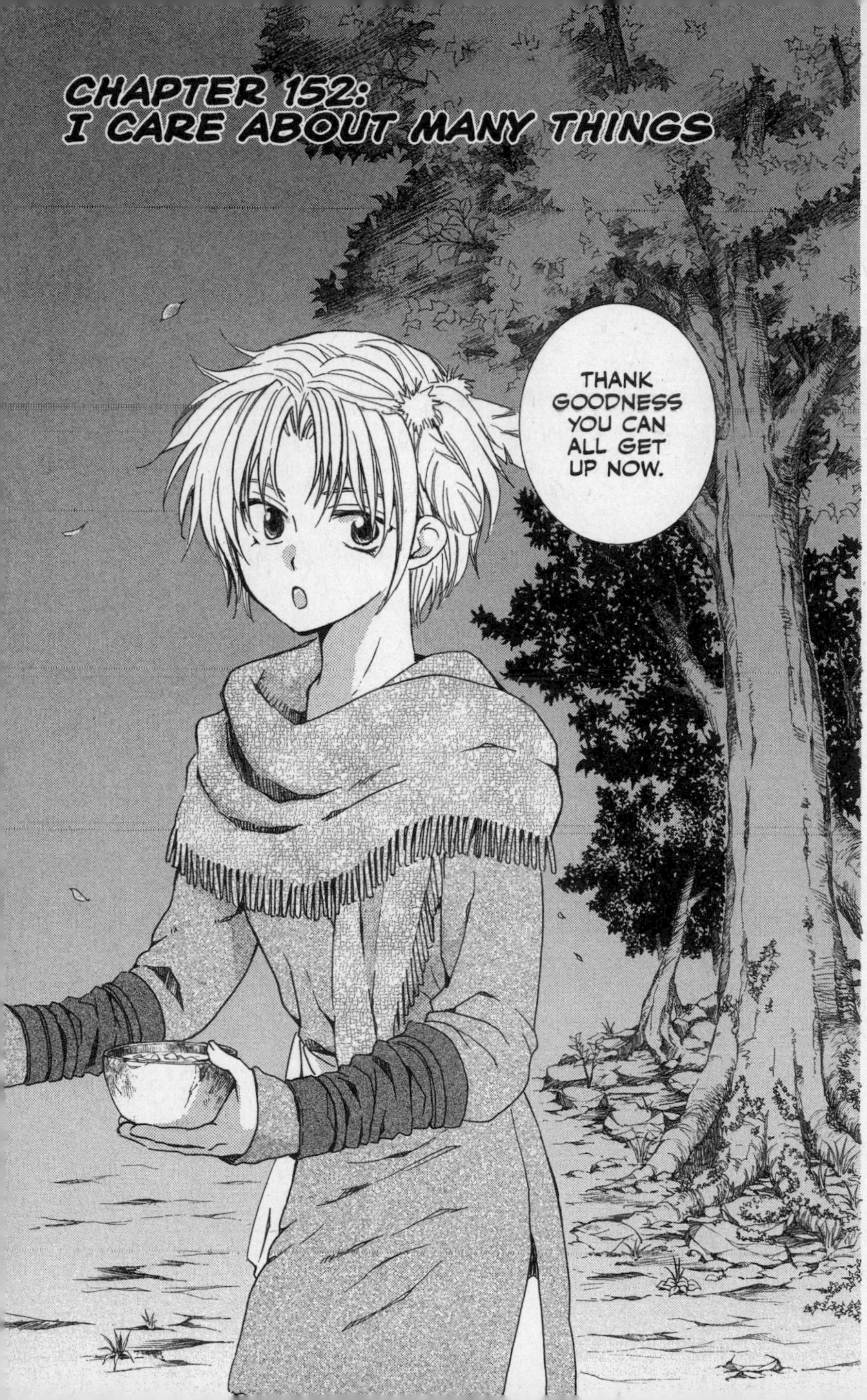
CHAPTER 152:
I CARE ABOUT MANY THINGS
THANK GOODNESS YOU CAN ALL GET UP NOW.

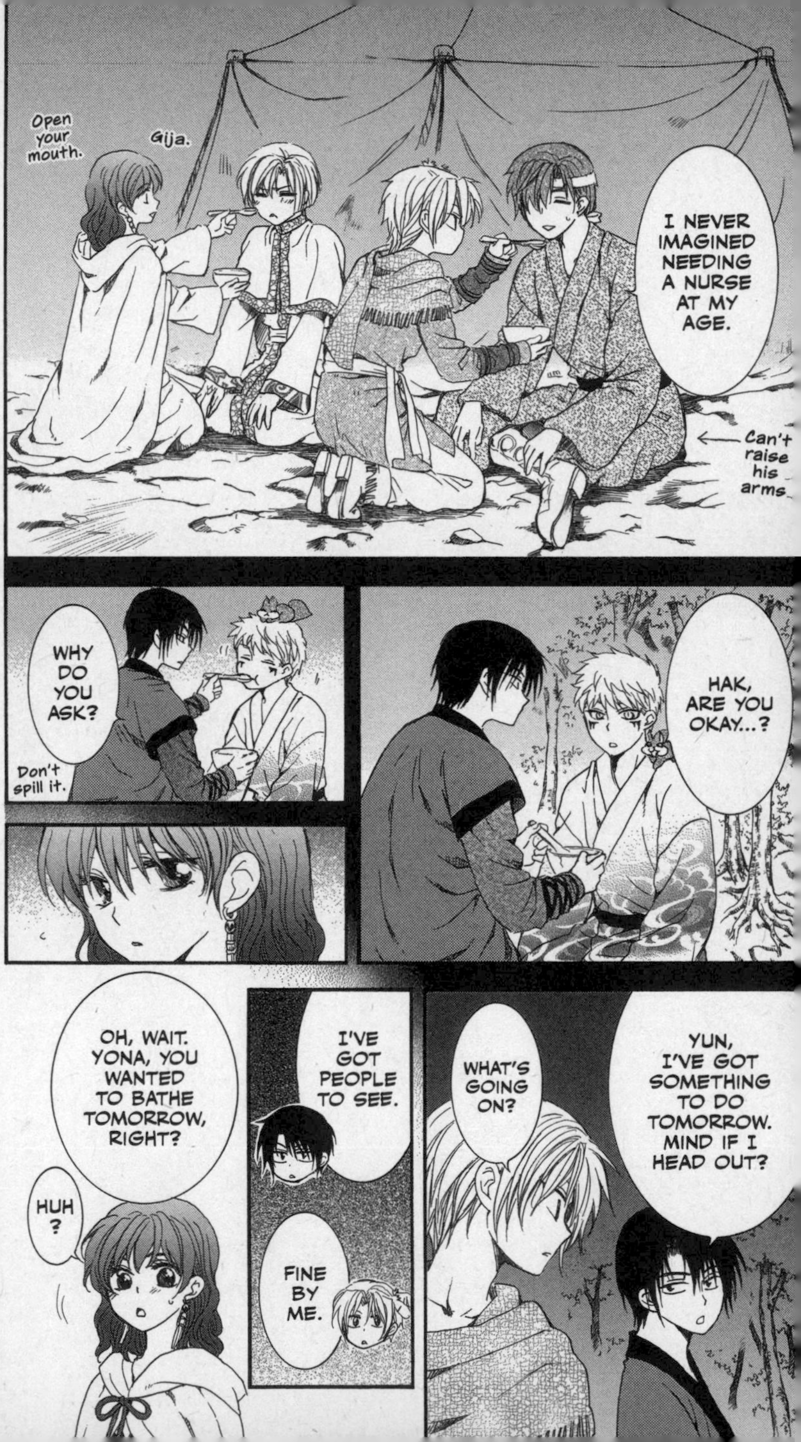
I NEVER IMAGINED NEEDING A NURSE AT MY AGE.
Can't raise his arms
Gija.
Open your mouth.
HAK, ARE YOU OKAY...?
WHY DO YOU ASK?
Don't spill it.
YUN, I'VE GOT SOMETHING TO DO TOMORROW. MIND IF I HEAD OUT?
WHAT'S GOING ON?
I'VE GOT PEOPLE TO SEE.
FINE BY ME.
OH, WAIT. YONA, YOU WANTED TO BATHE TOMORROW, RIGHT?
HUH?

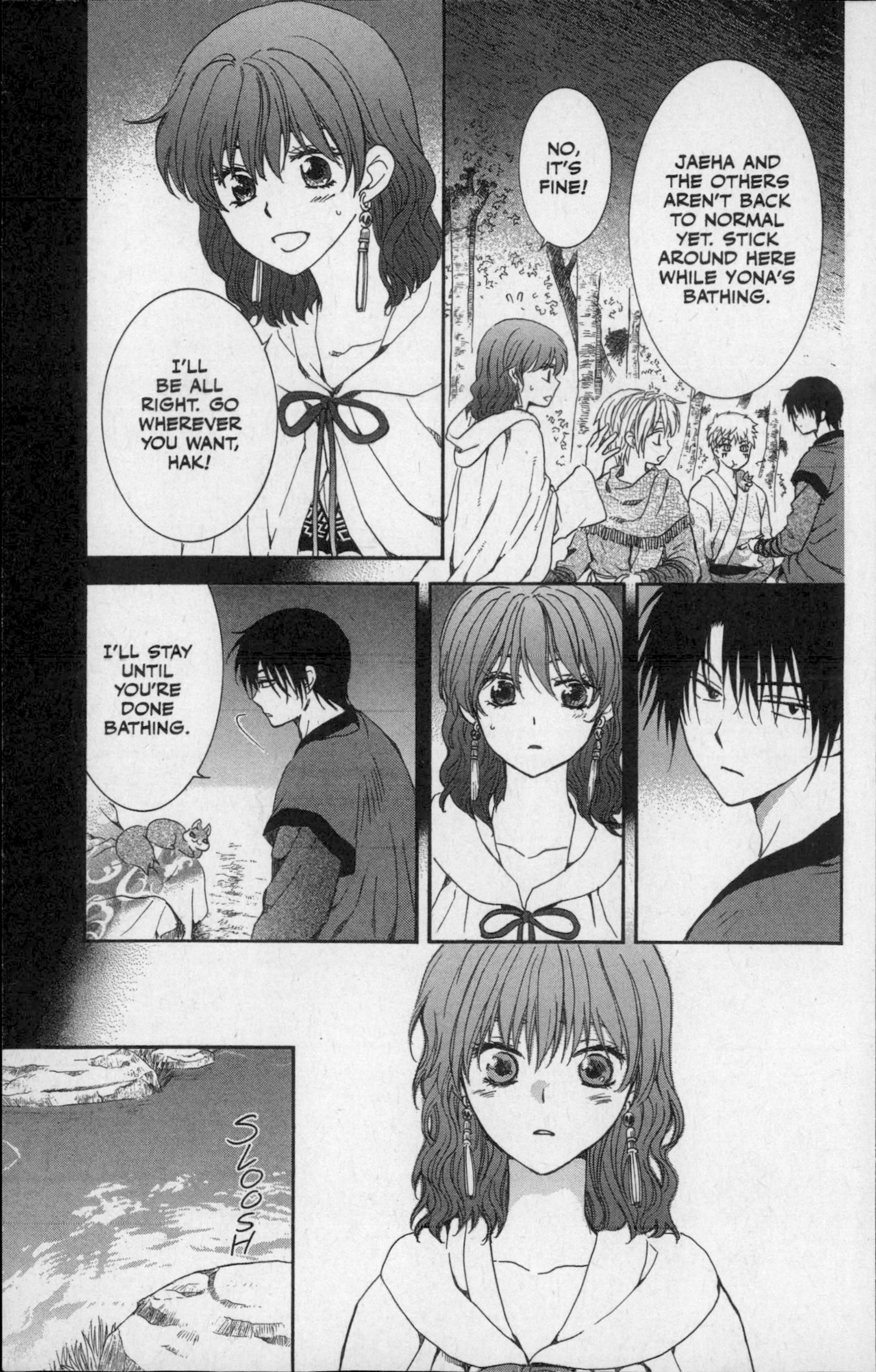
JAEHA AND THE OTHERS AREN'T BACK TO NORMAL YET. STICK AROUND HERE WHILE YONA'S BATHING.
NO, IT'S FINE!
I'LL BE ALL RIGHT. GO WHEREVER YOU WANT, HAK!
I'LL STAY UNTIL YOU'RE DONE BATHING.
SLOOSH

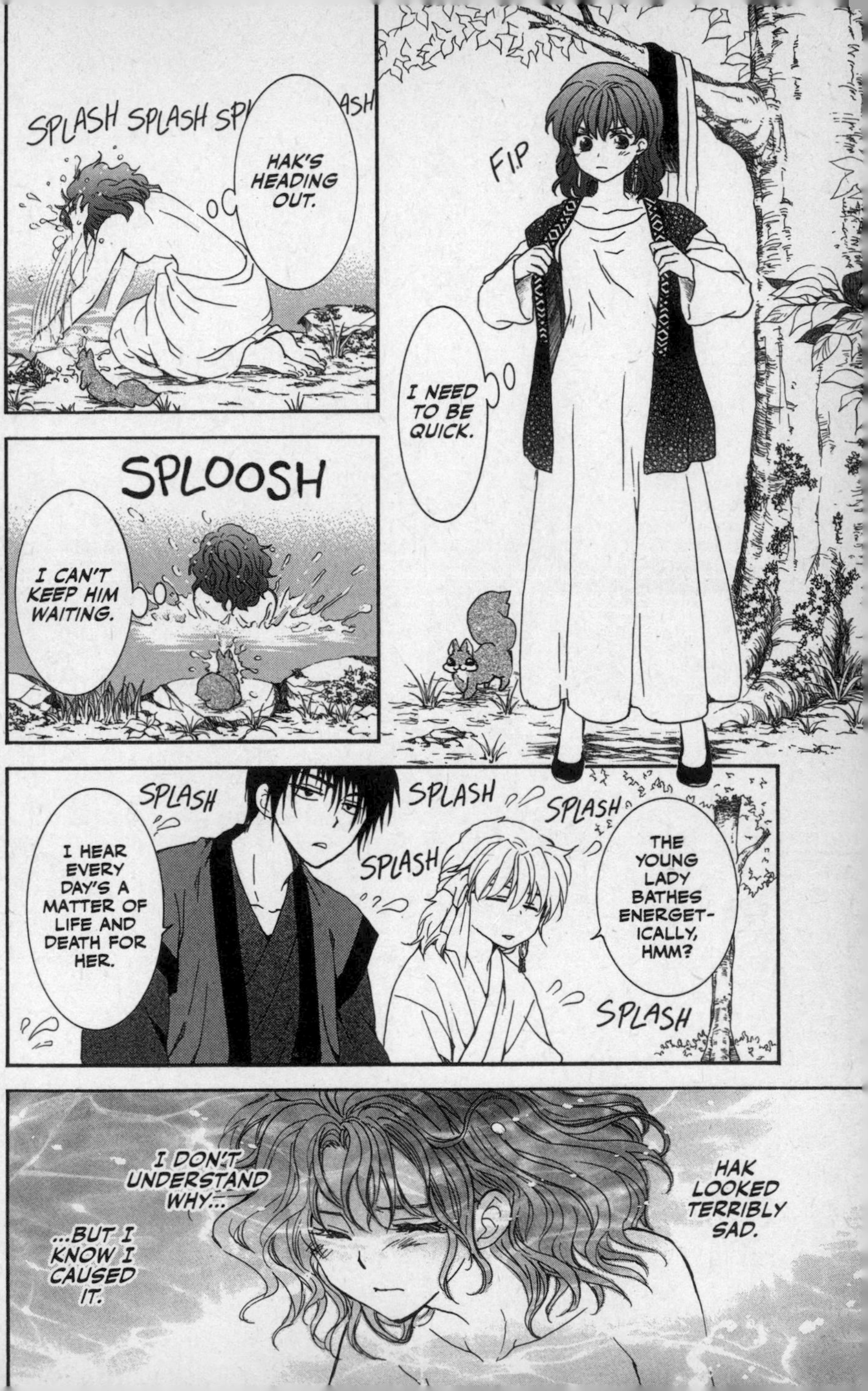
FIP
I NEED TO BE QUICK.
SPLASH SPLASH SPLASH
HAK'S HEADING OUT.
SPLOOSH
I CAN'T KEEP HIM WAITING.
SPLASH
THE YOUNG LADY BATHES ENERGET-ICALLY, HMM?
SPLASH
SPLASH
SPLASH
I HEAR EVERY DAY'S A MATTER OF LIFE AND DEATH FOR HER.
SPLASH
HAK LOOKED TERRIBLY SAD.
I DON'T UNDERSTAND WHY...
...BUT I KNOW I CAUSED IT.

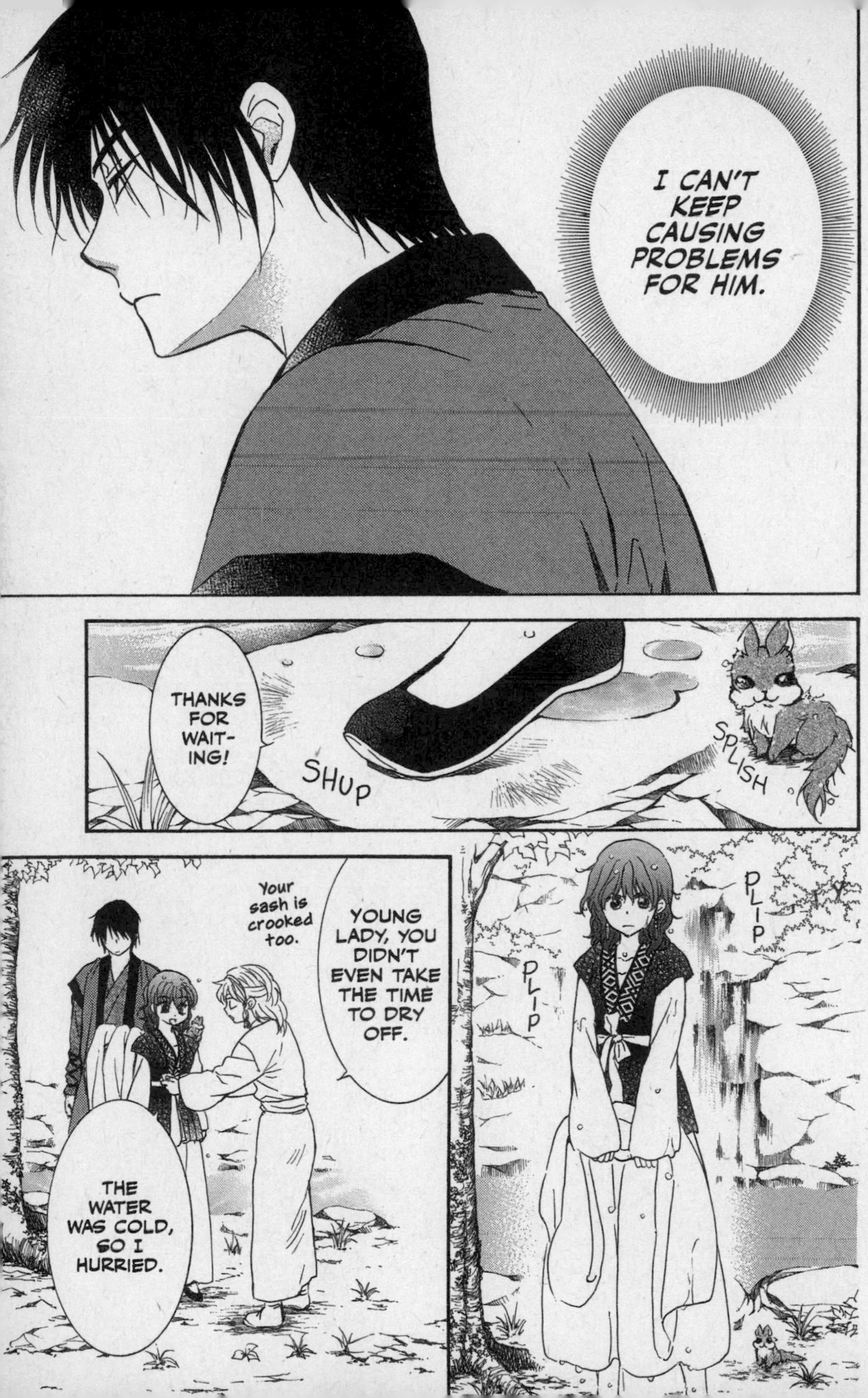
I CAN'T KEEP CAUSING PROBLEMS FOR HIM.
SPLISH
SHUP
THANKS FOR WAIT-ING!
PLIP
PLIP
YOUNG LADY, YOU DIDN'T EVEN TAKE THE TIME TO DRY OFF.
Your sash is crooked too.
THE WATER WAS COLD, SO I HURRIED.

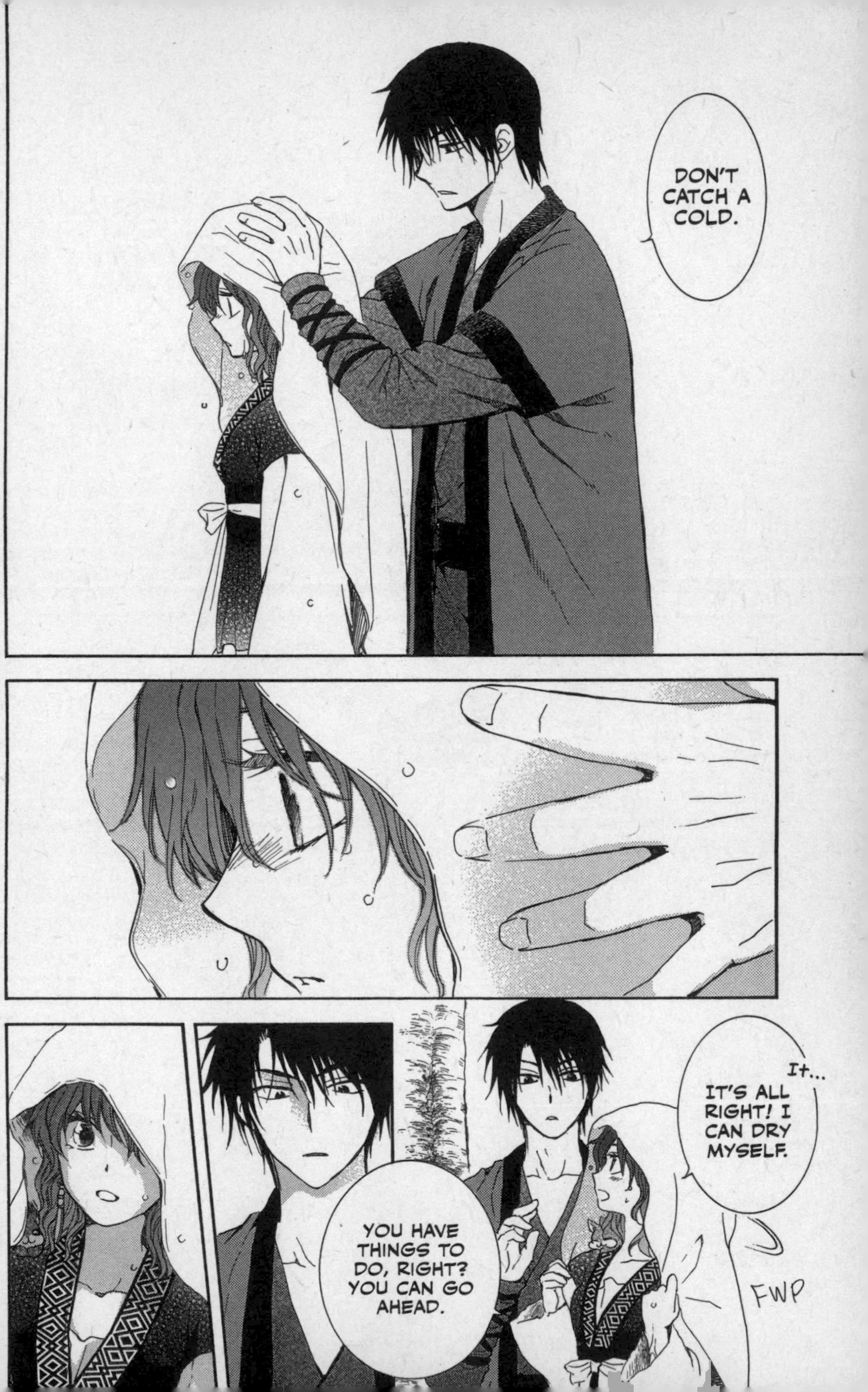
DON'T CATCH A COLD.
FWP
It... IT'S ALL RIGHT! I CAN DRY MYSELF.
YOU HAVE THINGS TO DO, RIGHT? YOU CAN GO AHEAD.

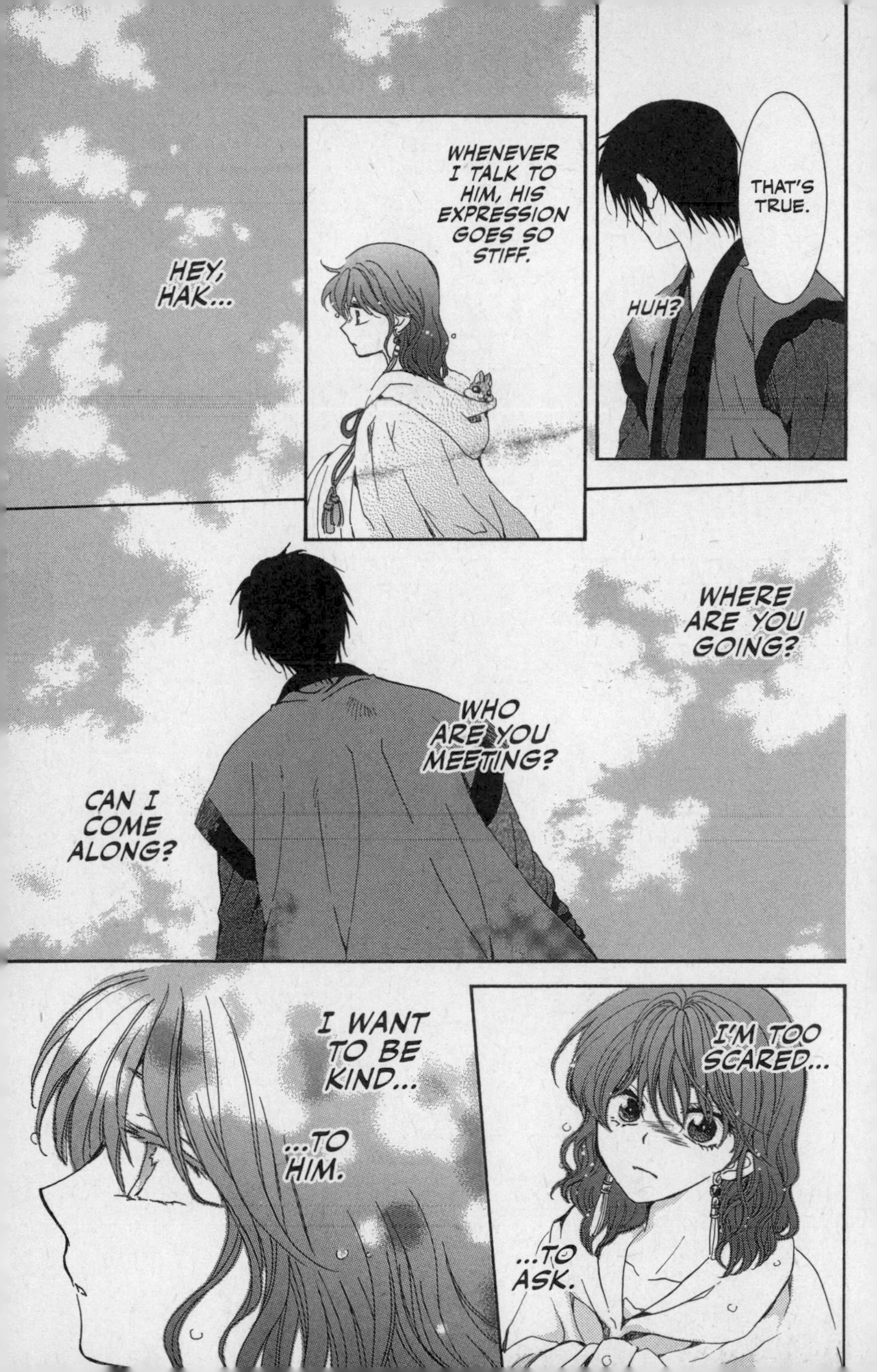
THAT'S TRUE.
HUH?
WHENEVER I TALK TO HIM, HIS EXPRESSION GOES SO STIFF.
HEY, HAK...
WHERE ARE YOU GOING?
WHO ARE YOU MEETING?
CAN I COME ALONG?
I'M TOO SCARED...
...TO ASK.
I WANT TO BE KIND...
...TO HIM.

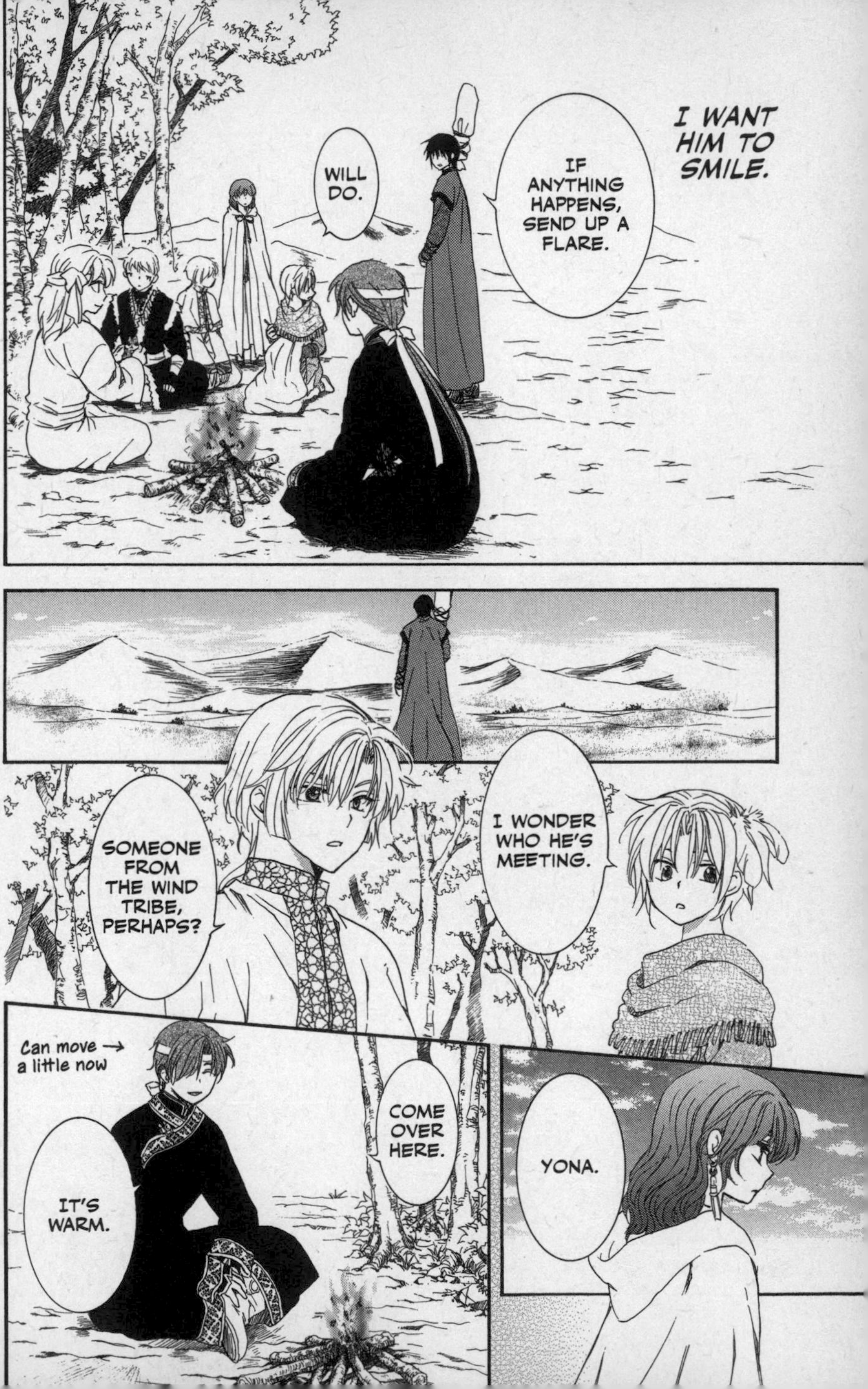
I WANT HIM TO SMILE.
IF ANYTHING HAPPENS, SEND UP A FLARE.
WILL DO.
I WONDER WHO HE'S MEETING.
SOMEONE FROM THE WIND TRIBE, PERHAPS?
YONA.
COME OVER HERE.
IT'S WARM.
Can move → a little now

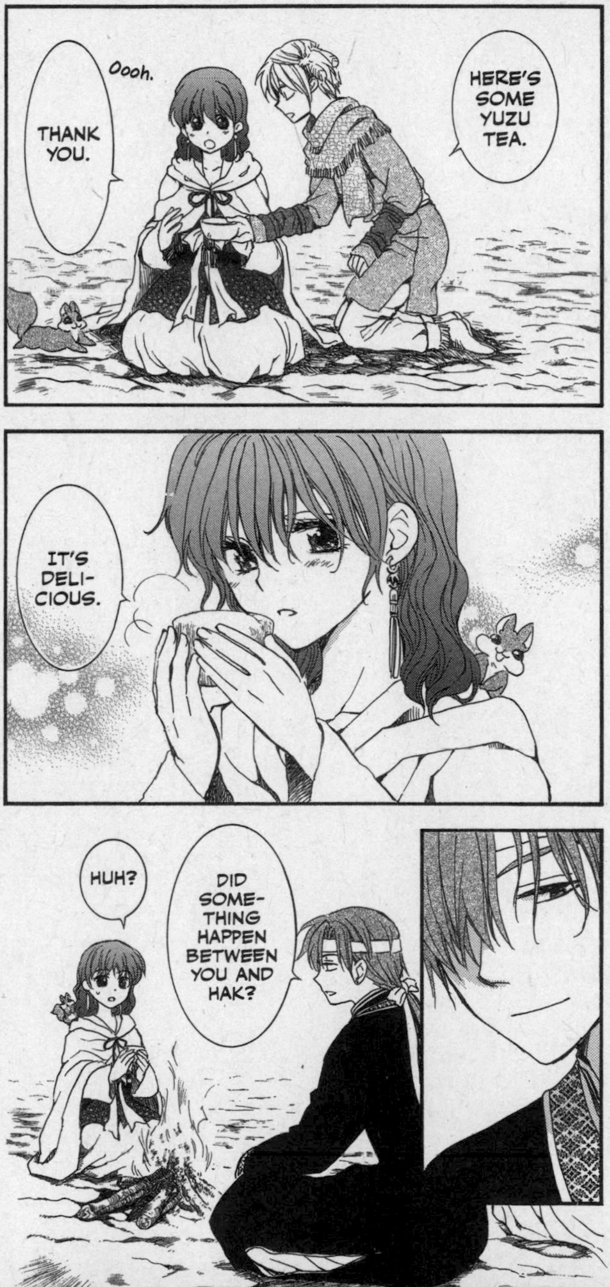
HERE'S SOME YUZU TEA.
Oooh.
THANK YOU.
IT'S DELI-CIOUS.
DID SOME-THING HAPPEN BETWEEN YOU AND HAK?
HUH?

I wanted to draw more about Xing, but I still had Yona's story to tell. The Nation of Xing arc is over for now. (I didn't have many extra pages in this volume.)

I always have to do my initial pages quickly, so when the story comes out in new volumes, I clean up the art and adjust the expressions to be more like what I'd imagined. But sometimes after I touch up the faces, people tell me that the first version was better.

This time around I didn't like the changes I made to many of the panels I fixed, so I reverted them to the way they were published in the magazine. I wish I could draw things the way I imagine them on the first try.

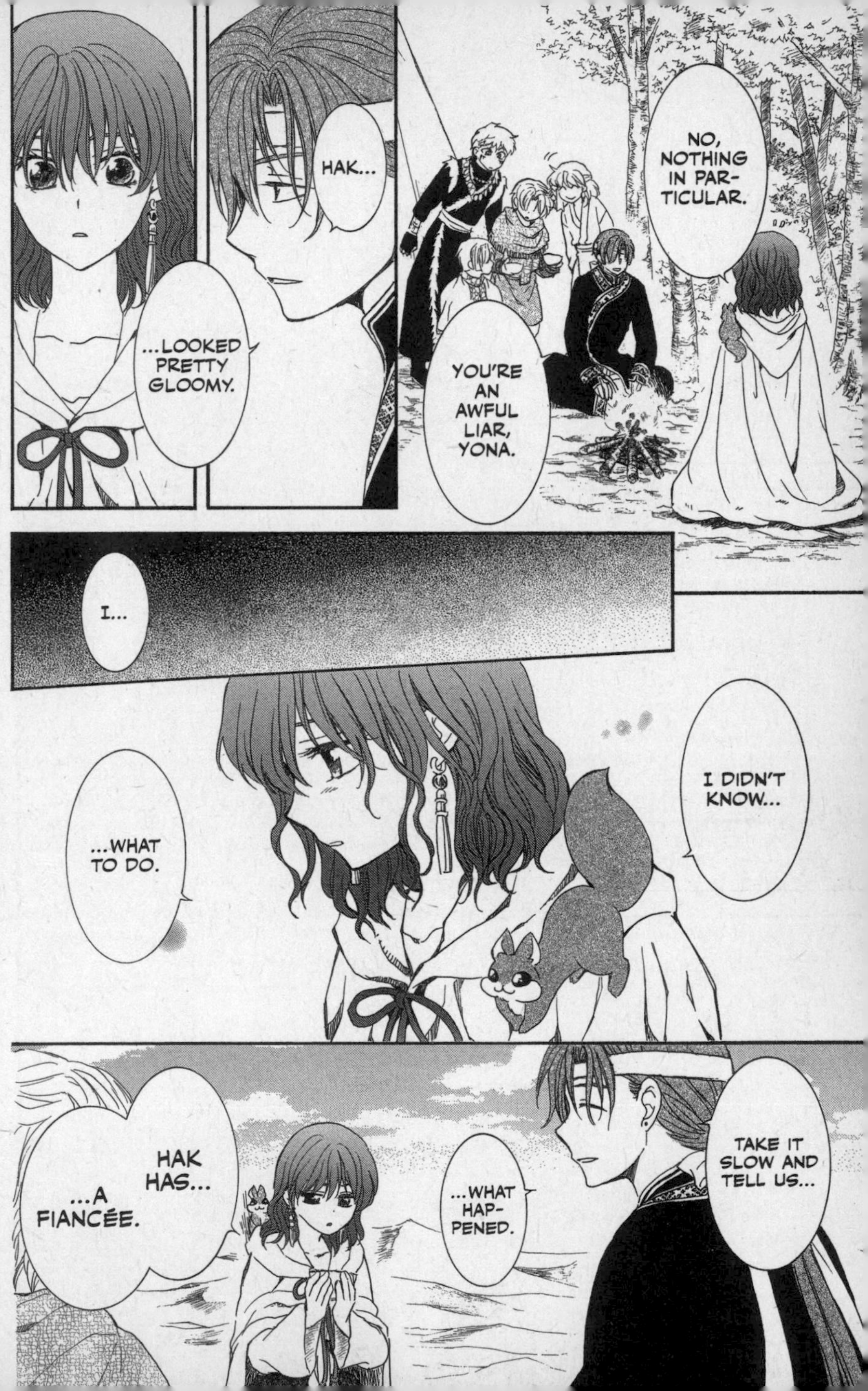
NO, NOTHING IN PARTICULAR.
YOU'RE AN AWFUL LIAR, YONA.
HAK...
...LOOKED PRETTY GLOOMY.
I...
I DIDN'T KNOW...
...WHAT TO DO.
TAKE IT SLOW AND TELL US...
...WHAT HAPPENED.
HAK HAS...
...A FIANCÉE.

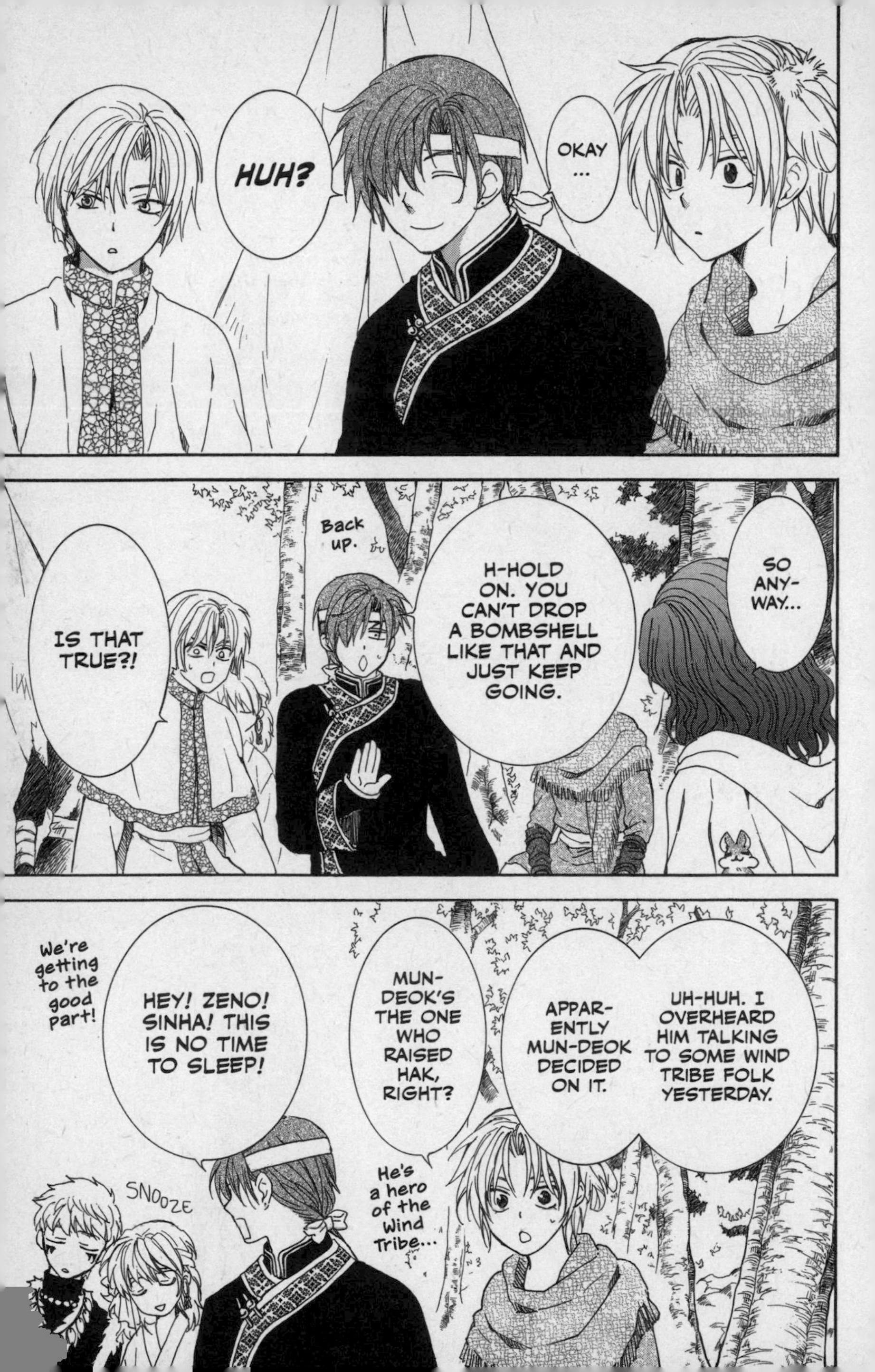
OKAY ...
HUH?
SO ANY-WAY...
H-HOLD ON. YOU CAN'T DROP A BOMBSHELL LIKE THAT AND JUST KEEP GOING.
Back up.
IS THAT TRUE?!
UH-HUH. I OVERHEARD HIM TALKING TO SOME WIND TRIBE FOLK YESTERDAY.
APPAR-ENTLY MUN-DEOK DECIDED ON IT.
MUN-DEOK'S THE ONE WHO RAISED HAK, RIGHT?
He's a hero of the Wind Tribe...
HEY! ZENO! SINHA! THIS IS NO TIME TO SLEEP!
We're getting to the good part!
SNOOZE

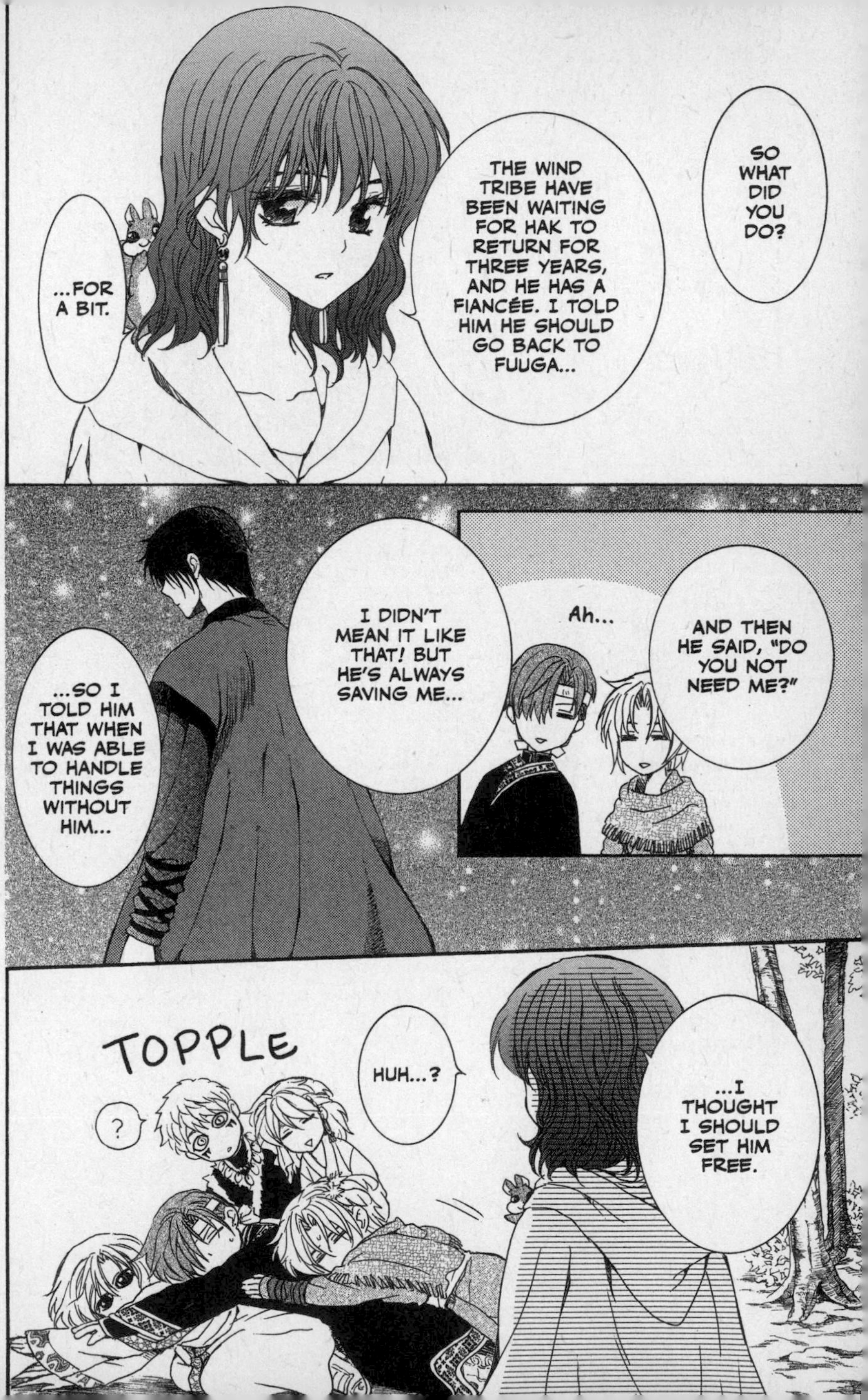
SO WHAT DID YOU DO?
THE WIND TRIBE HAVE BEEN WAITING FOR HAK TO RETURN FOR THREE YEARS, AND HE HAS A FIANCÉE. I TOLD HIM HE SHOULD GO BACK TO FUUGA...
...FOR A BIT.
AND THEN HE SAID, "DO YOU NOT NEED ME?"
Ah...
I DIDN'T MEAN IT LIKE THAT! BUT HE'S ALWAYS SAVING ME...
...SO I TOLD HIM THAT WHEN I WAS ABLE TO HANDLE THINGS WITHOUT HIM...
...I THOUGHT I SHOULD SET HIM FREE.
HUH...?
TOPPLE
?

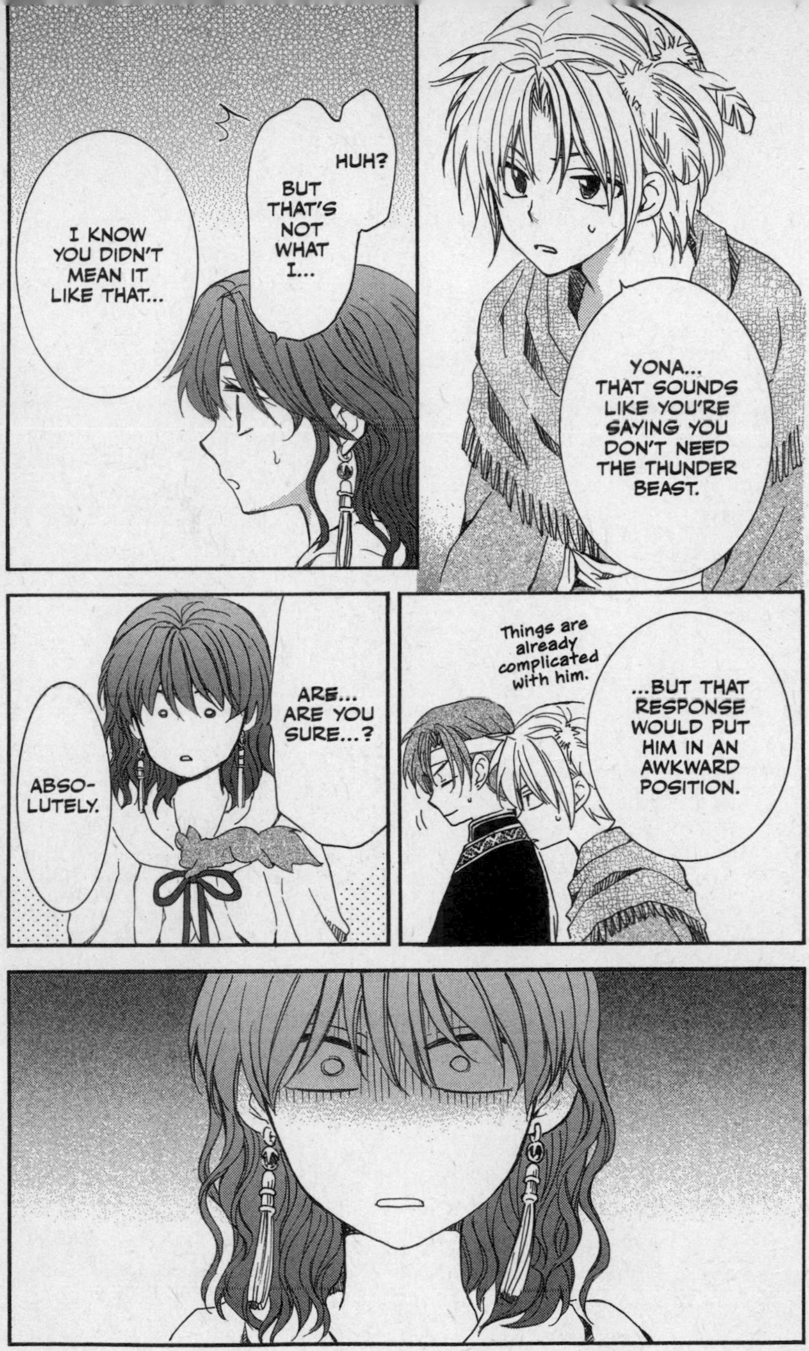
YONA... THAT SOUNDS LIKE YOU'RE SAYING YOU DON'T NEED THE THUNDER BEAST.
HUH? BUT THAT'S NOT WHAT I...
I KNOW YOU DIDN'T MEAN IT LIKE THAT...
...BUT THAT RESPONSE WOULD PUT HIM IN AN AWKWARD POSITION.
Things are already complicated with him.
ARE... ARE YOU SURE...?
ABSO-LUTELY.

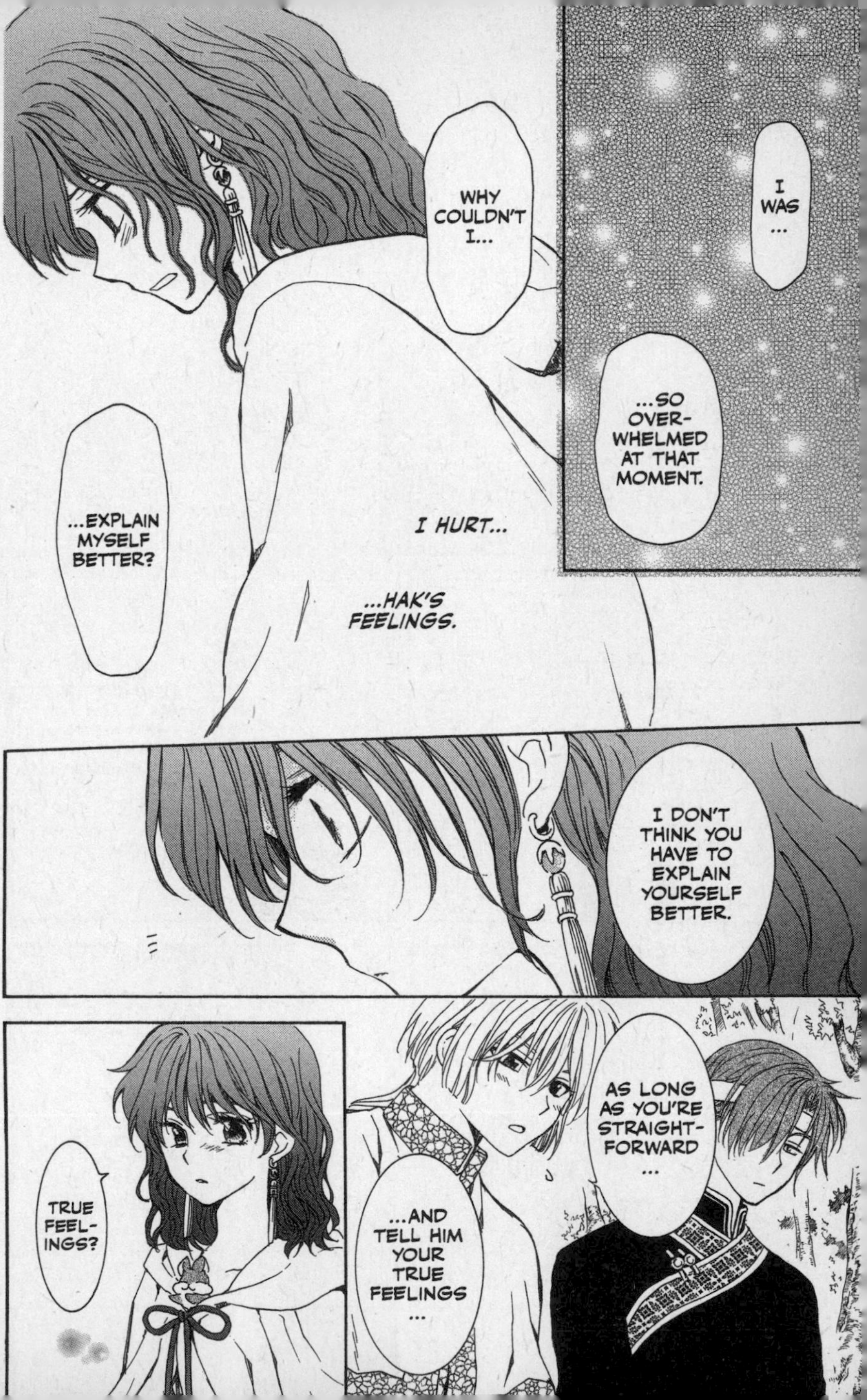
I WAS ...
...SO OVER-WHELMED AT THAT MOMENT.
WHY COULDN'T I...
I HURT...
...HAK'S FEELINGS.
...EXPLAIN MYSELF BETTER?
I DON'T THINK YOU HAVE TO EXPLAIN YOURSELF BETTER.
AS LONG AS YOU'RE STRAIGHT-FORWARD ...
...AND TELL HIM YOUR TRUE FEELINGS ...
TRUE FEEL-INGS?

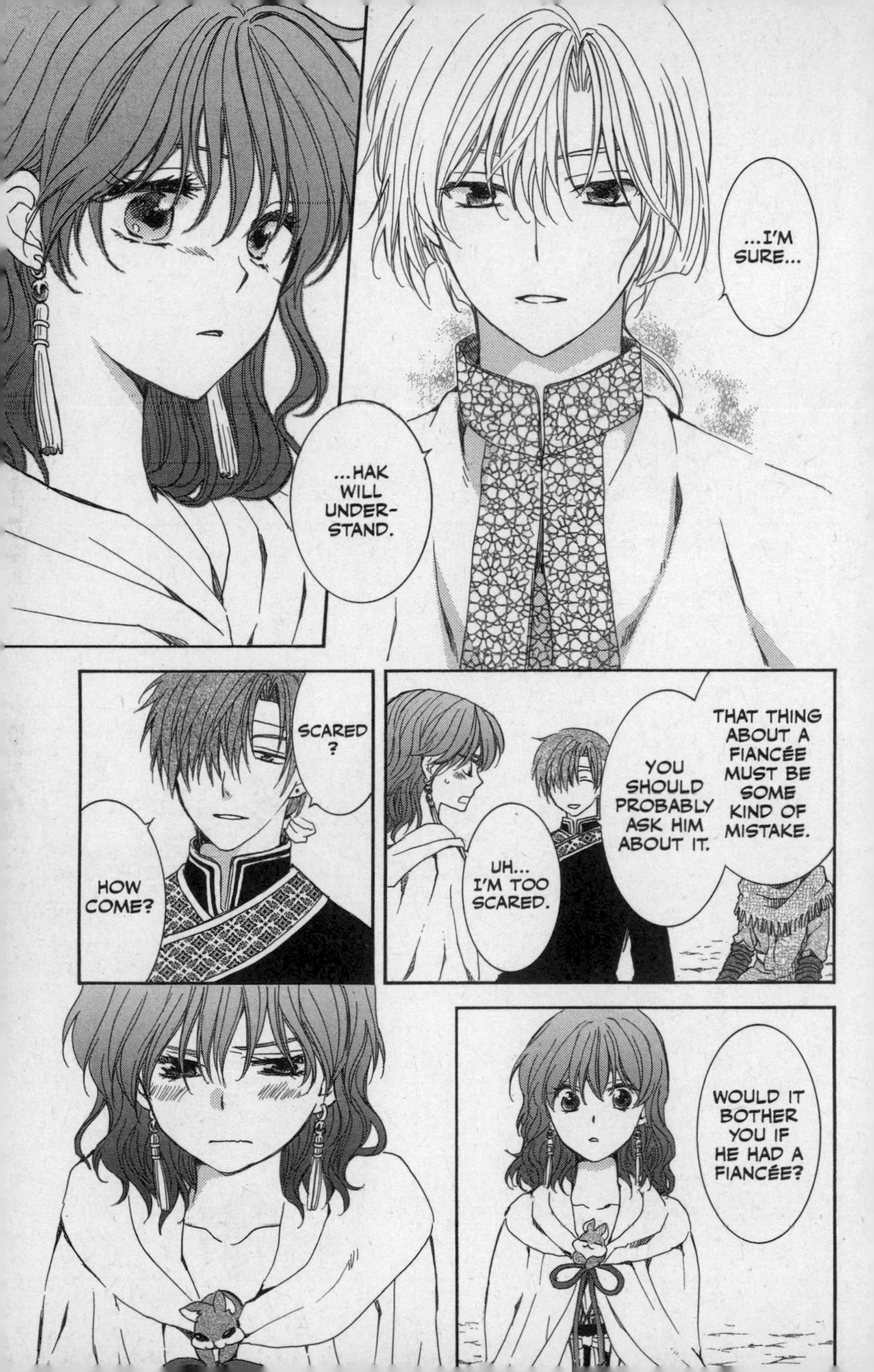
...I'M SURE...
...HAK WILL UNDER-STAND.
THAT THING ABOUT A FIANCÉE MUST BE SOME KIND OF MISTAKE.
YOU SHOULD PROBABLY ASK HIM ABOUT IT.
UH... I'M TOO SCARED.
SCARED?
HOW COME?
WOULD IT BOTHER YOU IF HE HAD A FIANCÉE?

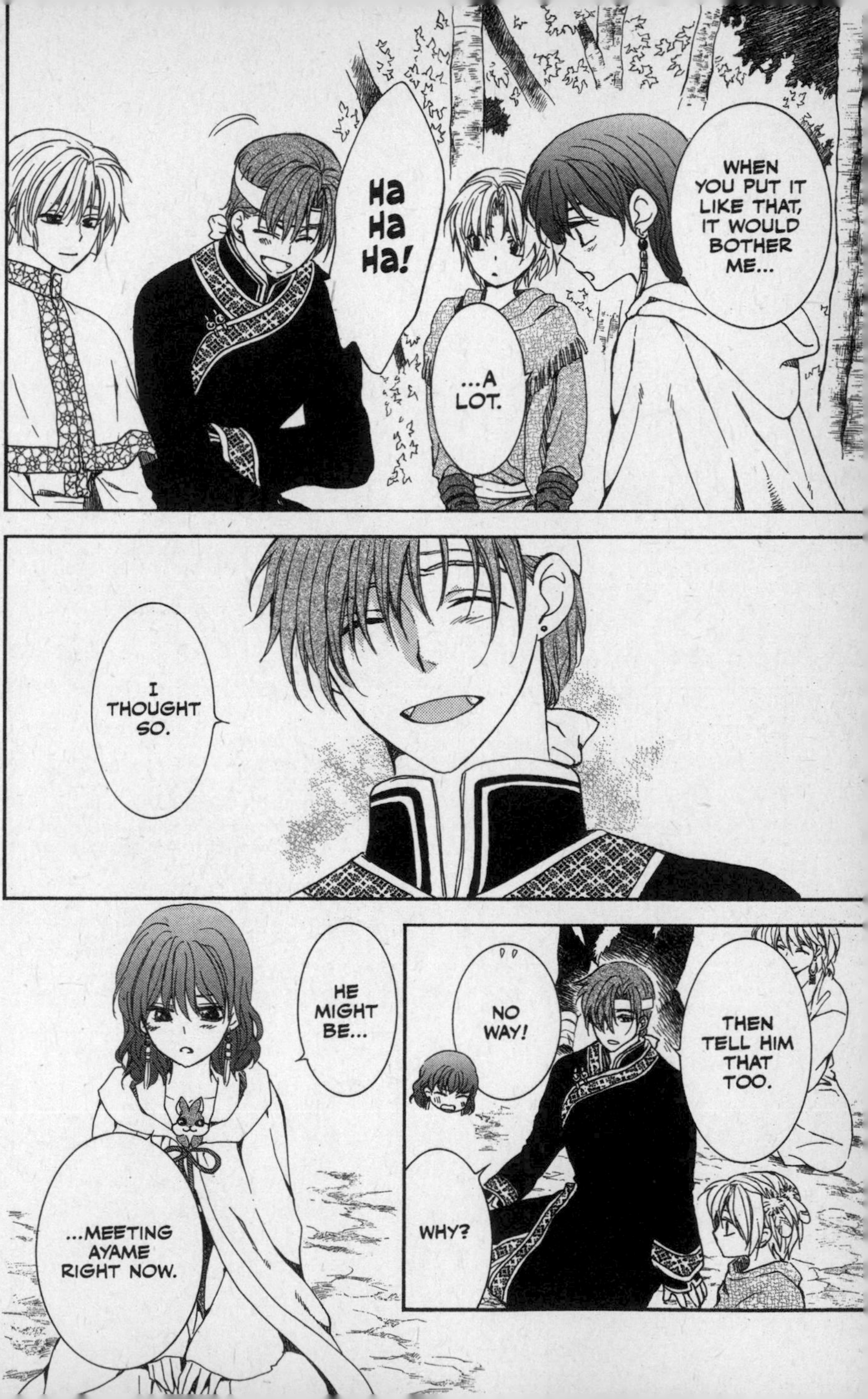
WHEN YOU PUT IT LIKE THAT, IT WOULD BOTHER ME...
...A LOT.
HA HA HA!
I THOUGHT SO.
THEN TELL HIM THAT TOO.
NO WAY!
WHY?
HE MIGHT BE...
...MEETING AYAME RIGHT NOW.

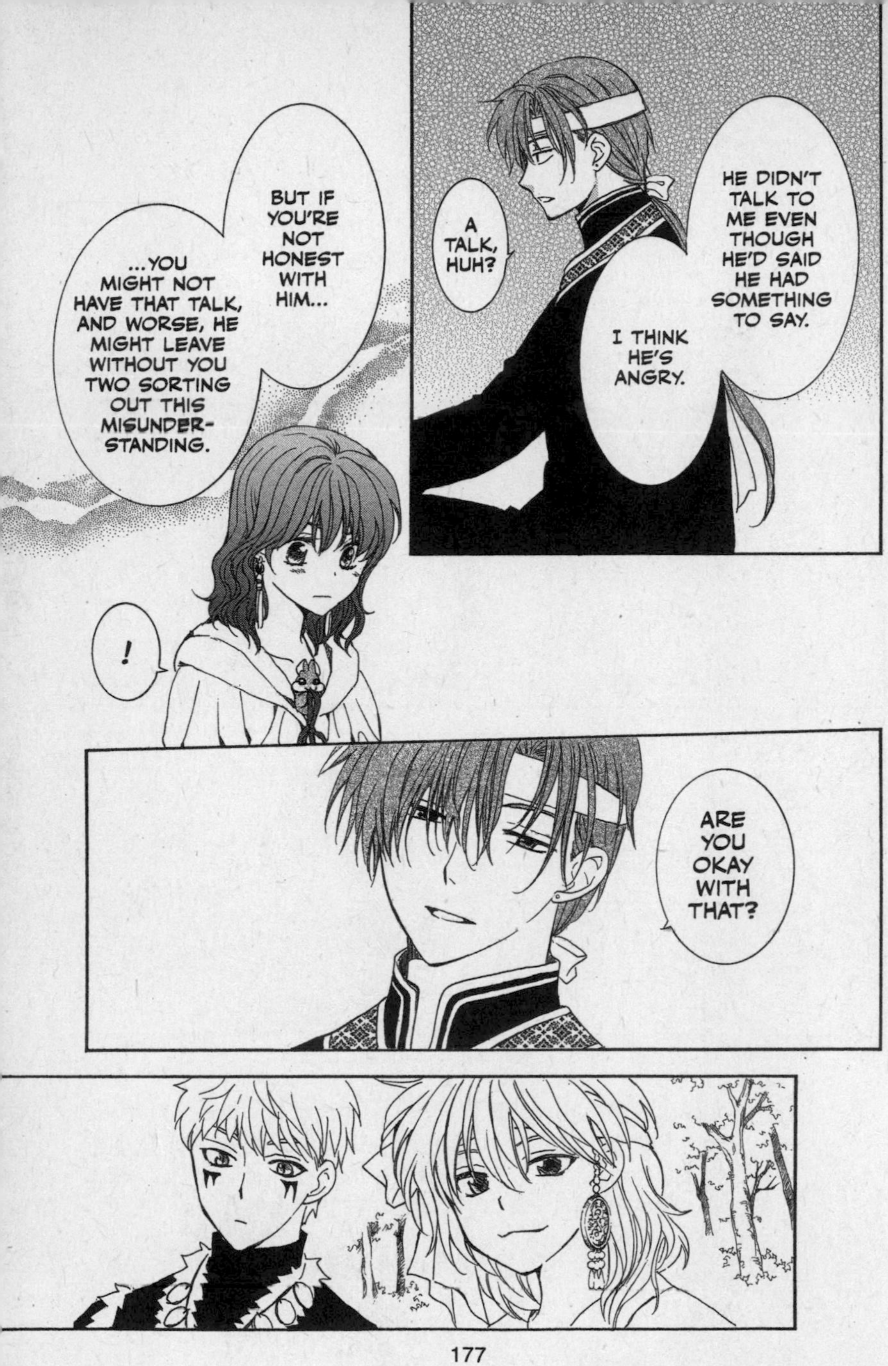
HE DIDN'T TALK TO ME EVEN THOUGH HE'D SAID HE HAD SOMETHING TO SAY.
I THINK HE'S ANGRY.
A TALK, HUH?
BUT IF YOU'RE NOT HONEST WITH HIM...
...YOU MIGHT NOT HAVE THAT TALK, AND WORSE, HE MIGHT LEAVE WITHOUT YOU TWO SORTING OUT THIS MISUNDERSTANDING.
!
ARE YOU OKAY WITH THAT?

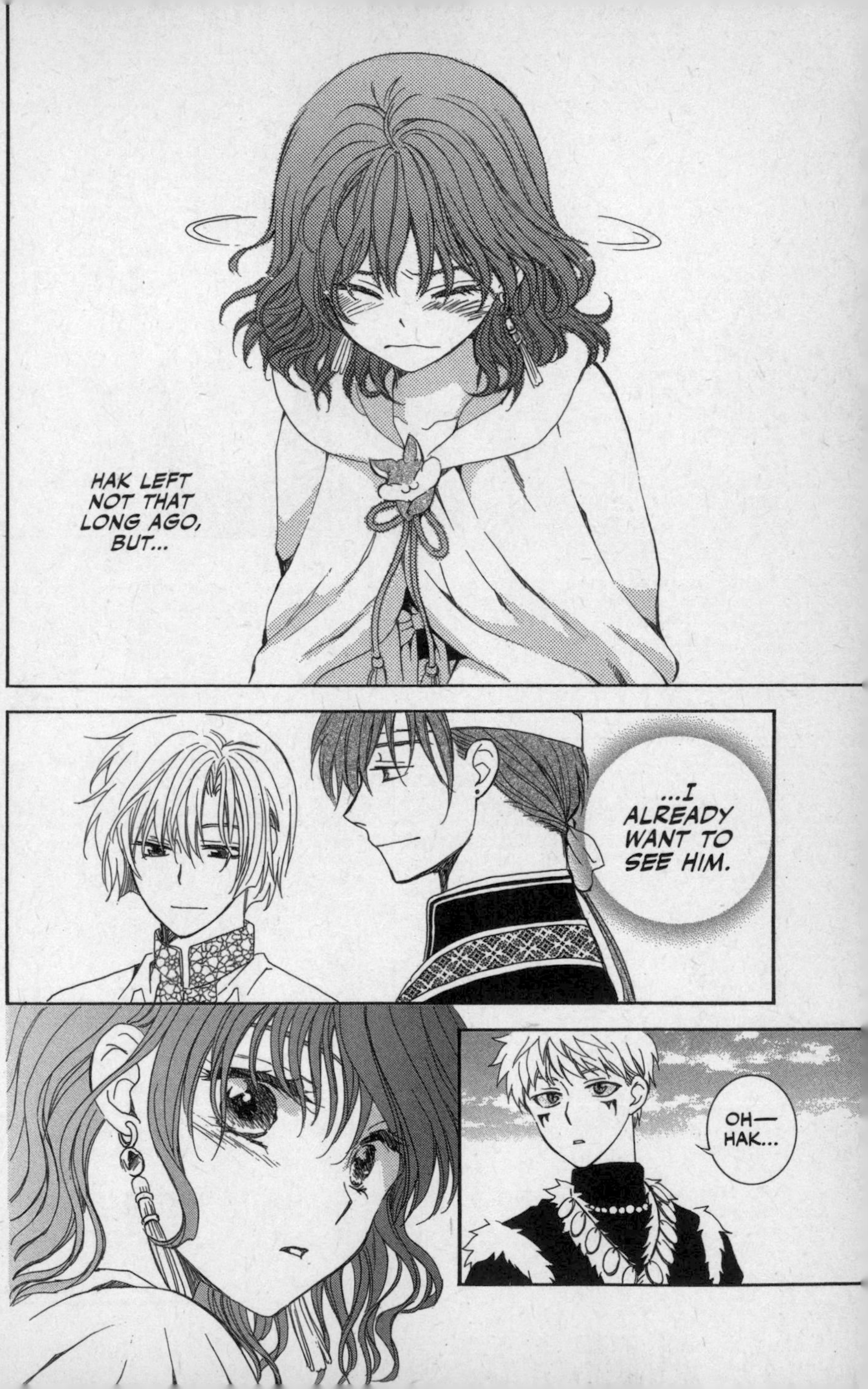
HAK LEFT NOT THAT LONG AGO, BUT...
...I ALREADY WANT TO SEE HIM.
OH— HAK...

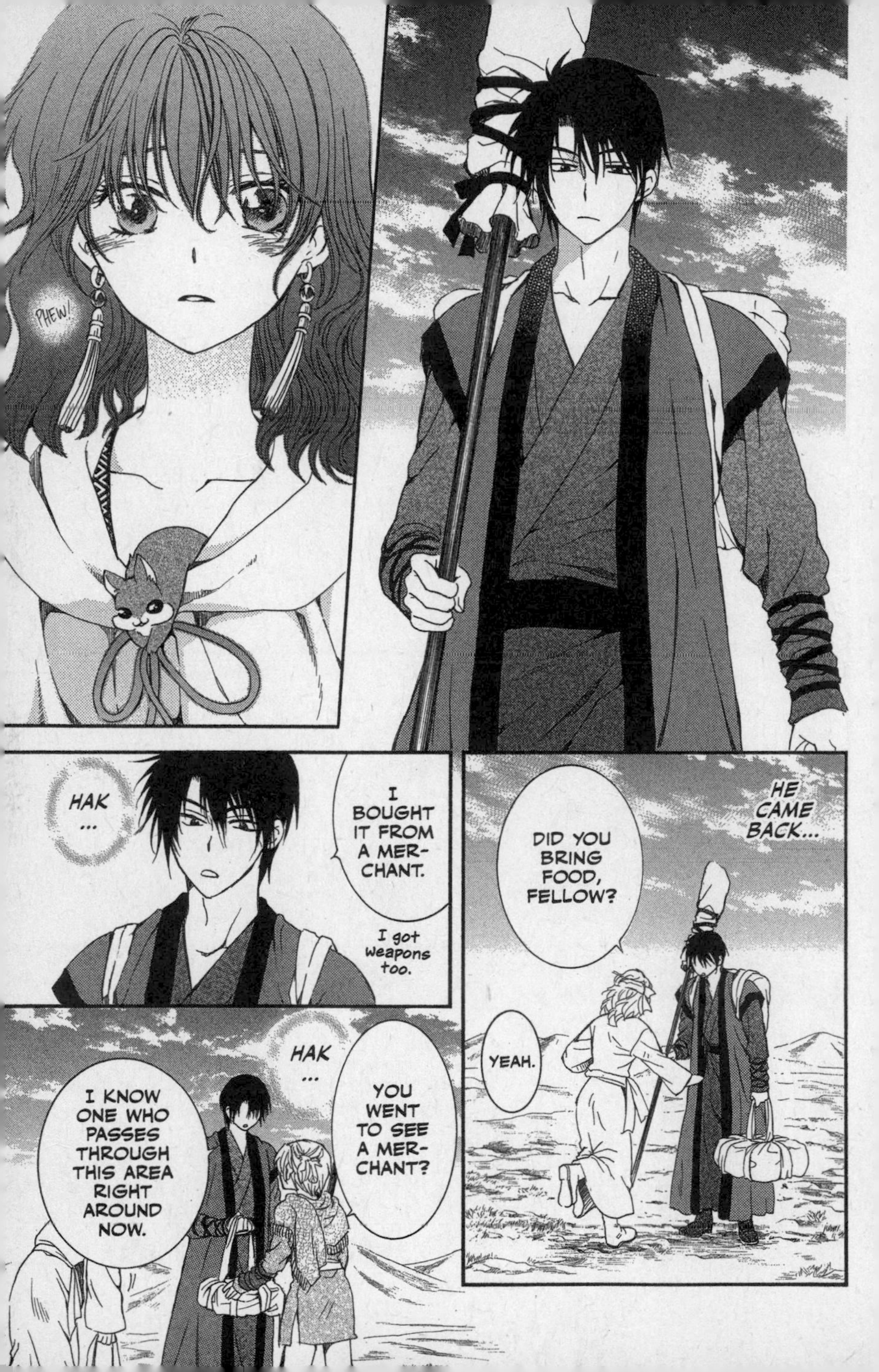
PHEW!
HE CAME BACK...
DID YOU BRING FOOD, FELLOW?
YEAH.
HAK ...
I BOUGHT IT FROM A MER-CHANT.
I got weapons too.
HAK ...
YOU WENT TO SEE A MER-CHANT?
I KNOW ONE WHO PASSES THROUGH THIS AREA RIGHT AROUND NOW.

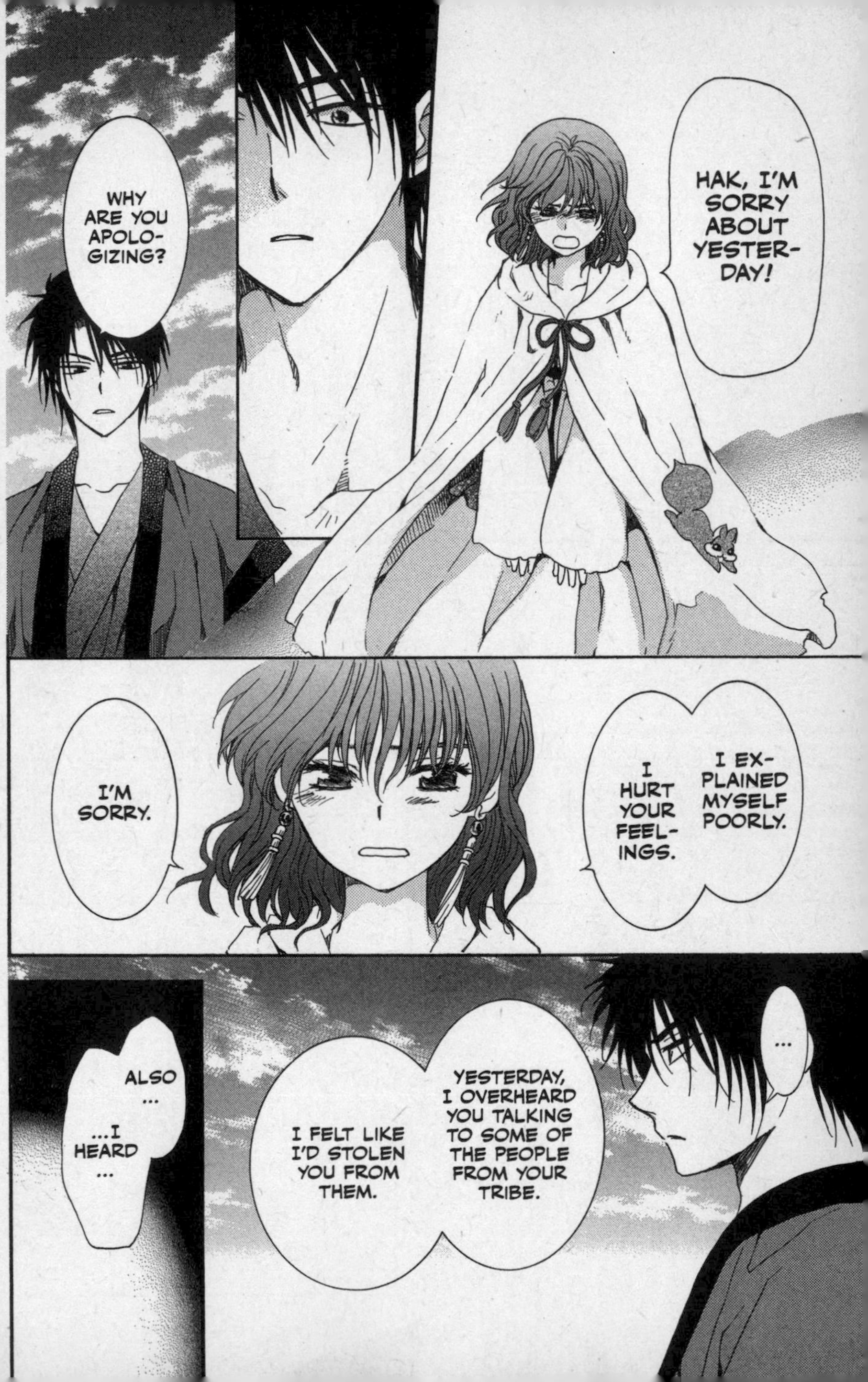
HAK, I'M SORRY ABOUT YESTER-DAY!
WHY ARE YOU APOLO-GIZING?
I EX-PLAINED MYSELF POORLY.
I HURT YOUR FEEL-INGS.
I'M SORRY.
...
YESTERDAY, I OVERHEARD YOU TALKING TO SOME OF THE PEOPLE FROM YOUR TRIBE.
I FELT LIKE I'D STOLEN YOU FROM THEM.
ALSO ...
...I HEARD ...

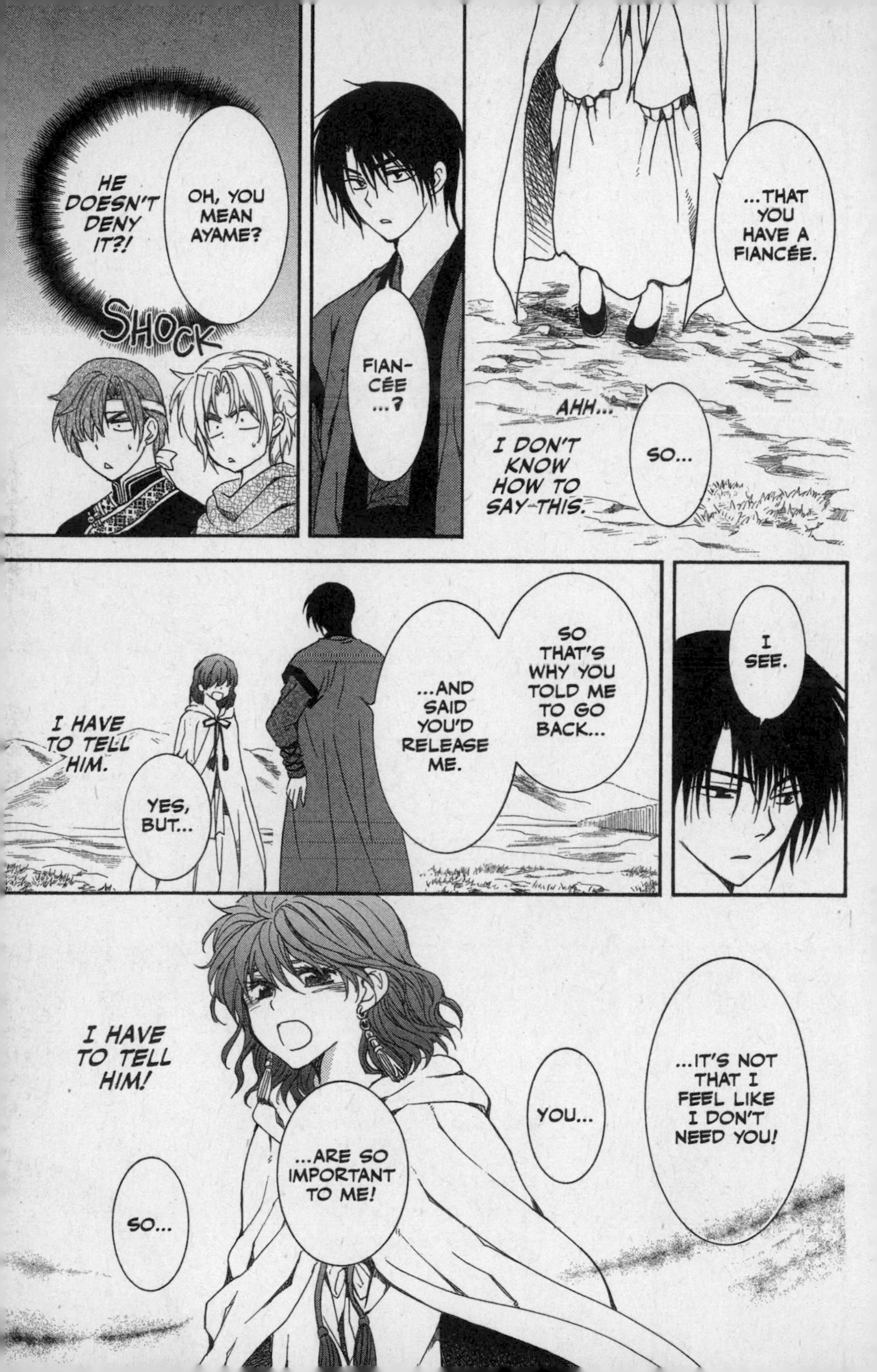
...THAT YOU HAVE A FIANCÉE.
AHH...
I DON'T KNOW HOW TO SAY THIS.
SO...
FIAN-CÉE ...?
OH, YOU MEAN AYAME?
HE DOESN'T DENY IT?!
SHOCK
I SEE.
SO THAT'S WHY YOU TOLD ME TO GO BACK...
...AND SAID YOU'D RELEASE ME.
I HAVE TO TELL HIM.
YES, BUT...
...IT'S NOT THAT I FEEL LIKE I DON'T NEED YOU!
YOU...
I HAVE TO TELL HIM!
...ARE SO IMPORTANT TO ME!
SO...

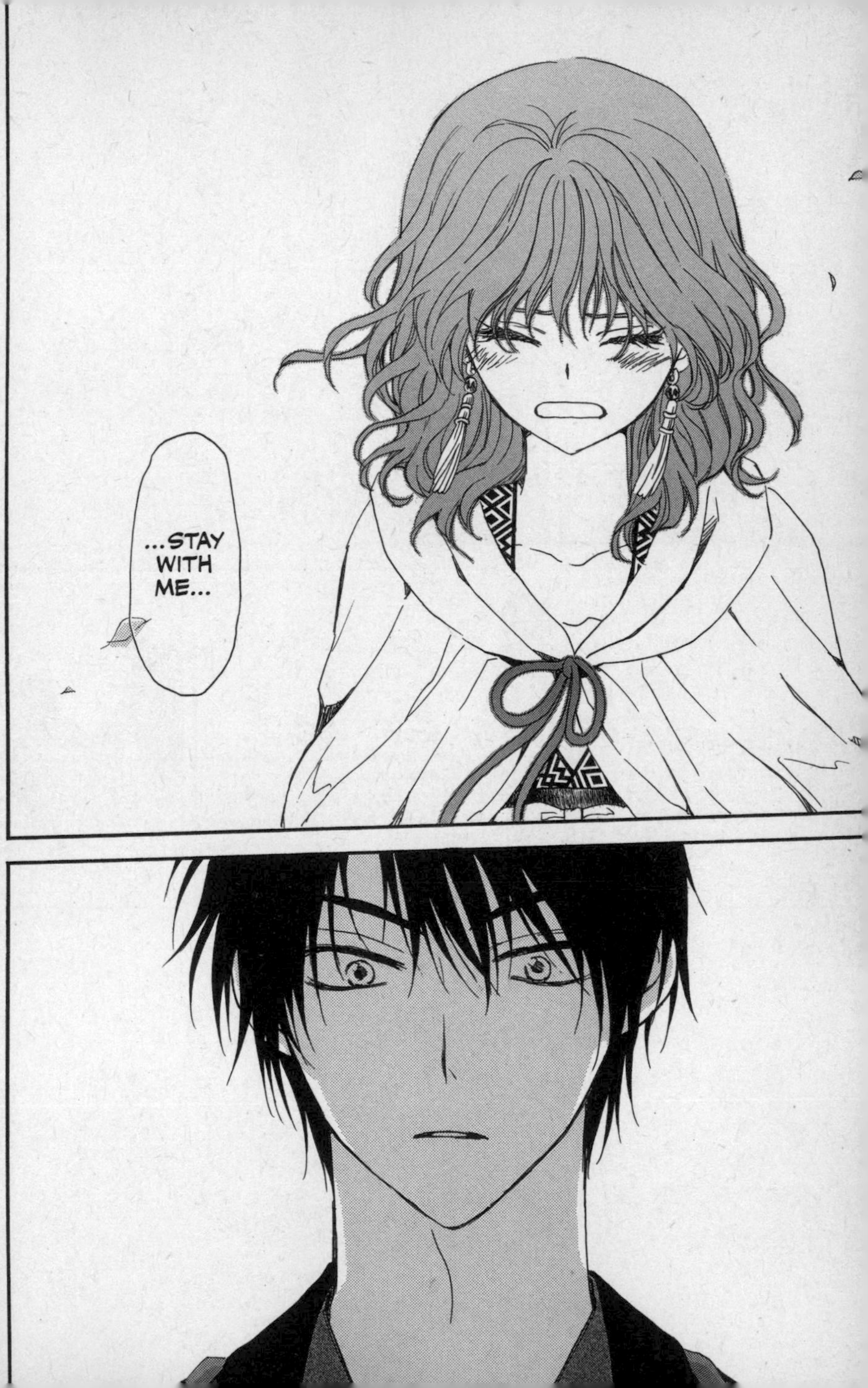
...STAY WITH ME...

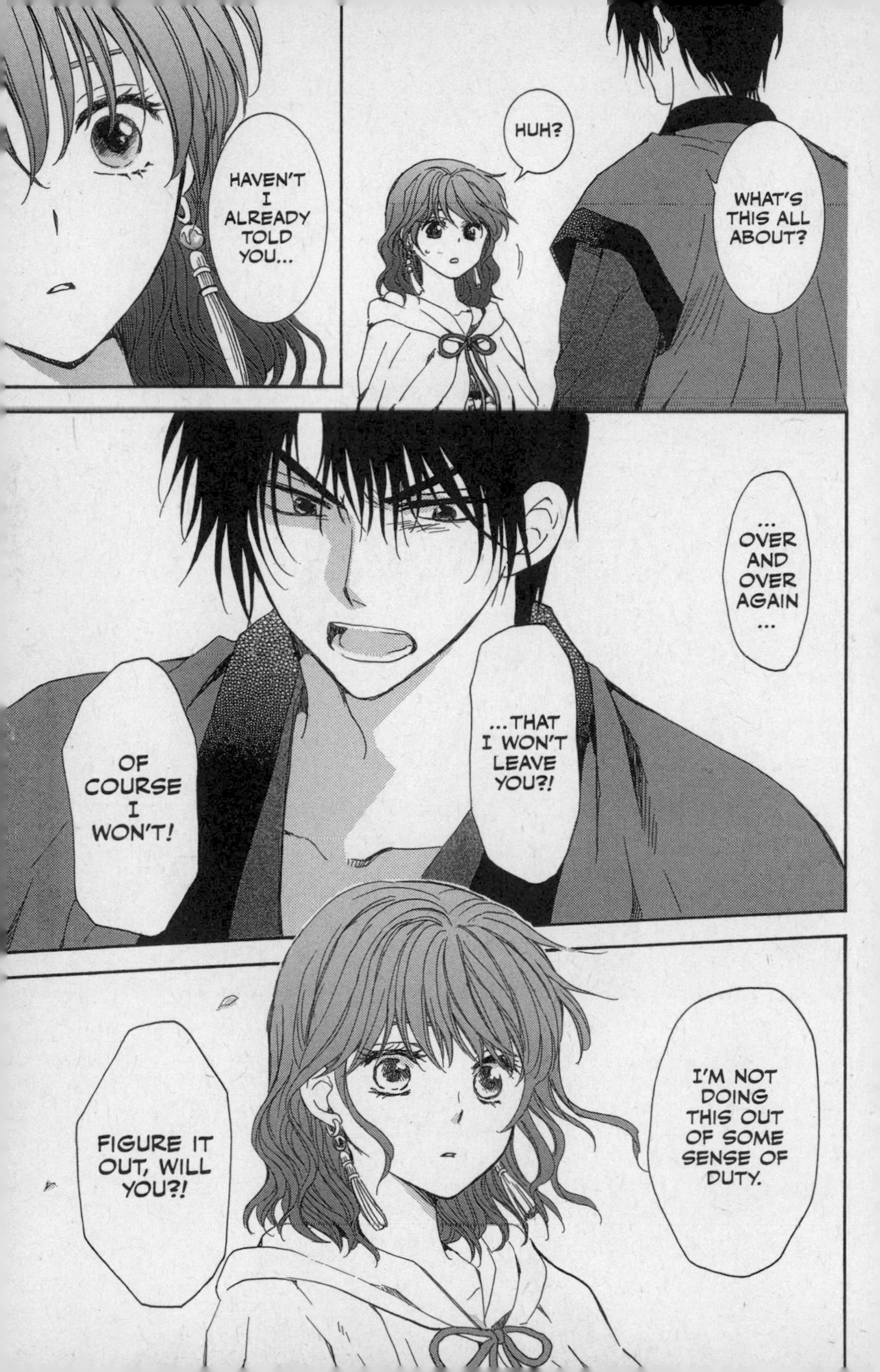
WHAT'S THIS ALL ABOUT?
HUH?
HAVEN'T I ALREADY TOLD YOU...
...OVER AND OVER AGAIN...
...THAT I WON'T LEAVE YOU?!
OF COURSE I WON'T!
I'M NOT DOING THIS OUT OF SOME SENSE OF DUTY.
FIGURE IT OUT, WILL YOU?!

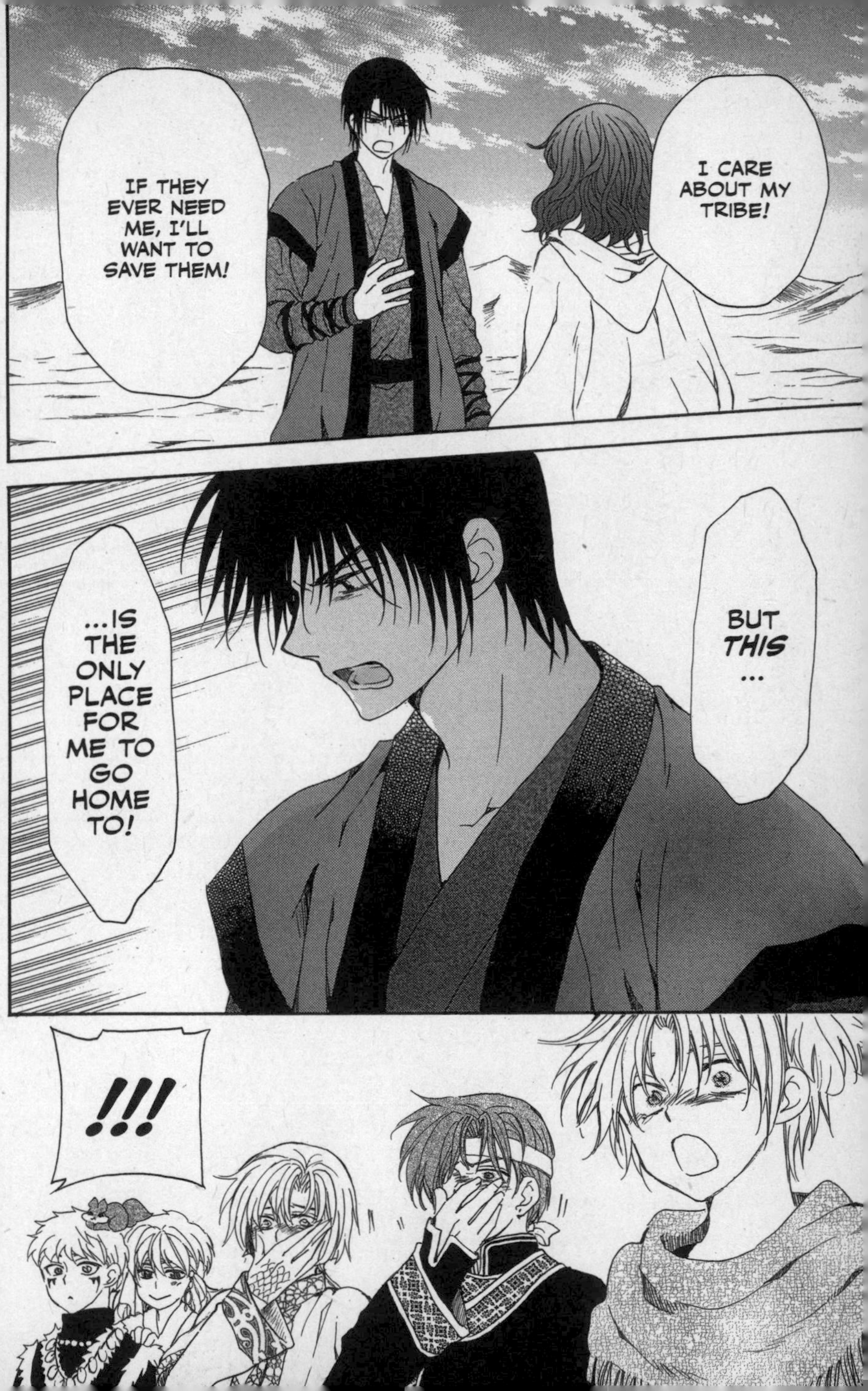
I CARE ABOUT MY TRIBE!
IF THEY EVER NEED ME, I'LL WANT TO SAVE THEM!
BUT *THIS* ...
...IS THE ONLY PLACE FOR ME TO GO HOME TO!
!!!

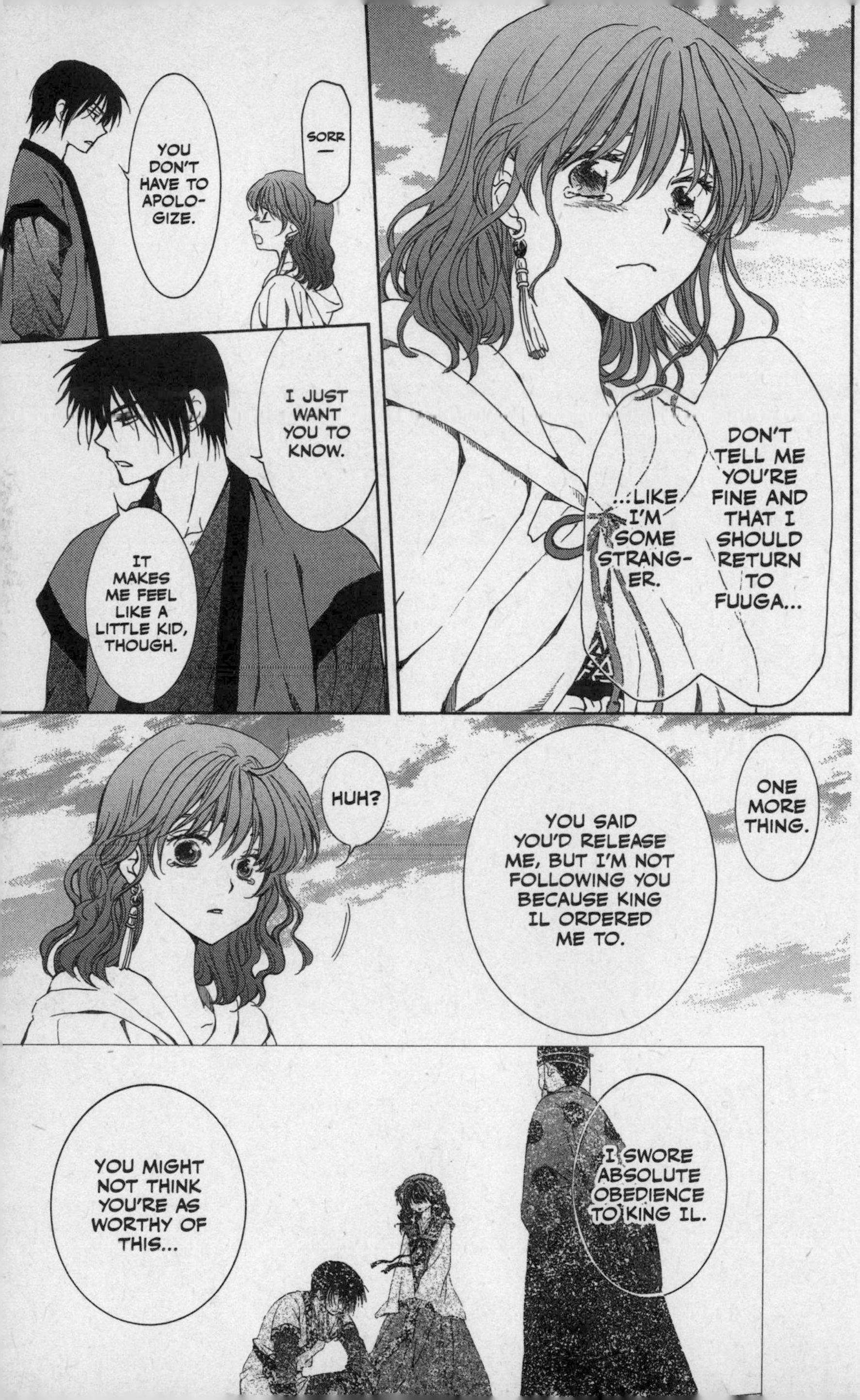
DON'T TELL ME YOU'RE FINE AND THAT I SHOULD RETURN TO FUUGA...
...LIKE I'M SOME STRANGER.
SORR—
YOU DON'T HAVE TO APOLOGIZE.
I JUST WANT YOU TO KNOW.
IT MAKES ME FEEL LIKE A LITTLE KID, THOUGH.
ONE MORE THING.
YOU SAID YOU'D RELEASE ME, BUT I'M NOT FOLLOWING YOU BECAUSE KING IL ORDERED ME TO.
HUH?
I SWORE ABSOLUTE OBEDIENCE TO KING IL.
YOU MIGHT NOT THINK YOU'RE AS WORTHY OF THIS...

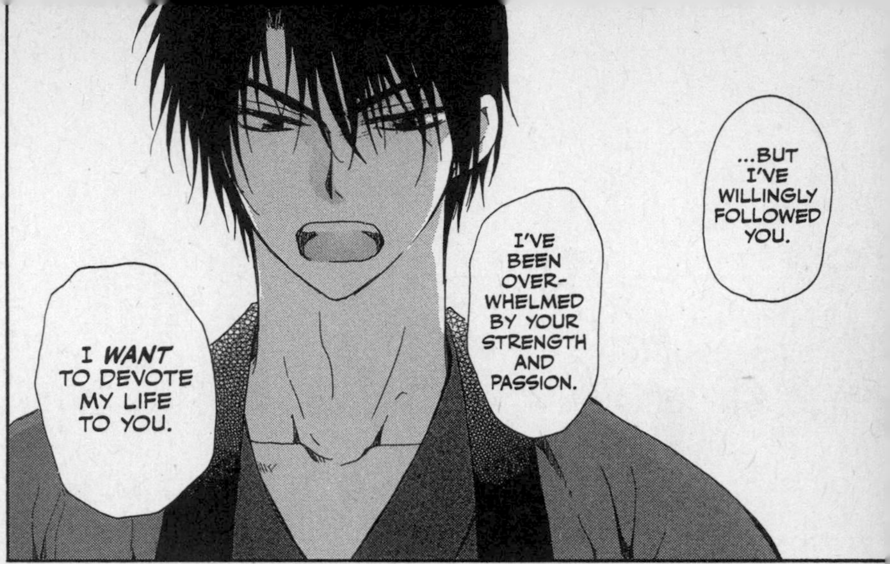
...BUT I'VE WILLINGLY FOLLOWED YOU.
I'VE BEEN OVER-WHELMED BY YOUR STRENGTH AND PASSION.
I *WANT* TO DEVOTE MY LIFE TO YOU.
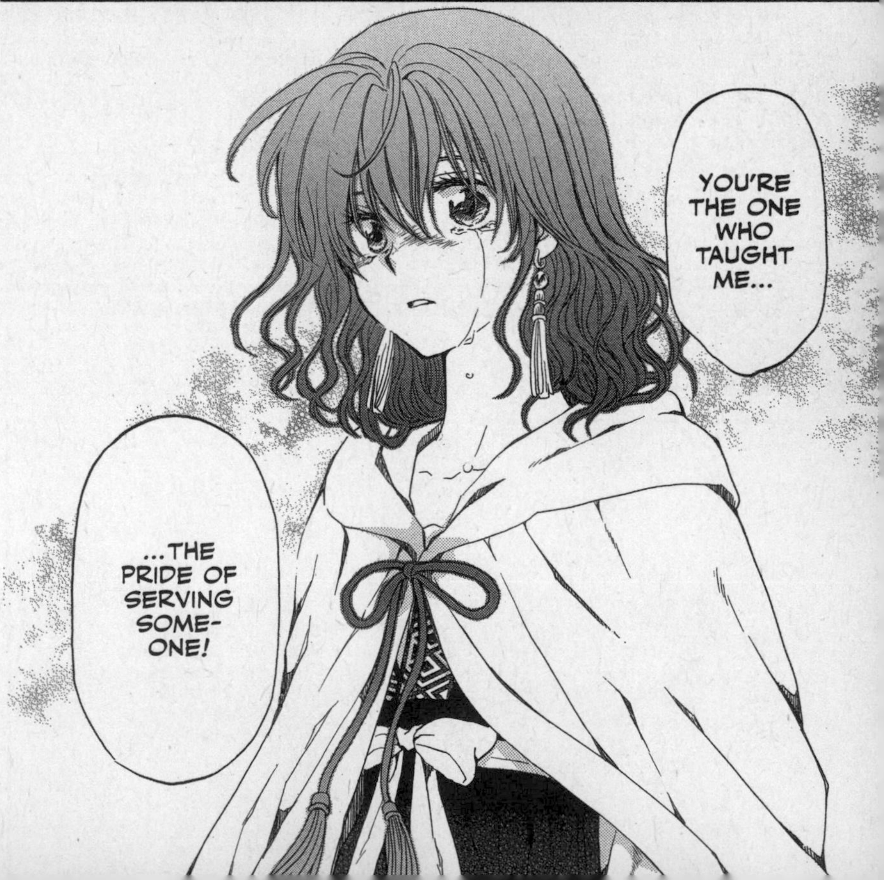
YOU'RE THE ONE WHO TAUGHT ME...
...THE PRIDE OF SERVING SOME-ONE!

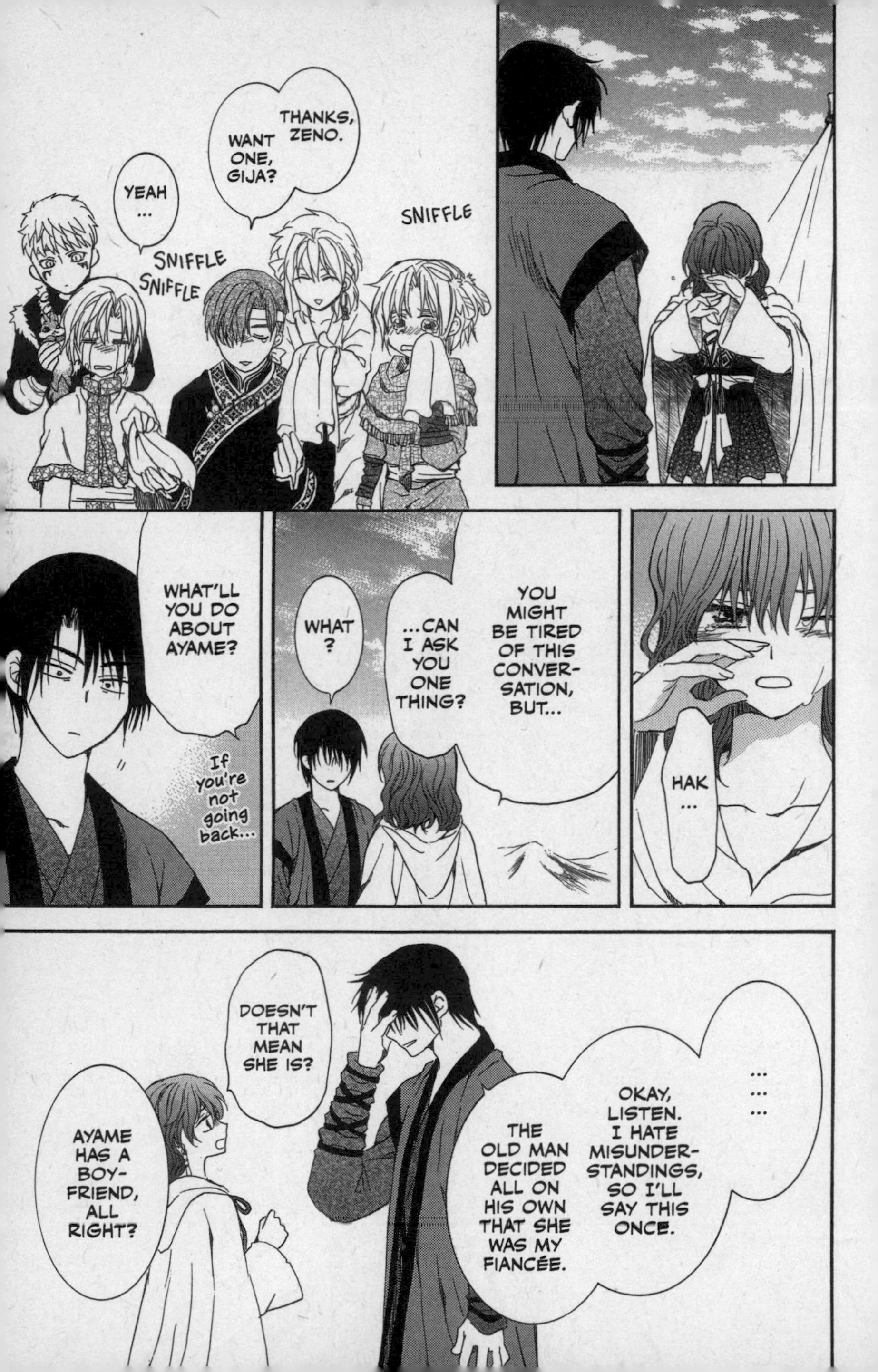
SNIFFLE
THANKS, ZENO. WANT ONE, GIJA?
YEAH ...
SNIFFLE
SNIFFLE
HAK ...
YOU MIGHT BE TIRED OF THIS CONVERSATION, BUT...
...CAN I ASK YOU ONE THING?
WHAT ?
WHAT'LL YOU DO ABOUT AYAME?
If you're not going back...
... ...
OKAY, LISTEN. I HATE MISUNDERSTANDINGS, SO I'LL SAY THIS ONCE.
THE OLD MAN DECIDED ALL ON HIS OWN THAT SHE WAS MY FIANCÉE.
DOESN'T THAT MEAN SHE IS?
AYAME HAS A BOYFRIEND, ALL RIGHT?

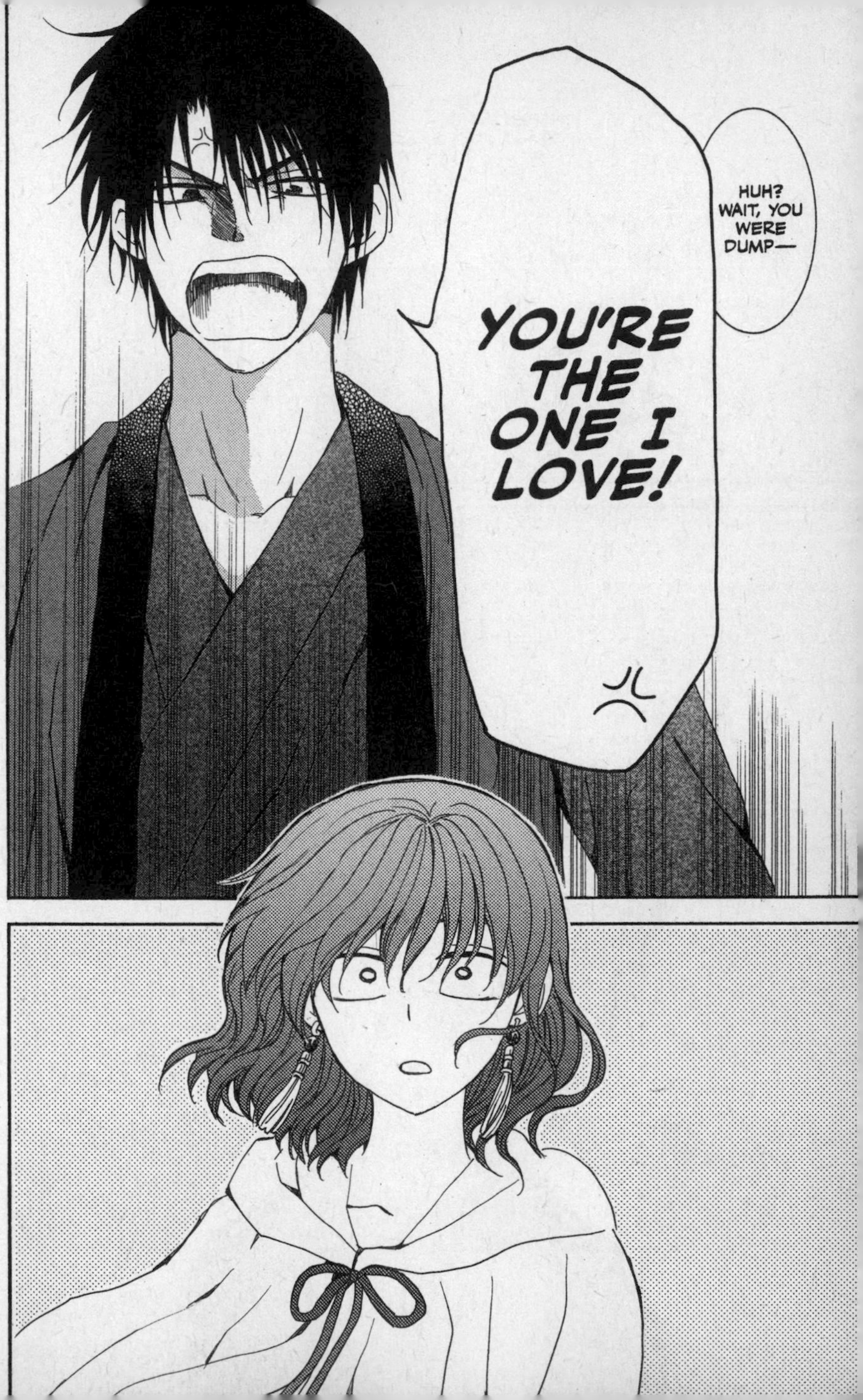
HUH? WAIT, YOU WERE DUMP—
YOU'RE THE ONE I LOVE!

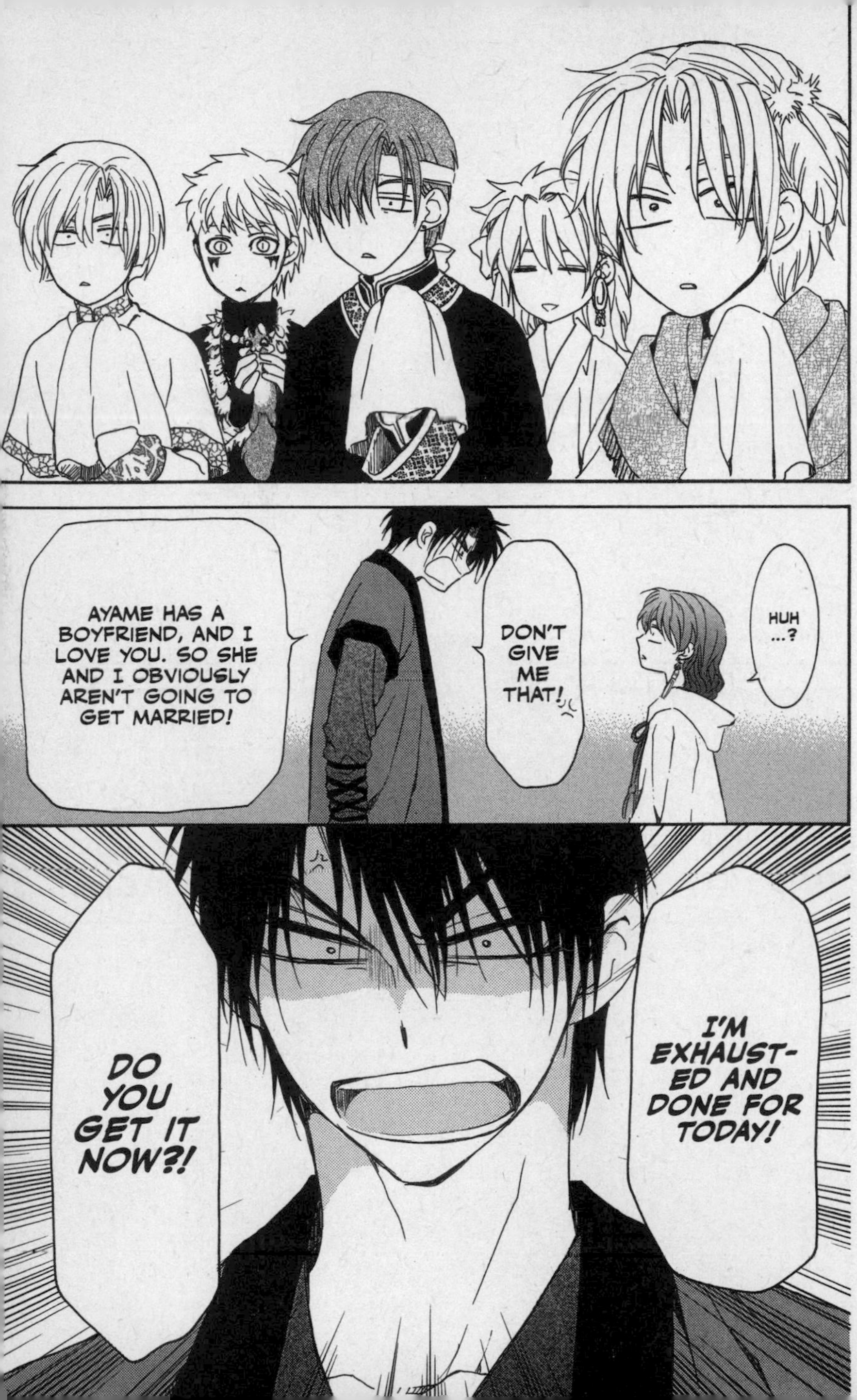
HUH ...?
DON'T GIVE ME THAT!
AYAME HAS A BOYFRIEND, AND I LOVE YOU. SO SHE AND I OBVIOUSLY AREN'T GOING TO GET MARRIED!
I'M EXHAUST-ED AND DONE FOR TODAY!
DO YOU GET IT NOW?!

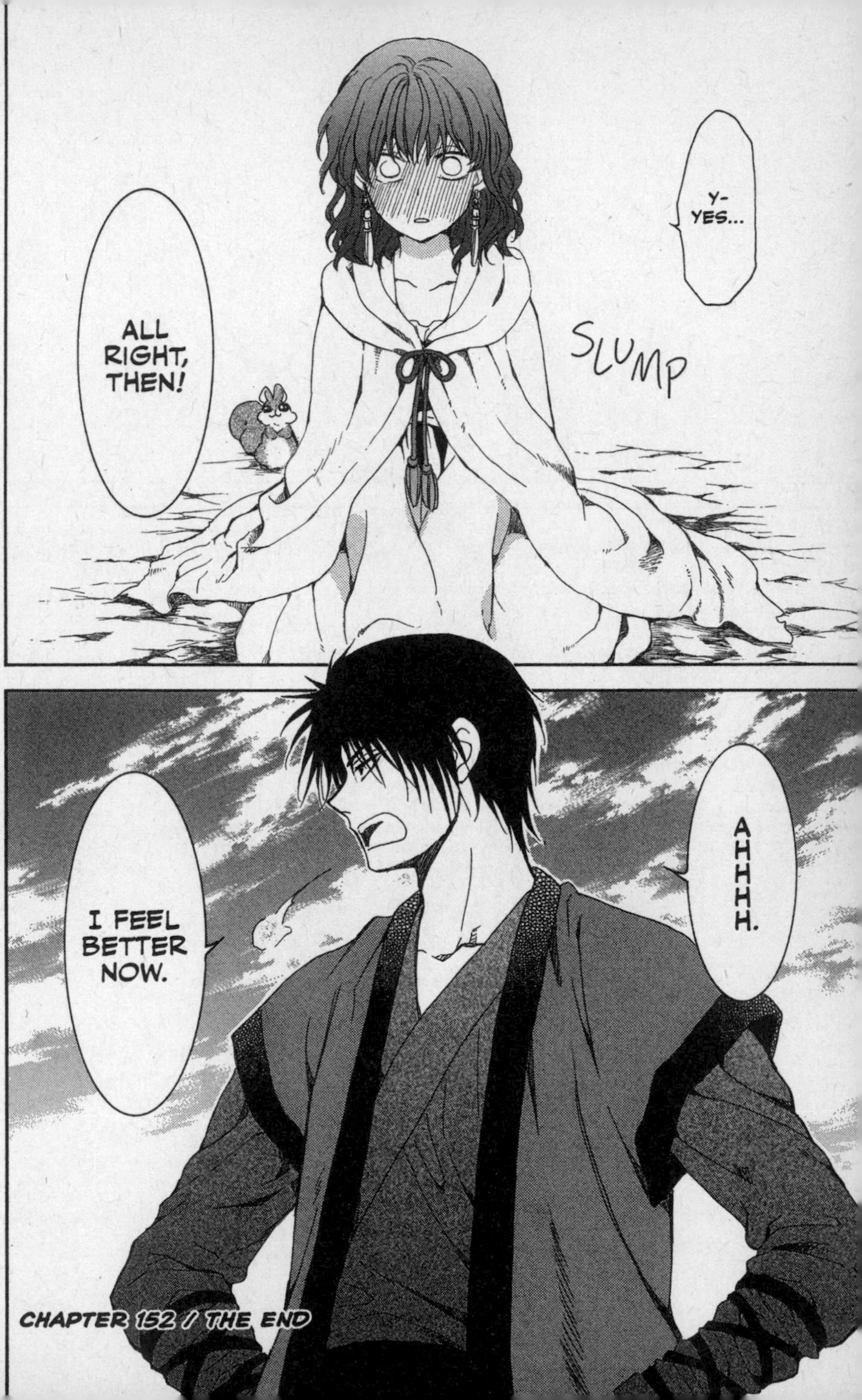
Y-YES...
SLUMP
ALL RIGHT, THEN!
AHHHH.
I FEEL BETTER NOW.
CHAPTER 152 / THE END

There were some characters that I wanted to draw more of, but it was difficult to do so while I was drawing the Nation of Xing arc... I placed these three on the back cover since it was my last chance to draw them in color.

—Mizuho Kusanagi

Born on February 3 in Kumamoto Prefecture in Japan, Mizuho Kusanagi began her professional manga career with *Yoiko no Kokoroe* (The Rules of a Good Child) in 2003. Her other works include *NG Life*, which was serialized in *Hana to Yume* and *The Hana to Yume* magazines and published by Hakusensha in Japan. *Yona of the Dawn* was adapted into an anime in 2014.

YONA OF THE DAWN
VOL.26
Shojo Beat Edition

STORY AND ART BY
MIZUHO KUSANAGI

English Adaptation/Ysabet Reinhardt MacFarlane
Translation/JN Productions
Touch-Up Art & Lettering/Lys Blakeslee
Design/Philana Chen
Editor/Amy Yu

Akatsuki no Yona by Mizuho Kusanagi
© Mizuho Kusanagi 2018
All rights reserved.
First published in Japan in 2018 by HAKUSENSHA, Inc., Tokyo.
English language translation rights arranged with
HAKUSENSHA, Inc., Tokyo.

Printed in the U.S.A.

Published by VIZ Media, LLC
P.O. Box 77010
San Francisco, CA 94107

10 9 8 7 6 5 4 3 2 1
First printing, October 2020

viz.com   shojobeat.com